RELIGION AND SOCIETY
IN THE AGE OF SAINT AUGUSTINE

Religion and Society
in the Age of Saint Augustine

PETER BROWN

HARPER & ROW, PUBLISHERS
New York, Evanston, San Francisco, London

FIRST U.S. EDITION

STANDARD BOOK NUMBER: 06-010554-2

LIBRARY OF CONGRESS CATALOG CARD NUMBER: 70-181609

CONTENTS

CONTENTS

Part II: ROME

Part III: AFRICA

RELIGION AND SOCIETY
IN THE AGE OF SAINT AUGUSTINE

The putting together of these articles has provided me with an opportunity to explain to myself why I wrote them. For they grew up under the pressure of obscure if tenacious preoccupations. They formed part of an evolution towards the writing of a biography—that of Augustine of Hippo (354–430).* It is this unpremeditated convergence on biography that now strikes me as a unifying theme. How this should be calls for some explanation.

There are many good reasons for starting on a biography of Saint Augustine. He is a central figure in the development of Western thought. He lived in an age better and more diversely documented than any period of ancient or medieval history before the thirteenth century. Unlike Tertullian and Ambrose, his intellectual development can be traced immediately, in a prolific succession of securely-dated works. Above all, he was a man who changed. The reader of many Late Roman authors will find his way into a vivid and firmly-orientated world. It is, indeed, one of the delights of the period that we can enter so many, and such different, worlds. We can immerse ourselves in the old-fashioned Rome of Symmachus, in the exuberant Antioch of Libanius, in the *petit noyau* of depressed pagan intellectuals grouped around Julian the Apostate, and, later, in the deeply-loved life of the Auvergne of Sidonius Apollinaris. But no author takes us into a world that changes with such convincing and intimate momentum, as does Augustine. A man open to headlong change in himself, he was able to register with uncanny sensitivity the changing climate of the Roman world in the last century of the Western Empire.

Yet all these good reasons would not, I think, have held me, if I had not felt that Augustine was providing something more than

* *Augustine of Hippo: a biography*, Faber & Faber, 1967.

abundant and differentiated evidence for a crucial period of history. Augustine, also, lent me a language.

Augustine is still close to us, less through what he believed, as through what preoccupied him. He faced squarely and he expressed in words, 'words those precious cups of meaning', the problem of the relation between the inner and the outer life of a man. Whenever he talked, he was acutely aware of the 'long, twisting lanes of speech' through which his thought had to pass to reach his hearers. When he saw a friend, he looked at his eyes, hoping to catch in them some hint of the deep movements of a soul hidden behind the heavy cloud of the flesh; and he thought, wistfully, that in some far-distant transformation, in the resurrection of the dead, the whole of that dull body might have the sensitivity of a glance. Later, as he sat on his bishop's *cathedra* and spoke to his congregation in the basilica at Hippo, he scanned the rows of faces, and thought: 'One deep calling to another.'

Augustine's *Confessions* are constructed around the abiding paradox of the relations between the inner and the outer world. Nothing is quite what it appears on the surface. For who could expect that the reading of a run-of-the-mill textbook might kindle in one student 'an incredible blaze'; that a passing joke in a lecture could be taken to heart by another as 'burning coals'? To remember a book is not to oblige us by telling us what the book said—it is to recapture the sudden 'flash' of creativity in a young man that followed a year of bitter mourning, and to re-live the delicate indecisions involved in sending a presentation copy to an admired professor. To leave a mistress is to let the 'heart' alone speak to us— 'my heart was battered till it ran blood'.

Augustine's curiosity is one of his great claims upon us. He has watched jealousy in babies; he has isolated a 'murky shadowing of God's omnipotence' in the gratuitous vandalism of an adolescent; he has paused to wonder why he enjoyed crying at the theatre. We would not trust a man who had not scrutinized so minutely and with such evident impatience of stereotypes, the strands of his feelings, nor sensed so acutely the gulf between the hidden, unplumbed world within a man, and the opaque, noisy and supremely inquisitive throng of mankind outside it. Still less would it have been possible to follow Augustine the old theologian out on to the more windswept promontories of his thought on grace, freewill and predestination, if it were not for the authentic sense of puzzlement with which he still peered into himself, to wonder how so turbulent a world, so ringed with shadows and flawed with mysterious crevasses, could ever ally itself with the enduring purposes of God. 'He has found peace,' wrote the old man, 'for he has found amazement.'

Augustine did not write for us, though he can make us forget this. He wrote for his contemporaries. In his *Confessions* he was giving to sensitive men of the late fourth-century world a language with which to understand themselves. Such men had every reason to feel 'amazement' at themselves. Many had experienced, like Augustine, a mounting tension between their inner and their outer life, between the demands of their personal experience and the patterns of life so confidently handed down to them by an ancient society. He may choose to transpose the language of Augustine into very different terms; but the historian who wishes to understand the Later Roman Empire just cannot avoid the tension to which Augustine has pointed.

For, on the most straightforward level, nothing is quite what it appears in the Later Roman Empire. This is the first and most lasting attraction of that age of change. Seldom were the externals of traditional Roman life so strenuously maintained: seldom did the aristocracy feel so identified with their inherited classical tradition and with the myth of Eternal Rome. Seldom had the authority of the Roman Emperors been supposed to reach so far—into the definition of their subjects' beliefs, into what oaths they swore when gambling, into the 'irrepressible avarice' that might lead a man, if undeterred by beheading, to sell edible dormice above the market price. When we enter a museum, we peer at the fourth-century ivories to catch some hint of the profound changes that raced beneath their surface: the smooth, neo-classical faces stare us down.

Yet we know that the surface of ancient life was being betrayed at every turn: it was being abandoned in the clothes men wore, in the mosaics they walked on, in the beliefs they held, or in the beliefs of the women they married, in the very sounds that filled their streets and churches with the strange chants of Syria. Like bizarre reflections of a building in troubled water, the façade of Greco-Roman life shifts and dissolves. The gods of classical Greece live a fairy-tale existence in and out of the vinescrolls of Coptic textiles; and, in the popular literature of the Christian communities, we look upwards at the Roman world from the rank undergrowth of the towns and villages of the Near East. In a sixth-century Syriac chronicle of Edessa, we can learn more about what it was like to live (and to starve) on the streets of an ancient city, than we can ever know about the Rome of Cicero. It is in Late Roman sources such as these, that we gain a liberating sense of how large and how diverse the ancient world really was—how far it extended beyond the narrow image of classical civilization which has been bequeathed to us by the governing classes of the Roman Empire.

The extent to which the provincials of the Roman world continued to participate in classical civilization, the terms on which some equilibrium was reached between unity and diversity in a province such as Africa—this theme has been hotly debated in the last generation (pp. 237 sq. and 279 sq.). If, in many of these articles, I have refused to regard the Roman Empire as having been undermined by the revolt of unabsorbed and militant ethnic groups, it is because I regard the true distances between men in the Late Roman period to have had little to do with differences of race or language, and little even with the much-vaunted contrast between the 'classical' governing classes, and the 'non-classical' provincials. The distance between Rome and the provinces was not as unbridgeable as were the private distances that had somehow opened up between men of very similar background. The young Augustine performed a classical oration before Symmachus, the Prefect of Rome, in 384. On that occasion, they spoke the same language to each other. But each went home to a different world. Symmachus was a tenacious pagan of the old school. He was genuinely most at his ease, sitting with colleagues of the Priestly College, discussing the meaning of a prodigy that had appeared at Spoleto. Augustine was a Manichee. He left the Forum to consort with the pale 'Electi', and to seek comfort for his sense of guilt and pardon for his disquieting ambition, in the revelations of a Mesopotamian visionary.

These articles attempt to explore how men came to feel so different from each other, and by what ways they sought to find expression for their differences. I was drawn into the problems posed, for the historian of North African society, by the rise of a great schismatic church—the Donatist Church (pp. 237 sq.). The resonance of Donatist ideas of 'separateness', the Donatist cult of the martyr, the Donatist symbolism of ritual purity, the Donatist insistence on a man's need to live by a 'Divine Law' as a self-conscious alternative to the common pressures of society appealed to me; and this, in turn, led me to similar topics—to obscure and desperate movements of militant rejection, as in the North African Circumcellions (p. 333), to the fate of persecuted groups (pp. 301 sq.), to the radical self-assertion of Pelagius and his followers (pp. 183 sq.), to the fortunes in the Roman world of 'cells' of a new, exotic religion—the Manichees (pp. 94 sq.).

Under the influence of this perspective, I have at times tended to think of the Roman Empire as a landscape that was slowly veined and folded, from the third century onwards, by innumerable little earth-tremors, welling up from deep inside the inner lives of its inhabitants. The long-term repercussions of the sharp thoughts of men in their loneliness, form part of the story I have wanted to tell: and my first debt is to those Late Roman sources and to their modern interpreters, who have told me most about such thoughts. ... Yet I have become increasingly aware that this is not the whole story. The Late Antique period has too often been dismissed as an age of disintegration, an age of other-worldliness in which sheltered souls withdrew from the crumbling society around them, to seek another, a Heavenly, City. No impression is further from the truth. Seldom has any period of European history littered the future with so many irremoveable institutions. The codes of Roman Law, the hierarchy of the Catholic Church, the idea of the Christian Empire, the monastery—up to the eighteenth century, men as far apart as Scotland and Ethiopia, Madrid and Moscow, still turned to these imposing legacies of the institution-building of the Late Antique period for guidance as to how to organize their life in this world. I find it increasingly difficult to believe that these great experiments in social living were left there inadvertently by an age of dreamers, or that they happened through some last, tragic twitching of a supposed 'Roman genius for organization'. They were, many of them, the new creations of new men; and the central problem of Late Roman religious history is to explain why men came to act out their inner life through suddenly coagulating into new groups, and why they needed to find a new focus in the solidarities and sharp boundaries of the sect, the monastery, the orthodox Empire. The sudden flooding of the inner life into social forms: this is what distinguishes the Late Antique period, of the third century onwards, from the classical world. In the second century A.D. men had thought more dark (because more private) thoughts than in any later age. It has long been recognized that the radically otherworldly mood of the Gnostic and Hermetic literature, that reached its peak in the age of the Antonines, provided the humus from which the Late Antique revolution sprang: but such very private dreams could not, of themselves, create a Papacy, a Christian Empire, a Califate. It took the men of Late Antiquity to do that.

One feature of Late Roman society—usually seen more clearly by the medievalist than by the classical scholar—is the slow emergence of a society ever more sharply contoured by religious belief. The heretic, the Jew, the pagan become second-class citizens (pp. 303 sq.). The bishop, the holy man, the monastic community rise in increasing prominence above the *saeculum*, the world of the average man. The community is ringed by the invisible frontier between the 'saved' within the Christian fold and the 'damned' outside it.

Only constant acquaintance with the realities of Late Roman social life can make us realize, however, how very slowly and as a result of how many paradoxical developments, this medieval contouring of society emerged. Hence preoccupation with the theory and practice of religious coercion in the Later Roman Empire (see pp. 260 sq. and 301 sq.). Religious coercion belongs to the pornography of Late Roman history. Like pornography, it has too often fascinated and repelled by treating certain human habits in undue isolation. The way that a bishop made up his mind on the issue of religious coercion; the unspoken aims, assumptions and safeguards that governed its application; the ways in which the Imperial laws against heretics took on different meanings by being applied differently in the various parts of the Empire—these topics enable us to approach the wider problem of the manner in which a newly-Christianized society groped for an image of itself, and took up a stance towards the world outside it. A study which began with the practical problems of local administration in fourth-century North Africa took me insensibly from the formation of the idea of the Christian society in the early Middle Ages to the impingement of Christian Europe on the non-Christian world at the time of the Spanish Conquest of America (see pp. 92–93).

Throughout I have been struck by the manner in which the small decisions, the half-articulated prejudices, the imaginative patterns of the average inhabitants of the Roman world came to 'charge' the atmosphere around them. Events whose outlines we take so much for granted in our text-books of the Late Roman period come to be 'refracted'. An imperial law, an economic crisis, a barbarian raid: these can be presented as such obvious matters in themselves; but to the men who lived through them, they came as so many confirmations of hopes and fears, or as so many opportunities, the ability to experience and take advantage of which had been shaped and delimited by the small thoughts and habits of previous generations. It is to this area of Late Roman history that we must go to find some of the deepest changes. Changes in popular feeling and in the cultural equipment of the governing classes carried along the seemingly fixed points of Roman law and politics like a hidden current. We suddenly find that we have been swept out into strange waters, and are looking back at a very different landscape. In the long routines spent maintaining their local position by means of the Imperial laws, the Catholic bishops of the West find they have imperceptibly invested the fading court of Ravenna with the aureole of a Holy Roman Empire. The outlook of the townsfolk of the Mediterranean world tacitly hardens, throughout the fourth century, to exclude the barbarian and the man of war. In the later decades of the sixth century, the neutral sub-pagan façade of the East Roman state comes to be underpinned by an upsurge of popular Christian devotion, and strengthened by a new sense of solidarity as a 'people of God'. As in these examples, silent evolutions of collective attitudes very often preceded the more spectacular events of the Late Roman period: the nature of the settlement of the barbarians in the West was, to a large extent, dictated by a previous sharpening of prejudice against the 'foreigner'; and the Arab and Slav invasions merely brought into the open the resilience of the small towns of the Byzantine Empire. The fate of the Roman Empire, in its different provinces, was moulded by the debates of ordinary men as to who they were, to whom they would be loyal, where they felt they belonged, whom they were prepared to accept, and whom they would persist in rejecting.

An elementary sense of reality can save the historian of the Roman Empire from brushing aside such intangibles. The Roman Empire was a very big place. Its economy and its communications were of the most primitive. The great Roman roads passed through little towns which derived most of what they ate, lived in and wore from a radius of some thirty miles. We shall never understand the life of the towns of the Greco-Roman world unless we re-live, through the texts, the creeping fear of famine. However we may draw our maps of the grandiose road-system of the Roman world, each small town knew that they would have to face out alone a winter of starvation, if ever their harvest failed.

The Empire had been created and intermittently defended by calculated and wide-ranging political action; but it survived very largely through what people wanted to do, year in and year out. It survived through what its inhabitants did in winter. For, for many months every year, the 'realities' that have been so confidently invoked in standard accounts of the development of the Roman world—armed force, commerce, fiscal control—were simply washed away. The passes filled with snow, the great flagstones of the Roman roads sunk into the mud, the stores of fodder dwindled in the posting-stations, and the little boats rocked at anchor. The Mediterranean ceased to exist; and the distance between the Emperor and his subjects trebled.

Yet, by A.D. 400, the Roman Empire had survived over four hundred such winters. For the Empire had become part of daily life. It was bathed in the elusive glow of shared sentiments, of unquestioned loyalties, of those half-sensed images of security and of the good life that guided the interests of its governing classes. The Spaniards have a word for it, when they describe the bonds of affection in a married couple—*illusión*. When the elements that made up this *illusión* changed, in the Late Antique period, the Empire itself changed. A historian of Late Antiquity, therefore, should never be ashamed to be known as the historian of *illusión*.

He must not be ashamed: but he would be ill-advised to attempt to teach others. For what he has stumbled on is nothing less than the need to study, in the past, the nexus that links the inner experiences of men to the society around them. This is too great a subject for measured generalizations—one might as well try to dictate the course of an ocean current. It is enough to say that this is the current which has swept me through the articles that follow, and to hope that it has taken me into sufficiently new and interesting territory to encourage others to believe that they, also, might commit themselves with profit—and greater success—to a similar course.

Debts of gratitude, however, must be made plain. Fate has done us proud. Seldom has so vast a mass of material on the most intimate fears and hopes of men survived from the distant past, as in the superabundant religious literature of the Late Antique world. The art of the age, also, speaks directly to us. Seldom has the great tradition of English pragmatic history been challenged to reach such heights, as in an almost unbroken succession of great works on the social and political structure of the Later Roman Empire.

Faced by such an *embarras de richesse*, one has to choose which vein to follow. I have found, increasingly, that, to find out why Late Roman society changed as it did, I have had to go to the intimate realities of men's lives—to their patterns of deportment, to their relations with women and children, to their methods of education, their tastes, their use (and abundant misuse) of leisure, to the heavy lumber of ideas at the back of their minds, and to the intimate, but no less real, diasters and excitements involved in their attempts to live at peace with themselves, their families and their near neighbours. In so doing, I am well aware that I have wandered off some of the royal roads of ancient history. In asking myself why the Roman aristocracy became Christian, I found myself more concerned with their wives and their poetry, than with the edicts of their Emperors (see pp. 161 sq.); just as, in discussing the supposed prevalence of sorcery in Late Antiquity (see pp. 119 sq.), I have attempted to point away from the somewhat prurient interest in the 'Decline of Rationalism', evinced by most standard accounts of Late Antique religion, to the more intimate, if prosaic, facts about how Late Roman men grappled with suffering and misfortune in their lives, by what means they maintained their image of themselves, and what they expected in their relations with others. The historian of religion, precisely because he is a historian of religion, must keep his eyes firmly on the ground. He cannot look closely enough at the abundant Late Roman evidence for the ways in which men related themselves to each other and to their own experience.

In studying the evolution of Late Roman society, from the third century onwards, I have found myself obscurely dissatisfied with accounts that invoke the melodramatic and the catastrophic, that posit sudden moments of dislocation and calamity. Whether I am right to be dissatisfied, I cannot yet tell—the matter is still *sub judice*, as a problem which only greater knowledge of the strangely-neglected last century of the classical Roman Empire, the Antonine and the Severan age, can illuminate. I have owed most to those recent studies that have shown me how Late Roman men continued to draw on their long classical past, and how many features of the society in which they lived had grown slowly and without major dislocation (if unpredictably) out of the classical Empire. The crevasse that separated many Late Roman men from the past had opened, first, in their own minds; and the development of the rift between the classical and Late Antique worlds must be approached

17

as much through what the men of the third and fourth centuries wrote in books, were prepared to patronize in art, and on what they were prepared to spend their time and money, as through the fate of the Roman armies. It cannot be stressed too strongly that Late Roman men were not men who lived in a society that had failed to remain a classical Roman society, by reason of some overwhelming external calamity (usually located in the conveniently little-known generations of the later third century). In their religion, in their thought, in their arts and in their styles of public behaviour, these men had found it quite possible, even desirable, to be different from classical Romans.

To study Late Roman society in this way, has meant facing the paradoxical manner in which change is observed to happen, both in individuals and in society. In trying to understand problems such as these, a large debt should be owed to some of the most exciting aspects of the culture of our age. The writing and practise of psycho-analysis, as far as it is readily available to the receptive layman; the disciplined and erudite study of living societies by the social anthro-pologist; the sense of perspective and of unexpected combinations in much sociological literature—these are there for him to use.

Yet the historian's debt to his contemporary helpers has to be expressed with some delicacy. For, like keen mountain-climbers, historians tend to be suspicious of complicated 'ironmongery'. Such 'ironmongery'—and not always the most practical—is pressed con-fidently upon them by a wide variety of other disciplines. On the whole, historians have preferred to travel light. To the dismay of their solicitous colleagues, they set off to tackle the most giddy peaks of human experience—the evolution of complex minds, the detonation of irrational hatreds, the rise of potent religious sym-bols—with an old-world *aplomb*, and a certain heroic indifference to up-to-date gadgetry.

There is, indeed, something very precious in the lightness of heart with which scholars continue to dangle over the precipices involved in the study of alien men in long-dead centuries. An in-tuitive, unselfconscious sensitivity, developed through a long dia-logue with ancient remains, can not be cherished too warmly. It is largely incommunicable, and quite irreplaceable. Yet this quality, though a *sine qua non*, need not be invoked to exclude help from others. The historian, when criticized by the representatives of other human sciences, tends to react by presenting to the world at large a somewhat idyllic picture of 'The Historian at Work'. Such a picture makes capital out of the happy fact that the study of history is, at its best, an unaffected and urbane discipline. Yet, I can only confess that the feline ease which such accounts convey, has somehow passed me by. Far too often, I have found myself dealing with phenomena which I do not readily understand in the world around me, and in myself, any more than I do in the distant past. To understand such things, I have found that I had frequently to reach out for help from other disciplines, and to scrutinize as vigilantly as my ignorance permitted, the relevance of what they had to say.

The difficulty of understanding the past begins with the present. It is all too easy to slur over, as due to distance in time, or to the paucity of the evidence, difficulties of interpretation and sympathy that lie far nearer home. The long-dead men that we study are at least frank with us: they are not at our sides to lull and confuse us. But once we ask whether we really know why a child is sad, why the young will not follow the ways of their fathers, why Negroes and Jews can be so hated, and why men write poems—then we come up against a patina of stereotypes, of conventional formulae that can cover the true nature of human action so effectively, as to make our neighbours, and even ourselves, as distant from our understanding as are the men of the fourth century A.D.

The patina of the obvious that encrusts human actions: this is the first and last enemy of the historian. He needs to draw gratefully on every available skill that will teach him how to remove that patina.

This is a heavy debt to incur. The historian can repay it only by treating other disciplines as he would wish to be treated himself— with diffidence, that is, and with a canny respect for the particularities of scientific traditions, that have passed through as many peculiar evolutions in the course of their development as has his own. Instant 'transplants' between disciplines are no substitute for the slow digestion of new ways of seeing the world. The historian has much to learn from many modern exponents of psycho-analysis, of social anthropology, of sociological theory. Yet he will never learn to use these insights, if he is content only to apply them as so many 'tools' to an understanding of the past. It is deceptively easy, in modern conditions, to load one's bookshelves with new tomes, to marshal curious erudition in footnotes, to invoke modern 'authorities' in order to lend a progressive air to the handling of old-fashioned problems. The building-up of a historical 'culture' is a slower and more painful affair. It does not begin with understanding the past, but with opening oneself to the present. It involves containing, in oneself, the confusion and dismay that ensues from the rejection of stereotypes, and from the tentative and hotly-debated elaboration of new ways of understanding human affairs. It is only when the insights of other disciplines have worked themselves into his mind, so that they help him to read his newspapers and to listen to conversations in a 'bus queue, that the historian can bring them to the study of the past.

Human beings are difficult to understand at the best of times. It is a tribute to the culture of our own times, that this has been clearly recognized by a wide variety of scholars. The gap between ourselves and others, that once so preoccupied Augustine, has been the spur to some of the most fertile exercises of curiosity in the modern age. It has driven us to scrutinize more closely than ever previously, the development of the inner life of the individual; it has challenged us to seize the logic of alien systems of belief in far away tribes, even to seek to enter into the different universes implicit in the different structure of primitive languages. Respect for the challenge posed by this gap between ourselves and others cannot be asserted and defended too often. For it is alarming, and at times a source of obscure anger, that people can be so different from ourselves, and ourselves so different from what we would like to think. Our sense of the gap, therefore, is frequently smothered by the need to tailor ourselves, and our awareness of others, to the comfortable proportions of the common stereotypes; and (even among the most learned) it has often been flatly denied by cocksure and 'knowing' attempts to reduce the disquieting multiplicity of human motives to some simple, magical formula.

The historian meets the gap between himself and others at its most sharp and uncompromising. The dead are irreducible. The men and women of the Late Roman Empire lived out their lives in their own way; they have left us stark evidence of this, without having given a thought to our delicate sensibilities, without having worried for a moment whether their hopes and fears ran counter to the common-sense of men of the twentieth century. In short, saved by the passing of fifteen hundred years from the need to reassure us, they could appear exactly as they were—every bit as odd as we are, as problematical, as difficult of access. To explore such people with sympathy, with trained insight, and with a large measure of common cunning, is to learn again to appreciate what one of the greatest of them said: *'Grande profundum est ipse homo* . . . Man is a vast deep . . . the hairs on his head are easier by far to number than are his feelings, and the movements of his heart.'

(In adding, between square brackets, selected references to recent literature, I have concentrated on those articles where I originally intended to provide a survey of learned opinion and, for the others, on those points where my arguments have been modified or expanded by later work.)

PART I

Religion and Society

SAINT AUGUSTINE*

Isidore of Seville once wrote that if anyone told you he had read all the works of Augustine, he was a liar.[1] From the time of his conversion to Catholic Christianity, in 386, until his death in 430, Augustine wrote some 117 books.[2] Of these books, not a single one is devoted to political theory. Even the title of the book, in which we study his 'political ideas'—*'City of God'*, *De civitate Dei*—is misleading. Augustine treated this as a technical term, taken from the Psalms,[3] to express what we might call 'The Communion of Saints'.

The book itself took thirteen years to write, that is, from 413 to 426. Even Augustine thought it a bit too long; and we tend to dis-

---

* *Trends in Medieval Political Thought,* ed. Beryl Smalley, 1963, pp. 1–21.

[1] 'Mentitur qui te totum legisse fatetur,
    Aut quis cuncta tua lector habere potest?'

Lines placed above the cupboard containing the works of Augustine in the library at Seville: Migne, *Patrologia Latina*, 83 col. 1109, cf. Possidius, *Vita Augustini*, xviii, 9.

[2] See H. I. Marrou, *St. Augustine and his influence through the ages* (Men of Wisdom), New York—London, 1957, for succinct summary of Augustine's life, thought and influence, and a full table of the usual editions and of English translations of his works, pp. 183–6. C. Andresen, *Bibliographia Augustiniana*, Darmstadt, 1962, is a full bibliography, and E. Lamirande, 'Un siècle et demi d'études sur l'ecclésiologie de S. Augustin', *Revue des Etudes augustiniennes*, viii, 1, 1962, 1–124, covers exhaustively all studies of Augustine's views on Church and State. Of innumerable editions and translations of the *De civitate Dei*, the best edition is in the *Corpus Christianorum*, Series Latina, xlvii and xlviii, 1955 (cited here by book, chapter, line and page), and the best bilingual text, that of the *Bibliothèque augustinienne*, vols. 33–6, R. H. Barrow, *Introduction to St. Augustine, The City of God*, London, 1950, contains a summary, commentary and thoughtful translations of select passages, to all of which I am particularly indebted. [See now, P. Brown, *Augustine of Hippo*, Faber, 1967, esp. pp. 287–329.]

[3] *Gloriosa dicta sunt de te, civitas Dei*, Ps. lxxxvi, 3. Augustine deliberately chose this title, rather than the classical word for a just community, *res publica De civ. Dei*, ii, 21, 116 (p. 55).

miss it, as Henry James dismissed the Russian novels of the last century, as a 'loose, baggy monster'. Above all, De civitate Dei is a book of controversy. It should never be treated as though it were a static, complete photograph of Augustine's thought. It reads like a film of a professional boxing championship: it is all movement, ducking and weaving. Augustine is a really stylish professional: he rarely relies on the knock-out; he is out to win the fight on points. It is a fight carried on in twenty-two books against nothing less than the whole of the pagan literary culture available to him.[1] Thus he is reluctant to follow an argument through to its conclusion in one move: instead, he twists a definition here, demolishes another there, proposes one to annoy an opponent, ignores it in the next few chapters, then takes it up again, no less than seventeen books further on, that is, ten whole years later.[2] To try to extract from this infinitely flexible book a rigidly coherent system of political ideas is like trying to square the circle: it is a problem that has fascinated many great minds and baffled all of them.

Yet this book dominated the political thought of the early middle ages; and Augustine is one of the few thinkers of the Early Church who can be called 'contemporary' to ourselves. In this, he is like a planet in opposition: given the vast distance of time and culture that separates him from us, he has come as close as possible to the preoccupations of our own age. Why is this so? Perhaps it is because the whole emphasis on what is fruitful in political theory has shifted. The texts which the student usually has to study for his examinations, and especially the works of the 'classical' political theorists, Hobbes, Locke and Rousseau, already belong to the past. But the attitudes of Augustine and of many medieval theorists, though expressed in a foreign language and forming part of a framework of ideas to which we are unaccustomed, somehow remain relevant.

'Classical' political theory, from the seventeenth century onwards, was based upon a Rational Myth of the State. By myth I mean the habit of extrapolating certain features of experience,

---

[1] Augustine's qualities as a writer, and the literary taste of his age, have been brilliantly characterized by H. I. Marrou, St. Augustin et la fin de la culture antique, Paris, 1938, esp. pp. 39–76 (with handsome modifications, pp. 665–72). J. C. Guy, Unité et structure logique de la 'Cité de Dieu', Paris, 1961, is an excellent introduction to the shape of the work. [See Brown, Augustine of Hippo, pp. 304–312.]

[2] De civ. Dei, xix, 21, 2 (p. 687), of a promise made in ii, 21 (pp. 52–5), transl. Barrow, pp. 110–18.

isolating them, in abstraction or by imagining an original state in which only those elements were operative, and using the pellucid myth thus created as a means of explaining what should happen today. The tendency, therefore, was to extrapolate a rational man; to imagine how reason, and a necessity assessed by reason, would lead him to found a state; and to derive from this 'mythical' rational act of choice, a valid, rational reason for obeying, or reforming, the state as it now is. By contrast, medieval thought, like modern thought, is neither concerned with a myth of the state, nor to base the fact of political obedience upon this myth. Both regard it as impossible to extrapolate and isolate man in such a way. Political society exists concretely: whether because of God, or history, does not matter; it is there. Above all, the link between the individual and the state cannot be limited to a rational obligation. As it exists, in fact, it is mysterious. We are linked to political society by something that somehow escapes our immediate consciousness: by a whole tangled skein of pressures and motives, some rational, many more not so. It is the nature of this tangled skein that perplexed medieval, as it now perplexes modern, thinkers. A man just finds himself in a situation in which men, for all the world like himself, are in a position to kill him, or to order him to kill others. Should this be so? Is it worth it? Is it right? In what circumstances may it be resisted? By what means may it be controlled? Thus, Augustine will not give us a fully-worked out 'myth'. Instead, he will do something more important when dealing with an intractable reality: he will tell us where it is worthwhile looking; and, in so doing, he will direct very bright beams into crucial areas of the human situation.

For this reason, our paper will not claim to summarize the political ideas of St. Augustine:[1] rather, it will attempt to delineate

[1] This has been done, admirably, by J. N. Figgis, *The Political Aspects of St. Augustine's 'City of God'*, London, 1921, and N. H. Baynes, 'The Political Ideas of St. Augustine's "De civitate Dei",' *Historical Association Pamphlet*, N. 104, London, 1936 = *Byzantine Studies and Other Essays*, London, 1955, pp. 288–306. See also H. A. Deane, *The Political and Social Ideas of St. Augustine*, New York-London, 1963. Recent studies have emphasized the manner in which Augustine's thought on this, and on every other subject, was constantly changing: see E. Cranz, 'The Development of Augustine's Ideas on Society before the Donatist Controversy', *Harvard Theological Review*, xlvii, 1954, pp. 255–316, and B. Lohse, 'Augustins Wandlung i. seiner Beurteilung d. Staates', Studia Patristica, vi, *Texte u. Untersuchungen*, 81, 1962, pp. 447–75. [See R. A. Markus, *Saeculum: History and Society in the Theology of St. Augustine*, 1970.]

the distinctive manner in which he thought; to introduce the general reader to Augustine's assumptions, to what problems he thought were important, to the particular viewpoint from which he chose to impose meaning on the 'blooming, buzzing confusion' of human political society. Augustine's spontaneous reactions, therefore, as they appear at random in his sermons and letters, will often provide us with material that throws quite as vivid a light on his basic assumptions as do his professed formulations of political theory. Such a study must also, with regret, leave to one side the problem of the sources of Augustine's ideas, and their destiny throughout the middle ages; it can only claim to be a portrait, not a landscape.

The central problem of Augustine's thought is one which we all have to face: to what extent is it possible to treat man as having a measure of rational control over his political environment? The discovery that the extent of this control is limited has revolutionized political theory. Half the world is committed to some form of Marxist determinism: and the other half, far from rallying to Hobbes, Locke and Rousseau, studies Freud, the social psychologists, and the sociologists. On this point, Augustine is quite explicit: 'For no one is known to another so intimately as he is known to himself, and yet no one is so well known even to himself that he can be sure as to his own conduct on the morrow. . . .'[1] This is the specifically Augustinian contribution to the problem of free will and determinism: for him, man is so indeterminate, so discontinuous, so blind in his intentions and haphazard in his attempts to communicate, that he must be determined by some forces outside the horizon of his immediate consciousness—for Augustine, of course, by God.

For this reason, one should begin studying Augustine's political theory in Book Ten of his *Confessions*, which he wrote around 397 or 400, that is, a good thirteen years before he wrote the *City of God*. Here we have Augustine's man, revealed by meditation on his own 'memory', in fact on his whole inner world: 'Great is this power of memory . . . a spreading, limitless room within me. Who can reach its uttermost depths? Yet it is a faculty of my soul, and belongs to

[1] Ep. 130, ii, 4, transl. Dods, *The Letters of Saint Augustine*, ii, Edinburgh, 1875, p. 145.

my nature. In fact, I cannot totally grasp all that I am.'[1] Above all, man is discontinuous: he is incapable, by himself, of maintaining a continuous moral intention: 'As for the allurement of sweet smells, I am not much troubled. . . . At least, so I seem to myself; perhaps I am deceived. For that darkness is lamentable in which the possibilities in me are hidden from myself: so that my mind, questioning itself upon its own powers, feels that it cannot rightly trust its own report.'[2] And, if man is discontinuous, his communication with others remains an unfathomable mystery. It is here that we can see most plainly how Augustine must invoke God to give meaning to this mystery. Communication is like putting a trunk-call through a vast telephone exchange: God is the operator, and it is He, and He only, who puts you through to what He thinks best: 'For you, O Lord, the most just ruler of the universe can so act by Your secret influence upon both those who consult and those who are consulted—neither of them knowing what they do—that when a man consults he hears what it behoves him to hear, given the hidden merits of souls, from the abyss of Your just judgement. Let no man say to You: What is this? or Why is this? He must not say it, he must not say it. For he is a man.'[3] Now if man cannot determine himself entirely in consciousness, in moral intention, in communication, how much less can he claim complete self-determination in politics: how can he presume to claim to impose an intention planned by his reason on that scrambling box of human wills, presided over by God. It is typical of Augustine that he should cite the biblical text which is central to the Christian idea of kingship throughout the middle ages and beyond—*cor regis in manu Dei*, 'the heart of the king is in the hand of God'—but that he should deliberately complete the quotation: '*Just like a running stream*, so is the heart of the King in the hand of God: He deflects it wherever He wants.'[4]

[1] *Conf.* X. viii, 15; transl. F. J. Sheed, *The Confessions of St. Augustine*, London–New York, 1944, p. 147. [Brown, *Augustine*, pp. 178–180.]

[2] *Conf.* X. xxxii, 48; transl. Sheed, p. 194.

[3] *Conf.* VII, vi, 10: transl. Sheed, p. 109.

[4] *Prov.* xxi, 1, in *De gratia et libero arbitrio*, c. 42 (426/7). In this, and other passages of his late works, Augustine appears to have deliberately made a study of the political history of the Old Testament, in order to show that it was God only who controlled the outcome of the policies and conscious intentions of the protagonists: see A. M. de la Bonnardière, in *Revue des Etudes augustiniennes*, ix, 1–2, 1963, pp. 77–85.

It is from this direction that we must approach Augustine's contribution to the Christian doctrine of passive obedience. He is a man for whom the delusion of self-determination appears as far more dangerous than any tyranny: 'Hands off yourself' he says. 'Try to build up yourself, and you build a ruin.'[1] It is important to note the way in which this obedience is seen to rest on the individual. Augustine makes frequent use of the crucial passage of the thirteenth chapter of St. Paul's Epistle to the Romans: *Omnis anima potestatibus sublimioribus subdita sit, non enim est potestas nisi a Deo: quae autem sunt a Deo ordinatae sunt . . .*: 'Let every soul be subject to the governing powers, for there is no power but from God; these, coming from God, are subject to His ordering.'[2] This is a free translation, in Augustine's sense. In it, the weight shifts to the last part—*quae autem sunt a Deo ordinatae sunt*. This does not mean that the 'powers that be' are divinely sanctioned in a crude sense: it is more that they are obeyed for the sort of reasons that would induce a man to obey any aspect of God's ordering of the world. A man is humble before his rulers because he is humble before God. His political obedience is a symptom of his willingness to accept all processes and forces beyond his immediate control and understanding. Thus, he can even accept the exercise of power by wicked men. In this, Augustine's view of obedience is strictly analogous to his view of illness, another phenomenon plainly beyond man's control and constantly frustrating his intentions. What does he do, he once wrote to a friend, when he feels depressed, and cannot preach well? *Flectamur facile ne frangamur*—'Let us bend easily, lest we be broken'. 'No man plans what he should do better than one who is more prepared not to put into action what is checked by the divine power, than he is avid to insist on doing what is thought out by his human calculations. For *many are the thoughts in the heart of man, but the counsel of the Lord endureth for ever*.'[3]

Because this obedience is based upon a religious attitude, it cannot be absolute. After all, the Christian Church had, in Augustine's

---

[1] *Sermon* 169, c. 11.

[2] *Rom.* xiii, 1 ff. By a characteristic slip, Augustine, quoting from memory, once wrote 'Omnis *ordo* a Deo', instead of 'Omnis *potestas . . .*': *De vera religione*, xli, 77; *Retractationes*, i, 12, 8.

[3] *De cathecizandis rudibus*, xiv, 20. The citation—*Prov.* xix, 2—recurs when Augustine discusses his own dealings with the Imperial authorities on behalf of a town which had been severely punished for rioting: *Ep.* 104, iii, 11.

opinion, grown because of the *pia libertas*[1]—the pious independence of the martyrs, who had refused to obey orders to sacrifice. The cult of the martyrs was the only form of popular devotion in the Early Church; and, in Africa, the accounts of how these 'prize-fighters of the Lord' had snubbed raging governors were read from the altar on innumerable anniversaries. But we must remember that these accounts are all courtroom scenes; and, as in a courtroom, the individual's heroic gesture is strictly cut off from the outside world. It is framed in a straightforward protocol of correct behaviour. There is no appeal to the outside world—to political movements, to mobs, to immediate action of any kind. The martyrs remain, in the minds of late Roman bishops, courageous, but, like themselves, punctilious. Occasions for disobedience do not worry Augustine: what concerns him is the correct way to express and overriding love of God. One incident shows this plainly. That thoroughly un-Augustinian body of men, Augustine's own congregation at Hippo, had lynched the commander of the local garrison. Augustine is profoundly shocked. He agrees entirely that the man was a very wicked man; that his flock had been victimized by him. But the true, humble Christian, St. Laurence, on whose martyrdom he had been preaching, had limited his disobedience to a courteous refusal to sacrifice. Such a Christian would have nothing to do with an act of arbitrary violence against a man set above him by God for good or ill.[2] Perhaps no thinker except Confucius has placed so great an emphasis on obedience as being produced and determined by the need to maintain an exacting standard of personal integrity and inner equilibrium; and on the need to avoid 'rancour', whose ideogram, derived from a 'closed up heart', plays such a part in the opening columns of the *Classic of Filial Piety*.[3]

An acute sense of the spiritual dangers of excessive claims to self-determination lies at the root of Augustine's doctrine of passive obedience: and it forms a somewhat oppressive feature of his political activities as a bishop. But it is only the negative facet of a positive doctrine. It is the positive doctrine of *ordo*—of the divine order of the universe—that predominates in the *City of God*. Man cannot claim complete self-determination because of his place in the

---

[1] *Contra litteras Petiliani*, ii, xcii, 211.

[2] *Sermon* 302, 10–17.

[3] *Hsiao Ching*, ed. Creel, Chang and Rudolph, 'Literary Chinese by the Inductive Method', Chicago, 1948², p. 68.

divine order of things: in that order, he is tuned to one pitch and to one pitch only.[1]

We need only look around us to be surprised by the beauty of this order: '*Omnis ordo a Deo:* All order is from God. We must admit that a weeping man is better than a rejoicing earthworm. But I could still expatiate in praise of the earthworm. Consider his shining complexion, his rotund body, the perfect way in which his top fits his middle, and his middle, his tail-end; how, in his humble way, all his parts strive to make up a united whole. There is no single part of him so formed as not to harmonize with the proportions of any other.'[2] But man, unlike the earthworm, is an extremely complicated and notoriously erratic being. Above all, he is capable of a bewildering variety of loves. In his sermons, Augustine's men appear, not as 'dust and ashes', but as sturdy sinners, whose capacity to enjoy what they do strikes him as quite natural. 'The world', he says, 'is a smiling place.'[3] Little wonder, then, that it is enjoyed immoderately. The tenacity of their affections amaze him: think of highwaymen, tortured because they will not reveal the names of their accomplices. 'They could not have done this without a great capacity for love.'[4] Augustine is acutely aware of the juxtaposition of these two elements. On the one hand, there is the self-evidence of a divine order of supreme beauty, to be contemplated in nature and in the absolute certainties of the laws of thought: on the other hand, the fact that, in this beautiful universe, the human soul tends to disperse itself in a baffling multiplicity of intense but partial loves. Such human loves only hint at a lost harmony: and it is the re-establishment of this harmony, by finding man's proper place and rhythm, that constitutes, for Augustine, the sum total of Christian behaviour.

Augustine's moral thought, therefore, is devoted to the re-

---

[1] For the complex idea of *ordo* as it affects Augustine's ethical thought, see two brilliant studies, J. Burnaby, *Amor Dei*, London, 1938, esp. pp. 113–37, and R. Holte, *Béatitude et Sagesse:* St. Augustin et le problème de la fin de l'homme dans la philosophie ancienne, Paris-Worcester (U.S.A.), 1962, esp. pp. 193–300. The essentially dynamic and interior nature of this idea is well stressed by G. Madec, in *Revue des Etudes augustiniennes*, ix, 1–2, 1963, p. 140: 'Or il me semble que la spéculation augustinienne ne s'appuie sur la base statique d'un univers hiérarchisé que pour s'épanouir en recherche de Dieu par l'ascension spirituelle'.

[2] *De vera religione*, xli, 77.

[3] *Sermon* 158, 7.

[4] *Sermon* 169, 14.

establishment of a lost harmony. Because of this, human action is judged in terms of its relations. A good action is one that is undertaken in the light of a relation to a wider framework: the word *referre*, 'to refer', or 'relate', is central to Augustine's discussion of human activity; and for Augustine, of course, this human activity, of whatever kind, can only reach fulfilment when it can take its place in a harmonious whole, where everything is in relation to God.[1]

It is from this direction, then, that Augustine approaches problems of political behaviour in a Christian ruler. The exercise of power, the establishment of order, the administration of punishment and the fighting of wars have their place in the order of human loves and human needs: Augustine is the last man to ignore their existence. Along with art and learning, political activity is among the 'great things' that human beings just do keep on doing with characteristic intensity.[2] In Book Five of the *City of God*, the problem of political activity is dealt with at length in this fashion. To Augustine, his present age of Christian emperors is different from the pagan past, because the Christian emperors are aware of this true harmony, and the pagans were not. In Augustine's treatment of them, the ancient Romans emerge as undeniably heroic figures: Augustine plainly regarded them with the same sort of intense ambivalence as we, now, regard our own Eminent Victorians. But they were utterly unaware of the true nature of man's harmony. Instead, they set about establishing their own. It was a harmony based upon rigid self-control: they cowed their lesser vices with a stupendous pride and by a love of praise that led to exemplary public conduct.[3] They had their reward. God allowed them to conquer lesser men and to establish a remarkable city; but it was a mere *forma*—a perfect, but dead, shell.[4] God, who laughs the

[1] The classic summary of this idea is in *De doctrina Christiana*, i, xxii, 21; transl. D. Robertson, Saint Augustine, *On Christian Doctrine*, The Library of Liberal Arts, New York, 1958, p. 19. [See Brown, *Augustine*, pp. 324–329.]

[2] *De quantitate animae*, xxxiii, 72.

[3] *De civ. Dei*, v, 13 (pp. 146–7). Characteristically, Augustine allows a classical author, Sallust, *Catilina*, vii, 6, to provide the material for this description; see F. G. Maier, *Augustin u. das antike Rom*, Stuttgart, 1955, a sound, if studiously negative treatment. [See Brown, *Augustine*, pp. 309–312.]

[4] *De civ. Dei*, v, 19, 50–51 (p. 155); *secundum quandam formam terrenae civitatis*. The translation of Barrow, p. 56, 'if judged by the rough standards of the earthly city', misses the sharpness of the word *forma*, cf. *Sermon*, 268, 2: baptized Christian outside the Church is like a perfectly formed, but dead, amputated limb.

c

proud to scorn (with a rather bloodyminded humour characteristic of African authors), had used all this feverish activity to spell out words in a language which the old Romans could not have understood; they were to provide stirring examples of fortitude to inspire Christian martyrs and the dispirited members of the 'redeemed family', the Church,[1] 'while they themselves conduct their own cases down below—whether successfully or not, is not at all relevant'.[2] Thus, the pagan empires of the past grew, prospered and fell for reasons of which the protagonists were entirely unconscious; from the point of view of God they were the incidental by-product of an experiment which, to put it mildly, has little to do with political theory.

With a Christian ruler the picture changes dramatically, to an historian, somewhat unconvincingly. Augustine's summary of the virtues of a Christian prince, and his portraits of Constantine and Theodosius, are, in themselves, some of the most shoddy passages of the *City of God*.[3] But in the framework of Augustine's ideas they are quite explicable. The Christian ruler differs from the pagan, not in the amount of power he wields, nor in the nature of the state which he maintains: he differs only in his awareness of where this power stands in God's order, to what it is related, what ends it may serve.[4] Above all, he will admit no illusion as to the ultimate source of what Augustine would have us regard as the by no means despicable 'consolations'[5] of political success. In Book Five of the *City of God*, Constantine, the first Christian prince, appears very much as he appears on his coins: decked out in the massive finery of his imperial robes, but with his eyes raised to Heaven.[6]

By now it should be plain that what we call Augustine's political thought gravitates around problems of man's behaviour in politics.

[1] *De civ. Dei*, v, 18 (pp. 151–4).

[2] *De civ. Dei*, iv, 5, 19 sq. (p. 102).

[3] esp. the sketchy and superficial panegyric of Theodosius the Great: *De civ. Dei*, v. 26 (pp. 161–2). [On which, now see Y. M. Duval, 'L'éloge de Théodose dans la "Cité de Dieu" (v. 26, 1). Sa place, son sens et ses sources', *Recherches augustiniennes*, iv, 1966, pp. 135–79.]

[4] *De civ. Dei*, v, 24 (p. 160): transl. Barrow, pp. 58–60.

[5] *De civ. Dei*, v, 24, 6 (p. 160).

[6] *De civ. Dei*, v, 25, 1–14 (pp. 160–61). For the difficulty experienced by his first biographer, Bishop Eusebius of Caesarea, in fitting Constantine into the stereotype of a pious man, see A. D. Momigliano, 'Pagan and Christian Historiography in the Fourth Century A.D.', *The Conflict between Paganism and Christianity in the Fourth Century*, ed. Momigliano, Oxford, 1963, pp. 93–4.

The Christian subjects to whom he preached, and the Christian officials to whom he wrote advice, were not, for Augustine, 'natural political animals'; they were men faced with a whole range of aims and objects of love, of which those created by living in political society were only some among many others. They reacted to these aims not because they lived in a particular type of state, but because they were particular types of men. Put briefly, Augustine's political theory is based upon the assumption that political activity is merely symptomatic: it is merely one way in which men express orientations that lie far deeper in themselves. The Christian obeys the state because he is the sort of man who would not set himself up against the hidden ways of God, either in politics or in personal distress. The Christian ruler rules as he does because he is humble before God, the source of all benefits.

These remarks on the duties of the subject and the quality of the Christian ruler were welcome at the time. They showed that Christian ethics could absorb political life at a moment when pagans had begun to fear that Christianity had proved itself incompatible with Roman statecraft. They influenced the middle ages profoundly, because they provided a totally Christian criterion of political action in an unquestioningly Christian society. They do not, however, exhaust Augustine's thought on the state: they provide no answer to the question of why this form of political life exists at all. Indeed, in Augustine's opinion, one swallow did not make a summer. When he wrote the *City of God*, he was convinced of the collective damnation of the human race, with the exception of a small few, predestined to be 'snatched' from that 'damned lump'. The symptoms, therefore, which tend to predominate in his description of human political activity can only be thought of as symptoms of a disease. The roots of this disease go very deep indeed: it is first diagnosed, not even in Adam, but in the Fall of the Angels. The most blatant symptom of this fall is the inversion of the harmonious order established by God.[1]

It is characteristic of Augustine that he should regard the most

[1] Thus, a promise of a book dedicated to the nature of the two 'cities' caused by the Fall of the Angels is contained in Augustine's commentary on Genesis: *de Genesi ad litteram*, xi, xv, 20. For this reason, I would reject, with Guy, pp. 9–10, the widespread and facile opinion that the *City of God* was provoked entirely by the Sack of Rome, in 410: a 'City of God' might well have been written by Autustine without such an event.

basic relationship in the divine order as one of dependence,[1] and so the most basic symptom of the dislocation of this order, as one of domination—of the need to secure the dependence of others.[2] Augustine's own sense of personal dependence on God is particularly acute, it provides what is, perhaps, the sharpest note in his *Confessions*: 'Let the proud of heart deride me, and all who have never been brought low and broken by Thee unto salvation. . . . For, without Thee, what am I but a guide to my own destruction? Or at my best what am I but an infant suckled on Thy milk and feeding upon Thee. . . . What indeed is any man, seeing that he is a man? . . .'[3] For such a man, the only Fall could be one that upset this relationship of omnipotence and dependence. Thus, first the Devil, then Adam, chose to live on their own resources; they preferred their own *fortitudo*, their own created strength, to dependence upon the strength of God.[4] For this reason, the deranged relationships between fallen angels and men show themselves in a constant effort to assert their incomplete power by subjecting others to their will.[5] This is the *libido dominandi*, the lust to dominate, that was once mentioned in passing by Sallust, as an un-Roman vice, typical of aggressive states, such as Assyria, Babylon and Macedon.[6] It was fastened upon by Augustine as the universal symptom *par excellence* of all forms of deranged relationships, among demons as among men. Seen in this bleak light, the obvious fact of domination, as a feature of political society, could make the world of states appear as a vast mental hospital, ranging from the unhealthy self-control of the early Romans to the *folie de grandeur* of a Babylonian tyrant. This was a bitter pill, which many lay rulers were forced to swallow in later ages. But, as always with Augustine, the outward expression of this 'lust' in the form of organized states is merely a symptom. The extent, and even the admitted injustice of the state-building that Augustine observed, and commented on in blistering terms, was of purely secondary importance. A *libido*, for Augustine, was a desire that had somehow got out of control: the real problem, therefore, was why it had got out of control, what deeper disloca-

[1] esp. *De Genesi ad litteram*, viii, vi, 12.

[2] esp. *De Genesi ad litteram*, xi, xv, 20.

[3] *Confessions*, iv. i, 1: transl. Sheed, p. 45.

[4] See the massive summary in *De civ. Dei*, xii, 6, 1–14 (pp. 359–60): transl. Barrow, pp. 30–32.

[5] *De civ. Dei*, xiv, 28 (pp. 451–2): transl. Barrow, pp. 36–8.

[6] Sallust, *Catilina*, ii, 2, in *De civ. Dei*, iii, 14, 50 (pp. 76–7).

tion this lack of moderation reflected. So, to say, as Lord Acton would, that 'all power tends to corrupt, and absolute power corrupts absolutely', would have struck Augustine as being rather like saying that a man got measles from having spots.

We emphasize this aspect of Augustine's thought because we tend to treat the state in isolation. But this is something which Augustine never did, at any time. The object of his contemplation, the aspect of human activity that he sought to make intelligible and meaningful, is not the state: it is something far, far wider. For him, it is the *saeculum*. And we should translate this vital word, not by 'the world', so much as by 'existence'—the sum total of human existence as we experience it in the present, as we know it has been since the fall of Adam, and as we know it will continue until the Last Judgement.[1]

For Augustine, this *saeculum* is a profoundly sinister thing. It is a penal existence, marked by the extremes of misery and suffering,[2] by suicide,[3] madness,[4] by 'more diseases than any book of medicine can include',[5] and by the inexplicable torments of small children.[6] It is also marked by a disquieting inanity. Like a top set off balance, it wobbles up and down without rhyme or reason. Huge states can just happen, 'like passing mist';[7] a gang of slaves almost overturns the Roman Republic at its height;[8] elderly bishops, vowed to poverty, are tortured by their conquerors for buried treasure they have no part in.[9] There are no verbs of historical movement in the *City of God*, no sense of progress to aims that

---

[1] This aspect of Augustine's thought is made particularly clear by H. I. Marrou, *L'Ambivalence du Temps de l'Histoire chez S. Augustin*, Montreal-Paris, 1950.

[2] *De Genesi ad litteram*, xi, xxxv, 48: *omnis contritio saeculi*, above all, *De civ. Dei*, xxii, 22 (pp. 842–5).

[3] *De civ. Dei*, xix, 4, 110–31 (pp. 666–7).

[4] *De civ. Dei*, xix. 4, 43–61 (p. 665).

[5] *De civ. Dei*, xxii, 22, 89–94 (p. 844).

[6] See a moving passage in *Contra Julianum*, v, i, 4: 'There is no other reason why the mass of Christians detest your new-fangled ideas [the Pelagian denial of collective punishment for an Original Sin] . . . but that they think of God as both the Creator of men and as absolutely just, and then witness with their own eyes the sort of agonies suffered by their own little babies. . . .' [See Brown, *Augustine*, pp. 393–397.]

[7] *De civ. Dei*, iv, 5, 19 (p. 102).

[8] *De civ. Dei*, iv, 5 (p. 102).

[9] *De civ. Dei*, i, 10, 70 ff. (p. 12).

may be achieved in history.[1] The Christians are members of a far country. Even to call them 'pilgrims' somewhat weakens the impact of Augustine's terminology: they are *peregrini* in the full classical sense; they are registered aliens, existing, on sufferance, *in hoc maligno saeculo*. Above all, they are in the *saeculum*, as in a vast experimental laboratory: to bring this point home, Augustine uses the familiar image of an olive press, squeezing the olives for oil.[2] The religious life of all members of the Christian Church is quite inconceivable for Augustine without this constant *pressura*—this constant pressing—inside the *saeculum*. It is important to note this. A whole study of the relations between the Catholic Church and society might be written around changes in the meaning of this one word, *saeculum*. For Augustine, it is all-embracing and inescapable: for other writers, it can become narrow, it can stand for a 'lay world' outside the Church, as a sort of primeval swamp of unregenerate politics that demands reclamation by the Catholic Church. This last view would contradict Augustine's most firmly held assumptions on the religious life: the true Christian was here to be pressed in the selfsame press as the bad; to suggest anything else would be like suggesting that, in our experimental laboratory, the guinea-pigs should take over control of the tadpoles.[3]

The most obvious feature of man's life in this *saeculum* is that it is doomed to remain incomplete.[4] No human potentiality can ever reach its fulfilment in it; no human tension can ever be fully resolved. The fulfilment of the human personality lies beyond it; it is infinitely postponed to the end of time, to the Last Day and the glorious resurrection. Whoever thinks otherwise, says Augustine:

---

[1] Augustine's view was not shared by other Christian writers of his century: v. E. Th. Mommsen, 'St. Augustine and the Christian Idea of Progress', *Journ. of the History of Ideas*, xii, 1951, 346–74 = *Medieval and Renaissance Studies*, ed. E. F. Rice, jr., Ithaca–New York, 1959, pp. 265–88.

[2] *Sermon* 19, 6. [See Brown, *Augustine*, pp. 292–293.]

[3] This alternative is dismissed as irrelevant: *de Trinitate*, iii, iv, 9: 'But since we have not reached that state [in which 'the government and direction of human affairs are in the hands of men who are devoutly and perfectly submissive to God'] (for we must be exercised in this exile after the manner of mortal men, and be forcibly instructed by scourges in meekness and patience), let us think of that higher and heavenly country itself, from which we are separated during this exile', transl. Stephen McKenna, 'Saint Augustine's *The Trinity*', Catholic University of America, Washington, D.C., 1963, p. 103.

[4] See Burnaby, pp. 53–60, for a brilliant evocation of Augustine's attitude.

'understands neither what he seeks, nor what he is who seeks it'.[1]

For Augustine, human perfection demands so much, just because human experience covers so very wide an area, a far wider area than in most ethical thinkers of the ancient world. It includes the physical body: this dying, unruly thing cannot be rejected, it must be brought into its proper place and so renewed.[2] It includes the whole intense world of personal relationships:[3] it can only be realized, therefore, in a life of fellowship, in a *vita socialis sanctorum*.[4] It is inconceivable that such claims can be met in this world; only a morally obtuse man, or a doctrinaire, could so limit the area of human experience as to pretend that its fulfilment was possible in this life. Thus, in opening his Nineteenth Book of the *City of God* by enumerating and rejecting the 288 possible ethical theories known to Marcus Varro as 'all those theories by which men have tried hard to build up happiness for themselves actually within the misery of this life',[5] Augustine marks the end of classical thought. For an ancient Greek, ethics had consisted of telling a man, not what he ought to do, but what he could do, and, hence, what he could achieve.[6] Augustine, in the *City of God*, told him for what he must live in hope. It is a profound change. In substituting for the classical ideal of an available self-perfection the idea of a man, placed as a stranger in an uncomprehending land, a man whose virtue lies in a tension towards something else, in hope, in faith, in an ardent yearning for a country that is always distant, but made ever-present by the quality of his love, that 'groans' for it, Augustine could well be called the first Romantic. Thus we should never isolate Augustine's reflections on the state and society. They are part of an anxious search for at least some echo, for some stunted analogy, that might lead men, in the misery of this life, to share with him some appreciation of the fulfilment of the human being that will be achieved beyond the *saeculum*. Anyone who reads the whole of Book Nineteen of the *City of God*—

---

[1] *De consensu Evangelistarum*, ii, 20. The statement is all the more poignant as Augustine in his early days had once hoped for just such fulfilment; see Burnaby, pp. 35–6. [See Brown, *Augustine*, pp. 148–151.]

[2] *Sermon* 115, 15. 'Take away death, the last enemy, and my own flesh shall be my dear friend throughout eternity'.

[3] *De civ. Dei*, xix, 8 (pp. 672–3): transl. Barrow, pp. 78–80.

[4] *De civ. Dei*, xix, 5, 5–6 (p. 669), transl. Barrow, p. 70.

[5] *De civ. Dei*, xix, 1, 4 ff. (p. 657).

[6] Max Pohlenz, *Die Stoa*, i. Göttingen, 1948, p. 111.

and it can be done with a most intelligent translation in Barrow's *Introduction to St. Augustine, The City of God*—will realize this immediately. It will be a salutary lesson in the true perspective of Augustine's thought.

Augustine attempts deliberately and persistently to see in human society the expression of the most basic and fundamental human needs. For only when he has hit upon what is truly fundamental in this life, can he feel that he has caught a partial hint of how these needs will reach fulfilment in his 'most glorious City'. For this reason, he is impatient with classical Roman theories of the state: these exclude too much of the realities of human behaviour. Augustine's political theory, therefore, is marked by the search for an all-embracing lowest common denominator of human needs that seek realization in social life. It is concerned with what is fundamental.

He finds this fundamental need in the human desire for peace. 'So great a good is peace', he writes, 'that even in earthly and mortal conditions to hear of it is pleasant, and nothing more desirable can be desired, nothing better, in fact, can be found. I should like to speak a little longer about this, and I think I shall not burden the reader: I do it because peace is the end of the city which I am describing, and also because of its inherent attractiveness, since peace is dear to all of us.'[1] This *pax*, for Augustine, means far more than tranquillity, unity and order. These things are only preconditions for its attainment. For Augustine, the obverse of peace is tension—the unresolved tension between body and soul and man and man, of which this life is so full. Peace, therefore, is the avoidance and in its final form, the resolution of these tensions. Such a meaning of peace is characteristic of Augustine. He was a sensitive man, with an acute sense of violence and tension. His concern with peace as something absolutely fundamental to human happiness made him welcome any feature of organized society that might at least cancel out some of those tensions of which he was so intensely conscious.[2]

[1] *De civ. Dei*, xix, ii, 26 ff. (p. 675): transl. Barrow, p. 84.

[2] 'His learning is too often borrowed, and his arguments are too often his own...', Gibbon, *Decline and Fall*, c. xxviii, note 79. The sources of Augustine's idea of peace have been exhaustively studied by M. Fuchs. *Augustin u. der antike Friedensgedanke*, Stuttgart, 1936. But the danger of treating the history of the idea *in vacuo* is that Augustine's concern, in Book XIX, is to persuade the reader of the Resurrection as a final resolution of tensions. H. J. Diesner, 'Die "Ambivalenz" des Friedensgedankens u.d. Friedenspolitik bei Augustin', *Kirche u. Staat im spätrömischen Reich*, Berlin, 1963, 46–42, in presenting this

For this reason, Augustine could accept the domination of man over man that had arisen from the Fall. This domination at least cancelled out certain tensions—although at a terrible cost, as anyone who has witnessed judicial torture and executions, would admit if he had any sense of human dignity.[1] But at least an ordered hierarchy of established powers can canalize and hold in check the human lust for domination and vengeance. For Augustine, like Hobbes, is a man for whom a sense of violence forms the firmest boundary stone of his political thought. The North Africa of his age was a notoriously 'tough' province. Augustine narrowly escaped assassination by his ecclesiastical rivals.[2] What Augustine feels particularly acutely is the manner in which violence is a two-way affair, as demoralizing for the avenger as for the victim.[3] It is this that shocks him in the lynching of the commander of the garrison at Hippo. *Ordinata est respublica* he says: 'The state is an ordered affair'; if he was wicked, let him be executed by a properly vested, impersonal authority, and not by the most degrading of all forms of action for all who take part in it, *privata licentia*, taking the law into one's own hands by mob violence.[4]

The weakness of Augustine's position is, of course, that it implies a very static view of political society. It is quite content merely to have some of the more painful tension removed. It takes an ordered political life for granted. Such an order just happens among fallen men. Largely because he feels he can take it for granted, Augustine can dismiss it. For him, it is a 'peace of Babylon' that should only be 'used' by the citizens of the Heavenly City. Like the Jews, they are 'captives' in this Babylon, although they are urged, as Jeremiah urged the Jews, to *Let its peace be your peace.*[5] Even in a model prison all the inmates can do is to accept, gratefully, whatever benefits may come their way.

But this is only the most negative facet of his attitude. The structure of political society, its vested order of command and

---

attitude as purely static and conservative, seems to have missed the subtle alchemy by which Augustine will transform a traditional *idée reçue* by incorporating it in a novel argument.

[1] *De civ. Dei*, xix, 6 (pp. 670–71), transl. Barrow, pp. 72–6.
[2] Possidius, *Vita Augustini*, xii, 2.
[3] *Sermon*, 302, xi, 10.
[4] *Sermon*, 302, xiv, 13–17.
[5] *Jerem.* xxix, 7 in *de civ. Dei*, xix, 26 (pp. 695–7): transl. Barrow, pp. 126–8.

obedience, is what Augustine would take for granted: what really interested him deeply was the quality of such ordered societies, above all, the quality of the reasons for their coherence. He, therefore, rejects as too narrow the classical definition of the *res publica*: such a definition would make it appear as if political society were a mere structure designed to protect certain rights and interests. For Augustine, this misses the point. Men, because they are men, just do cohere, and work out some form of normative agreement—an *ordinata concordia*. What cannot be taken for granted is the quality of this ordered life; and, for Augustine, this means the quality of the motives and aims of its individual members. 'Suppose therefore', he writes, 'that a different definition of *populus* is proposed . . . like this: A people is a gathering of a multitude of rational beings united in fellowship by sharing a common love of the same things. In that case, to see the character of each people, you have to examine what it loves . . . it is a better or a worse people as it is united in loving higher or lower things.'[1]

This definition is typical of Augustine. It is deliberately fundamental and all-embracing. Such a definition is so wide that it could include a football crowd on a Saturday afternoon; indeed, the atmosphere of the Roman circuses, with their amazing manifestations of mob-psychology, is never far from Augustine's discussion of the motives of human groups.[2] It hits upon a fundamental motive: *dilectio*, which, for Augustine, stands for the orientation of the whole personality, its deepest wishes and its basic capacity to love, and so it is far from being limited to purely rational pursuit of ends. It is dynamic; it is a criterion of quality that can change from generation to generation. 'History tells us', he writes, of how the quality of the Roman Republic did change; 'what were the things the Roman people loved in its earliest days, and in its later days.'[3] In short, Augustine's definition deliberately focuses attention upon that 'middle distance' of human habits, values and instincts, which, far

[1] *De civ. Dei*, xix, 24, 1-3 (p. 695): transl. Barrow, p. 124, *rationalis* in this case means 'possessing reason', as distinct from a herd of animals.

[2] *Confessions*, vi, viii, 13: transl. Sheed, pp. 90-91, for an acute description of this reaction of his friend, Alypius, to the gladiatoral shows—'He was no longer the man who came there, but one of the crowd to which he had come, a fit companion for those who had brought him'. In *De doctrina Christiana*, i, xxix, 30; transl. Robertson, pp. 24-5, he can explain the Christian fellowship in terms of the fan-club of an actor!

[3] *De civ. Dei*, xix, 24, 11-16 (p. 695): transl. Barrow, p. 124.

more than its structure, remains the greatest mystery of political society.

Today, perhaps, we can appreciate the importance of this shift of emphasis. Previously, it could be assumed that political theory was a matter of structure, in an almost mechanical sense. In discussing this structure, we had tended to analyse it into its component parts, and, hence, to isolate the individual on the one hand, and the state, on the other, as the only two parts whose relations are relevant to thought on political society. In fact, this isolation is a deliberately self-limiting myth. So much of our modern study in sociology and social psychology has shown the degree to which political obedience is, in fact, secured, and political society coheres by the mediation of a third party, of a whole half-hidden world of irrational, semi-conscious and conscious elements, that can include factors as diverse as childhood attitudes to authority, crystallized around abiding inner figures, half-sensed images of security, of greatness, of the good life, and, on the conscious plane, the acceptance of certain values.[1] These make up an orientation analogous to Augustine's *dilectio*.

The problems which this perspective poses, therefore, cannot be ones of structure, so much as of the quality of the needs that seek expression in obedience and coherence. Viewed in such a way, the state becomes a symbol: it is one of the many moulds through which men might be led to express needs and orientations that lie deep in themselves; and the expression of these needs through an organized community provides a far more tenacious bond of obligation than the purely rational agreements of a social contract. For Augustine, this need to express loves through political society can be very sinister, just as human loves can be sinister: 'the earthly (or fallen) city worships its own strength in its rulers'.[2] But it can also provide his successors with the foundations of a theory of the Christian state. For, as it was expressed at the time, and in the middle ages, this emphasis on quality, on the direction of a *dilectio*, as the criterion of an organized society, appealed to very different preoccupations than that of a modern sociologist. It offered a way to recreate the

---

[1] Among many abstract treatments, see esp. the precise study of I. Menzies, 'A Case Study of the Functioning of Social Systems as a Defence against Anxiety: a Report on a Study of the Nursing System of a General Hospital'. *Human Relations*, xiii, 1960, pp. 95–121.

[2] *De civ. Dei*, xiv, 28, 7–12 (p. 451); transl. Barrow, p. 36.

link between a given form of political structure and what could be broadly called a civilization—a set of traditionally accepted values. Augustine is content, in Book Nineteen, to demonstrate that the quality of a state ultimately depends upon the values of its members; but the natural inference, drawn throughout the Augustinian tradition in the middle ages, was that the state exists precisely in order to maintain specific values, to preserve the true ends and loves dictated by the Christian religion.[1] Augustine did not draw this conclusion in the *City of God*, partly, I suspect, because he could, by that time, take such an inference for granted.

The Christian emperors of his generation had made the possibility of an official Christian state seem quite natural to Augustine. They were proud to be 'limbs of the Church' as well as Roman emperors.[2] They indulged in spectacular acts of piety, the penance of Theodosius before St. Ambrose, told in a surprising number of Christian sources, had already begun a popular image of Christian kingship that would have a long future.[3] Above all, they had suppressed pagans and heretics. Augustine was deeply involved in this last change. He is the only bishop in the Early Church whom we can actually see evolving, within ten years, towards an unambiguous belief that Christian emperors could protect the Church by suppressing its rivals. He is the only writer who wrote at length in defence of religious coercion; and he did this with such cogency and frequency that he has been called *le prince et patriarche des persécuteurs*.[4]

Augustine is also a crucial figure in the symbiosis between bishop and politician that is the most obvious feature of fifth-century life.[5] The provincial governors who came from Ravenna to Carthage, most of them good Catholic Christians, would have found themselves obliged both to praise 'the solicitude of the bishops' in massive

[1] esp. H. X. Arquillière, *L'Augustinisime politique*, Paris, 1955².

[2] *De civ. Dei*, v. 26, 47 (p. 162).

[3] *De civ. Dei*, v. 26, 50 ff. (p. 162).

[4] This evolution took place less abruptly and with far less hesitation than many commentators would admit. See R. Joly, 'S. Augustin et l'intolérance religieuse', *Revue belge de philologie et d'histoire*, xxxiii, 1, 1955, 263–94, and P. R. L. Brown, 'The Attitude of St. Augustine to Religious Coercion', *Journal of Roman Studies*, liv, 1964, pp. 107–116 [pp. 260–78] [and Brown, *Augustine*, pp. 234–240].

[5] P. R. L. Brown, 'Religious Coercion in the Later Roman Empire: the case of North Africa', *History*, xlvii, 1963, pp. 283–305 [pp. 301–31].

edicts against heretics, and, from 415 onwards, they were expected to read presentation copies of instalments of the *City of God*. Augustine could write to one such man: 'I tell you this: If your administration, inspired as it is by the qualities I have just mentioned, is limited to the one aim that men should suffer no inconveniences in their material life, and if you do not think that it is your business to be concerned with the end . . . to which they relate this quiet, that is, to put it bluntly, how they should worship the true God, in Whom lies the fulfilment of all quiet in this life, all such hard work on your part cannot advance you to the blessed life. . . .'[1] Here we have, already in Augustine's correspondence, the subtle and all-important difference between reading the *City of God* for oneself, and being told it by a bishop. In later centuries, in a society where the external role of the Church will become more explicit, Augustine's subtle, dynamic doctrine in which values form a field of forces, linking what men really want in their hearts with what they want from a state, will settle down as a static hierarchy of duties. In the letter of Pope Gregory the Great to Queen Brunhilde, the *dilectio* of Augustine has become, quite simply, *dilectio sacerdotum*,[2] and 'love', 'love of the see of S. Peter'.[3]

Augustine would not have said this. We are left with a dichotomy: an acute awareness of the actual condition of man in this *saeculum*; and a yearning for a City far beyond it. Augustine never overcame this dichotomy. And for this reason, his most considered reflections on political society, as they appear in the *City of God*, are no more than the anxious questioning of a shadow; they are a hint of a full peace and of a full realization of hidden loves, in the Heavenly Jerusalem, whose name signifies '*Visio pacis*'. In a sermon which he preached at Carthage in the same year as he sat down to write the *City of God*, we can see, better than anywhere else, the force and the true direction of the momentum that led Augustine to pile up this great work for future ages to puzzle on: 'When, therefore, death shall be swallowed up in victory, these things will not be there; and there shall be peace—peace full and eternal. We shall be in a kind of City. Brethren, when I speak of that City, and especially when scandals grow great here, I just cannot bring myself to stop.'[4]

[1] *Ep.* 155, 10.
[2] Greg., *Reg.* viii, 4.
[3] Greg., *Reg.* vi, 5. See Arquillière, pp. 131–41.
[4] *Ennaratio in Ps.* lxxxiv, c. 10.

45

THE LATER ROMAN EMPIRE*[1]

I

Not only has the appearance of the work of Jones been an event of the first importance in the study of the Later Roman Empire: it is a monument to a distinctive approach to ancient history. For the book is an intellectual triumph: it is marked by the mastery of a vast quantity of texts, by a never-failing felicity of interpretation, above all, by a massive independence of mind.

It is the splendid isolation of Jones that most strikes the student of Later Roman history. This is a period that is more in danger of being taken for granted than of being ignored. Guiding-lines towards an understanding of the period from 284 to 602, that had begun as brilliant essays in interpretation by ancient and medieval historians of the early decades of this century, have imperceptibly hardened into *Schultraditionen*, piously handed down from footnote to footnote. There is, indeed, a 'sacred rhetoric' of Later Roman social history, which is all the more hypnotic for being based on a genuine anxiety to master the profound and disquieting changes of the Roman Empire, whose decline and fall has always stirred the sensitive European as, in some way, a *memento mori* for his own age.[2]

* *Economic History Review*, 'Essays in Bibliography and Criticism', lvi, 2 ser. XX, 1967, pp. 327–43.

[1] A review of A. H. M. Jones, *The Later Roman Empire, 284–602. A Social Economic and Administrative Survey* (Oxford: Basil Blackwell, 1964. 3 vols. Vols. I–II: pp. xiv + 1068; Vol. III: pp. 448. £14 14s.). Here abbreviated as *L.R.E. The Decline of the Ancient World* (Longmans, 1966) presents the substance of *L.R.E.* in an abbreviated form.

[2] For example, M. Rostovtzeff, *Social and Economic History of the Roman Empire*, 2nd ed. revised by P. M. Fraser (1957), 1, 541, and G. I. Brătianu, 'Vers le Bas-Empire', *Etudes byzantines d'histoire économique et sociale* (1938), 15–22. S. Mazzarino, *The End of the Ancient World*, trans. Holmes (1966), is a suggestive if sketchy *aperçu* of the historiography of the decline of the Roman Empire;

There has been a tendency to take for granted, both that the main social and economic developments of the Late Roman period provide the clue to the decline and fall of the Roman Empire, and that the transition between the ancient world and the Middle Ages is best understood in terms of the replacement, in this period, of an 'ancient' by a 'medieval' style of society.[1] These developments have been summed up in the growth of great estates,[2] the abandonment of a monetary for a natural economy,[3] the decline of the urban middle classes,[4] the collapse of trade,[5] the regimentation of society into a caste-system;[6] the immediate circumstances of the fall of the Western Empire have been understood in terms of a decline of population,[7] of the barbarization of the Roman army,[8] of the rise of

---

A. Piganiol, *L'Empire chrétien* (Histoire romaine, IV, 2), 1947, esp. 411–22, remains the best introduction to modern views. [See S. D'Elia, *Il basso impero nella cultura moderna dal quattrocento ad oggi* (1967).]

[1] See notably L. M. Hartmann, *Kapitel vom spätantiken und mittelalterlichen Staate* (1913). The same concern is fundamental to H. Pirenne, *Mohammed and Charlemagne*, trans. Miall (1937); see A. Riising, 'The Fate of Henri Pirenne's thesis on the consequences of the Islamic Expansion', *Classica et Medievalia*, XIII (1952), 87–130. It is shared, from a different perspective, by Soviet historians, most notably by E. M. Schtajerman, *Die Krise der Sklavenhalterordnung im Westen des römischen Reiches*, trans. Seyfarth (1964), and 'Programmes politiques à l'époque de la crise du iii. siècle', *Cahiers d'histoire mondiale*, IV (1958), 310–29.

[2] See M. Weber, *Die sozialen Gründe des Untergangs der antiken Kultur* (1896). Contrast *L.R.E.* II, 781–8. [Now see J. Percival, 'Seigneurial Aspects of Late Roman estate management', *English Historical Review*, LXXXIV (1969), 449–473].

[3] See F. Lot, *La fin du monde antique et le début du moyen-âge*, 2nd ed. (1951), esp. 96. Contrast *L.R.E.* I, 26–32, 61–6, and 101–9.

[4] See S. Dill, *Roman Society in the Last Century of the Western Empire* (1899), 245–81, and Rostovtzeff, *Social and Economic History*, I, 467–541. Contrast *L.R.E.* II, 737–63 and 1053.

[5] See F. W. Walbank, *The Decline of the Roman Empire in the West* (1946) [re-edited as *The Awful Revolution*, (1969)]. Contrast *L.R.E.* II, 844–72 and 1038–9.

[6] See Lot, *La fin du monde antique.* 115–46. Contrast *L.R.E.* II, 1047–53.

[7] See A. E. R. Boak, *Man Power Shortage and the Fate of the Roman Empire in thr West* (1955). Contrast *L.R.E.* II, 1040–5.

[8] See *L.R.E.* II 619–23 and 1036–8. Compare, most recently, R. Macmullen, *Soldier and Civilian in the Later Roman Empire* (1963), esp. pp. 119–77. On the Romanization of Germanic generals, see especially K. Stroheker, 'Zur Rolle der Heermeister fränkischer Abstammung im späten 4. Jahrhundert', *Historia*, IV

provincial nationalism in the guise of Christian heresies; and it has
been held that the divergent destinies of the Eastern and the
Western Empires merely ratify our impression of the deep-seated
weaknesses of Roman society in the West of the third and fourth
centuries A.D.[1] These broad outlines having once been presented,
recent scholars of the period have been content, with some notable
exceptions, to execute intricate manœuvres in well-charted seas, such
as the vicissitudes and programmes of the pagan aristocracy of
Rome[2] and the social position and *Tendenz* of the leading contemporary historians,[3] and to lavish their ingenuity on the political
message of frivolous texts, such as the *Scriptores Historiae Augustae*.[4]

Jones, by contrast, takes very little for granted. It is not only the
caution of a great scholar which strikes us, as when Jones writes of

---

(1955), 314-30 (= *Germanentum und Spätantike*, 1966, 9–29). On the co-opera-
tion of general and Roman landowner to maintain the agrarian system of the
Empire, see A. D. Momigliano, in *Rivista storica italiana*, LXIX (1957), 282,
and E. A. Thompson, 'The Settlement of the Barbarians in Southern Gaul,'
Journal of Roman Studies, XLV (1956), 65–75.

[1] See Brătianu, 'La distribution de l'or et les raisons économiques de la
division de l'empire romain', *Etudes Byzantines*, 59–91, and E. Demougeot,
De l'unité à la division de l'empire romain, 395–410 (1951), esp. pp. 33–89. See
L.R.E. II, 1064–8.

[2] See especially A. Alföldi, *A Conflict of Ideas in the Later Roman Empire. The
clash between the Senate and Valentinian I* (1952). F. Paschoud, 'Réflexions sur
l'idéal religieux de Symmaque', *Historia*, XIV, (1965), 215–35, is a recent
example. [See now his *Roma Aeterna*, 1968.]

[3] See the excellent studies of E. A. Thompson, *The Historical Work of Ammianus Marcellinus* (1947) and A. D. Momigliano, 'Cassiodorus and the Italian
Culture of his time', *Proc. Brit. Acad.* XLI (1955), 207–45 (= *Studies in Historio-
graphy* (1966), 181–210), and 'Gli Anicii e la storiografia del VI. sec. d. Cr.', *Rend.
Accad. Lincei*, ser. 8, XI (1956), 279–97. Unfortunately studies of East Roman
historiography are notably less satisfactory: see R. Rubin, *Prokopios von
Kaisareia* (1954), cols. 75–80 (=*Pauly-Wissowa-Reallexikon*, XXIII, 1 (1957),
cols. 349–54) and *Das Zeitalter Justinians*, I (1960), 168–244; M. V. Levčenko,
'Vizantijskij istorik Agafii Mirinejskij i ego mirovozzrenie', *Vizantijskij
Vremennik*, III (1950), 62–84; and O. Veh, *Zur Geschichtsschreibung und
Weltauffassung des Prokops von Caesarea: 3. Teil, Der Geschichtsschreiber
Agathias von Myrina* (1953). [A defect handsomely remedied by Averil Cameron,
Agathias, 1970.]

[4] See most recently J. Straub, *Heidnische Geschichtsapologetik in der christ-
lichen Spätantike. Untersuchungen über Zeit und Tendenz der S.H.A.* Antiquitas
4, 1 (1963) and *Historia Augusta-Colloquium, Bonn*, Antiquitas 4, 2 (1964). [Sir
Ronald Syme, *Ammianus and the Historia Augusta* (1968) and *Emperors and
Biography* (1971), provides a welcome relief.]

the widely accepted superiority of the Eastern to the Western parts of the Empire, that 'this is a question which needs investigation', that 'this again must be demonstrated' (II, 1027). Far more, it is the inimitable manner with which he will approach any problem: a mastery of the available material, a sense of the concrete, an inspired commonsense will unfailingly dissolve the cruder outlines of the textbooks into an exquisitely shaded mosaic of known facts. One masterly example, among many, is his analysis of the structure of landholding and of the legal categories and actual living-conditions of the peasantry: it is outstanding not only for its felicity of inter- pretation, but for its humane sense, when handling a subject known to us largely from juridical sources, of the manifold loopholes and small compensations of real life in an agricultural community.[1] It deserves the attention and gratitude of ancient and medieval his- torians alike. Altogether, in the present state of Late Roman studies, this book is like the arrival of a steel-plant in a region that has, of late, been given over to light industries.

Behind this *Survey* there lies an amazing work of digestion. Jones has attempted to make all the evidence his own. Inevitably, this means that Jones's evidence is the sort of evidence that one man can make his own. It is confined almost exclusively to texts (includ- ing papyri); secondary literature, archaeological reports on Late Roman sites, numismatic evidence, and the flotsam and jetsam of inscriptions ('since many are so cunningly concealed in the *corpora* and periodicals' [p. vii]), cannot be handled with such certainty, and so they appear only subliminally in Jones's study.

The most lasting impression of the central chapters of this *Survey* is that the study of Late Roman society began in the sixteenth and seventeenth centuries with the study of the Roman law codes of Theodosius II and Justinian,[2] and that it is likely to end with them. Quite crucial considerations have to be deduced from such adminis- trative documents: the impression that agriculture, and not the trade and industry of the towns, contributed the overwhelming bulk of the national income, has to be based, largely, on a belief that 'the apportionment of the burden of taxation probably corresponded

[1] *L.R.E.* II, ch. xx, 'The Land', esp. 773–812.
[2] On the origins of Byzantine scholarship, see most recently, A. Pertusi, 'Le siècle de l'érudition', *Jahrbuch der österreichischen byzantinischen Gesellschaft*, XV (1966), 3–25, and in *Quaderni dell' Istituto di filologia greca dell' Università di Palermo*, III (1966).

roughly to the economic structure of the empire' (II, 1039). If Jones's overall picture of Late Roman society is to be reversed, this must be done along the lines taught us by Jones himself, by the patient re-examination and resetting of every piece of his vast mosaic of legislative texts.[1]

The reliance on such material, is the most obvious feature of this *Survey*. It is not, however, the most original.[2] For Jones has gone on to exploit the immense reserves of the Christian literature of this period, as no other author has done before him. The popular literature of the Christian Church has ensured that the 'man in the street' exists for us, in the Later Empire, as in no other period of ancient history.[3] And in the letter-books of the Fathers of the Church and in the acts and canons of its councils, Jones has found lush pasture for his evident fascination with the mechanisms of organization. As a result, this *Survey* is the first social history of the

[1] Hence the importance, for instance, of Jones's views on the *Notitia Dignitatum* (*L.R.E.* III, 347-80), for his assessment of the military weaknesses of the Western Empire at the time of the barbarian invasions (*L.R.E.* I, 194-9). Disagreement with Jones has tended to concentrate on his interpretation of administrative texts: see, for example, L. Ruggini, 'A proposito del follis nel iv secolo', *Rend. Accad. Lincei*, ser. 8, XVI (1961), 306-19, and in *Rivista storica italiana*, LXXVII (1965), 201-11, and A. Chastagnol, in *Rev. études latines*, XLII (1965), esp. 162-5. [For further examination of points of significant detail, see, for example, C. Lepelley, 'Déclin ou stabilité de l'agriculture africaine au Bas-Empire? À propos d'une loi d'Honorius,' *Antiquités Africaines*, I (1967), 135-144 and A. Cerati, 'À propos de la *conlatio equorum* dans le Code Théodosien', *Latomus* XXIX (1970), 998-1025.]

[2] See most recently J. Karayannopulos, *Das Finanzwesen des frühbyzantinischen Staates* (1958), and W. Seyfarth, *Soziale Fragen der spätrömischen Kaiserzeit im Spiegel des Theodosianus* (1963).

[3] Brilliantly demonstrated by N. H. Baynes: for example, 'The *Pratum Spirituale*', *Byzantine Studies and Other Essays* (1955), 271-70, and E. Dawes and N. H. Baynes, *Three Byzantine Saints* (1955), xi-xiv. See most recently, F. Halkin, 'L'hagiographie byzantine au service de l'histoire', *Thirteenth International Congress of Byzantine Studies*, Oxford 1966. [Now see E. Patlagean, 'À Byzance: ancienne hagiographie et histoire sociale', *Annales* XXIII (1968), 106-138 and P. Brown, 'The Rise and Function of the Holy Man in Late Roman Society', *Journal of Roman Studies* LXI (1971)—to appear.] The one serious omission in the *L.R.E.* is the evidence of the *Talmud*, well exploited by M. Avi-Yonah, *Geschichte der Juden im Zeitalter des Talmud* (1962) [and whose evidence is relevant to discussion on price-levels during the 'inflation' of the third century: see D. Sperber, 'The Cost of Living in Roman Palestine', *Journal for the Social and Economic History of the Orient*, XI (1968), pp. 233-74 and 'The Inflation in 4th-century Palestine', *Archiv orientalní*, XXXIV (1966), 54-66].

established Christian Church.[1] Invaluable pages on the wealth and social origins of the clergy culminate in a remarkable conclusion: the Christian Church is caught *in flagrante delicto*, as an institution harbouring more idle mouths, taking a larger share of the national wealth than the notorious Imperial bureaucracy, and equally accomplished in extracting wealth from the peasantry.[2] Any further study of the role of Christianity in Late Roman society must begin with these lucid pages.

To attempt to mould so much evidence is, inevitably, to be partly moulded by it. Jones presents this book, quite candidly, as a *Survey*. It is most effective in describing the way in which Late Roman people organized their lives—the structures of their administration, the organization of their army, the mechanisms of legislation, the collection of rents and taxes, the sources from which the state and the wealthier classes drew their wealth. One must read Jones often to realize how rich and how amazingly differentiated in his presentation of these aspects of Late Roman life. But it must be remembered, that not only are these precisely the aspects of the Later Empire that have been rendered most explicit for us in contemporary evidence: this evidence, itself, is the only evidence that can lend itself to unambiguous canons of interpretation, to the clinching of an argument through the sifting of 'proof texts'. They are the aspects of Late Roman social history that are, as it were, the most easy to 'verbalize'. But just because they are the most obvious, they are not always the most important: for what one often misses is a sense of the subtlety and the dynamic quality of the relations of change and continuity in these last centuries of the classical Roman Empire.

Jones's conclusions on the fall of the Roman Empire in the West, and on the quality of the Roman State that survived in the East, faithfully mirror the scope of the evidence he has handled. He maintains that his evidence 'suggests that the simple but rather unfashionable view that the barbarians played a considerable part in the decline and fall of the empire may have some truth in it', indeed, that 'barbarian attacks probably played a major part in the fall of the West' (II, 1027); while, in his description of the internal

---

[1] *L.R.E.* II, 920–9; a necessary complement to J. Gaudemet, *L'Eglise dans l'Empire romain* (IV–V. s.), Histoire du droit et des institutions de l'Eglise en Occident, III (1958).

[2] *L.R.E.* II, 894–914 and 933–4.

condition of the Empire, he emphasizes a theme that he has pursued relentlessly and demonstrated with amazing skill from a variety of sources throughout his *Survey*, that 'the basic economic weakness of the Empire was that too few producers supported too many idle mouths' (II, 1045). Such conclusions have the irrefutable merit of being intelligible to any Late Roman reader. Whether we accept them as sufficient and comprehensive, depends largely on what we think of the degree of awareness of Late Roman men. I would suggest that certain crucial developments have been passed over lightly by this *Survey*, because the evidence for them, being less explicit, has to be mobilized and assessed by different methods from those used by Jones. These concern: (i) changes in the attitude of the civilian population to the barbarian; (ii) the degree to which the continuity of the basic orientations of the economic and cultural life of the Roman Empire, from the age of the Severi to Theodosius I, excluded a necessary adjustment to the new form of the barbarian menace, created by new conditions along the Roman frontier; (iii) the extent to which the continuity of traditional social groupings hindered the initiative of the Roman state, by preventing the growth of a distinct bureaucratic class; (VI) the relation, in certain areas and in certain periods of the Later Empire, between the accumulation of the national wealth by the state, the church and private persons, and the rate of growth in trade and agriculture.

II

In his chapter on 'Religion and Morals' (xxiii), Jones limits himself to estimating the precise effect of Christian teaching on the behaviour of the average man. We have brilliant pages on the use of wealth,[1] on the survival of secular attitudes to divorce,[2] a salutary emphasis on the slowness with which Christianity abandoned the mentality of a minority religion,[3] and a shrewd estimate of the Church's failure.[4] What is ignored, is the slow merging of pagan prejudice with Christian intolerance.

[1] *L.R.E.* II, 970–2.
[2] Ibid. 973–6.
[3] Ibid. 984–5. The existence of a pagan tradition critical of ideas of a 'Heavenly City' and concerned with the practical responsibilities of government has been traced in Arabic sources by R. Walzer, 'Aspects of Islamic Political Thought', *Oriens*, XVI (1963), 40–60, esp. 44 and 55.
[4] Ibid. 979–82.

This merging took very different forms in the Eastern and the Western provinces of the Empire. In the West, Christian opinion, in the late fourth century, was prepared neither to respect those who kept the barbarian outside the Empire, nor to tolerate and absorb the barbarian, once inside. Western Christianity was not 'pacifist'. Rather, it became respectable through crystallizing the latent anti-militarism of the civilian population:[1] this is already evident in the 'senatorial' apologetic of Lactantius.[2] Unlike the medieval Byzantine Empire, Western society of the early Middle Ages failed notably to find an honourable place for the Roman soldier.[3]

At one and the same time, to be respectable involved keeping the barbarian at arm's length. Ambrose, for instance, will expect his readers to assume that the barbarian must be a heretic, and the heretic a barbarian.[4]

The barbarian raids and settlements in the Western Empire were

[1] Ibid. 922-4 shows that the bishops on the whole were drawn from the average civilian middle classes of the Empire.

[2] See J. Moreau, *Lactance: De la mort des persécuteurs*, I, Sources chrétiennes, 39 (1954), 51–5.

[3] See H. Delehaye, *Les légendes grecques des saints militaires* (1909). [Sulpicius Severus studiously minimized the military background of his hero, Martin of Tours: J. Fontaine, *Sulpice Sévère: Vie de Saint Martin*, II (Sources chrétiennes 134), 1968, pp. 436–508.]

[4] Clearly seen by M. Meslin, 'Nationalisme, État et religion à la fin du IVe siècle', *Archives de Sociologie des Religions*, XVIII (1964), 3–20. St. Patrick had to excuse himself for trying to convert the Irish: see *Confessio*, esp. c. XV (*Patrol. Lat.* LIII 808–9). There was no attempt to evangelize beyond the Roman frontier: see E. A. Thompson, 'Christianity and the Northern Barbarians', *The Conflict between Paganism and Christianity in the Fourth Century A.D.*, ed. Momigliano (1963), 56–78, esp. 62–4. This contrasts with later Byzantine diplomatic practice: see G. Moravcsik, 'Byzantinische Mission im Kreis der Türkvölker an der Nordküste des Schwarzen Meeres', *Thirteenth International Conference of Byzantine Studies*, Oxford 1966. [See now, Lellia Cracco-Ruggini, ' "De morte persecutorum" e polemica antibarbarica nella storiografia pagana e cristiana', *Rivista di storia e letteratura religiosa* IV, 1968, pp. 433–47 and 'Pregiudizî razziali, ostilità politica e culturale, intolleranza nell' impero romano'. *Athenaeum* n.s., XLVI, 1968, pp. 139–52 with J. Vogt, 'Kulturwelt und Barbaren,' *Akademie der Wissenschaften und Literatur in Mainz, Abh. d. Geistes- und Sozialwiss. Klasse*, 1967, W. Speyer-I. Opelt, 'Barbar: Nachträge zum Reallexikon für Antike und Christentum', *Jahrbuch für Antike und Christentum* X (1967), 251–290, and I. Opelt, 'Das Nationalitätsproblem bei Eunapios von Sardis', *Wiener Studien* LXXXII (1969), 23–36; and my remarks, inf. pp. 90–91.]

a protracted, piecemeal process. They might have taken on a very different meaning, if they had not been consistently experienced, by the most influential and articulate leaders of the civilian population, as the arrival of men condemned forever to remain 'outsiders'— men of war and heretics.[1] One cannot resist the impression that it was the new intolerance of the 'respectable' Catholicism of the later fourth century which kept the barbarian kingdoms 'barbaric': it forced the Visigothic, Vandal and Ostrogothic ruling classes in on themselves; it fostered their Arianism; it checked their 'detribalization', and so it ringed the Mediterranean of the late fifth and sixth centuries with precarious, encapsulated minorities, the *regna gentium*.[2]

The feature of East Roman society that contrasts most significantly with Western developments passes unnoticed in Jones's *Survey*. His insistence, in the face of much fashionable opinion, that the great theological controversies of the fifth and sixth centuries did not act as a cover for the 'separatist' aspirations of the Eastern provinces, but 'were in reality what they appeared to be' (II, 970), masks a whole judgement on the quality of the Christian culture of the Greek world. This culture was remarkably homogeneous. The Monophysite controversy is inconceivable without such a cultural framework: it is a 'centripetal' controversy, *par excellence*, in which the experts disagreed so vehemently precisely because each was convinced that it was possible to achieve agreement on a shared body of doctrine.[3] Nor was this rancorous creativity ever limited to theology: the Alexandrian Monophysite, John Philoponos found time to drub opponents on subjects as diverse as

[1] For example, E. Diehl, *Inscriptiones Latinae Christianae veteres*, I (1961), no. 1516, implies that a barbarian was delivered by Catholic baptism both from original sin *and* from his 'barbaric race'. [See P. Brown, *The World of Late Antiquity: From Marcus Aurelius to Muhammad* (1971), pp. 122–125.]

[2] E. A. Thompson, 'The Conversion of the Visigoths to Catholicism', *Nottingham Medieval Studies*, IV (1960), 4–35, esp. 29–33, and M. Wallace-Hadrill, 'Gothia and Romania', *The Long-Haired Kings* (1962), 45–6 [now add E. A. Thompson, *The Goths in Spain*, 1969 and Marc Reydellet, 'Les intentions idéologiques et politiques dans la *Chronique* d'Isidore de Séville', *Mélanges d'Archéologie et d'Histoire* LXXXII (1970) 363–400].

[3] C. Moeller, 'Le chalcédonisme et le néo-chalcédonisme en Orient de 451 à la fin du VIe siècle', *Das Konzil von Chalkedon*, I (1953), 637–720. [See John Meyendorff, 'Justinian, the Empire and the Church', *Dumbarton Oaks Papers* XXII (1968) 43–60.]

the perishable nature of the stars (thus anticipating Galileo)[1] and the spherical nature of the earth.[2]

By the end of the sixth century, the inhabitants of the Eastern Empire had come to feel themselves to be members of a totally Christian community, whose governing classes were attached to the same forms of religious life as the populace. The change is anticipated by the all-embracing character of the religious legislation of Justinian;[3] it is confirmed in the savage treatment of the 'outsider' *par excellence* in a Christian society, the Jew;[4] it is shown in the new quality of popular devotion to images,[5] and in the fact that the early seventh century is the golden age of hagiography.[6]

We miss this development if we concentrate exclusively on the theological divisions of the Eastern Empire. In theology, for instance, Egypt is 'perhaps the supreme example in human history of the triumph of non-co-operation'.[7] Yet we are only beginning to appreciate how this province contributed more to the general cultural life of the Empire than at any previous period of Roman rule,[8] and the extent to which its inhabitants remained united against the outsider, the pagan barbarian, praying in Greek and

[1] S. Sambursky, *The Physical World of Late Antiquity* (1962), 154–75.

[2] W. Wolska, *La Topographie chrétienne de Cosmas Indicopleustes*, Théologie et science au VIe siècle (1962), 147–92. See also B. Tatakis, *La philosophie byzantine*, Histoire de la philosophie, fasc. supplém. 2 (1949), 1–95, and G. L. Huxley, *Anthemius of Tralles. A Study in Late Greek Geometry*, Greek, Roman, and Byzantine Monographs, I (1959). [See now, *The Cambridge History of Later Greek and Early Medieval Philosophy*, ed. A. H. Armstrong (1967).]

[3] See L.R.E. I, 285–6 and A. Berger, 'La concezione di eretico nelle fonti giustinianee', *Rend. Accad. Lincei*, ser. 8, X (1955), 353–68.

[4] *L.R.E.* II, 949–50.

[5] E. Kitzinger, 'The Cult of Images in the Age before Iconoclasm', *Dumbarton Oaks Papers*, VII (1954), 83–149, esp. 127–8, and A. Frolow, 'Le culte de la relique de la Vraie Croix à la fin du VIe siècle', *Byzantino-Slavica*, XXII (1961), 320–39. [See now P. Brown, *The World of Late Antiquity*, pp. 172–87.]

[6] H.-G. Beck, *Kirche und theologische Literatur im byzantinischen Reich*, Handbuch der Altertumswissenschaft, XII, 2, 1 (1959), 402–13.

[7] N. H. Baynes, 'Alexandria and Constantinople. A Study in Ecclesiastical Diplomacy', *Byzantine Studies*, 101.

[8] See A. Cameron, 'Wandering Poets: A Literary Movement in Byzantine Egypt', *Historia*, XIV (1965), 470–509, and C. Detlef G. Müller, 'Die koptische Kirche zwischen Chalkedon und dem Arabereinmarsch', *Zeitschr. für Kirchengeschichte*, LXXV (1964), 271–308. [Now add P. du Bourguet, *L'Art copte*, 1968.]

Coptic for the success of the Roman army, now thought of as the host of the people of Israel.[1]

This contrast must be taken into account in considering the divergent fate of the Eastern and Western provinces of the Empire in the early Middle Ages.

For Jones the problem of the decline of the Roman Empire appears deceptively simple: in the East, it did not decline, it survived very well.[2] Jones's point is reinforced by recent studies of Byzantine society in the later seventh century.[3] These show that the Empire survived the Arab and Slav invasions of that time on an administrative, social, and military framework, that was not altogether different from that described by Jones for the reigns of Justinian and Maurice: there was no radical 'renewal' of the structure of East Roman society, such as had once been ascribed to the reign of Heraclius.[4] The decisive factor, perhaps, was the new homogeneity: it ensured that a population that was always ready to submit to catastrophic barbarian raids as a 'scourge of God' might also rally to repel the invader with something like the spirit of a crusade.

In the West, the fate of the Empire was sealed by Christian prejudice. Judged by 'Byzantine' standards, the barbarian kingdoms of the West must appear vaguely disgusting: the Merovingians granted tax-exemptions (I, pp. 261-2) and sold bishoprics (II, 920). But it is only too easy to underestimate the primitive bedrock of Roman law and administrative practice in the West, and to fail to appreciate the determination with which the Frankish kings and the mixed aristocracy of their court continued to rule a sub-Roman society effectively far into the seventh century.[5] The problem,

---

[1] P. J. Photiades, 'A semi-Greek, semi-Coptic Parchment', *Klio*, XLI (1963), 234-5. [See J. Barns, 'Schenute as an Historical Source', *Actes du Xème Congrès des Papyrologues*, Warsaw (1964), 153-157.]

[2] *L.R.E.* II, 1025-7.

[3] See especially A. Pertusi, 'La formation des thèmes byzantins', *Berichte zum XI. internationalen Byzantinistenkongress*, 1958 (1960), 1-40, and J. Karayannopulos, *Die Entstehung der byzantinischen Themenordnung*, Byzantinisches Archiv, 10 (1959). [See now W. Kaegi, 'Some Reconsiderations on the Themes', *Jahrbuch der österreichischen byzantinischen Gesellschaft* XVI (1967), 39-54.]

[4] P. Lemerle, 'Quelques remarques sur le règne d'Héraclius', *Studi medievali*, 3rd ser. 1 (1960), 347-61.

[5] See esp. M. Wallace-Hadrill, *The Long-Haired Kings*, 185-223, and R. Sprandel, 'Struktur und Geschichte des merowingischen Adels', *Histor. Zeitschr.* CXCII (1961), 33-71.

therefore, for the Western medievalist is not only why the Western Empire 'fell', but why it could not be recreated, like the many 'barbarian' Empires established in Northern China in the early Middle Ages. Part of the answer may be found in the history of intolerance in the fifth and sixth centuries.

III

The study of Later Roman history had, once, been content to concentrate exclusively on those features that separated Late Roman society from its classical roots. The views of Lot and Rostovtzeff are what a theologian would call 'sub-lapsarian': the 'fall' of the 'crisis' of the third century ensured that the Roman Empire as reorganized by Diocletian and Constantine bore only a superficial resemblance to an ancient society. Jones's *Survey* is an implicit rebuttal of this view. It comes after a generation of research that has been stimulated, above all, by surprising discoveries of the degree to which the ancient forms of life survived the 'crisis' of the third century. The transformations of urban life, in the Later Empire, have been found to be far more paradoxical than had once been thought.[1] A realization of the continuing role of a monetary economy has altered our picture of the 'style' of Late Roman society.[2] The traditional elements in the ideology of the Imperial power have come to be recognized.[3] Above all, the intellectual transformation of Late Antiquity can be seen as a continuous arc, linking the age of

---

[1] For example, S. Mazzarino, *Aspetti sociali del quarto secolo* (1951), 217–69; P. A. Février, 'Ostie et Porto à la fin de l'Antiquité', *Mélanges d'archéologie et d'histoire*, LXX (1957–8), 295–330; P. Petit, *Libanius et la vie municipale à Antioche* (1955) and P. A. Février, 'Notes sur le développement urbain en Afrique du Nord', *Cahiers Archéologiques* XIV (1964), 1–47 [see now the most important study of D. Claude, *Die byzantinische Stadt im 6. Jht.* (Byzantinisches Archiv 13), 1969.]

[2] For example, H. Geiss, *Geld- und naturalwirtschaftliche Erscheinungsformen im staatlichen Aufbau Italiens während der Gotenzeit*, Vierteljahrschrift für Sozial- und Wirtschaftsgeschichte, Beiheft 27 (1931); G. Mickwitz, *Geld und Wirtschaft im römischen Reich des vierten Jahrhunderts* (1932); A. Piganiol, 'Le problème de l'or au IVe siècle', *Annales d'histoire sociale* (1945), 47–53; and Mazzarino, *Aspetti sociali*, 169–216.

[3] For example, H. Gelzer, 'Altertumswissenschaft und Spätantike', *Histor. Zeitschr.* CXXXV (1926), 173–87. J. Karayannopulos, 'Der frühbyzantinische Kaiser', *Byzantinische Zeitschrift*, XLIX (1956), 369–84, provides a useful survey.

Marcus Aurelius to that of Constantine, and quietly overspanning the spectacular external events of the third century:[1] it is no longer surprising to find Plotinus and his senatorial circle in the Rome of Gallienus,[2] and an Italian gentleman portrayed in the 'Asiatic' manner of the Antonines, on the eve of the accession of Diocletian.[3]

It is, precisely, a balance sheet of the speed and direction of change in the third and fourth centuries that we need, to understand the problems facing the Roman Empire.[4]

For the problem posed by this continuity is, in part, a psychological one. One cannot understand the mentality of the governing classes of the fourth century, if one does not realize the extent to which they seemed to themselves to have coped successfully with the disorders of the mid-third century, in terms of ideals of government and society that merely continued the aspirations of the prosperous days of the Severi: Dio Cassius already wanted 'a stable, centrally governed, sharply graded society of which the primary object is to avoid at all costs disorder and change';[5] Jones's *Survey*, with its great emphasis on the achievement of just these qualities in Dio's native, Eastern provinces, would have reassured him. Dio and his senatorial colleagues, of course, would have less of a hand in bringing about that state of affairs than they had hoped; but the inscriptions of the Later Empire show that men who shared his

[1] See E. R. Dodds, *Pagan and Christian in an Age of Anxiety* (1965).

[2] R. Harder, 'Plotins Leben', *Kleine Schriften* (1960), 257–95. [Now add *The Cambridge History of Later Greek and Early Medieval Philosophy*, ed. A. H. Armstrong, 1968 and, on the resilience of traditional scholarship, see A. D. Momigliano, 'L'età del trapasso fra storiografia antica e storiografia medievale'. *Rivista storia italiana*, LXXXI, 1969, pp. 286–303.]

[3] C. E. Vermeule, 'A Graeco-Roman portrait of the 3rd century A.D.', *Dumbarton Oaks Papers*, XV (1961), 1–22. [Now add I. Lavin, 'The Ceiling Paintings in Trier and Illusionism in Constantinian Painting'. *Dumbarton Oaks Papers*, XXI, 1967, pp. 99–113.]

[4] *L.R.E.* I, 25–32, is particularly sane on the economic crisis. See especially G. Walser, T. Pekary, *Die Krise des römischen Reiches. Bericht über die Forschungen zur Geschichte des 3. Jahrhunderts (193–284 n. chr.) von 1939 bis 1959* (1962), and the excellent surveys of R. Rémondon, *La crise de l'empire romain* (1964), 97–114, esp. 102–5, and F. Millar, *Das römische Reich und sein Nachbarn. Die Mittelmeerwelt im Altertum, IV.* Fischer Weltgeschichte (1966), esp. 146–7, 217–20, and 241–9: now available as *The Roman Empire and its Neighbours* (1967), at pp. 144–45; 213–17; 239–48. [See J. P. Callu, *La politique monétaire des empereurs romains de 238 à 311* (1969).]

[5] F. Millar, *A Study of Cassius Dio* (1964), 108.

attitudes continued to govern the Greek provinces, from the late third to the late sixth century.[1]

It has always been dangerous to govern the Mediterranean with attitudes that have become fixed with success. One has only to read Jones's sober pages on the cost of transport, 'the greatest incubus on the empire' (II, 1048),[2] and to compare this with the abundant literature on the famines of Rome in the fourth century, in which all parties emphasize that the solution of their ills was *only* a matter of transport,[3] to realize this. As for the relations of these men with the barbarians: from the battle of Adrianople to the reign of Justinian II,[4] the worst catastrophes of the Roman Empire were precipitated by the belief that the primitive methods applied to the inhabitants of the Empire by its bureaucracy—the eternal short-cut of the coercion of social groups (II, 1051)—could be successfully extended to embrace the transfer of barbarian populations.

The Roman Empire of the fourth century, therefore, was an empire that had successfully maintained itself around the Mediterranean. Jones's explanation of the fall of this Empire in the West merely reflects faithfully the great blind spot of such a society: the northern barbarian is the unwelcome intruder, seemingly more importunate than ever, but of whom nothing is known. Most students of Ammianus Marcellinus, for instance, are merely following the grain of their author, by piling up studies of the affluent 'Mediterranean' societies of Rome and Antioch, and passing over what he

[1] L. Robert, 'Epigrammes du Bas-Empire, II: Epigrammes relatifs à des gouverneurs', *Hellenica*, IV (1948), 35–110, esp. 108. [See now G. Dagron, 'L'Empire romain d'Orient au IVe siècle et les traditions politiques de l'Hellénisme'; *Travaux et Mémoires du Centre de Recherche d'Histoire et Civilisation byzantines* III (1968), 1–235 and A. Pertusi, 'I principi fondamentali della concezione del potere a Bisanzio. Per un commento al dialogo "Sulla scienza politica" attribuito a Pietro Patrizio (secolo VI), *Bull. Instituto storico per il Medio Evo e Archivio Muratoriano* LXXX (1968), 1–23.]

[2] *L.R.E.* II, 827–34 and 841–4. See also J. Rougé, 'Quelques aspects de la navigation en Méditerranée du Ve siècle et dans la première moitié du VIe siècle', *Cahiers d'Histoire*, VI (1961), 131–54, and his *Recherches sur l'organisation du commerce maritime en Méditerranée sous l'empire romain* (École pratique des Hautes Etudes. Ports, Routes, Traffics, 21, 1966).

[3] See H. Kohns, *Versorgungskrisen und Hungerrevolte im spätantiken Rom* (Antiquitas 6, 1961), esp. 63–77.

[4] See Ammianus Marcellinus, *Res gestae* XXXI, 4, 4–5, and Theophanes, *Chron.* ad ann. mundi 6183 (Bonn Corpus, pp. 559–61). See P. Charanis, 'The Transfer of Populations as a Policy in the Byzantine Empire', *Comparative Studies in Society and History*, III (1961).

has to say about the northern barbarians.[1] He has, indeed, far less to say than he should: he and his audience plainly sympathized with the Emperor Julian in dismissing the Visigoths as a mere backward tribe, ravaged by slave-traders, and in regarding Persia as the traditional enemy.[2] A complete study of the social and diplomatic relations between *Germania* and *Romania* on the eve of the invasions has yet to be written, for the simple and depressing reason that few people thought about such things at the time. The Byzantime Empire of the early Middle Ages, a state chastened by bitter experience, is infinitely superior in this respect to the omnipotent and obtuse colossus of the fourth century: 'in these centuries was forged, in reply to the northern challenge, by steadfast faith and lucid thinking, by careful study and observation, by trial and error, that essential weapon of East Roman policy—the imperial diplomacy which remains one of Byzantium's lasting contributions to the history of Europe'.[3]

This is not to be isolated as a purely political failure. It reflects a tension in the orientation of Late Roman society, between the Mediterranean and the northern provinces of the Western Empire. For one of the most remarkable developments of the third and fourth centuries is the fact that for the first time, Roman civilization—Roman urban life, Roman villas, a Roman style of life, and a Roman standard of living—had reached the political frontier of the Empire in just those areas that faced the most restless parts of the barbaric world. In the Balkan peninsula, for instance, in the second and early third century, the 'barbarian' could exist inside the Empire. By the fourth century the frontier provinces of the Danube were as much part of *Romania* as any other; and so the only 'barbarian' was

[1] Most recently, for example, A Demandt, *Zeitkritik und Geschichtsbild im Werk des Ammianus* (1965). E. A. Thompson, *The Early Germans* (1965), esp. 72–108, 'Roman Diplomacy and the Barbarians', and *The Visigoths in the Time of Ulfilas* (1966) are brilliant exceptions. [Now see J. F. Matthews, 'Olympiodorus of Thebes and the History of the West', *Journal of Roman Studies* LX (1970), 79–97.]

[2] Ammianus Marcellinus, XXII, 7.8. Compare P. Petit, *Libanius. . .* 182–7, for an excellent characterization of the horizons of his compatriot, Libanius.

[3] D. Obolensky, 'The Empire and its Northern Neighbours, 565–1018', *The Cambridge Medieval History*, IV. *The Byzantine Empire: I. Byzantium and its Neighbours*, (1966), 473. [On sixth-century attitudes, see two excellent studies by Averil Cameron, 'Agathias and the early Merovingians', *Annali della Scuola Normale di Pisa*, ser. ii, XXXVIII, 1968, pp. 95–140; and 'Agathias on the Sassanians', *Dumbarton Oaks Papers*, XXXIII, 1969, pp. 69–183.]

the one across the military frontier,[1] faced directly, for the first time, with a society whose higher standard of living and intolerance of his own way of life must have seemed to increase with every development of the third and fourth centuries. 'Envy', not the aimless motion of tribes,[2] drew the barbarians on to a land where the bait— the great villas and Imperial residences of Pannonia[3] and the Rhineland[4]—dangled provocatively close.

Yet, at just this time, the personnel of the Late Roman government continued to come, predominantly, from the Mediterranean.[5] Their style of life remained Mediterranean, based on the laborious transport of grain to the traditional urban centres of the ancient world.[6] Their armies had to be fed from Aquitaine;[7] and, in the end, they will both abandon their Romanized colleagues in Britain, and will shroud this withdrawal from the northern world in a silence that becomes ever more shocking the more we learn of the high

---

[1] Compare Dio Cassius, in the early third century, on Pannonia—'The Pannonians . . . lead the most miserable existence of all mankind. For they are not well off as regards either soil or climate; they cultivate no olives and no wine . . .' (*Dios' Roman History*, transl. Cary, Loeb, v. 415), with a fourth-century source: '. . . *Pannoniae regio, terra dives in omnibus, non solum fructibus et iumentis, sed et negotiis et mancipiis, in qua semper imperatorum est habitatio delectabilis'* (*Totius Orbis Descriptio*, c. 57, Geographi Graeci Minores, II, 525 and ed. J. Rougé, *Expositio Totius Mundi et Gentium*, Sources chrétiennes, 1967, 124). [M. Meslin, *Les Ariens d'Occident*, 335–430 (1964), 59–102, is a discovery of the intellectual activity of this province.]

[2] Ambros. *Ep.* XVIII, 21: the good harvest of Rhaetia Secunda had 'lured the enemy upon her'.

[3] A. Mócsy, s.v. 'Pannonia', *Pauly-Wissowa-Reallexikon*, Suppl. IX (1962), cols. 516–776, esp. 667–701 and E. B. Thomas, *Römische Villen in Pannonien*, 1964. [Now see A. Mócsy, *Gesellschaft und Romanisation in der römischen Provinz Moesia Superior* (1970).]

[4] For the high standard of urban life in fourth-century Trier, see, for example, H. Eiden, 'Spätrömische Figurenmosaik im Kornmarkt in Trier', *Aus der Schatzkammer der antiken Trier. Neue Forschungen und Ausgrabungen* (1959), 54–93. For the frontier policy, see most recently, E. Demougeot, 'La Gaule nord-orientale à la veille de l'invasion germanique', *Revue historique*, CCXXXVI (1966), 17–46. [Now see Edith Wightman, *Roman Trier and the Treveri* (1970).]

[5] One such resident was even taken home, to be buried in Italy: E. Gabba-G. Tibiletti, 'Una signora di Treviri sepolta a Pavia', *Athenaeum*, n.s. XXXVIII (1960), 253–62, at p. 254.

[6] See J. Teall, 'The Grain-Supply of the Byzantine Empire', *Dumbarton Oaks Papers*, XIII (1959), 137–8, on the continuance of a grain-trade between Mediterranean cities as late as the seventh century.

[7] *L.R.E.*, II, 1064–5.

quality of the Late Roman life of that province.[1] Two studies are still vital to our understanding of the failure of the Western Empire: that of C. E. Stevens, which emphasizes the technological failure to develop a 'Northern' agrarian society, as an alternative to that of the Mediterranean,[2] and that of W. H. C. Frend, which stresses a parallel failure to absorb a non-Mediterranean society in the hinterland of Africa.[3] The medievalist, who is aware of the degree to which the agrarian society of Northern France was able, seven centuries later, to bear the weight of an architecture as ambitious and a nobility as parasitic and given over to 'pot-latch' behaviour as the urban aristocracies of the age of the Antonines,[4] must conclude that, in the conditions of the fourth and early fifth centuries, the Mediterranean was a *damnosa haereditas*, tying the Roman governing class of the West to the double rigidity of a Mediterranean style of life and the intolerance of a Mediterranean, urban religion.

IV

The social history of the Later Roman Empire must be studied, largely, in terms of the role of the State in Late Roman society. Jones shows healthy scepticism on the extent to which the Imperial laws either intended to impose, much less succeeded in imposing, a rigid control on the social system of the Empire.[5] The more precise problem remains: the place which a newly created and powerful bureaucracy had gained in Roman society from the fourth century onwards: to what extent, for instance, its regulations on the colonate colluded with the needs of the great landowners,[6] to what extent its

[1] See most recently studies of Pelagianism that imply a high standard of culture and theological life in early fifth-century Britain: J. N. L. Myres, 'Pelagius and the End of Roman Rule in Britain', *Journ. Rom. Studies*, L (1960), 21–36, and J. Morris, 'Pelagian Literature', *Journ. Theolog. Studies*, n.s. XVI (1965), 26–60. [See Sheppard S. Frere, *Britannia. A History of Roman Britain*, 1967.]

[2] C. E. Stevens, 'Agriculture and Rural Life in the Later Roman Empire', *The Cambridge Economic History*, I (1942), 89–117.

[3] W. H. C. Frend, *The Donatist Church* (1952), esp. 25–59.

[4] Lynn White Jr. *Medieval Technology and Social Change* (1962), 39–78.

[5] *L.R.E.* I, viii, and II, 1051. See R. MacMullen, 'Social Mobility and the Theodosian Code', *Journal of Roman Studies*, LIV (1964), 49–53—a dossier of successful evasions.

[6] *L.R.E.* II, esp. 796.

demand for payment in kind damaged the interests of important classes;[1] to what extent the structure and methods of the tax system encouraged the rapid accumulation of wealth through profiteering by privileged members of the bureaucracy;[2] to what extent the salaries and standards of living of public servants could compete with those of private individuals:[3] to what extent, generally, it is possible to regard the Late Roman period as marked by the formation of a new class, a 'nobility of service', sensitive to the initiative of the Emperors, and so providing the sociological foundations of the Imperial absolutism.

Jones's views on this subject are of the greatest interest. The Later Roman Empire, in his opinion, was marked by an exceptional degree of social mobility. In the Eastern Empire, this social mobility favoured the growth of a loyal administrative class; while, in the West, this mobility was brought to a halt by the power of the senatorial aristocracy, who, by the middle of the fifth century, enjoyed a monopoly of high office.[4] The amazing spread of Christianity after the conversion of Constantine illustrates this clearly: for this, 'the most audacious act ever committed by an autocrat in disregard and defiance of the vast majority of his subjects',[5] is now seen to coincide with a regrouping of the Roman social hierarchy around the Imperial court.[6]

Continued study of the 'speed' and the 'area' of such mobility is not only vital to our understanding of the general 'sensitivity' of the upper classes of the Empire to the initiative of the Emperor: it affects our view of the religion and culture of the age;[7] it can be invoked to explain both the 'classicizing' of Christianity,[8] and the

[1] Mickwitz, *Geld u. Wirtschaft*.
[2] Mazzarino, *Aspetti sociali*, 110–18 and 169–216.
[3] *L.R.E.* II, ch. XVI, 'The Civil Service', and 1055–8.
[4] *L.R.E.* I, 207, and II, 1066.
[5] J. B. Bury, *History of the Later Roman Empire* (1923), I, 366.
[6] Jones, 'The Social Background of the Struggle between Paganism and Christianity', *The Conflict between Christianity and Paganism* (1963), 17–37, esp. 35–7. Compare, Mazzarino, *Aspetti sociali*, esp. 114.
[7] See the excellent studies of K. M. Hopkins, 'Social Mobility in the Later Roman Empire: the evidence of Ausonius', *Classical Quarterly*, n.s. XI (1961), 239–48, and 'Elite Mobility in the Roman Empire', *Past and Present*, XXXII (1965), 12–26.
[8] See P. R. L. Brown, 'Aspects of the Christianisation of the Roman Aristocracy', *Journal of Roman Studies*, LI (1961), esp. 9–11. [v. inf. p. 177–82.]

corresponding cheapening of classical culture, as a mark of status hastily acquired by the new professional classes.[1]

Such a study requires caution and due attention to the nuances implied in this *Survey*. There is the very difficult problem of the continuity of the provincial aristocracies in the third and fourth centuries. I find it difficult to believe that the 'crisis' of the third century created a *tabula rasa* in every province of the Empire. The platitude of Late Roman authors, that 'nobility' was merely newly amassed riches should not be taken too seriously:[2] Jones is, surely, right to suggest that the vast properties of some Roman senatorial families had 'snowballed' slowly, since the High Empire.[3] The only provincial aristocracy that has been studied in detail—that of Gaul— may be the least representative;[4] in that this was an area where the insecurity of the third century had been at its greatest, and where the residence of the Emperors at Trier encouraged exceptional fluidity. In Italy, by contrast, it is possible to find families who continue from the age of Marcus Aurelius to beyond the end of the Western Empire.[5] Such families may have covered many provinces of the Western Empire like ground ivy. If anything, it was the power of the State and not the traditional way of life of the provincial upper classes of the Western Empire which had been weakened by

---

[1] See the excellent remarks of Alföldi, *A Conflict of Ideas*, 96–124 and Momigliano, 'Pagan and Christian Historiography in the Fourth Century A.D.', *The Conflict between Paganism and Christianity*, esp. 85–6.

[2] Gaudentius, *Sermo*, XV (*Patrol. Lat.* XX, col. 949), and Salvian, *de gubernatione Dei*, III, 10 (*Patrol. Lat.* LIII, col. 68).

[3] *L.R.E.* II, 555.

[4] See K. Stroheker, *Der senatorische Adel im spätantiken Gallien* (1948) [and 'Spanische Senatoren der spätröm. und westgot. Zeit', *Germanentum und Spätantike* (1965), 54–87].

[5] E.g. the Naeratii of Saepinum, near Beneventum; see s.v. Naeratius, *Pauly-Wissowa-Reallexikon*, XVI, 2539 ff. We can anticipate a study of such a family, the Rufii Festi of Volsinii, by J. F. Matthews. [*Historia*, XVI, 1967, pp. 484–509.] See also, J. Morris, 'Munatius Plancus Paulinus', *Bonner Jahrbücher*, CLXV (1965), 88–96, esp. the remarks on p. 96. [Fergus Millar, 'P. Herennius Dexippus, The Greek World and the Third Century Invasions', *Journal of Roman Studies*, LIX, 1969, pp. 12–29, is a fundamental contribution to this problem in the Greek world. A. H. M. Jones–J. R. Martindale–J. Morris, *The Prosopography of the Later Roman Empire*, vol. I: 260–395 A.D. (1971) has now placed an indispensable tool in the hands of scholars; see also the remarks of A. Chastagnol, 'La prosopographie, méthode de recherche sur l'histoire du Bas-Empire', *Annales* XXV (1970), 1229–1235.]

the 'crisis' of the third century,[1] and, for this reason, the sinister efflorescence of aristocratic government and of traditional culture in fifth-century Italy may have very deep roots indeed.[2]

Even in the Eastern Empire, the creation of a continuous 'administrative' governing class was a 'dam' close-run thing'.[3] Spectacular instances of social mobility and genuine administrative efficiency among the Praetorian Prefects should not blind us to the slow and unremitting pressure of the average, well-educated member of the Greek urban upper classes on the lower reaches of the bureaucracy and on the provincial administration. As governors and officials, these men received epigrams that hardly changed throughout this period.[4] They may not have been landowners on the same scale as the Western senators, but they shared a common human wish to avoid high taxation, and knew well enough how to protect themselves against its incidence. Their culture had impressive elements of continuity with the classical past, which rendered them 'sound-proof' to the religious preoccupations of their masters.[5]

[1] Studies of the forms of political influence in the Roman world rightly emphasize that these forms were continuous, while it was the needs of the State which changed in the third century: G. E. M. de Ste Croix, 'Suffragium: from Vote to Patronage', *British Journal of Sociology*, V (1954), 33–47, and L. Harmand, *Le Patronat sur les collectivités publiques des origines aux Bas-Empire* (1957). [See now P. Garnsey, *Social Structure and Legal Privilege in the Roman Empire* (1970).]

[2] *L.R.E.* I, 204–7. See A. Cameron, 'The Date and Identity of Macrobius', *Journal of Roman Studies*, LVI (1966), 25–38. [For the case of the *Anicii* and their traditional connections with Africa, see now A. Beschouach, 'Uzappa et le proconsul d'Afrique Sex. Cocceius Anicius Faustus Paulinus'. *Mélanges d'Archéologie et d'Histoire* LXXXI (1969), 195–218, esp. 215–218.]

[3] 'Outbursts of professionalism were the exception, the rule was a victory of the aristocratic ethos', Hopkins, 'Elite Mobility', *Past and Present*, XXXII (1965), 19. The only truly distinctive 'administrative' class was formed by the eunuchs: see Hopkins, 'Eunuchs in Politics in the Later Roman Empire', *Proc. Cambridge Philological Soc.*, CLXXXIX (1963).

[4] See Robert, 'Epigrammes du Bas-Empire', *Hellenica*, IV (1948), and Gervase Mathew, *Byzantine Aesthetics* (1963), esp. 54–77—a brilliant characterization. [See now, G. Dagron, 'Aux origines de la civilisation byzantine: langue de culture et langue d'État', *Revue historique*, CCXLI (1969), pp. 23–56.]

[5] See most recently Averil and Alan Cameron, 'Christianity and Tradition in the Historiography of the Late Empire', *Classical Quarterly*, n.s. XIV (1964), 316–28, and Averil Cameron, 'The "Scepticism" of Procopius', *Historia*, XV (1966), 466–82. [See now A. Cameron, 'The End of the Ancient Universities', *Cahiers d'histoire mondiale* X (1967), 653–673; H. D. Saffrey–L. G. Westerink, *Proclus: Théologie platonicienne*, Éditions Guillaume Budé (1968), IX–LIV; Ph.

It is a pity that studies of the traditional aristocracies of the Later Empire should have concentrated almost exclusively on the Western Empire.[1] It means that it is difficult to know what to look for, to find their equivalent in the East. To seek a Symmachus or a Sidonius Apollinaris among the Cappadocian Fathers is to court disappointment.[2] But patient work along the fringes of the bureaucracy at Constantinople, on the poetry, for instance, patronized by officials and private persons, can reveal the extent of a more stable, more backward-looking, more amateurish world.[3]

Altogether, the Late Roman bureaucracy remained dangerously embedded in the aristocratic values of the ancient world. This new class had to compete with long-established ideas of status. The standard of living of its members always fell below that of the possessors of inherited wealth. Its inflated titles[4] and notorious corruption[5] merely reflect an uphill struggle to maintain its position. Its frontiers were never, for a moment, secure against the encroach-, ments of the traditional upper classes of the Empire;[6] as the Em-

Merlan, 'Ammonius Hermiae, Zacharias Scholasticus and Boethius', *Greek Roman and Byzantine Studies* IX (1968), 193–203; and A. Cameron, 'The Last Days of the Academy at Athens', *Proc. Cambridge Philol. Society* CXCV (1969), 7–29.]

[1] See the excellent studies of A. Chastagnol, *La Préfecture urbaine à Rome sous le Bas-Empire* (1960), *Les Fastes de la Préfecture urbaine* (1962), and *Le Sénat romain sous le règne d'Odoacre* (1966), and M. A. Wes, *Das Ende des Kaisertums im Westen des römischen Reichs*, 1967; see inf. pp. 227–34.

[2] For example, B. Treucker, *Politische und sozialgeschichtliche Studien zu den Basilius-Briefen* (1961), criticized by S. Giet, 'Basile, était-il sénateur?', *Revue d'histoire ecclésiastique*, LX (1965), 429–43.

[3] Averil and Alan Cameron, 'The Cycle of Agathias', *Journal of Hellenic Studies*, LXXXVI (1966), 6–25. For a pre-Constantinian administrative family, still active in the fifth century, see L. C. Cantarelli, 'L'iscrizione onoraria di Giunio Quinto Palladio', *Bulletino Communale di Roma*, LIV (1926), 35–41, and W. M. Ramsey, 'A noble Anatolian family of the Fourth Century', *Classical Review*, XXXIII (1919), 1–9.

[4] R. Guilland, 'Etudes sur l'histoire administrative de l'Empire byzantin. Les titres nobiliaires de la haute époque (IVe–VIe siècles)', *Mélanges G. Ostrogorsky*, 1 (1963), 117–33, for the inflation of honours.

[5] *L.R.E.* II, 1054–6.

[6] As is shown in attitudes to influence: W. Liebeschuetz, 'Did the Pelagian Movement have Social Aims?' *Historia*, XII (1963), 227–41, esp. 228–32, and O. Collet, 'La pratique et l'institution du suffragium au Bas-Empire', *Revue historique de droit français et étranger*, 4 ser. XLIII (1965), 185–221. [See R. I. Frank, '*Commendabilis* in Ammianus Marcellinus', *Amer. Journal of Philology* LXXXVIII (1967), 309–318.]

peror was forced to admit, 'the collection of [tax] arrears flags when the exactor pays deference to the debtor.'[1]

V

Jones characterizes the Later Roman Empire as an increasingly 'top-heavy' society. For, to the traditional accumulations of landed wealth and the traditional demands of an urban civilization, that had already reached sinister proportions under the Antonines, the Late Roman Emperors added a vastly increased army and bureaucracy, and patronized an established church that absorbed men and wealth like a sponge. The long-term effects of this imbalance were, briefly, that land fell out of cultivation and the population slowly receded, because the combined weight of rents and taxes left the peasants unable to rear sufficient children to counterbalance the very high death-rate.[2] Few pre-modern societies have been described, in cross-section, with such patient detail, and their weaknesses revealed with such austerity, as in this *Survey* of the Roman Empire.

The precise extent and progress of the imbalance which Jones senses can never, of course, be measured statistically. Such a characterization of the Later Empire is bound, therefore, to remain 'impressionistic'. More important, this characterization is tied to the level of consciousness of contemporary writers, and is determined by the angle of vision permitted by the material that Jones handles.

Given the rigid structure of any pre-industrial Mediterranean society, from fourth-century Rome to eighteenth-century Naples, many of the phenomena which Jones deplores—notably the accumulation of property and the high consumption and conspicuous waste of the Late Roman aristocracy—are inevitable.[3] The

---

[1] *L.R.E.* II, 545. [See J. F. Matthews, 'Symmachus and the *magister militum* Theodosius', *Historia* xx (1971), 122–128 esp. 127–128, 'The Gallic Supporters of Theodosius', *Latomus* xxx (1971) and *Western Aristocracies and the Imperial Court*—to appear.]

[2] Ibid. 810–23 and 1038–47.

[3] R. P. Duncan-Jones, 'Wealth and Munificence in Roman Africa', *Papers of the British School at Rome*, xxxi (1963), esp. 161–2. Compare Patrick Chorley, *Oil, Silk and Enlightenment. Economic Problems in XVIIIth Century Naples* (1965), esp. 11–15. [What we lack is a study of the continuity and transformation of ancient ideals on public expenditure in the late classical period, for which the remarks of L. Robert, in *Hellenica* xi–xii, 1960, pp. 569 sq., would be a starting-point.]

culprits may merely have changed without necessarily increasing: in the early third century, contemporaries blamed the extravagance of the Greek cities;[1] by the early fourth century, they were blaming the army and the bureaucracy.[2] As for the Christian Church, contemporaries, on the whole, welcomed its growth to affluence, and so let it pass largely unnoticed. We may never know whether a Christian basilica of the Late Roman period was as expensive as a portico of the age of Marcus Aurelius. What we do know, from Late Roman sources, is that the basilica was welcomed as an avatar of the forum.

For the anatomy of any 'top-heavy' society cannot be divorced from a study of the 'vertical' links between classes. In the Later Empire, people felt that they needed protectors. They even sought them in Heaven as well as on earth.[3] Our judgement on Late Roman society, in many cases, depends largely on our estimate as to how effective this protection was. The Gaul of the fifth and sixth centuries, for instance, provides an example of the strengthening of the local, 'vertical' links of society around an effective aristocracy, whose role is summed up, with justifiable self-congratulation, in the works of Gregory of Tours.[4] Such men provided some degree of security for the civilian population in the time of the barbarian kingdoms.[5] There was always a need, in East and West, for such people: 'a man who could do harm to his enemies and good to his friends'.[6] Yet more patient work on the agrarian history of the age may reveal, for instance, that absenteeism and a lack of interest in one's estate were not as common among Late Roman landowners as Jones's picture suggests. The *agricola bonus* may have been un-

[1] Millar, *Cassius Dio*, 109.

[2] Lactantius, *De mortibus persecutorum*, VII (ed. Moreau, *Lactance*, 84–5).

[3] See most recently František Graus, *Volk, Herrscher und Heiliger im Reich der Merowinger. Studien zur Hagiographie der Merowingerzeit* (česk. akad. věd. 1965). [See F. Lotter, 'Illustrissimus vir Severinus', *Deutsches Archiv* XXVI (1970)), 200–207 and P. Brown, 'The Rise and Function of the Holy Man', *Journal of Roman Studies* LXI (1971).]

[4] On the reputation enjoyed by the family of Ecdicius on account of his organization of famine relief: Gregory of Tours, *Hist. Francorum*, II, 24. For the role of the bishop in the life of the towns, for instance, see R. Latouche, *The Birth of the Western Economy*, trans. Wilkinson (1961), esp. 103–6.

[5] For a wholesale ransoming and resettlement of the agricultural population of Liguria after a barbarian invasion, see Ennodius, *Vita Epifanii*, esp. cc. 171–7 (Mon. Germ. Hist., Auct. Antiq. VII, 1885, 105–6).

[6] *L.R.E.* II, 915.

fashionable in the literature of the time: but we do catch frequent glimpses of him in less refined sources—in sermons and in the lives of saints.[1]

Ultimately, Jones's brilliant anatomy suffers from the nature of the evidence. An economic historian of this period is condemned to remain at a 'pre-Harveyan' stage: he can trace the veins and arteries of the society; he has only a hint of capillaries (banking, for instance, appears in only one document);[2] he has to refuse to know how the blood may have circulated.

Jones's picture of the Later Roman Empire is deliberately static. He sees no areas in which substantial changes in the national wealth could happen. He insists, for instance, that trade and industry never played an important role in Roman society.[3] The economic and social history of the Later Roman Empire, therefore, turns on the fate of agriculture; and, as Jones can see no change in agriculture more significant than a general recession partially offset by isolated instances of a gain in cultivation, he must concentrate on the depressing efficiency of the mechanisms by which money and food passed from the overwhelming majority of the population to the houses of the few. Furthermore, the *Survey*, in treating taxation, the cities, and the land in strictly separate chapters, implicitly denies that the functional relationship between the different areas of Late Roman economic life was any more complicated than this sad process. Altogether this *Survey* shows that we still know very little about what it was like to live in a Late Roman town,[4] or a Late

---

[1] See, for instance, Augustine, *Enarratio in Ps.* 136, 5, and Teall, 'The Grain Supply of the Byzantine Empire', *Dumbarton Oaks Papers*, XIII (1950), 130-1, for the considerable evidence in Byzantine lives of saints. [See L. Robert, *Hellenica* XI-XII (1960), 321-327—inscriptions of farmers in the Hauran.]

[2] See Rémondon, *La crise de l'empire romain*, 309-10, who points to the possible role of the church in banking.

[3] *See L.R.E.* II, esp. 841-50 and 855-8.

[4] Ibid. 1018-20, for instance, tacitly dismisses the view that the activities of the circus-factions are in any way symptomatic of the social structure of the East Roman cities: see Manojlović, 'Le peuple de Constantinople', *Byzantion*, XI (1936), 617-716, criticized by J. Jarry, 'Hérésies et factions de cirque à Constantinople du Ve au VIIe siècle', *Syria*, XXXVII (1960), 348-71, esp. 349-59, whose alternative view, however, is less convincing; and, most recently, Ch. Pietri, 'Le Sénat, le peuple chrétien et les partis de cirque à Rome, sous le pape Symmaque (498-514)', *Mélanges d'archéologie et d'histoire*, LXXVIII (1966), 123-39. [On the early Byzantine town, we now have D. Claude, *Die byzantinische Stadt im 6. Jht.* (Byzantinisches Archiv 13), 1969 and, on circus-factions,

Roman village, and, even less, about the full complexity of the relations between the two.

The form of Jones's *Survey* is, indeed, a tacit rebuttal of an alternative approach to Late Roman economic history.[1] This other approach concentrates on the economic development of specific regions of the empire; it is based on an exhaustive analysis of whatever material throws light on the relations between the various facets of the economic life of a region, on the varied participation and role of classes, and on the shifts in these relationships throughout the Late Roman period. The fragmentary nature of the evidence for any single region in this period makes such studies hazardous in the extreme; but the conclusions of some such regional studies may not only qualify, but transmute Jones's judgement on the general structure of Late Roman society. In Northern Italy in the late fourth century, for instance, there is some evidence for the role of the towns and of the Imperial bureaucracy, resident in Milan, and of the army, stationed in the area, as factors promoting the growth of agriculture.[2] It has been suggested, less plausibly, that high taxation might even have encouraged more efficient farming;[3] while the existence of large centres of consumption stimulated a trade in agricultural produce whose importance in the economic life of the Later Empire may have been unduly minimized by Jones.[4] Similar conclusions may be reached for regions of the Eastern Empire in the fifth and sixth centuries. The villages of Syria, for instance, rose to unparalleled affluence in the Late Roman period because of a development of olive-plantations, made possible by the coexistence of great landed wealth and increased consumption by the cities, the bureaucracy,

---

A. Cameron, *Porphyrius the Charioteer* (1971). Archaeological surveys may add some indications on the rise and decline of the population of some Late Roman sites: see N. Duval, 'Notes sur l'urbanisme tardif à Sufetula', *Cahiers de Tunisie* XLV–XLVI (1964) and, for Alexandria in the late sixth century, M. Rodziewicz, *Études et travaux du centre d'archéologie méditerranéenne*, III (1969), 134–145.]

[1] Most notably, the studies of L. Ruggini, 'Ebrei e Orientali nell' Italia settentrionale tra il IV. e il VI. secolo d. Cr.', *Studia et Documenta Historiae et Juris*, XXV (1959), 186–308; *Economia e Società nell' 'Italia Annonaria'*, *Rapporti fra agricoltura e commercio dal IV. al VI. secolo d. Cr.* (1961); and 'Vicende rurali dell' Italia antica dall' età tetrarchica ai Langobardi', *Rivista storica italiana*, LXXVI (1964), 261–86.

[2] Ruggini, *Economia e società*, esp. 19–56.

[3] Ibid. 29–30.

[4] Ibid. 84–152.

and the army.[1] Archaeological surveys of Palestine, also, may yet reveal a Late Roman society whose thriving agriculture and high technical achievements were directly related to the progressive accumulation of wealth and manpower around the Holy Places.[2]

Jones's firm, negative conclusion on the role of trade in the Later Roman Empire is based on a cross-section of a society that is assumed, rather than proved, to be static. The issue is not so much whether the merchant was an important figure in Late Roman society,[3] nor whether, in the general tax system of the Empire, the towns were expected to contribute only a small proportion;[4] it is, rather, the extent to which the role of trade varied from region to region, and fluctuated from century to century. In a society as rigid as that of the Roman Empire, even a small relative change in the sources of the national wealth might make a great difference. One cannot but be impressed, for instance, by the cumulative evidence for the greater degree of commercial activity in the Eastern Empire: it is reflected even in the difference between the industrious life of the first monastic communities of Egypt and Syria and that of their otiose equivalents in the West.[5] By the age of Justinian, this commercial activity may have found more outlets than previously. The Western provinces have been suggested as one such outlet, where a wealthy aristocracy of cosmopolitan tastes survived throughout

---

[1] G. Tchalenko, *Villages antiques de la Syrie du Nord. Le massif du Bélus à l'époque romaine*, Institut français d'archéologie de Beyrouth, L, 3 vols. (1953–8). See M. Rodinson, 'De l'archéologie à la sociologie historique', *Syria*, XXXVIII (1961), 170–200, esp. 194–9. [See now E. Patlagean, 'Sur la limitation de fécondité dans la haute époque byzantine', *Annales* XXIV (1969), 1353–1359, at 1358]

[2] M. Avi-Yonah, 'The Economics of Byzantine Palestine', *Israel Exploration Journal*, VIII (1958), 39–51, esp. 48–51.

[3] *L.R.E.* II, 864–72. The inhabitants of Edessa may have thought otherwise. During the plague of 501, they prayed for the continued good health of the merchant community, on whose presence they depended: Joshua the Stylite, *Chronicle*, ed. Wright, 1882, c. 44.

[4] *L.R.E.* I, 464–5 and 871–2. One should remark that the assessment and collection of a tax on agricultural produce was considerably more simple than that of a tax on industry, and so the victimization of the small man was even more obvious in the latter case—as is shown by the passage of Libanius, cited in *L.R.E.* II, 872. On the exceptional mobility enjoyed by a merchant in the Later Empire, see also Augustine, *Enarratio in Ps.* 136, 3.

[5] *L.R.E.* II, 931–2.

71

the sixth century.[1] To the East, the renewed building activity of a city such as Jerash may betray a revival of the caravan trade.[2] Altogether, a regional study of the economic life of the eastern frontier of the Empire in the sixth and early seventh centuries has yet to be written: further exploitation of archaeological material, and of the evidence of Syriac, Hebrew, and Arabic texts, might yet reveal the vigour of these local roots of the achievements of the sixth century.[3]

VI

If further studies of the social and economic life of some provinces in the Later Empire reveal to us more of the 'underpinning' of the society described in this *Survey*, they will serve to reinforce an impression already given by Jones—that, viewed against the background of the history of the Roman Empire, the 'Later' Roman period could boast its own solid achievements.

The *Survey* resolutely refuses to decribe the social and administrative conditions of the Later Empire in terms of causes of decline. For Jones approaches the Later Roman Empire with an unrivalled knowledge of the history of the classical world. This history has left him with few illusions. He is not concerned to single out catastrophic causes of decline, for the very good reason that he has never rated too highly any previous form of Roman society. A passionate identification with one feature or another of the classical world seems to be a prerequisite for grand hypotheses on the decline and fall of the Roman Empire. Jones withholds this identification: Gibbon's age of the Antonines is already suspect to him;[4] Rostov-

[1] Suggested by Rémondon, *La Crise de l'Empire romain*, 310–12. See also H. L. Adelson, *Light Weight solidi and Byzantine Trade during the sixth and seventh centuries*, Numismatic Notes and Monographs, cxxxviii (1957), and, for China, S. Nai, 'Zolotaja vizantijskaja moneta, naidennaja v mogile perioda dinastij Sui', *Vizantijskij Vremennik*, xxi (1962), 178–82.

[2] *Gerasa, City of the Decapolis*, ed. C. H. Kraeling (1938), esp. 62–7, and the most suggestive remarks of R. Paret, 'Les villes de la Syrie du Sud et les routes commerciales d'Arabie à la fin du VIe siècle', *Akten des XI. Byzantinistenkongresses 1958* (1960), 438–44 [and, now, U. Monneret de Villard, *Introduzione allo Studio dell' archeologia islamica* (*Civiltà veneziana, istudi 20*), 1966, esp. pp. 1–104; 147–64 and J. B. Segal, *Edessa. The Blessed City* (1970)].

[3] See most notably N. V. Pigulevskaja, *Vizantija na putjakh v Indiju* (1951) [now transl. *Byzanz auf den Wegen nach Indien* (1969)] and *Arabi u granic vizantji i Irana v IV–VI vv* (1964).

[4] *L.R.E.* i, 3–14.

tzeff's urban bourgeoisie are revealed as idle rentiers, who continued to look after themselves only too well;[1] and, 'As all readers of Tacitus know, the Roman army of the Principate was not impeccable' (II, 1036). Viewed in this perspective, the Later Roman period becomes a period of Roman history like any other, marked by distinctive advances: the fourth century saw a more reliable and more professional army;[2] the Eastern Emperors prevented civil war in their domains for periods of over a century;[3] Greco-Roman culture extended far wider than at any other time.[4]

Jones's perspective is 'Byzantine'. His material, his methods of interpretation, his love of organization, place Jones at the centre of affairs. He views Roman society from the elevated standpoint of the central government: like the great historians of the early Byzantine period, Jones keeps close to the court, and scans the world from Constantinople. We leave his *Survey*, therefore, with the great satisfaction of knowing that, up to A.D. 602, men in the Eastern Empire continued to rule like Romans—and to manage their matrimonial affairs like Romans. These men are the heroes of the *Survey*: Marinus the Syrian, for instance: 'And at night also, he had a pen-and-ink stand hanging by his bedside, and a lamp burning by his pillow, so that he could write down his thoughts on a roll; and in the daytime he would tell them to the king, and advise him as to how he should act.'[5] In writing about such men, Jones has written, not a complete social history of the Later Roman Empire, but the first, irreplaceable chapter in the history of the Byzantine state. It is to Jones that we will continue to go in order to begin to understand the unique position of the medieval Byzantine Empire, 'the complexity of an emperor's task, the vast extent of his rule, the infinite variety of that imperial forethought which was the sovran's duty'.[6]

---

[1] *L.R.E.* II, 737–63 and 1053. On Rostovtzeff, see especially A. Momigliano, 'M. I. Rostovtzeff', now in *Studies in Historiography*, pp. 91–104, esp. 97–8 [and now, the differentiated discussion of M. A. Wes, 'Geschiedenis en late oudheid van Rostovtzeff tot Jones', *Tijdschrift voor Geschiedenis*, (LXXXII) 1969, 453–68].

[2] *L.R.E.* II, 1036–8.

[3] Ibid. 1033.

[4] Ibid. 1008.

[5] *The Chronicle of Zachariah of Mitylene*, VII, 9, trans. Hamilton and Brooks, 178.

[6] N. H. Baynes, 'The Byzantine State,' *Byzantine Studies*, 47–66, at 54.

APPROACHES TO THE RELIGIOUS CRISIS
OF THE THIRD CENTURY A.D.*

The simultaneous appearance of works by two such highly individual scholars as Professor E. R. Dodds[1] and Dr. W. H. C. Frend[2]
made 1965 an *annus mirabilis* for the study of the religious history of
Late Antiquity. Professor Dodds describes 'the general attitude to
the world and the human condition', and 'some specific types of
experience', in numerous individuals, from the period from Marcus
Aurelius to Constantine. Dr. Frend, though he writes a history of
the persecution of Judaism and Christianity in the Graeco-Roman
world, is notable for having transcended the Pontius-Pilate-complex
that has tended to relegate the fate of the Christians to a by-way
of Roman administrative law. Instead, he has concentrated on the
abundant and fascinating material for the varying attitudes of the
persecuted. We are introduced to the important people first: we
come across the Devil on page 33 (as early on, proportionately, as
we meet Him with Professor Dodds), and this reviewer, at least, was
happy to wait until page 165 for a brisk discussion of the *institutum
Neronianum*.[3] And when the divergent attitudes of Christians to the
world around them are conveyed in a series of vivid portraits of
Tertullian, Clement of Alexandria, Cyprian, Origen and Gregory

* *English Historical Review*, LXXXIII, 1968, pp. 542–58.

[1] *Pagan and Christian in an Age of Anxiety*, London: C.U.P., 1965. 27s. 6d.

[2] *Martyrdom and Persecution in the Early Church* (Oxford: Blackwell, 1965.
£4 12s. 6d.).

[3] [This article did not intend to review the juridical problems of the persecution of the Christians: this has been admirably done by T. D. Barnes, 'Legislation against the Christians', *Journal of Roman Studies*, LVIII, 1968, pp. 32–50.
Nor would I suggest that such problems are of no importance for the religious
historian. What we think both of the reaction of Roman society to the Christians
and of the evolution of Christian opinion, depends on our knowledge of the precise source, incidence and chronology of pagan persecutions—as is made clear
by T. D. Barnes, 'Tertullian's *Scorpiace*', *Journal of Theological Studies*, n.s.,
xx, 1969, pp. 105–32 and *Tertullian*, 1971.]

Thaumaturgos, we find ourselves back in the same century as Professor Dodds, and faced with the same problem—with varieties of religious experience. Thus, if this review suggests some ways of putting the very lonely men of Professor Dodds back into the cities and churches conjured up with such gusto by Dr. Frend; and if it tries to focus the bright, clinical light which Professor Dodds shines down impartially on pagan and Christian alike, on to some areas of the Christian attitudes described by Dr. Frend, it is not to deny the independent merits of each book. The religious changes of the Late Antique world need to be understood on as many levels as possible. Lastly, by juxtaposing these two subtly different accounts of the forces at work in the period between Marcus Aurelius and Constantine, this review would like to continue the exploration of a problem, raised by Professor A. H. M. Jones' *Later Roman Empire*, of 1964 (pp. 3–36) and posed acutely by two highly original surveys (R. Rémondon, *La crise de l'empire romain*, 1964, pp. 97–114 and F. Millar, *The Roman Empire and its Neighbours*, 1967, at pp. 144–5, 213–17, 139–48): the problem of the exact significance of the notorious 'Crisis of the Third Century'—a crisis which both writers accept, a little unwarily perhaps, as the 'watershed between the Ancient World and the European Middle Ages' (Frend, p. 389).

To begin with the shorter book. In his four chapters—'Man and the Material World', 'Man and the Daemonic World', 'Man and the Divine World' and 'The Dialogue of Paganism with Christianity'—Professor Dodds has given us a masterpiece of precise analysis. Each topic builds up like the articulations of a crystal. The student of ancient and medieval religion, alike, will have to read this book constantly, to find crucial clarifications (to take instances from one chapter only) on the difference between a Hellenic and a gnostic view of evil in the cosmos (pp. 12–17), on the origins of asceticism (pp. 27–33) and, as one would expect from Professor Dodds, an authoritative outline of the evolution of Plotinus' ideas on the fall of the soul (pp. 24–25). What must strike the less specialized reader as novel is the explicit alliance which Professor Dodds has made with Freudian psycho-analysis. Historians of inflation in the crisis of the third century would regard it as imprudent—not to say uncultivated—to approach the baffling fluctuations of the *denarius* without a sensitivity to monetary phenomena that is, at least, kept in tune by modern economic theory. Yet historians of the rise of Egyptian monasticism, faced with equally baffling and headlong shifts in men's relations to their own bodies, still feel licensed, for some reason, to be innocent of modern knowledge. One may question the psycho-analytic theory which Professor Dodds chooses as an ally; but without it, the lucid, paradoxical and deeply convincing pages on the origins of asceticism just could not have been written (pp. 27-9).

The alliance of disciplines inevitably involves a selection of the strands within each discipline. The historian and the social anthropologist have, as a whole, favoured orthodox Freudian psychoanalysis, because it claims to meet its allies half-way: such Freudians have retained a faith, not shared by many of their colleagues, that behaviour can be reduced to 'historical' happenings in childhood (such as the known conduct of a father) which need not, *per se*, escape the diligent biographer, and to the impingement on the child of certain social factors, that can often be known to the historian—patterns of child-rearing, family structure and early education. Erikson's *The Young Luther* and *Childhood and Society*, and, above all, Professor Dodds' own brilliant essay of interpretation 'From Shame Culture to Guilt Culture' in the second chapter of his *Greeks and the Irrational* (1963), have made plain that it is on these terms that an *entente cordiale* with Freudian psycho-analysis is acceptable to the historian.

Freudian orthodoxy, however, tends to take away with one hand what it offers us with the other. It is overwhelmingly diagnostic. It is extremely useful as a tool to diagnose dreams, whether these dreams are private (as those of Marcus Aurelius on p. 29, n. 1, Aelius Aristides, on pp. 41-5 and Perpetua, on pp. 51-3) or collective (as with the Gnostic systems, on pp. 19-20, or with the millennial ideologies of Professor Norman Cohn's *Pursuit of the Millennium*). But diagnosis isolates. Many of Professor Dodds' figures seem 'trapped in the loneliness of the neurotic', partly because it is only their neurosis that strikes his cold and clinical eye. The result is an unduly static view of the religious crisis of the third century. One cannot know, from these brilliantly etched casehistories, how this crisis came about, and one is left wondering what could possibly follow. What one misses is what Professor Dodds has already given us in his *Greeks and the Irrational*, that is, an authentically psycho-analytic interpretation of historical change. There, he had juxtaposed the style of Archaic with Classical Greek society and had introduced a well-known historical event (changes in the structure of the early Greek family) as a catalyst provoking the transformation of the one into the other. By contrast, apart from a few discreet hints, we do not have a convincing psycho-genesis of the Late Antique 'Age of Anxiety'.

The reviewer is challenged to be indiscreet. For conventional explanations of the religious crisis of the third century plainly do not convince Professor Dodds. Indeed, the labour-saving formula of most historians of the end of the Roman Empire, that 'misery and mysticism are related facts', wears very thin indeed in this highly-differentiated account. The 'wave of pessimism that swept over the West' (p. 18), coincides with the age of the Antonines and the Severi, a period when, as Dr. Frend says, 'the barometer was Set Fair' (Frend, p. 310). Quite apart from the psychological naïvety of formulae that link the growth of otherworldliness in the Later Empire with the political unrest of the mid-third century, it may well be asked whether the political 'crisis' itself has not been understood in too melodramatic terms. Take Plotinus. Here is a man who lived precisely at the nadir of the public fortunes of the Roman Empire. What emerges in Professor Dodds' account of him, is his robust Hellenic optimism on the beauty of the material world and his faith in human reason; yet these assertions sprang from a vigorous dialogue with the gnostic Valentinus—a man who wrote black thoughts in the palmy days of the mid-second century! What is more: recent studies of the Roman environment of Plotinus, of the survival of the traditional forms of life in Italy, of the continuity of local families and the stability of aristocratic art forms throughout the third century (for which, see P. Hadot, *Plotin*, 1963, pp. 139 ff.; F. Millar, *The Roman Empire* . . . pp. 144–5; John Matthews, 'Continuity in a Roman Family; the Rufii Festi of Volsinii', *Historia*, xvi (1967), 484–509 and C. E. Vermeule, 'A Graeco-Roman portrait of the 3rd century A.D.', *Dumbarton Oaks Papers*, xv (1961), 1–22) make one suspect that, psychologically as well as physically, the sacking of Byzantium and Autun was as far away from Campania as Antwerp would be from Avila.[1]

There seems to be nothing inconsistent in looking for the genesis of the 'Age of Anxiety' long before its conventional forcing-ground, the disturbances of the mid-third century. One still has not yet

[1] [See now, Fergus Millar, 'P. Herennius Dexippus: the Greek World and the Third-Century Invasions', *Journal of Roman Studies*, LIX, 1969, pp. 12–29, and further, sup. pp. 58 and 64–66.]

assessed the price at which the self-confidence of the Antonine and Severan periods had been bought. We have long had direct access to the souls of the men of the late second century and the early third century; surprisingly, apart from the monumental work of Rostovtzeff on the *Social and Economic History of the Roman Empire*, we do not know nearly as much as we could know about their families and their cities. With a few notable exceptions, the vast amount of material for the outlook of the provincial aristocracies of the Greek East and (to a lesser extent) of Africa, has remained untilled.[1] To what extent, for instance, did these men suffer from the results of that old-fashioned affliction, loss of liberty? (On Aelius Aristides, for instance, the comments of A. D. Momigliano, in 1933, 'Aspetti di Michele Rostovzev', *Contributo alla storia degli studi classici*, 1955, pp. 330–1 remain relevant.) Plutarch had invoked the idea to explain the vast scale of games and public expenditure, which had reached ominous proportions by the time of Marcus Aurelius (see Jones, *The Later Roman Empire*, i. 12–14). But this was only one of many patterns of extroverted, traditional behaviour that had settled down into costly and meaningless routines. (On the stresses and strains of the Imperial court, for instance, see F. Millar, 'Epictetus and the Imperial Court', *Journal of Roman Studies*, lv (1965), 141–8). With Dr. Frend, we meet the bourgeoisie of the Greek world as men dangerously identified with the *status quo*: they were genuinely afraid of atheism, and anxious about disrespect for one's superiors (pp. 260 and 275); their political ideal, we have been reminded, was 'a stable, centrally governed, sharply graded society of which the primary object is to avoid at all costs disorder and change' (F. Millar, *A Study of Cassius Dio*, 1964, p. 108); their most gifted children were supposed to be reared, from an early age, in the straitjacket of a revived Attic Greek (Philostratus, *Life of Apollonius of Tyana*, I, 7). It is, perhaps, not altogether surprising that the 'crevasse of the inner life'—the *abyssus conscientiae*—should open in a very drastic form across so rigid a surface.[2]

At the other end of the period, we are left, in Professor Dodds'

[1] [But now see T. D. Barnes, 'The Family and Career of Septimius Severus', *Historia* xvi, 1969, pp. 87–107 and 'Philostratus and Gordian', *Latomus* xxvii, 1968, pp. 581 sq., G. W. Bowersock, *Greek Sophists in the Roman Empire*, 1969, and E. L. Bowie, 'The Greeks and their Past in the Second Sophistic', *Past and Present*, xlvi, 1970, pp. 3–41.]

[2] [Bowersock, op. cit., pp. 71–5 has interesting remarks on the prevalence of hypochondriacal anxiety in the age of the Antonines.]

analysis of the ascetic movement, with very lonely men: their disgust for the material world has been introjected as disgust for their own bodies; they are not inclined 'to utilise or improve the external world'. Yet one need only pass from this cold account of the early manifestations of asceticism to the deeply human narrative of early monasticism by Derwas Chitty, *The Desert a City* (1966), to suspect that something is lacking in the principles governing Professor Dodds' selection of the evidence. To isolate, in a Freudian diagnosis of great perceptiveness, the element of personal neurosis in the origins of asceticism is to deprive asceticism of its future. What we miss is what Chitty's account challenges us to seek: an insight (psycho-analytic if need be), into the extraordinary momentum that rapidly transformed asceticism into monasticism—that is, into one of the most remarkable institutional achievements of the early medieval period. What both historian and psychologist must explain is why, without exception, the most effective politicians and organizers of the fourth century were either men of ascetic taste or leaders of ascetic movements—Pachomius, Athanasius, the Emperor Julian, Basil of Caesarca, Ambrose and Augustine.

One could take Professor Dodds a little further: the resentment against the world which, as he suggests, was *introjected* by the ascetic as hatred of his body, was, also, massively *projected*—in the drastic form of hostility to the religious outsider (the pagan, heretic or schismatic) or, more subtly, as a guilty sense of obligation to restrain and repair the damaged and the fallen. The idea of public office as a 'press-ganging', remained a mere courtesy among the secular governing-class of the Empirc (Symmachus, *Relatio*, xvii. 2; Marcian, *Novella* i, pr; adapted by Augustine to the Christian governor—*Enarr. in Ps.* 61, 8. The formula was probably used to disclaim imputations of sale of office, as with the forcible ordination of bishops; *Cod. Just.* I, 3, 30, 4). But it was taken on with deadly earnest by the Christian bishops. *Licentiosa libertas*: God, Augustine suspected, had not allowed this to Augustine; he would not allow it to himself, and he certainly did not allow it to the sinners and schismatics of his diocese. The blatant *Wille zur Macht* of the ecclesiastical leaders of the Later Roman period has this deep strain in it. Hence, perhaps, the psychological paradox by which the drastically otherworldly developments described by Professor Dodds for the century before Constantine, paved the way for the great power in society of the fourth-century ascetic bishop. The organization of the Christian church did more than save men from loneliness: it enabled resentment and depression to pour into the mould of a measured paternalism, a White Man's Burden whose guilt-laden imagery, in the liturgy of episcopal ordination, for instance, is of equal interest to the historian of medieval political thought and to the psychologist.

There is another point on which too exclusive an attention to individual neurosis can obscure the function of this neurosis in society at large. We meet Montanus the Phrygian prophet described by Professor Dodds with delightful detachment (pp. 63–5); but we must go to Dr. Frend to realize the extent to which people needed a Montanus. Tertullian needed Montanus because his 'New Prophecy' offered a hope of change—the belief that, because of the Holy Spirit, Christianity would always have something new to say (Frend, p. 371). In many traditional societies, the possessed prophet and the dreamer have acted as the mid-wife of change (see, especially K. O. L. Burridge, *Mambu, A Melanesian Millennium*, 1960, esp. pp. 179–81 and 217–83). The Roman society of the age of Tertullian has been called 'pathologically traditionalist' (S. Mazzarino, *The End of the Ancient World*, transl. Holmes, 1966, p. 130). We should take this epithet seriously (see Dodds, p. 131, n. 3). The self-confidence of the age had been associated with a successful cultural reaction. How much was excluded in this reaction, is shown in the gulf that opened increasingly between an archaic and *précieux* literary culture and a new, partly exotic creativity in the arts (R. Bianchi-Bandinelli, 'Forma artistica tardo antica e apporti Parthi e Sassanidi nella scultura e nella pittura', *Persia e il mondo greco-romano*, 1966, p. 329). For many people, what was new had to come violently. The conservatism of the age of the Antonines coincides, significantly, with the Gnostic 'revolt against Time'—the *contrarietatem et dissolutionem praeteritorum* of Marcion (Irenaeus, *Adv. haer.* IV, i; see H-C. Puech, 'La Gnose et le temps', *Eranos Jahrbuch*, xx (1951), 57–113). Tertullian and Montanus were thrown together for similar reasons. The 'Age of Anxiety' became, increasingly, the age of converts. Professor Dodds has made us realize how much the social and religious historian, the psychologist and the sociologist must keep together, in order to understand the fateful ramifications of the increasing urge of so many members of the Roman Empire to become 'new' men. 'Adversus haec igitur nobis negotium est, adversus institutiones maiorum, auctoritates receptorum, leges dominantium,

argumentationes prudentium, adversus vetustatem, consuetudinem
. . .' (Tertullian, *Adversus Nationes*, ii. 1). And with Tertullian, of
course, we rejoin Dr. Frend.

To any reader already acquainted with Dr. Frend's *Donatist
Church*, to say that this present book is an even better book by thirteen years, is praise enough. We have the rare intellectual treat of
watching the further unfolding of a seminal preoccupation. This is
a wider book than the *Donatist Church* in many ways. The constricting effect of a great French tradition of North African studies,
which, in archaeology and religious history alike, had emphasized
what was local and ethnic in North Africa in the Roman and
Islamic periods, at the expense of the relations between this province
and the outside world, has been sloughed off in this book. We begin
now where we end in the *Donatist Church*: with a brilliant juxtaposition of two radically different attitudes of the Christian Church
to civilized society. One had always felt that this contrast, as it
affected Africa in the fourth and fifth centuries, could never be
explained in terms of speculations on the social and religious origins
of Numidian Donatism; and that the ideas at stake in the Donatist
controversy had both a longer prehistory and a far wider resonance.
Martyrdom and Persecution has dealt handsomely with these criticisms: Dr. Frend has lavished 500 years of ancient history and the
whole Mediterranean basin on us. More subtly and decisively, he
has enlarged the width and depth of his historical sympathies. One
would have expected a masterly treatment of the Judaism and the
Christianity of protest, of separation—of the Maccabees, the Qum-
ran sect, of Tatian, Tertullian and Cyprian. To our delight, we also
get a perceptive, even a poignant, evocation of the religious optim-
ists, of the men who were not 'twice born', who saw no necessary
discontinuity between Judaism or Christianity and the classical
world—Philo, Clement, Origen and Gregory Thaumaturgos. Furthermore, for Dr. Frend, this parallel development in Judaism and
Christianity coincided with the parallel manners in which Jewish and
Christian communities reacted to their concrete social environment;
so that the old story of the Hellenization of Christianity, as Dr. Frend
presents it, now reads as if Michael Rostovtzeff had re-written the
Dogmengeschichte of Adolf von Harnack. For just this reason, it is
a book that will be obligatory to any student of the Ancient World.

In *Martyrdom and Persecution* Dr. Frend has allied himself with
yet another great tradition of scholarship. The book is a warning of

the urgent relevance of recent advances in Jewish studies. His emphasis on the Maccabaean background to the Christian idea of martyrdom is central to the book. So is his explanation of the emergence of distinctively 'Maccabaean', Jewish ideas in African Christianity, which, in his opinion, account for the harsh attitude to the world at large which has distinguished the Western Church from its more optimistic Eastern counterpart, in all later centuries. Scholars need to be reminded of these close links with Judaism. Confident appeals to the Romanity of St. Cyprian, for instance, have long been a labour-saving formula for students of the Latin idea of the church in general, and the idea of papal authority in particular. Now, it is not even certain that Cyprian was ever a Roman lawyer (G. W. Clarke, 'The Secular Profession of St. Cyprian of Carthage', *Latomus*, xxiv (1965), pp. 633–8); and to seize his thought on the unity of the church, for instance, we must learn to have the patience to wander a little off the beaten track of Cicero and the *Digest*, into the schools of philosophy and the *Talmud*. This is an alliance formed by intuition. We may regard the intuition as fruitful while still feeling that Dr. Frend has over-played his hand (see the severe critique of F. Millar, in *Journal of Roman Studies*, lvi (1966), 232–4). To take one example only: the fact that the Old Testament is vital to the ecclesiastical thought of St. Cyprian, for instance, does not necessarily prove what Dr. Frend (a good Donatist bishop at heart, one suspects, who values the reassuring concreteness of a physical presence and the guarantees of precise physical continuity) would suggest—that the Christian church in Africa had exceptionally close links with the local synagogues, nor that Christianity was offering 'a powerful Semitic religion' to 'those who still spoke the Punic language and hankered after its religion and culture' (p. 332). (On the cultural and linguistic context of the rise of Christianity in Africa, see my disagreement in 'Christianity and Local Culture in Late Roman Africa', *Journal of Roman Studies*, vol. lviii, 1968, pp. 85–95, see inf. pp. 279–300.)

We may be dealing with something more interesting: with a neo-Judaism—a reception of the Old Testament as a literal rule of life for a religious group. This reception foreshadows the later adaptation of the Old Testament to the needs of a Christian governing class, from S. Ambrose onwards, and its further application, by the Irish, to the needs of Christian asceticism in a tribal environment (see R. Kottje, *Studien zum Einfluss des Alten Testaments auf Recht und Liturgie des Frühen Mittelalters (vi–viii Jht.)*, 1964). Here, Professor Dodds could help Dr. Frend. Dodds frequently stresses the extent of the 'crisis of identity' and of the need to belong that especially afflicted those men of the late second and third centuries, who were no longer held in their traditional background (pp. 77–8, n. 1 and pp. 137–8). Social death—a fate whose gravity has struck many anthropologists (see, for instance, C. Lévi-Strauss, *Anthropologie structurale*, 1958, pp. 183–4)—was precisely the fate that lay in store for the proselyte to Judaism and, even more so, to Christianity. Men like Tertullian and Cyprian thought of themselves as having totally discontinued their previous life, and stressed the need to separate themselves from their previous environment. They found themselves faced with the problem of creating a code of social living *ex nihilo*: in describing the Christian community Tertullian passes desperately from one form of group-language to another— from the jargon of a Roman legion to the taboos of the New Prophecy. By Cyprian's time, the Old Testament was fully available in Latin, and it was desperately needed by Christians to whom social death was an alternative to an identity elaborately and precariously modelled on the ritual decrees of Leviticus.

Recent emphasis on direct borrowings from Judaism has obscured the crucial importance of a dividing of the ways between the organization of the Jewish and the Christian communities. At just this period, Judaism was moving towards a greater 'democratization' and 'de-specialization' of the religious life. The rabbis, men who exemplified a religious culture which all believers might achieve, had come to replace the priest as the leaders of the community (see, for instance, the vivid description of the careers and position of leading rabbis in Mesopotamia, in J. Neusner, *A History of the Jews in Babylonia*, ii, *The Early Sassanian Period*, 1966, esp. pp. 147–50 and 282–7). By contrast, the Christian community was marked by a growing differentiation and hieratization. Even an evident Jewish legacy such as veneration for a martyr, was being adapted to enhance the position of the bishop in the Christian community (see esp. Theodor Klauser, *Christlicher Märtyrerkult, heidnischer Heroenkult und spätjüdische Heiligenverehrung* (Arbeitsgemeinschaft für Forschung des Landes Nordrhein-Westfalen, 91, 1960, esp. pp. 37–8). The Judaism which a Christian bishop received into his community was not the Judaism of his contemporaries, the rabbis, but the ancient Judaism of his exemplars, the priests. Hence the

83

importance of the 'neo-Judaism' of Christian adaptations of the priestly code of Leviticus: in a society greatly preoccupied, in the third and fourth centuries, with problems of organization, with hierarchy, with the divine sanctions of the Imperial power, the Christian Church stood out as a group that had organized itself most effectively on a hierarchy based on the division between the sacred and the profane, and, by implication, on the superiority of the spiritual over the lay world.

Martyrdom itself might be better understood in terms of the organization of the Christian Church. On this central subject, Dr. Frend blocks out his categories firmly and persuasively. What is not so certain is whether what he regards as the only authentically Christian form of martyrdom—a witnessing to the continued activity of the Spirit, in a form analogous to protest against the world— ever existed in a pure state. This outward-going movement, of martyrdom as protest, was sucked backwards, like the undertow of a wave, by a constant inward-going anxiety: an anxiety to maintain one's identity, and that of one's group, as separate from one's past and one's environment. Tertullian moved in this direction: his 'political warfare against the pagan Empire came to nothing', as his energies were increasingly directed inwards, towards maintaining the purity and identity of the Christian group (pp. 373-4). Donatism followed him. The concern to preserve the newly-bestowed identity of the Christian convert lasts longer than the idea of martyrdom as a seed-bed of radicalism: 'Christianus est . . . ut breviter multa concludam, qui post baptismi ablutionem alienus est a peccato' (*Ep. 'Honorificentiae tuae . . .'*, I. *P.L. Suppl.*, 1689)— the formula of a Pelagian letter shows that the idea will continue to disquiet Latin Christians for a long time to come.

It is not only as an historian of varieties of religious experience that Dr. Frend continues to challenge us. This history of the conflict of Judaism and Christianity with the Graeco-Roman world continues his *Donatist Church*: both turn Rostovtzeff's *Social and Economic History of the Roman Empire* on its head. In both books Dr. Frend emphasizes the role of extremist forms of Judaism and Christianity as movements that rendered articulate all those forces which the urban bourgeoisie of the Hellenistic and the Roman worlds had failed to include, and with which Rostovtzeff himself had little sympathy (see the exceptionally perceptive comments of A. D. Momigliano, 'Aspetti di Michele Rostovzev', pp. 332-4). Any debate with Dr. Frend is a debate with Rostovtzeff: more precisely, it is a debate on whether the triumph of Christianity was, in any way, a direct consequence of what had been, for Rostovtzeff, merely the blind and inarticulate outburst of the under-privileged sections of the Roman world in the 'crisis' of the third century.

The revolt of the Maccabees, regretted by Rostovtzeff as the story of 'how Rome permitted these barbarians to destroy everybody and everything Hellenistic with the greatest steadfastness and cruelty' (*Caravan Cities*, 1932, p. 64), is now hailed by Dr. Frend: 'Here was the first revolutionary outburst against what became the values of the Graeco-Roman world' (p. xiii). Indeed, he has turned Rostovtzeff's perspective into a pattern that sometimes smacks more of prophecy than of history. For, starting with his account of the Maccabees, we are presented with a series of stylized antetypes, foreshadowing what Dr. Frend holds to be the supreme religious revolt against the values and society of the ancient world, the Donatist schism. Of the Maccabaean period, he writes: 'Five hundred years later, the officers of the Tetrarchy were to find the same balance of acquiescence and resistance in Egypt and North Africa during the Great Persecution. In each case, the inspiration of the resistance was both cultural and religious, the "foreign ways" of the big town being resented by a rural population which was also open to exploitation and oppression by urban tax-collectors and land-lords' (pp. 43-4).

To begin at the end. The work of the archaeologist in North Africa has made it increasingly difficult to transpose the conflict of Donatism and Catholicism on to a map of relations between town and countryside, such as Dr. Frend inherited from Rostovtzeff. The main contours of this map are being eroded: it may no longer be helpful to describe Numidia as a 'rural' province, in a sense significantly different from any other part of North Africa, and so, to treat Donatism that was predominant there as in any way distinguished from Catholicism by being the religion of a 'rural' population (see P.A. Février, 'Toujours le Donatisme: à quand l'Afrique?', *Rivista di storia e di letteratura religiosa*, ii (1966), 228-40).

The social background of the Jewish resistance to Greek and Roman influence seems to stand in need of similar redefinition. There were many areas in the Near East—such as Palestine at the time of the Maccabees, and, later, the Syriac culture of Edessa—

where Hellenization never coincided with a class division. The local aristocracies continued to speak the local, Semitic languages, and had as little sense of being relegated to the status of a 'rural population' by so doing, as the cultivated canons of Lyons, when they wrote Provençal up to the seventeenth century. When Hellenization meant abandoning the ways of one's ancestors, resistance was *de rigueur* for the local leaders of such societies. In Palestine, moreover, religious conservatism and resistance to the outside had been associated precisely with a landed aristocracy (see esp. E. Würthwein, '*Der 'amm ha'arez im Alten Testament*, Beiträge zur Wissenschaft vom Alten- u. Neuen Testament, Folge iv, 17, 1936). The supporters of Bar Kochba who fled with their family-papers to the caves of Engeddi were considerable landowners (see Y. Yadin, 'The expedition to the Judaean Desert: Expedition D: The Cave of the Letters', *Israel Exploration Journal*, 12 (1962), 227–57, esp. pp. 235–48). As for the priests and, later, the rabbis, to be 'watchful in the study of the Torah' was to belong to a *Geistesadel*, carefully reared on a classical language and, so, with a hearty contempt for one's local *patois* (see Avi-Yonah, *Geschichte der Juden im Zeitalter der Talmud*, 1962, p. 72, on the attitude of the Jewish patriarchs to Syriac). Briefly, to believe that one's fathers had been right and the rest of the world wrong is an attitude quite consistent with the views of local aristocracies as selfconscious, as confident and as superior in their own terms as the Greek bourgeoisie; and, so, there are many pitfalls along the way of any outline of the history of the Maccabaean tradition that presents its Palestinian origins almost exclusively in terms of a blue-print for the revolt of the excluded and the oppressed rural elements in the Graeco-Roman world.

Chapters xiv—'The Triumph of Christianity, 260–303'—and xv, 'The Great persecution, 303–312'—are the *pièce de résistance* of Dr. Frend's narrative. According to his superbly-conducted marshalling of the evidence, rural paganism died a natural death in North Africa, Phrygia and Egypt in the generation after 260; it was assassinated, in the towns, by the municipal crisis of the age. It was Christianity which entered the vacuum in the countryside: in North Africa, Phrygia and Egypt, it harnessed the energies of an increasingly self-confident and embittered peasantry to a religion of protest; and having once established itself, in its most resilient and uncompromising form, across the grain-producing areas on which the Roman state depended, its triumph was certain. In the Great Persecution the

86

death-warrant of paganism was already signed: 'Times had changed radically since Decius (p. 498). . . . Then the Christians (of Egypt) were cowed, now they scented victory. This was a revolution on the point of success' (p. 516).

In his stirring narrative of the Great Persecution, Dr. Frend has come dangerously close to identifying himself with its first narrators —Lactantius and Eusebius of Caesarea—and so shares in their limitations, namely, exaggeration and hindsight. To imply that, in the eastern provinces of the Empire, the Great Persecution had assumed the proportions of a civil war is to take the military imagery of both authors a little too seriously. The age of the Tetrarchy was a very busy time for everybody. The government was constantly disturbing the provincials on more pressing matters than the Christians (witness the registers of an official in Egypt: *Papyri from Panoplis*, Chester Beatty Monographs, 10, ed. T. C. Skeat, 1964). In a period when the Roman armies, for instance, were recruited by regular depredations resembling the methods of the press-gang (see *Vita Pachomii*, *Vita prima*, c. 4: *Pachomii Vitae Graecae*, Subsidia Hagiographica, 1932, p. 3), a convoy of Christian 'confessors' on their way to the mines may not have attracted the attention that Dr. Frend considers it deserved.

The Great Persecution is important for other reasons. It is the particular merit of Dr Frend's narrative that he prefaces his account of this persecution with a comprehensive evocation of the religious and intellectual background to the conservatism of the Tetrarchy. The Great Persecution is significantly different from the persecution of Decius: for it is not only the last and greatest administrative action against the Christians, it is the first Pagan Revival. Dr. Frend seems more confident that this Pagan Revival was doomed to failure than were its Christian contemporaries. A rallying of the conservative forces of a society may never eradicate a religion; but it has often brought its expansion to a halt among the upper classes, as was the fate of Buddhism in late medieval China. The urban upper classes had survived the 'crisis' of the third century rather better than Dr. Frend allows [B. Brenk, 'Die Datierung der Reliefs am Hadrianstempel in Ephesos und das Problem der tetrarchischen Skulpturen des Ostens', *Instanbuler Mitteilungen* XVIII, (1968, pp. 238–258 gives a vivid example of the ideology to which these classes still clung tenaciously]. The vast output of traditional literature in the fourth century points backwards to the solid spadework of pagan schoolmasters of the age of Diocletian; and an Emperor like Galerius (whom Dr. Frend describes entirely in the spirit of Lactantius) was no fanatical boor. His family could afford to emigrate from the evacuated trans-Danubian provinces. He would have been no more of a barbarian than any member of a displaced colonial upper class. [Sir Ronald Syme, *Emperors and Biography*, 1971, esp. pp. 179–193, has shown how misleading contemporary invective can be on the social origins, and, hence, on the cultural and religious attitudes of important third-century emperors such as Maximin Thrax.] He would have spoken the somewhat stilted, standardized Latin of the Danubian provinces (see Mihaescu, *Limbia latină in provincii le dunărene ale imperiului roman*, 1960); and he would have continued the solemn *Romanitas* of a Diocletian with unnerving sincerity. At Nicomedia, a cultivated Christian such as Lactantius found his beliefs treated, once more, as 'a religion unworthy of a sane individual's credence' (p. 497). It is only in the light of the sudden revival of pagan philosophical opinion that we can appreciate the desperate manner in which Lactantius would seek to redress a balance that had suddenly tilted in favour of paganism, by allying himself with the most extreme elements in the religious thought of his age, with a Hermetic Gnosticism that runs like an icy current beneath the placid surface of the 'Christian Cicero' (see esp. A. Wlosok, *Laktanz und die philosophische Gnosis*, Abhandlungen der Heidelberger Akademie der Wissenschaften, 1960). We have been warned that: 'The revolution of the fourth century . . . will not be understood, if we underrate the determination, almost the fierceness, with which the Christians appreciated and exploited the miracle that had transformed Constantine into a supporter, a protector, and later a legislator of the Christian Church' (A. D. Momigliano, 'Pagan and Christian Historiography in the Fourth Century', *The Conflict between Paganism and Christianity in the Fourth Century*, ed. Momigliano, 1963, p. 80). But this fierceness, in turn, is quite inexplicable if we continue to treat the Great Persecution as an inevitable prelude to the victory of the Church, and fail to do justice to the fear of definitive outlawry in a reorganized, conservative society, that lay in the immediate past of all educated Christians of the age of Constantine.

To dissent from Dr. Frend, it is not sufficient to indulge oneself in the grey task of cutting his evidence down to size. This reviewer would suggest that changes in the relationship between town and countryside did indeed influence the establishment of Christianity in the Later Roman Empire; but in a very different manner from that proposed by Dr. Frend. The fragmentary indications for the religious evolution of the countryside in this period do not show that paganism died a natural death, being immediately replaced by Christianity; but they do show that the paganism which an educated townsman would recognize and welcome did, indeed, regress. (The evidence has been read in this way, for instance, by R. MacMullen, *Enemies of the Roman Order*, 1967, esp. at pp. 229–34.) By the late third century, indeed, there was a sinister *caesura* between official Roman paganism and an equally urban Christianity, neither form of which religion held much appeal for large areas of the Roman world. The countryside had come to wear an alien look; in Britain and in Syria, for instance, the most dynamic cults were the ones least acceptable to the standardized 'Roman' religion of a Diocletian. There were disquieting reminders that millions of men who were, technically, Romans continued to live in a way that contradicted an increasingly rigid conservative image of 'Roman antiquity and religious uniformity' (p. 476): Diocletian was genuinely shocked to discover, in Egypt and elsewhere, that these 'Romans' had continued to marry their sisters. But, twenty years later, Lactantius is telling educated men that Diocletian's protector, Jupiter, had also behaved in as un-Roman, in as barbarous a fashion as any Egyptian peasant. Many were prepared to believe him. Men brought up in the towns of the late third and early fourth centuries still identified civilization with the survival of their towns and with the possession of an elevating literary tradition: anyone who reads Eusebius' attack on the pagan Hierocles, or Professor Dodds' summary of the 'Dialogue of Paganism with Christianity' (esp. pp. 116–31), must realize that, compared with the vast and menacing stretches of their own countryside and the new horizons of the barbarian world, a hair's breadth separated pagan and Christian members of the intelligentsia. In the Great Persecution, the pagan wing of this intelligentsia tried to outlaw their Christian rivals. They failed. What a Lactantius and a Eusebius could offer, by way of negotiation, was to shelter the elevating traditions of classical education under the umbrella of a revealed religion. Their price was sloughing-off the ill-behaved gods of classical paganism as barbarous. The bargain seems unattractive only if we forget that men of the Late Roman period were fanatically dedicated to their elevating education (a dedication vividly illustrated, in a small facet, by the incapacity of authors to appreciate the irrational in any traditional social function, not even in the pantomime: see J. Bayet, 'Les vertus du pantomime Vincentius', *Mélanges de littérature latine*, 1967, esp. pp. 450–6), and were genuinely less certain about their traditional religion. The average good Roman of Diocletian, 'pious, religious, quiet and chaste' is not so very different from the average good Christian of Lactantius, with the crucial difference that the Christian is steeled for survival, in an insecure world, by baptism and by the possession of a supernatural Wisdom—a Wisdom that, nevertheless, bears a surprising, and reassuring, resemblance to a conventional digest of the thoughts of the old philosophers and oracles.

Constantine was to seal this bargain with the intelligentsia of the towns by turning his back on the religion of the only effective group in the Roman world that had remained overwhelmingly opaque to Christianity, and closely in touch with the countryside—that is, the Roman army. Instead, he opted for the religion of men whose most acceptable spokesmen were identified with the traditional culture of the urban centres of the Roman world, whose hierarchy, as bishops, after the Council of Nicaea, would maintain the *status quo* of the provincial *metropoleis*, whose values were entirely civilian, and whose hatred of the persecutors (in the pages of Lactantius) thinly masks a townman's fear and contempt of the highly-effective and unashamedly military *junta* that we dignify by the grandiose title of 'The Diocletianic Tetrarchy'. In so many ways the 'soft' son of a soldier father and a good bourgeois, Constantine even builds himself a city, decorated with classical Greek antiques. [Now see P. Brown, *The World of Late Antiquity*, 1971, pp. 82–94.]

This was a fateful alliance. Groups that claim to be protecting civilization seem to generate barbarians. Far from making the processes of Romanization more flexible, the Christian church made them more rigid by equating civilization with orthodoxy. The inhabitants of the Val di Non, for instance, who had become civilized in an old-fashioned way, would be dismissed by the bishop of Trent as a *natio barbara*: for though Roman, they had remained pagan (Vigilius of Trent, *Epistula* I, 1 P.L. 13, 550 D).

This greater inflexibility played a disastrous role in the relations of the Empire with the barbarians. In the fourth century, the barbarian chieftain could be accepted without comment on becoming

Romanized (see K. Stroheker, 'Zur Rolle der Heermeister fränkischer Abstammung im späten 4. Jahrhundert', *Historia* iv (1955), 314–30 = *Germanentum u. Spätantike*, 1966, pp. 9–29; A. Demandt, *Zeitkritik und Geschichtsbild im Werk Ammians*, 1965, pp. 31 ff.). The policy by which the Emperor Theodosius hoped to save the Empire from the Gothic menace assumed that the bridge between the barbarian world and the Roman was still open: the rank and file of the tribesmen would be deprived of their leaders and would be controlled by a Gothic aristocracy, skilfully seduced by the offer of full participation in the benefits of Roman civilized life (see E. A. Thompson, 'The Visigoths from Fritigern to Euric', *Historia*, xii (1963), 105–26). But just such a policy was being sabotaged by the intolerance of the Catholic bishops patronized by the same Emperor: for a bishop, orthodoxy was the only bridge over which a barbarian could enter civilization; and in the eyes of John Chrysostom, a Goth who was fully identified with the Roman order by pagan standards but who had remained an Arian, might just as well have stayed in his skins, across the Danube (see Theodoret, *Historia Ecclesiastica*, v. 32). [See p. 53–4.]

The Great Persecution and its sequence, the conversion of Constantine, cannot be written, in the manner of Rostovtzeff, as if it were an epilogue to the urban civilization of the Ancient World: it is the most paradoxical episode in that pseudo-morphosis by which the classical tradition and a classical, urban style of life survived up to the rise of Islam.

Many books will grow out of *Martyrdom and Persecution*. An orientalist could bring the ideas blocked out by Dr. Frend to the more fragmentary history of the Christian church in Persia. Here we have Christian attitudes to the world evolving in laboratory conditions: a strongly Jewish background, a vast and irremovable pagan Empire, evidence for the slow evolution by which the *benai qeiāmā*, the Sons of the Covenant, an encratite core of true believers, living in total discontinuity with their environment, mellow, by the late seventh century, into the Nestorian missionary-bishops of Central Asia and the Far East, whose statement of belief to the Emperor of China, of 635–638, is the very last, quite unmistakable echo of the optimism of the Greek apologists described by Dr. Frend.

Dr. Frend writes, rather, for the Western medievalist. The poignant theme of his book is the separation of Eastern and Western

Christianity. His opinion, that the die was already cast as early as in the contrast between the Latin Tertullian and the Greek Clement of Alexandria, is an original answer to an old problem—that of the Eastern Schism, for long a skeleton in the cupboard of cultivated Western Europeans. It is as a book on the building up of the harsh contours of the Latin idea of the Church that Dr. Frend opens windows that look straight out to Gregory VII and beyond. Donatism is part of the Western ecclesiological tradition: it can no longer be treated just as an opening vignette for supercilious accounts of the ravages of enthusiasm on the fringes of the Catholic Church. Everybody in the Middle Ages read Cyprian, while the more cautious formulae in Augustine's anti-Donatist works were largely ignored. [Now see H. E. J. Cowdrey, 'The Dissemination of St. Augustine's Doctrine of Holy Orders during the Later Patristic Age', *Journal of Theological Studies* xx, 1969, pp. 448–481.] Some of the most precious roses in the garden of the medieval church, therefore, were grafted on to this harsh and primitive root-stock. Dr. Frend makes one wonder who would have felt more comfortable in the company of Gregory VII—Augustine, Catholic bishop of Hippo, or Petilian, Donatist bishop of Constantine? Above all, Dr. Frend has given us new tools to write the history of the parting of the ways between Byzantium and Western Europe. In the Eastern world, he hails 'the Christian optimism, the hope of salvation for all, . . . the reconciliation of rival political and social systems as differing aspects of the Eternal Word of God . . .' which, in his view, laid the foundation of Byzantine theology and Byzantine political theory. Students of Byzantine relations with the outside world (and, so also, of the history of Eastern Europe in the early modern period), could well profit by reading *Martyrdom and Persecution*. Human nature being frail, of course, to hope that all rational men will be saved usually means to expect all good Byzantine citizens to be like oneself (the citation that 'God wishes all men to be saved' is used, by the Emperor Heraclius, to order the forcible baptism of all Byzantine Jews). But, given the intellectual equipment which Dr. Frend describes in the Greek apologists—a robust faith that, in a stable and civilized community, the tensions between religious belief and secular peace can be reconciled—it is not surprising that the most lasting legacy of Byzantine ecclesiastical statecraft should have been the idea of the Peace of the Church (on whose relevance, in the Reformation period, see, especially, C.

Vivanti, *Lotta politica e pace religiosa in Francia fra Cinque e Seicento*, 1963, on the *eirenic* circles around Henri of Navarre), and of Byzantine diplomacy, the civilized idea of a family of Christian princes (A. Grabar, 'God and the "Family of Princes" presided over by the Byzantine Emperor', *Harvard Slavic Studies*, ii (1954), 117–23). In Western Europe, the propounders of the idea of the Church, and, consequently, the idea of the Christianized society, were less certain that such tensions could be resolved, and, for that reason, were more aggressive: a church that always thought of itself as a separate élite could either be persecuted or dominant; and the world outside it, regarded either as actively hostile or as inferior, as a backward colony to be ruled firmly, with a heavy, guilt-laden paternalism. Augustine provides the alchemy that turned the persecuted élite of Cyprian into the persecuting élite of later times. In the West, therefore, the Christian society will always be pushing against its frontiers: a distinctive idea of the Church, held in varying degrees of crudity, blesses the impingement of Western Europe on the outside world in the Crusade, in the Reconquista, in the constant pressure against the pagans in Eastern Europe and along the shores of the Baltic (on which see, esp., H.-D. Kahl, '*Compellere intrare*. Die Wendenpolitik Bruns von Querfurt im Lichte hochmittelalterlichen Missions-und Völkerrechts', *Zeitschrift für Ostforschung*, vol. iv, 1955, now in *Heidenmission und Kreuzzugsgedanke*, ed. Beumann. Wege der Forschung, vii (1963), 177–274). Not surprisingly, the catechism which Augustine wrote to aid a Carthaginian priest in absorbing demoralized pagans after the destruction of their great temples in 399—a catechism in which the 'gathered' church of Cyprian has been subtly transposed into the triumphant élite of the age of Theodosius the Great—forms the basis of the first catechism published by the Spaniards in the New World (see Adolfo Etchegaray-Cruz, 'Saint Augustin et le contenu de la catéchèse prétridentine en Amérique Latine', *Revue des études augustinennes*, xi (1965), 277–90). That Dr. Frend has made us appreciate the deep roots and the fateful repercussions of divergent Christian attitudes forged in the period between Marcus Aurelius and Constantine is, perhaps, the crowning claim of *Martyrdom and Persecution* to be a contribution to the understanding of the history of Europe.

THE DIFFUSION OF MANICHAEISM
IN THE ROMAN EMPIRE*

A study of the fate of Manichaeism in the Roman Empire derives its interest from three main problems. First, Manichaeism was invariably associated with Persia: to study the growth of Manichaeism in the eastern provinces of the Roman Empire, and to trace the attitude of the Roman governing-class to its expansion, is to touch on an important sector of the cultural relations between the Sassanian Empire and the Roman world. Secondly, the repression of Manichaeism in the Christian Empire was the spear-head of religious intolerance: the only Christian heretics to be executed in the Early Church were Manichees or those, such as Priscillian, on whom the accusation of Manichaeism could be made to stick. Thirdly, Manichaeism was a missionary religion: its rapid expansion in the third and fourth centuries makes it the last religion from the eastern provinces to attempt to make headway in Roman society, just as its appearance in the T'ang Empire of China, alongside Buddhism and Nestorian Christianity, place it among the leading 'barbarian' religions that spread into an Empire which had suddenly opened to the Western World. Conversely, the withering away of Manichaeism in the Roman Empire is a symptom of the growth of a new, more exclusive, more localized society, that foreshadows the embattled Christendom of the Middle Ages.

* *Journal of Roman Studies*, LIX, 1969, pp. 92–103.
[The same year as this article was published, a biography of Mani in a fifth-century Greek papyrus came to light in Egypt: see A. Henrichs–L. Koenen, 'Ein griechischer Mani-Codex. (P. Colon inv. nr. 4780)', *Zeitschrift für Papyrologie und Epigraphik*, v, 1970, pp. 97–216. It is with deep gratitude to these scholars—and with a pardonable sense of relief—that I can draw attention to their report (as 'Mani-Codex') as having substantially corroborated and much extended what 1 wrote on the immediate background and origins of Manichaeism.]

I

The Rescript of Diocletian, of A.D. 297, to Julianus, Proconsul of Africa, is our first evidence of the official reaction to the spread of Manichaeism:

'Eos [*sc.* Manichaeos] audivimus nuperrime veluti nova et inopinata prodigia in hunc mundum de Persica adversaria nobis gente progressa vel orta esse . . . et verendum est, ne forte . . . conentur per execrandas consuetudines et scaevas leges Persarum innocentioris naturae homines, Romanam gentem modestam atque tranquillam, et universum orbem nostrum veluti venenis anguis malivoli inficere.'[1]

The Emperor has been taken a little too seriously. Many scholars have simply assumed that, because Manichaeism entered the Roman Empire from across the political frontier, it was a Persian religion.[2] More precisely, others have argued that Manichaeism could find a place in the religious beliefs of the Iranian governing class of the Sassanian Empire,[3] and that both its expansion within the Sassanian Empire and its missionary activity in the eastern provinces of the Roman Empire served the statecraft of the King of Kings.[4] The unquestioning identification of Manichaeism with Persia has acted, also, as a labour-saving device for students of religious intolerance in the Later Empire: it has lulled us into

[1] *Mosaicarum et Romanarum Legum Collatio* xv, 3, §4, ed. E. Seckel-B. Kuebler, *Jurisprudentiae anteiustinianae reliquiae* ii, 2, 1927, pp. 381 ff., whose text I follow: see below p. 107, n. 3 on the imagery of the *anguis malevolus*. Now in A. Adam, *Texte zum Manichäismus* (Kleine Texte für Vorlesungen und Übungen, 175), 1954, no. 56, pp. 82–3.

[2] Recently accepted by E. Volterra, 'La costituzione di Diocleziano e Massiminiano contro i Manichei', *Persia e il mondo greco-romano* (Accademia dei Lincei, anno 363, quaderno 76), 1966, pp. 27–50 at pp. 40–44.

[3] G. Widengren, *Mesopotamian Elements in Manichaeism* (Uppsala Universitets Årsskrift) 1946, p. 179: 'By propagating a syncretistic religion, Mani was able to offer the Sassanian King of Kings a religion well-suited to be acceptable both to his Iranian and Mesopotamian subjects'.

[4] Notably by W. Seston, 'L'Égypte manichéenne', *Chronique d'Égypte* xiv, 1939, pp. 362–27; 'Le roi Narsès, les Arabes et le manichéisme', *Mélanges R. Dussaud*, 1939, pp. 227–34; and *Dioclétien et la Tétrarchie* (Bibliothèque de l'école française d'Athènes et Rome, 162), 1946, pp. 149–59; and accepted, for instance, by A. Chastagnol, *La préfecture urbaine sous le Bas-Empire*, 1960, p. 156: 'Ce sort particulier s'explique sans doute par *les origines iraniennes de la doctrine* et par *la crainte de trahisons au moment des guerres entre la Rome et la Perse*', (My italics).

95

believing that we know precisely why this group, at least, was so hated.

Manichaeism was not a 'Persian' religion in the strict sense. It is unfortunate that the first and only study of the diffusion of Manichaeism in the Roman Empire, by de Stoop, in 1909, should have been the work of a pupil of Cumont, and written at a time when the 'Iranian' interpretation of Manichaeism was at its height, recently fed, as it had been, by the discovery of Manichaean manuscripts in their most 'Iranian' form, in Central Asia.[1] For Cumont, Manichaeism was the direct successor of Mithraism in the Western world.[2]

The general reassessment of the nature of Manichaeism,[3] followed by the discovery of the Coptic Manichaean documents in the Fayyūm in Egypt[4] has made it increasingly difficult to represent Manichaeism as a development of Iranian religion.[5] The Manichees entered the Roman Empire, not as a final version of the *Mages Hellenisés*, but at the behest of a man who claimed to be an 'Apostle of Jesus Christ': they intended to supersede Christianity, not to

[1] G. de Stoop, *Essai sur la diffusion du manichéisme dans l'empire romain* (Université de Grand. Recueil de travaux publiés par la faculté de philosophie et lettres, 38) 1909. For the development of Manichaean studies, and its relation to the finds in Egypt and Central Asia, the best account is by J. Ries, 'Introduction aux études manichéennes', *Ephemerides Theologicae Lovanienses* XXXIII, 1957, pp. 453–82; XXXV, 1959, pp. 362–409.

[2] See F. Cumont, *The Mysteries of Mithra* (trans. McCormack), Dover Editions, 1956, p. 207: 'The sect of Manichaeus spread throughout the empire during the fourth century, at the moment when Mithraism was expiring, and it was called to assume the latter's succession'.

[3] Most notably E. Waldschmidt—W. Lentz, *Die Stellung Jesu im Manichäismus* (*Abhandlungen der Akad. d. Wissenschaften*, Berlin 1933, 13); H. Schaeder, *Urform und Fortbildung des manichäischen Systems* (*Vorträge der Warburg-Bibliothek* IV, 1924–1925), 1927, and F. C. Burkitt, *The Religion of the Manichees*, 1925.

[4] C. Schmidt–J. J. Polotsky, *Ein Mani-Fund in Ägypten: Originalschriften des Mani und seiner Schüler*. (*Sitzungsberichte der preussischen Akademie der Wissenschaften, Philol.-Hist. Klasse*, 1933, I.)

[5] See A. Böhlig. 'Christliche Würzeln im Manichäismus', *Bulletin de la société d'archéologie copte* XV, 1960, pp. 41–61 [= *Mysterion und Wahrheit*, 1968, pp. 202–221], esp. p. 47–Zoroaster and Buddha are distant figures, compared to Jesus. The best statement of the nature of Manichaeism relates Mani to Gnosticism, not to Zoroaster: H. C. Puech, *Le Manichéisme: son fondateur, sa doctrine* (Musée Guimet, Bibliothèque de diffusion LVI) 1949, esp. pp. 69–70. [On Mani's close connection with the Judaeo-Christian Gnostic sect of the Elchasaïtes, now see 'Mani-Codex', pp. 133–160.]

spread the *scaevas leges Persarum*.[1] Diocletian had made the mistake, pardonable in a Roman if not in a modern historian of Near Eastern culture, of treating Persian-controlled Mesopotamia *tout court* as 'Persia'.

Mani belongs where he said he belonged, to the 'land of Babylon'. He came from southern Mesopotamia, the Sassanian province of Asorestan, 'Ασσύρια.[2] Of his seven great books, one only was written in Middle Persian: the rest, in an Aramaic closely related to Syriac.[3] He looks back to the Gnostic Christianity of Osrhoene: his dialogue is with Marcion and Bardaisan of Edessa;[4] Zoroaster is a distant figure to him. To study Mani and Manichaeism, is to study cultural frontiers that have nothing to do with the political frontiers of the two Empires. The history of Manichaeism is to a large extent a history of the Syriac-speaking belt, that stretched along the Fertile Crescent without interruption, from Antioch to Ctesiphon. 'The frontier territory between Rome and Parthia was neither a cultural barrier nor a mere gateway and point of passage between East and West. It was a vital creative centre in its own right, and it was this fact above all which enabled it to serve as an effective intermediary between the two great civilisations that flourished on its borders.'[5] What Ward-Perkins has said of the art of the Parthian period, remains true of the religious history of the whole Late Antiquity. Mesopotamia was the 'religiöse Wetterecke der Spätantike'. What we must first discover is why, from this *Wetterecke*, the wind of Manichaeism appears to have blown so strongly to the West.

This problem has been brought yet further from solution by ill-founded speculations on the relations between Mani, the Manichees

[1] See especially, J. Ries, 'Jésus-Christ dans la réligion de Mani', *Augustiniana* xv, 1964, pp. 437–54. [On the crucial rôle of Paul in detaching Mani from the Elchasaïte community, see 'Mani-Codex', pp. 114–15 and esp. p. 139.]

[2] On Asorestan-'Ασσύρια, see E. Honigmann—A. Maricq, *Recherches sur les Res Gestae Divi Saporis*, 1953, pp. 41–2 and 49, n. 2.

[3] Henning, 'Mitteliranische', *Handbuch der Orientalistik, I. Abt., IV Bd.* (*Iranistik*, 1958), 73: 'in seiner dem Syrischen naherverwandten ostaramäischen Muttersprache'. [The new biography was originally written in Syriac: 'Mani-Codex', pp. 104–105.]

[4] As rightly emphasized by Burkitt, op. cit. [p. 96, n. 3] and Böhlig, art. cit. [p. 96, n. 5], pp. 47 ff. [Mani's letter to the Edessenes: see 'Mani-Codex', pp. 108–9.]

[5] J. B. Ward-Perkins, 'Frontiere politiche e frontiere culturali', *Persia e 'l mondo greco-romano*, cit. [p. 95, n. 2], 395–409: from the English summary at p. 395.

and the Persian Kings, Shapur I, Ohrmizd I, Bahram I and Narseh I. These speculations ascribe to Shapur I the intention of using the message of Mani as a religious cement for his diverse Empire,[1] and to Narseh, the plan of rallying the Manichees in the Roman world as a Persian fifth-column, and, hence, of provoking the justified indignation of the Emperor Diocletian.[2] Such an interpretation of the rise of Manichaeism raises the general problem of the relations of the Sassanians to their non-Iranian subjects in general and to non-Zoroastrian religions in particular—a problem that has recently been handled by J. Neusner, for the case of the Jews in Babylonia, with exemplary caution and largely negative results.[3]

In the case of the relations between Mani and Shapur I the evidence is, quite literally, fragmentary: much has hinged on the possible reading of a lacuna in one Coptic papyrus.[4] Excited glimpses in the literature of a sect, of the confrontation of holy man and monarch, are hardly firm ground on which to build grandiose hypotheses on the relation of religion and statecraft in the Sassanian Empire: as Dr Maricq concludes, 'cette trâme est bien lâche encore'.

Such speculations are not so much groundless as misplaced. We are dealing with a religious movement of a very radical type. Faced by such a phenomenon, the historian should begin with enthusiasm, not with statecraft. To begin any other way in trying to understand Manichaeism, is to abandon a coherent body of vivid and contemporary religious literature in favour of a few dubious fragments.

We know three of the most important things about Mani.[5] He was a missionary: not for nothing did he borrow the Pauline title of 'Apostle of Jesus Christ' for his letters.[6] He was deeply preoccupied

[1] See Widengren, op. cit [p. 95, n. 3].

[2] See Seston, art. cit [p. 95, n. 4].

[3] J. Neusner, *A History of the Jews in Babylonia, II: The Early Sassanian Period* (Studia Post-Biblica, XI), 1966, pp. 2–3, 28 and 41.

[4] *Kephalaia* I, ed. H. J. Polotsky and A. Böhlig, 1940, p. 15, admirably re-examined by A. Maricq in Honigmann-Maricq, op. cit. [p. 97, n. 2], pp. 24–5. [The link between the preaching of Mani and the accession of Shapur I is now definitively disproved by 'Mani-Codex', pp. 125–132.]

[5] See esp. the summary of L. J. R. Ort, *Mani. A religio-historical description of his personality* (Supplements ad Numen, altera series, I), 1967.

[6] Schmidt-Polotsky, op. cit. [p. 96, n. 4], p. 23. Augustine, *Contra epistulam Fundamenti*, c. 1 = A. Adam, op. cit. [p. 95, n. 1] no. 10, p. 27: 'Manichaeus apostolus Jesu Christi providentia dei patris.' [On the influence of Paul on Mani's sense of his mission, see 'Mani-Codex', pp. 106–10, 138–9 and 198–9.]

with the problem of national boundaries.[1] He believed that he had founded a universal religion: unlike Christianity and Zoroastrianism, he would be able to spread the 'hope of life' in East and West alike. East had been East, and West had been West; and only in Mani had the twain met.[2] He was a man with a *daemon*. From the age of twelve, he had acted on the prompting of his 'Twin Spirit'. The final distillation of religious truth—the Holy Ghost that had been promised three centuries before Christ—had descended in him. With this belief he sent his disciples to East and West, and he himself lived a life of great missionary journeys.[3]

Now, the interest of Mani's journeys is that, radiating from Mesopotamia, they usually strike inland, into the traditional world of the Iranian plateau: only once did he hover on the frontiers of the Roman Empire.[4] Socially, he seems to have impinged intimately on the Iranian governing class: he acted on the fringes of the Sassanian royal family;[5] he converted client kings,[6] and female members of the Iranian aristocracy.[7] Thus for thirty years Mani had preached, performed exorcisms, conjured visions[8] near the heart of traditional Persian society, which knew him as 'the doctor from the land of Babylon'. When he was executed, in 276, it was at the instigation

---

[1] Puech, op. cit. [p. 96, n. 5] pp. 62–4. See esp. *Kephalaia* CLIV, cited in Schmidt-Polotsky, op. cit [p. 96, n. 4] p. 44; and F. C. Andreas, 'Mitteliranische Manichaica II' (*Sitzungsberichte der Akademie der Wissenschaften*, 1933, 5), p. 295 in A. Adam, op. cit. [p. 95, n. 1] no. 3d, p. 6.

[2] I know of no treatment of the possible source of this idea: it is far more drastic than any contemporary Christian statement of the supra-national quality of the Church—on which, see E. Peterson, 'Das Problem des Nationalismus im alten Christentum', in *Frühkirche, Judentum und Gnosis*, 1959, pp. 51–3.

[3] Mani as the Holy Ghost: Puech, op. cit. [p. 96, n. 5], pp. 43–4, nn. 164–6 at pp. 127–8. On Mani's journeys after his revelation: Puech, op. cit., pp. 44–9. Schaeder, op. cit. [p. 96, n. 3], p. 129: 'Er ist weniger Stifter als Missionär. Sein ganzes Lebenswerk, seine Reisen, seine Schriftstellerei sind Mission.' [Mani's 'Twin-Spirit': 'Mani-Codex', pp. 161–71. The Pauline background to Mani's visionary experiences: 'Mani-Codex', pp. 186–9.]

[4] *Kephalaia* I, ed. cit. [p. 98, n. 4], p. 15. [See now W. Sundermann, 'Zur frühen missionarischen Wirksamkeit Manis', *Acta Orientalia* XXIV, 1971, pp. 79–125.]

[5] M. 3: F. W. K. Müller, 'Handschrift-Reste in Estrangelo-Schrift aus Turfan', *Anhang, Abhandlungen preuss. Ak. Wiss.*, 1904, p. 87, pp. 81–2, in Ort op. cit. [p. 98, n. 5], p. 53.

[6] M. 6031 and *Manichäische Homilien*, ed. H. J. Polotsky, 1934, pp. 42–67. See O. Klíma, 'Baat the Manichee', *Archiv Orientalni* XXVI, 1958, pp. 342–6.

[7] Schmidt-Polotsky, op. cit. [p. 96, n. 4], p. 27, n. 2.

[8] M. 566 I Recto: in Ort, op. cit. [p. 98, n. 5], p. 51.

of the Zoroastrian clergy, led by the *mobedhan mobedh*, Karter, on the charge of having provoked apostasies from Zoroastrianism.[1] Mani was not the last religious leader in the Sassanian Empire to suffer for claiming that his was a universal faith, and that the 'Good Religion' of Zoroaster was both demonic and parochial.[2]

The fatal interview with King Bahram took place at Bēth-Lāpāt, Gundeshapur. Gundeshapur had been thoroughly 'westernized' by Shapur I: the Emperor Valerian was said to have died in captivity there;[3] it had been largely settled with prisoners of war from Shapur's great raids into the Roman Empire;[4] it boasted a centre of learning that drew on Greek sources;[5] it may have been decorated with sub-Antiochene mosaics like those at Bishapur;[6] Syriac would have been spoken in the streets. Yet, Mani would only be allowed to approach the Iranian Kings of Kings through an interpreter.[7] The execution of the 'doctor from Babylon' was a warning: Shapur I had wrested non-Iranian traditions, skills and manpower from *Anērān*— from Mesopotamia and the eastern provinces of the Roman Empire —and had placed them in the heart of *Ērān*;[8] Bahram I was to teach these non-Iranian elements to know their place. From 276 onwards, traditional Persian society, as a whole, was opaque to Manichaeism. Like a bow-sprit, its compact mass broke the Manichaean movement in two, scattering its missionaries to the North East into Soghdia and Central Asia (the Siberia of Persian dissidents),[9] and westwards into the Roman Empire.

[1] M. 3, Müller, op. cit. [p. 99, n. 5].

[2] M. 42: in Andreas, op. cit. [p. 99, n. 1], pp. 879-80. Compare the speech of Mâr Aba, Nestorian *catholikos* of the sixth century, *Vita*, c. 14 in Braun, *Ausgewählte Akten persischer Märtyrer*, 1915, pp. 198-9.

[3] *Chronicle of Seert, Patrologia Orientalis* IV, p. 220.

[4] *Chronicle of Seert, Patrol. Or.* IV, pp. 220-1: see N. Pigulevskaja, *Les villes de l'état iranien*, 1963, pp. 159-61.

[5] H. W. Bailey, *Zoroastrian Problems*, 1943, p. 81 and C. A. Nallino, 'Tracce di opere greche giunte agli Arabi per trafila pehlevica', *Raccolta di scritti* VI, 1948, pp. 285-303.

[6] See E. Will, 'L'art sassanide et ses prédécesseurs', *Syria* XXXIX, 1962, pp. 45-63.

[7] M. 3 in F. W. K. Müller, ed. cit. [p. 99, n. 5], p. 92.

[8] *Gesta Divi Saporis*, lines 34 f. in Honigmann-Maricq, op. cit. [p. 97, n. 2], p. 34.

[9] W. Henning, 'Neue Materialen zur Geschichte des Manichäismus', *Zeitschr. d. deutschen morgenländischen Gesellschaft* XC, 1936, pp. 11-14.

Thus at no time in Late Antiquity or the Middle Ages can Manichaeism be firmly identified with 'Persia'.[1] Under the Abbasid Caliphate, for instance, the revival of Persian aspirations and Persian literature in the ninth and tenth centuries involved not so much a revival of Manichaeism as a bitter revival of the *persecution* of Manichaeism. A courtier such as Ibn Khurdadbeh, whose grandparents had been Zoroastrian noblemen, and whose idea of the *adab* of a cultured Muslim gentleman had to include knowledge of 'to which princes Ardasher gave the title of king',[2] would have regarded the Manichees as his traditional enemies; his new Islamic orthodoxy only gave him an additional incentive to crush a religious group that he had continued to call by its ancient, pehlevi name—*Zindiks*, 'corruptors of the Law', the *Zend*.[3]

Mani, a man with a *daemon*, had overreached himself. But the Manichaean community remained. This community may have remained far closer to their Mesopotamian roots than had their ambitious, much-travelled leader.[4] I would suggest that the 'Christian' and 'Western' elements in Manichaeism asserted themselves immediately after the execution of Mani, as the basis of an organized Manichaean Church. For the next persecution of Manichaeism, in around A.D. 287, is a persecution of a group regarded as indistinguishable from the Christians in the Sassanian Empire.[5] This is hardly surprising. What we know of the Gnostic tendencies of Mesopotamian Christianity points inevitably to Manichaeism: as

[1] For this reason, I would not accept the statements of A. Abel, 'Les sources arabes sur le manichéisme', *Annuaire de l'Institut de philologie et histoire orientales et slaves* XVI, 1961–2, pp. 31–73, esp. at pp. 46 7.

[2] R. Paret, 'Contribution à l'étude des milieux culturels dans le Proche-Orient médiévale: l'encyclopédisme arabo-musulman de 850 à 950', *Revue historique* CCXXXV, 1966, pp. 47–100.

[3] See G. Vajda, 'Les Zindiqs en pays d'Islam au début de la période abbaside', *Rivista degli studi orientali* XVII, 1938, pp. 173–229 and B. Spuler, *Iran in der frühislamischen Zeit*, 1952, pp. 206–9.

[4] *Kephalaia* LXXVI, ed. cit. [p. 98, n. 4], pp. 183–8. The community at 'Gaukhai' is concerned at its leaders' constant absence. It is these communities, in southern Mesopotamia, that Mani visits on his last journey: see W. Henning, 'Mani's Last Journey', *Bulletin of the School of Oriental and African Studies* X, 1942, pp. 941–53. [On Mani's disciples as 'witnesses' in the new biography: 'Mani-Codex', pp. 110–114. His continued debates with the Mesopotamian Elchasaïtes: 'Mani-Codex', pp. 148–149.]

[5] *Chronicle of Seert, Patrol. Or.* IV, pp. 237–238.

Ephrem of Nisibis would say, Marcion had divided the sheep of Christ, Mani merely robbed the robber.[1] More important, the great raids of Shapur I had filled the areas where Mani preached with Syriac-speaking settlers, many of whom were Christians.[2] The new sect spread among these uprooted men; and from the late third century onwards, Manichaeism would dog, not the Zoroastrian establishment of Érān but the insecure Christian communities of the western parts of the Sassanian Empire.[3]

If this is so, we can appreciate with what ease and in what form Manichaeism entered the Roman world. The rapid conquests and retreats of Shapur I had ensured that a trail of expatriates linked Antioch to the heart of the Persian Empire.[4] Later, the fall of Palmyra and the establishment of Edessa and Nisibis as the bulwarks of the Roman defence in Northern Mesopotamia gave greater prominence to the areas that were Syriac-speaking, partly Christian, endemic with gnostic radicalism.[5]

As for the Manichees, they entered the Roman Empire as a group thoroughly alienated from the Sassanian state. They had lost Mani, then Sisinnios, at the hands of the Magi. Whether we are prepared to interpret the *détente* in persecution, granted by Narseh I in around 295, as part of a plan to rally the Manichees as a fifth-column in the Roman Empire, as Prof. Seston has done (and everyone after him), depends on whether we think it humanly possible for a tiny sect to forget overnight a generation of bloodshed. The

[1] Ephraem, *C. Haereses* xx, 3, ed. E. Beck, *Corpus Scriptorum Christianorum Orientalium*, Scr. Syr. LXXVIII, 1957. On the diffusion of Gnosticism, especially of Marcionism, in Mesopotamia, see A. von Harnack, *Marcion*, 1921, pp. 190 ff. and, especially, A. Vööbus, *History of Asceticism in the Syrian Orient: I, The Origin of Asceticism; Early Monasticism in Persia* (*Corpus Scriptorum Christianorum Orientalium*, vol. 184, Subsidia, 14) 1958, pp. 45–8. [Now see 'Mani-Codex', pp. 141–160.]

[2] See esp. M. L. Chaumont, 'Les Sassanides et la Christianisation de l'Empire iranien au IIIe. siècle', *Revue de l'Histoire des Religions* CLXV, 1964, pp. 165–202. [For the Mesopotamian Elchasaïtes, contact with Paul meant contact with a 'Hellene': 'Mani-Codex', pp. 146–149.]

[3] Excellently described, with much unpublished Syriac material, by Vööbus, op. cit. [p. 102, n. 1], pp. 159–62.

[4] Chaumont, art. cit. [p. 102, n. 2], p. 176: see Pigulevskaja, op. cit. [p. 100, n. 4], pp. 161–9, for a discussion of the diffusion of Syrian techniques in textile-production in the Sassanian Empire.

[5] See most recently, H. J. W. Drivers, *Bardaisan of Edessa* (Studia Semitica Neerlandica, 1) 1966, and Vööbus, op. cit. [p. 102, n. 1], pp. 187–9.

Manichaean Coptic Homilies that refer to events in the Persian Empire make this seem unlikely.[1] The Manichees had bitter memories: in this alone, they would have appeared in the Roman world in the same position as their Christian rivals; they were the first Christian or para-Christian group to be able to boast of suffering for their faith at the hands of 'the Magi, the servants of fire'.[2]

One can never ignore the Fertile Crescent. The Manichaean missionaries were only a small part of the steady trickle of Syriac-speakers across the frontiers of the two Empires: men like Aphraat who, in the mid-fourth century, moved from Southern Mesopotamia to Edessa, and only found it necessary to launch out from Syriac into pidgin-Greek when he reached Antioch;[3] or like Mâr Aba, who could travel easily, in the early sixth century, from Nisibis (by that time a Persian city) to Alexandria 'like a new Abraham from the land of the Chaldees'.[4]

Two points are worth noticing. First: it is the Christian communities and their radical off-shoots who do most to maintain the links across the Fertile Crescent in the Late Roman period. Tourists and philosopher-diplomats became rare;[5] Christian priests were more common.[6] It is only in the Christian community in Antioch, for instance, that there is a chink in the curtain that veiled the fate of the inhabitants of the surrendered city of Nisibis from Roman eyes.[7]

[1] *Manichäische Homilien*, ed. cit. [p. 99, n. 6], pp. 84–5, refers to bitter persecution in Persia.

[2] *Manichäische Homilien*, ed. cit. [p. 99, n. 6], p. 160.

[3] Theodoret, *Historia Religiosa*, c. viii (*Patrol. graeca* LXXXII, 1368 B). [Now see Fergus Millar, 'Paul of Samosata, Zenobia and Aurelian; the Church, Local Culture, and Political Allegiance in the Third Century', *Journal of Roman Studies* LXI, 1971.]

[4] See esp. W. Wolska, *La Topographie chrétienne de Cosmas Indicopleustes* (Bibliothèque byzantine), 1962, pp. 63–73.

[5] For which see recently J. F. Duneau, 'Quelques aspects de la pénétration de l'hellénisme dans l'Empire perse sassanide', *Mélanges Réné Crozet* I, 1966, pp. 13–22.

[6] Shown recently by E. Follieri, 'Santi persiani nell'innografia bizantina', *Persia e il mondo greco-romano*, pp. 227–242; see esp. G. Mercati, 'Per la vita e gli scritti di "Paolo il Persiano",' *Studi e Testi* V, 1901, pp. 180–206, esp. pp. 180–1.

[7] R. Turcan, 'L'abandon de Nisibe et l'opinion publique', *Mélanges André Pignaniol* II, 1966, pp. 875–90.

Secondly, Syria was the bridgehead of Manichaeism in the Roman world. The discovery of the Manichaean Coptic literature in Fayyūm has tended to distort our perspectives on this issue. The Manichaean Psalms were first written in Syriac;[1] Syriac Manichaean fragments were discovered alongside the Coptic documents;[2] the Manichaean community in Alexandria was a Syrian implantation (just as many Coptic Christian legends seem to echo the events of Antioch in the 260's).[3] The first Manichaean to settle in the Roman world was a characteristic figure of Roman religious history —a veteran, demobilized from Mesopotamia, returning with his own version of the sect to Palestine.[4] In the fourth century, Manichaeism was rife as a crypto-Christianity in Antioch and Palestine.[5] Most surprising of all is the group of well-known Syrians who stood, as it were, 'on the touch-line' of the Manichaean movement: Libanius intervened to protect them;[6] Strategius Musonianus whose culture (did it include Syriac?) led him to be commissioned by Constantine to examine the doctrines of the Manichees;[7] the *dux* Sebastianus, accused of being a Manichaean *auditor*;[8] Hierius, to whom Augustine addressed his first crypto-Manichaean treatise.[9] Plainly, Manichaeism became part of the Syrian scene. Wherever we meet a Syrian, indeed, we may meet a Manichee. At Salona, for instance, we find the inscription of a Manichaean nun in a town where the origins of the Christian community point to Nisibis;[10] at Carthage, a flourishing Manichaean 'cell' appears in the only wes-

[1] See T. Save-Söderbergh, *Studies in the Coptic Manichaean Psalm-Book*, 1949. [As was the new biography: 'Mani-Codex', pp. 104–105.]

[2] Ed. by Burkitt, op. cit [p. 96, n. 3], p. 111.

[3] J. Schwartz, 'Dioclétien dans la littérature copte', *Bulletin de la société d'archéologie copte* XV, 1960, pp. 151–66. For artistic relations between Egypt and Syria in the third century, see esp. E. Drioton, 'Art syrien et art copte', *Bull. soc. archéologie copte* III, 1937, pp. 20–40.

[4] Epiphanius, *Panarion* LXVI, 1 (ed. K. Holl, *Griechische Christliche Schriftsteller* 37).

[5] See de Stoop, op. cit. [p. 96, n. 1], pp. 61 sq. esp. Epiphanius, *Pan* LXVI, 87 and Cyril of Jerusalem, *Catecheses* VI, 21.

[6] Libanius, Ep. 1253, ed. Förster; Teubner XI, p. 329.

[7] Ammianus Marcellinus, XV, 13.

[8] Athanasius, *Historia Arianorum* 73.

[9] Augustine, *Confessiones* IV, xiv, 21.

[10] F. Cumont—M. A. Kugener, *Recherches sur le manichéisme* III, 1912, pp. 175 ff.: in Adam, op. cit. [p. 95, n. 1], no. 6, pp. 106–7. See R. Egger, *Römische Antike und frühes Christentum*, I, 1962, pp. 186–8.

tern city where the Syrian eccentricities of the Messalian—'The Praying'—monks seem to have gained a foothold.[1] The pattern continues as long as there are Manichaean communities at both horns of the Fertile Crescent. The journey of the philosophers from the Platonic Academy of Athens to the court of Khusro I in 531–532, is not quite as quixotic a flit as the account of Agathias would make us suppose.[2] It is part of the history of the Fertile Crescent. For it had been preceded by a visit of the Nestorian professors of Nisibis, Mâr Aba and Paul the Persian, to Constantinople.[3] The leader of the Athenian party was a Syrian, Damascius: he may well have discussed Plato in Syriac, the *lingua franca* of the sixth-century Near East.[4] While the exceptionally empathetic analysis of Manichaeism by Damascius' colleague, Simplicius, contains a fragment of the original mythology of the Mesopotamian Manichees—this may be a strange souvenir of his visit to Ctesiphon.[5] A little previously, a no less extraordinary encounter had taken place in Constantinople. In 529, the Manichaean leader, Photeinos, was confronted in debate by a nominee of the Emperor Justinian, Paul the Persian. Paul, also, would play his part in gratifying the philosophical taste of Khusro, by translating Aristotle into Syriac;[6] now, in Constantinople, he would debate in the stilted philosophical Greek of the Byzantine clergy and university professors.[7] The incidents are a reminder that right up to the sixth century, the diffusion of Manichaeism must be seen against the background of the extraordinary richness and homogeneity of the cultures of the Near East.

[1] G. Folliet, 'Les moines euchites à Carthage en 400–401' (Studia Patristica ii), *Texte und Untersuchungen* LXIV, 1957, pp. 386–99. Independently arrived at by Vööbus, op. cit. [p. 102, n. 1] II, 1960, p. 32, n. 72.

[2] Agathias II, 27. [See now Averil Cameron, 'Agathias on the Sassanians', *Dumbarton Oaks Papers*, XXIII–XXIV, 1969–70, pp. 164–176.]

[3] See Wolska, op. cit. [p. 103, n. 4] and Mercati, op. cit. [p. 103, n. 6].

[4] See P. Peeters, *Le tréfonds orientale de l'hagiographie byzantine*, 1950, pp. 20 sq., on the use of Syriac by diplomats.

[5] Suggested by Dr. Ilsetraut Hadot, 'Die Widerlegung des Manichäismus im Epiktetkommentar des Simplikios', *Archiv für Geschichte der Philosophie*, LI, 1969, pp. 31–57, though not accepted by Dr. Alan Cameron, 'The Last Days of the Academy at Athens', *Proc. Cambr. Philol. Soc.* CXCV, 1967, pp. 7–29.

[6] See Mercati, op. cit. [p. 103, n. 6], pp. 183 f.

[7] In *Patrologia Graeca* LXXXIX, coll. 528–78.

II

To return to the Emperor Diocletian. Students of the suppression of religious dissent too often forget that the declarations of persecuting authorities throw little light on the motives of the persecuted: what they do enable us to grasp are the fears and assumptions of the society that persecutes. As we have shown in Part I, Diocletian's edict has not taken us very far in our understanding of the Manichees. But it is vital evidence for his own form of Roman patriotism and for that of the officials and local notables in Africa who evidently regarded the arrival of Manichaean missionaries with horror.[1] As such it is a most revealing document. For it is a symptom of the increasing rigidity of the barrier that existed in the minds of the governing class of the later Empire, between 'Rome' and 'Persia'. The Manichees, as inhabitants of the open society of Mesopotamia, were caught between two professedly reactionary states—the 'Romanity' of Diocletian being matched by Narseh, a man 'driven on by praise of his ancestors'.[2]

This rigidity increases notably at the end of the fourth century: the laws against the Manichees are repeated with increasing severity from the reign of the Emperor Valentinian I onwards.[3] I would suggest the following reason: in the treatment of Manichaeism we have a clear index of the fusing of Roman prejudice with Christian doctrinal intolerance. Writing of Mani, Eusebios of Caesarea will use exactly the same language as the Emperor Diocletian: a poisonous snake, entering the Roman world from 'barbarous' Persia.[4] But the effects of this fusion, already so obvious in an educated court-bishop of the age of Constantine, were delayed for a few generations. Traditional pagans seem always to have regarded the Manichees with horror;[5] but the Christians were less certain.[6] Manichaeism existed on the fringes of the Christian community: the bishops might fulminate, but they were also prepared to

---

[1] The document is a rescript, see Volterra, art. cit. [p. 95, n. 2], p. 32.

[2] Lactantius, *De mortibus persecutorum* IX, 5.

[3] See E. H. Kaden, 'Die Edikte gegen die Manichäer von Diokletian bis Justinian', *Festschrift für Hans Lewald*, 1953, pp. 55–68.

[4] Eusebius, *Historia ecclesiastica* VII, 31.

[5] Augustine, *de utilitate credendi* 1, 2.

[6] It was to the credit of Saint Anthony, wrote Athanasius, that he did *not* associate with Manichees: *Vita Antonii*, c. 68.

debate.[1] The resumption of outright persecution of the Manichees coincides with the partial Christianization of the lay governing-class of the Roman world. It is the mysterious 'Ambrosiaster', a man in touch with the opinions of senators in Rome, who will cite the edict of Diocletian in his commentary on St. Paul: Manichaeism is a Christian 'heresy' for him; but it is also deeply hated as the 'new and unexpected monstrous-birth from Persia' that had disturbed conservative Romans.[2]

The Manichees, therefore, suffered a double outlawry. The Christianized Roman Empire, already chauvinistic in its attitude to Persia, now orthodox, would have little patience with 'snakes' from outside its frontiers. Manichaeism, at least, was a very small snake compared with the more imposing outsiders in the Roman world: Diocletian's image of the 'snake', amplified by a century and a half of religious zeal, will appear as a motto on the coins of Emperors committed to the most fateful of all confrontations with non-Roman heretics—on the coins of the Emperor Marjorian, on the eve of his luckless expedition against the Arian Vandal kingdom established in Africa.[3]

Altogether, the history of the original impetus of Manichaeism in the Roman Empire cannot be written as if it were a direct continuation of the spread of the oriental cults and of Mithraism. For the times had changed. Horizons had narrowed, frontiers hardened, in men's minds at least. In the second century, the doctrines of Elchasai would be warmly received in Rome: here was a 'Parthian book', to be treated with awe. But it is the open world of the second century that 'stands amazed' at the Wisdom of the East.[4] Some of this 'amazement' survives in pagan circles of the fourth century: the author of the *Kyranides* will claim to have discovered his occult

---

[1] See *P. Ryl.* 469 in Adam, op. cit. [p. 95, n. 1], no. 35, pp. 52–4. [Professor L. Koenen has kindly informed me of a record of an amicable discussion with Manichees in the circle of Didymus the Blind, in an unpublished papyrus of Didymus' *Commentary on Ecclesiastes*. A similiar debate, see *Apophthegmata Patrum*, Theodora 4 (*Patrol, Graeca*, LXV, 204A.)]

[2] 'Ambrosiaster', *Comment. ad II ep. Tim.* III, 6 (*Patrol. latina* XVII, 521).

[3] See P. Courcelle, 'Le serpent à face humaine dans la numismatique impériale du Vᵉ siècle,' *Mélanges André Piganiol* I, 1966, pp. 343–55.

[4] See esp. Festugière, *La Révélation d'Hermès Trismégiste* I, 1944, pp. 10–27, p. 20: 'le monde gréco-romain est comme en stupeur'. [The contrast is sharpened by the discovery that Mani was, indeed, connected with the followers of Elchasaï: 'Mani-Codex', pp. 141–160.]

recipes through a visit to Seleucia, guided by a plausible figure—an old Syrian who had been brought to Persia as a prisoner of war.[1] But most of the 'amazement' had worn off: 'Haec si aliquis Indus eloquitur, aut Persa commemorat, *suae genti* praecipiat . . . Cessa, Justine, cessa istius *vanitatis barbariem* diligenti cura captare, et *Romanus vir a Persico vel Armeniorum sacrilegio* nitere removeri'.[2]

To study Manichaeism is to study the fate of a missionary religion in a world of shrinking horizons.

III

There are two ways of approaching the way in which Manichaeism spread within the Roman Empire: the jig-saw puzzle and the Chinese boxes.

The approach of the jig-saw puzzle sees Manichaeism exclusively as a product of religious syncretism. The scholar asks what pieces in the jig-saw of Manichaean beliefs appealed to what religious groups in the Roman world: the pagans, it is said, were attracted by the Manichaean reverence for the Sun; the Christians, by the name of Christ.[3] This approach has severe limitations. I would prefer the approach of the Chinese boxes. To become a Manichee or to favour the Manichees meant favouring a group. This group had a distinctive and complex structure. Because of this structure, the Manichaean group impinged on the society around it in a distinctive way; and this structure, in turn, exposed it to distinctive pressures from its Roman environment.

First, the Manichaean religion was based on a rigid distinction between the perfect, the Elect (men and women), and the rank-and-file, the Hearers.[4] The *sancta ecclesia* of Mani was limited to the Elect.[5] The Elect secured the salvation of the Hearers, by forgiving

[1] Festugière, op. cit. [p. 107, n. 4], pp. 201 f.
[2] *Ad Justinum manichaeum* XVI, *Patrol. latina* VIII, 1008 C—D.
[3] This is the normal accusation of Christian polemists: v. Epiphanius, *Panarion* LXVI, 87, followed by Marc le Diacre, *Vie de Porphyre*, ed. H. Grégoire —A. Kugener, 1930, c. 86, p. 67. It is accepted by de Stoop, op. cit. [p. 96, n. 1], p. 33 *et passim*, and carried *ad absurdum* by H. J. Grondijs, 'Le diversità delle sette manichee', *Studi bizantini e neoellenici* IX, 1957, pp. 176–87 and 'Analyse du manichéisme numidien au IVe siècle', *Augustinus Magister* III, 1955, pp. 391–410. For my disagreement on one significant item—the meaning of the Manichaean worship of the Sun—see P. Brown, *Augustine of Hippo*, 1967, p. 56.
[4] Puech, op. cit. [p. 95, n. 5], pp. 88–91.
[5] Evodius, *de fide* 5 (*Corpus Scriptorum Ecclesiae Latinorum* xxv).

their sins and by purging their souls through entirely vicarious rituals.[1] The Hearers sheltered and fed the Elect.[2] Manichaeism, therefore, was a group with an unmistakable inner core: the Elect were vagrant, studiously ill-kempt, they carried exotic books, they were committed to elaborate liturgies and fenced in with drastic taboos.[3] The Hearers, by contrast, were indistinguishable from their environment.[4] The Manichaeism that we know most about in the fourth century is the Manichaeism of the Hearers—of the 'Fellow-Travellers'. Augustine and his friends were only Hearers.[5] A less-known example was the *dux* Sebastianus. This able and popular general was said to be a 'Hearer' of the Manichees.[6] At one moment, he might have become Emperor.[7] His eccentricity is a tribute to the Late Roman army as an oasis of religious freedom.

A religion that has to shelter behind patrons and half-adepts is an interesting phenomenon. Strange alliances could occur. Symmachus, the pagan, will choose Augustine, the Manichaean 'Hearer' for the chair of rhetoric in Milan at the behest of the Manichees.[8] He probably acted for the same reasons as a very similar pagan, Libanius, had done. Here was a small group suffering from the violence of the Christian communities; they were harmless, they were spread throughout the world in tiny enclaves, they worshipped the

---

[1] Hegemonius, *Acta Archelai*, 10; *Manichäische Homilien*, ed. cit. [p. 99, n. 6], p. 38; Augustine, *Contra Faustum* v, 10 and *Confessiones* IV, i, 1. The same mentality is vividly described in the twelfth-century Cathars, see R. Manselli, *L'eresia del male*, 1963, esp. p. 237.

[2] P. Alfaric, 'Un manuscrit manichéen', *Revue d'histoire et de littérature religieuses*, n.s. VI, 1920: in Adam, op. cit. [p. 95, n. 1] no. 16, pp. 34–5 and *Patrologia Latina Supplementum* II, 1378–1388.

[3] Vividly described by Vööbus, op. cit. [p. 102, n. 1], vol. I, pp. 117–31.

[4] This is a constant feature of such movements: see A. Abel, 'Aspects sociologiques des religions manichéennes', *Mélanges René Crozet*, I, 1966, pp. 33–46. It explains, in part, the success of Manichaeism along with Buddhism, among the nomads of Central Asia. Both were religions of groups of 'perfect', settled in the midst of laymen of totally different habits: see J. Maenchen-Helfen, 'Manichaeans in Siberia', *University of California Publications in Semitic Philology* XI, 1951, pp. 311–26, at p. 318–19 ... 'there is an aura of solemnity around them (the frescoes of Manichaean Elect), something ceremonial, a dignity which sets them worlds apart from the quick and fierce Qyrghyz noblemen'.

[5] Brown, op. cit. [p. 108, n. 3], p. 54.

[6] Athanasius, *Historia Arianorum*, 73.

[7] Ammianus Marcellinus, *Res Gestae* XXX, 10, 3.

[8] Augustne, *Confessiones* v, xiii, 23; see Brown, op. cit. [p. 108, n. 3], p. 70.

Sun.[1] In fact, they were an ugly reminder of what the pagans might become. It was a case of hang together or hang separately, such as would frequently cause the most unlikely religious minorities to strike up alliances throughout the Late Roman period.

Now these patrons and Fellow-Travellers were the most exposed to social pressures. For the heresy-laws of the Later Empire succeeded in one point only: they did damp the zeal of the upper-classes for religious non-conformity.[2] By the end of the fourth century, therefore, Manichaeism was already shorn of an intelligentsia that had come in equal numbers from pagan and Christian families.[3] African Manichaeism, for instance, was left with a rump of hard-core *Electi*, and with Hearers drawn exclusively from the fringes of the average Christian communities. The effect of persecution in the Christian Roman Empire, therefore, was to increase the 'Christianization' of Manichaeism, by encouraging occasional conformity and by cutting off its access to a large pool of post-pagan intellectuals.

Secondly, Manichaeism became a problem increasingly as a form of crypto-Christianity. Mani had trumped Christ: the Manichaean missionary had to prove it by dogging the Christian community; and his converts would tend to remain prudently hidden under the shadow of the Catholic Church. This accounts for the exceptional rôle of the Catholic bishop in the suppression of Manichaeism. The only studies of the rôle of the bishop in the trial of heretics in the Later Empire—because the only evidence—concern the trials of Manichees.[4] For, whatever the severity of the Imperial laws, only

[1] Libanius, *Ep.* 1253. For the violence with which Christian communities treated such small groups, see Julian, *Ep.* 41 (ed. Loeb. iii, p. 128).

[2] See P. Brown, 'Religious coercion in the Later Roman Empire', *History* XLVIII, 1963, at pp. 289–92. [v. inf., pp. 309 sq.]

[3] On such circles, see de Stoop, op. cit. [p. 96, n. 1], p. 6. The côteries of alchemists and philosophers, with their womenfolk, who were treated as 'sisters' and 'fellow-philosophers', were favourable to such ideas: e.g. Agapios, writing to his συμφιλόσοφς Urania, *apud* Photius, Βιβλιοθήκη, ed. P. Henry II, 1960, pp. 184–87. I feel, however, that such people were not representative: the eclecticism, even the confusion, of Gnostic literary remains at Nag Hammadi contrasts vividly with the organized dogmatism of the Manichaean scriptures. Manichaeism was a religion organized for survival in a harsher age than that which saw the spread of a *salonfähig* Gnosticism.

[4] See esp. E. Volterra, 'Appunti intorno all'intervento del vescovo nei processi contro gli eretici', *Bulletino dell'Istituto di diritto romano* XLII, 1934, pp. 453–68, and W. Ensslin, 'Valentinians II Novellen xvi u. xviii von 445', *Zeitschr. der Savigny-Stiftung für Rechtsgeschichte*, Rom. Abt. 57, 1937, pp. 367–78.

the bishop on the spot could find out to whom they applied. Thus the severe laws of Theodosius[1] were rendered practicable in Egypt by the zeal of the patriarch Theophilus. Theophilus imposed a food-test on his monks.[2] Hence the inquisitorial atmosphere accompanying the suppression of Manichaeism and that other form of Gnostic crypto-Christianity, Priscillianism: we hear of *agents provocateurs* (one zealous priest suggested adultery as a fine way of obtaining the names of heretics[3]). The discovery of Manichees would be accompanied by lurid public 'confession', before the bishop, throned in the apse of his basilica, like a Justice of the Peace.[4]

The suppression of religious dissent was rarely a victory for the Imperial administration: the *tertius gaudens* was always the bishop. The Manichees were the first to perceive this: they supported the Arian nominee of Constantius II against Athanasius; for they had far less to fear from the strict, but distant Emperor, than from a man of the calibre of Athanasius, established on their doorstep as the undisputed leader of the Christian community.[5]

The Christian Church appears as a labour-saving institution for the Roman state. For the problem of identifying the Manichee and of absorbing the convert devolved on the Christian clergy: the good faith of the converted Hearer would be guaranteed by his Catholic neighbours;[6] the converted Elect would spend a period under observation in a monastery; the Bishop would distribute certificates to both, protecting them against further trouble from the laws.[7]

Now it is interesting that this evidence is almost exclusively Western, and from the fifth and sixth centuries. We are reminded of the very different evolution of Church and State in the two parts of the Roman world. In Constantinople and the Eastern Empire, in 529, the problem of the converted Manichee was still being handled exclusively by the traditional police-mechanisms of the lay world: the bishop is peripheral.[8] In the West, the duty of identifying and

---

[1] *Cod. Theod.* XVI, 5, 9 (382).

[2] Eutychius, *Annales* (*Patrologia Graeca* CXI, coll. 1023-25).

[3] Augustine, *Contra Mendacium*, vii, 17.

[4] e.g. Leo, *Sermo* 16, 4 (*PL* LIV, 178B); Augustine, *de haeresibus* 46, 2 (*PL* XLII, 36), in Adam, op. cit. [p. 95, n. 1], no. 49, p. 67.

[5] Athanasius, *Historia Arianorum* 73.

[6] See the document in *Patrologia Latina* LXV, 25 B—C.

[7] See Brown, art. cit. [p. 110, n. 2], pp. 301-5.

[8] *Cod. Just.* I, V, 11 and 12.

absorbing heretics had long devolved on the clergy. It is a reminder that the more thoroughly 'Christianized' early Byzantine Empire will never be 'clericized' as rapidly as the less Christian but under-governed West.

Thirdly, Manichaeism was a missionary-religion. The Elect were obliged to travel; they would bring the seven great books of Mani with them; these scriptures, laid out on a high throne in front of the Hearers, were a reminder of the presence of Mani in his church, and a token that the 'cry of salvation', given forth in Babylon, had reached one's own town.[1] It is essential to remember this. Manichaeism did not grow out of any established group in a Late Roman town: it was not a schism or a peaceable deviation as the Gnostics had been. It had to come from the outside, through outsiders. What is more, in the fourth century the Manichees liked to come with *éclat*: the public dispute is a distinctive weapon of Manichaean propaganda;[2] and the arrival in the forum, or in front of the Christian church, of a group of pale men and women, clasping mysterious volumes and dressed with ostentatious barbarity, was a sight to be seen.[3]

Now the history of intolerance in the Later Roman Empire should never be treated in the abstract. More often than not, it is an aspect of the history of the Late Roman town. In the case of Manichaeism, it raised the problem of what to do with outsiders. The edicts are of misleading vehemence. The Manichaean 'Elect' was seldom 'deprived of the very elements' by execution; he was rarely 'exiled from Roman soil'; he was usually told, in no uncertain

[1] See esp. J. Ries, 'La Gnose manichéenne dans les textes liturgiques manichéens coptes', *Le Origini dello Gnosticismo. Colloquio di Messina*, 1967, pp. 614–24.

[2] Public debates: Addas in Alexandria: F. C. Andreas—W. Henning, M. 2 in *Sitzungsberichte der preuss. Akademie der Wissenschaften*, 1933, 7, p. 301. Challenge by Aphthonius to Aetius of Antioch: Philostorgius *Hist. Eccl.* III, 15 ed. Bidez, p. 461. Arrival from Antioch to Gaza; Marc le Diacre, *Vie de Porphyre*, c. 85, p. 66. Histrionic gestures: Augustine, *C. Felicem* i, 12—where Felix appears in the forum and offers to be burnt with his books if proved wrong. See Rufinus, *Historia Monachorum* 9 (*Patrologia Latina* XXI, coll. 426–7), for a gesture that misfired. [F. Decret, *Aspects du manichéisme dans l'Afrique romaine*, 1970, analyses the debate between Augustine and Manichaean leaders.]

[3] See esp. Marc le diacre, *Vie de Porphyre*, c. 85, p. 66. The Georgian version of this incident still further emphasizes the wild dress of the Elect: P. Peeters, *Analecta Bollandiana* LXI, 1941, p. 198.

terms, to 'get out of town'.[1] When Augustine unexpectedly left Carthage for Rome it was obvious to his enemies that, as a Manichee, he had been 'struck by sentence of exile' by the Proconsul.[2] The Manichaean Elect risked a fate suffered by many a religious mischief-maker, from St. Paul to St. Martin of Tours—a flogging and the open road.[3]

This fate, of course, is not without its compensations for a zealous missionary. Manichaeism was constantly scattering from the great cities, where officials and bishop were on the alert, to sleepy provincial towns and to the safety of remote villages[4]—Augustine retired from Carthage to Thagaste;[5] Pascentius, from Rome to Asturia.[6] The problem, therefore, is not why the Imperial legislation failed to stamp out Manichaeism—for it acted like a man scattering sparks as he beats out a fire—but why, despite the dispersing effect of this legislation, the Manichaean missionary endeavour had ceased, by the sixth century, to have the disturbing mobility of a plague.

The question is worth our while to ask. For, in the fifth century, the Western provinces of the Roman Empire lay wide open to Manichaean propaganda. Pope Leo was genuinely alarmed: the barbarian invasions had dislocated the security-system of the Catholic episcopate and had paralysed the Imperial authorities.[7] The spiritual atmosphere was chilly: it contained much the same raw admixture of asceticism and an obsession with the Devil as ruler of this world that would 'escalate' into neo-Manichaeism in

---

[1] See *Cod. Theod.* xv, 5, 18 (389): 'ex omni quidem orbe terrarum sed quam maxime ex hac urbe pellantur', The *Acta Archelai*, c. 65, reflects fourth-century conditions faithfully: 'valde enim hi qui missi fuerant ab eo per singulas civitates ab omnibus hominibus exsecrationi habebantur, maxime apud quos christianorum nomen veneratione erat'. Compare Rufinus, *Hist. Mon.* 9.

[2] Augustine, *C. litt. Petiliani* III, xxv, 30.

[3] Sulpicius Severus, *Vita Martini* VI, iv, 5.

[4] Gregory, *Reg.* v, 8, refers to Manichaean tenants on the estates of the Church in Sicily. For a similar 'de-urbanization' of heretics in medieval Italy, see the excellent study of C. Violante, 'Hérésies urbaines et hérésies rurales en Italie du xıème au xıııème siècles', *Hérésies et Sociétés dans l'Europe préindustrielle*, ed. J. Legoff, 1968, pp. 171–97, esp. pp. 179–88.

[5] See Brown, op. cit. [p. 108, n. 3], p. 54. In Carthage, by contrast, the Manichees lived under constant fear of denunciation: Augustine, *de moribus Man.* (II), xix. 92.

[6] Hydatius, *Chron.* no. 24 (*Patrol. Lat.* LI, 882).

[7] Leo, *Sermo* 16, 5 and *Ep.* 15 (*Patrol. Lat.* LIV, 680A).

Bulgaria, in Italy and in Southern France in the eleventh century.[1] The para-Manichaeism of the Priscillianists had already swept North-Western Spain.

I would suggest four reasons for the loss of momentum of the Manichaean movement.

First: by the fifth century, the Western town had become a very small place and had collapsed inwards around its bishop. We can see this most clearly with Augustine in Hippo. By 405, the Donatist bishop has gone; the local notables have rallied to Catholicism; he can meet the Manichaean missionary from the height of his own *cathedra* in his own basilica, while only ten years previously, he had met him on equal terms, on the neutral ground of a public bath-house, in front of an audience of mixed beliefs.[2] Later, when Arian propaganda reached Hippo, Augustine appealed to the *civitas* against the *peregrini*.[3] His activity is matched, at the far end of the Roman world, by bishops such as Rabbula of Edessa.[4] Later, one need only read Gregory of Tours to realize that religious eccentricity would receive short shrift in Gallic towns dominated by their bishop.[5]

Second: Manichaeism was out of date. It is often assumed that Manichaeism was one of the causes of the monastic movement. This is not so. The Manichees made great use of a common Christian literature of apocryphal gospels. These had always placed a heavy weight on chastity: and a young man who had gained access to these skilfully-inverted *erotica* through the Manichees did, indeed, end up in Augustine's monastery.[6] But Manichaeism had arisen some generations before monasteries. It represents a more primitive strand of asceticism: it continued the radical isolation from the world, the obligatory vagrancy of its Syriac homeland.[7] By

[1] See, most recently, C. N. L. Brooke, 'Heresy and religious sentiment: 1000–1250', *Bulletin of the Institute of Historical Research* XLI, 1968, pp. 115–31, and, now, R. I. Moore, 'The Origins of Medieval Heresy', *History* LV, 1970, pp. 21–36.

[2] See Brown, art. cit. [p. 110, n. 2], pp. 304–5; esp. *C. Felicem* i, 18.

[3] Augustine, *Tractatus in Johannem* XL, 7.

[4] See R. Duval, *Histoire politique, littéraire et religieuse d'Edesse*, 1892, pp. 169–71.

[5] Gregory of Tours, *Historica Francorum* IX, 6.

[6] Augustine, *Ep.* 64, 3.

[7] Vividly characterized by Vööbus, op. cit. [p. 102, n. 1], I, pp. 85 f. and II, pp. 22–35 and esp. pp. 187–92, on the well-merited tribulations of the vagrant Alexander the Sleepless. How little the Western authorities tolerated a religious

the 380's, the Western Manichees were already behind the times. A Manichaean Hearer in Rome, Constantius, tried to found a monastery for the Elect: he was embarrassed by their vagrant life.[1] Constantius was in touch with the atmosphere of late fourth-century Rome. In the 370's, the Manichaean Elect had already suffered from the Emperor Valentinian's 'new broom' in the city:[2] their conventicles had come to the notice of a government capable of introducing licensing-laws and concerned with all forms of vagrancy. The Christian community at Rome was also putting its house in order. Ascetic eccentricity was clamped into monasteries; and a powerful clergy would pray pointedly that God should protect their flock from ill-kempt ascetic *confessores*.[3]

Thirdly: Manichaeism lost its most characteristic lay supporter—the merchant. The merchant figured largely in Christian romances on Manichaeism.[4] The Soghdian merchants, known to the Chinese as men who 'travel all over the world in search of gain',[5] were the mainstay of Manichaeism in Central Asia and Northern China, in the seventh and eighth centuries.[6] Augustine converted one such Manichee—the rich merchant Firmus.[7] I suspect that, as a Catholic priest, Firmus continued to satiate his zeal and his wanderlust by travelling from Bethlehem, to Sicily, to Africa, to Rome, to Ravenna, as *factotum* of the senatorial ladies around S. Jerome and as literary agent of S. Augustine.[8] The merchant's life was still a good life in the fourth century: 'Navigare . . . et negotiari magnum est, scire multas provincias, lucra undique capere, non esse obnoxium in civitate alicui potenti, semper peregrinari, et diversitate negotiorum

---

vagrancy that was normal in the East, is shown in the total outlawry of the Circumcellions, whose oriental parallels have been shrewdly exposed by Salvatore Calderone, 'Circumcelliones', *La Parola del Passato* CXIII, 1967, pp. 94-109.

[1] Augustine, *de moribus Man.* (II), xx, 74.

[2] *Cod. Theod.* XVI, 5, 3 (372).

[3] L. Duchesne, *Christian Worship: its origin and evolution*, transl. McClure, 1919, p. 142.

[4] Scythianus: in Hegemonius, *Acta Archelai* 61-65.

[5] The New T'ang History, cited in E. G. Pulleybank, 'A Soghdian Colony in Outer Mongolia', *T'oung Pao* XLI, 1953, pp. 317-56 at p. 317.

[6] See Maenchen-Helfen, art. cit. [p. 109, n. 4], p. 324: 'Merchant and Manichaean must for some time have been practically synonymous'; and A. Adam, *Handbuch der Orientalistik*, I Abt., viii, 2, pp. 118-19.

[7] Possidius, *Vita* xv, 5.

[8] Augustine, Ep. 172, 2 and H. I. Marrou, 'La technique de l'édition à l'époque patristique', *Vigiliae Christianae* III, 1949, p. 218, n. 36.

et nationum animum pascere'.[1] And travelling broadens the mind. In sixth-century Alexandria the eccentric merchant survives: Cosmas Indicopleustes had contacts with Axum and the India trade. This had led him into a world dominated by Persia and by the Nestorian Christianity of the Persian dominions. This layman had the courage of his eccentricity, if not the scientific judgement, to attack the academic Establishment of his city—the proud professor, John Philoponos, ensconced as the protégé of the Patriarch of Alexandria and the self-appointed hammer of the Platonic Academy of Athens.[2] But in the West, trade receded and the merchant settled down as a local landowner, tied to the opinions of his locality. The Syrians of sixth-century Gaul are a harmless source of orthodox relics and pious legends. They are so 'integrated' into the Catholic community that one enterprising firm could invest money by buying up a Catholic bishopric.[3] Manichaeism would not revive until the eleventh and twelfth centuries; until the missionary activity fostered by the itinerant weavers of the new cloth-towns of Northern France and the 'tourist boom' of the Crusades marked the end of the rigid and parochial structure of early medieval Western society.[4]

Fourth: There was no reason why Manichaeism in the Eastern Empire should have been hamstrung in this way. Yet, after the savage purges of 527 and 530, there appears to be a complete standstill in Manichaean propaganda;[5] and there is no revival of Manichaeism during the fourteen years when the eastern provinces of the Roman Empire were part of the Persian dominions of Khusro II Aparvez.

I suspect a turning-point within Persian-controlled Mesopotamia itself. Up to the beginning of the sixth century, this region still 'bubbled' with radical Gnostic movements. These occasionally 'boiled-over', as the Catholic authorities put it, into the Roman

---

[1] Augustine, *Enarratio in Ps.* 136, 3.

[2] See esp. Wolska, op. cit. [p. 103, n. 4], pp. 3–11.

[3] On the identification of the merchant with the landowning classes, see L. Ruggini, 'Ebrei ed orientali nell'Italia settentrionale', *Studia et Documenta Historiae et Juris* XXV, 1959, pp. 186–308.

[4] See esp. C. Thouzellier, 'Hérésies et croisades au XIIème s.', *Revue d'Histoire Ecclésiastique* XLIX, 1954, esp. at pp. 864–5.

[5] I am unconvinced by most of the arguments propounded by J. Jarry, 'Les Hérésies dualistes dans l'empire byzantin du VIème au VIIème siècle', *Bulletin de l'Institut français d'archéologie orientale* LXIII, 1965, pp. 89–120.

Empire, as Manichaeism had done.[1] This is not surprising. In the late fifth century, Persia was the Sick Man of the Near East; the Iranian hold on Mesopotamia was seriously weakened.[2] But the savage suppression of the Mazdakite movement in 528 (a movement identified with Manichaeism in many sources[3]) is the beginning of the re-establishment of the traditional Persian monarchy, and an omen of the end of sectarian Mesopotamia. From 528 onwards, the Nestorian Church is increasingly assimilated to Persian society and, so, impervious to Manichaeism. Manichaeism itself became an exclusively Soghdian affair. The Manichaean Pilgrim Fathers of Samarkand looked down, from a safe distance, on their cowed brethren in Mesopotamia—'the damned Syrians'.[4] The heart of Manichaeism was burnt out.[5] No matter how impressive its diffusion might appear in Central Asia and China, Manichaeism was tied to the increasingly out-of-date landroutes through Central Asia to the Yangtse.[6] There is no evidence of Manichaeism along the new booming sea route, that linked Mesopotamia directly with Canton. We may be sure that there were no Manichaean stowaways in the ships of Sinbad the sailor.

This is the end of a great missionary religion. The Later Roman Empire has usually been presented as a society of growing anarchy and dislocation. A Manichee would have liked it better that way. I think the exact opposite is closer to the truth. Whatever the fate of the central government, the fifth and sixth centuries are marked by increasing tidiness and rigidity on the local level. The Christian

---

[1] For instance, the account of the Borboriani in Bar-Hebraeus, *Chronicon Ecclesiasticum* I, ed. Abbeloos, Louvain 1872, pp. 220–2.

[2] See esp. Pigulevskaja, op. cit. [p. 100, n. 4], pp. 218–21.

[3] See esp. Malalas, *Chronographia* (Bonn), pp. 309–20 and Theophanes, *Chron. Anno Mundi* 6016, ed. *De Boor* I, pp. 169–71. [J. Neusner, *A History of the Jews in Babylonia*, v, *The Late Sassanian Period*, 1970, confirms this impression.]

[4] Henning, art. cit. [p. 100, n. 9], p. 16.

[5] There may be one exception: Manichaean propaganda in Armenia may lie at the origin of the Paulician heresy, see D. Obolensky, *The Bogomils*, 1948, pp. 17–18. But even if it did spread into Armenia in the sixth century, Manichaeism lost its identity in the Paulician movement, where it is 'Christianised' beyond recognition. For an alternative explanation of the origin of Paulicianism, that minimises direct Manichaean influence, see N. G. Garsoian, *The Paulician Heresy. A Study of the Origin and Development of Paulicianism in Armenia and the Eastern Provinces of the Byzantine Empire*, 1964.

[6] O. Franke, *Geschichte des chinesischen Reichs* II, 1936, esp. p. 552, l. 27.

communities are better organized. The 'flock of the Lord' fills the Western towns right up to the narrow circle of their walls. The ascetic fringe knows its place, in the monasteries. The horizon of the average man is narrower, more firmly orientated. In such a world, the Manichees would have been an unwelcome reminder of the wider horizons of a past age. For us, the extraordinary activity of the Manichaean missionaries, who linked one end of the Fertile Crescent to the other within a generation, and who would spread the only *premeditated* universal religion in the history of thought from Babylon to Northern Spain, is a reminder of the blessings of political uncertainty and intellectual ferment that we are, perhaps, ill-advised to deprecate in the 'crisis' of the third century A.D.

SORCERY, DEMONS AND THE RISE OF CHRISTIANITY: FROM LATE ANTIQUITY INTO THE MIDDLE AGES*

My concern, in this paper, is to re-examine a small facet of the religious history of the Late Antique period, and to show how the historian may be helped by an extensive literature by social anthropologists on the problems of sorcery and spirit-possession.

The need to link disciplines is frequently expressed among us. Discussion of this need takes place in an atmosphere, however, that suggests the observation of an African chieftain on a neighbouring tribe: 'They are our enemies. We marry them.' Matchmaking should be a cautious process. The would-be linker of disciplines must be prepared 'to sigh throughout the long delays of courtship': in attempts to link social and religious history, classical and theological studies, I have observed that the unwary, or the precipitate, suitor has often ended up with the elderly, ugly daughter. I can only say that I have tried to keep abreast of a recent literature in social anthropology which, beginning with Professor Evans-Pritchard's *Witchcraft, Oracles and Magic among the Azande* of 1937, represents one of the most remarkable attempts to study, with precision and sophistication, an aspect of the role of the irrational in society.

To look again, with an insight schooled on other human disciplines, at the religious history of the Late Antique world is one of the most urgent tasks facing the ancient and the medieval historian. We have long possessed an overwhelming erudition on the religious ideas of the period from A.D. 200 to 600. We have begun to refine our views on the structure and functioning of Late Roman society. Yet, somehow, the nexus between the religious and the social evolution of Late Antiquity escapes us: worse still, it is a gap papered over, in most accounts, by textbook rhetoric.

---

* *Witchcraft Confessions and Accusations* (Association of Social Anthropologists Monographs, no. 9), 1970, pp. 17–45.

I

My first debt to the social anthropologists is that they have helped me to delimit the field of my inquiry. In his *Witchcraft, Oracles and Magic*, Evans-Pritchard has shown how fruitfully sorcery can be treated as 'a function of personal relations' and 'a function of situations of misfortune'.[1] Sorcery, therefore, need not be treated in isolation. It is not an unswept corner of odd beliefs, surrounding unsavoury practices: the anthropologists have shown that belief in sorcery is an element in the way in which men have frequently attempted to conceptualize their social relationships and to relate themselves to the problem of evil.

The historian of sorcery in Late Antiquity begins, however, where the anthropologist leaves off. The anthropologist meets beliefs and accusations surrounding the human figure of the sorcerer. He has a clear idea of how such a man fits in among his fellows. The most interesting advances in this aspect of his discipline have been connected with those insights into the structure of a society which may be elicited from the study of the witch and the sorcerer in it. The rites of the sorcerer are usually hidden from him.[2] By contrast, the historian makes his first acquaintance with this subject in the form of a vast collection of texts, principally magical papyri[3] and leaden cursing-tablets,[4] that minutely illustrate the 'technology' of sorcery in the ancient world. These highly circumstantial descriptions of a divine and demonic society would present any anthropologist interested in possible correlations between the structure of the spirit-world and social change with an *embarras de richesses*: perhaps he would be less disturbed than many students of ancient religion by the appearance of 'Jesus great god of the Hebrews' on a spell, hardened as he is by phenomena such as the

[1] Evans-Pritchard (1937, esp. pp. 63–117).
[2] Middleton & Winter (1963, pp. 3–4).
[3] See, for example. Eitrem (1925); Preisendanz *et al.* (1928 and 1931). The evidence is so widely dispersed that the beginner should utilize monographs which have mobilized the baffling range of references, most notably Abt (1908). For a discussion of demonology and magic between two learned men of the second and third centuries, skilfully translated and commented, see Chadwick (1953). Radermacher (1927) is essential for the Christian image of the sorcerer.
[4] See esp. Audollent (1904); Wünsch (1912). [See further, P. Roesch, 'Une tablette de malédiction de Tébessa', *Bulletin d'Archéologie Algerienne*, 2, 1966–67, 231–238 and D. Wortmann, 'Neue Magische Texte', *Bonner Jahrbücher* 168, 1968, 57–111.]

spirit which 'appeared in the curious guise of a small motor-car'.[1]
But in such manuals of the suprahuman world, the human agent
is lost to view. One meets sorcery as a *belief*, not as an event in
society. As a result, the study of sorcery in Late Antiquity—as,
indeed, in early Medieval Islam and in the Medieval and Renaissance periods—has been engulfed in the study of religion and of
the occult sciences.[2] More particularly, the topic has been harnessed to the problem of the 'decadence' of the ancient world. The
occult sciences have been studied as marking the nadir of the down-
ward curve of Greek scientific rationalism;[3] the rigmaroles of Gnostic demons, as a nadir in the decline of traditional Graeco-Roman
religion;[4] and the widespread opinion of historians, that a 'terror of
magic' was endemic in the fourth century A.D. is held to illustrate a
nadir in the morale and culture of the Roman governing classes.[5] It
is assumed, therefore, that the 'decadence' of the Later Roman
Empire is illustrated by a sharp increase in sorcery beliefs. The
reasons usually given are of studious generality: the general misery
and insecurity of the period; the confusion and decay of traditional
religions; and more specifically for the fourth century A.D., the rise to
power in the Roman state of a class of 'semi-Christians', whose new
faith in Christ was overshadowed by a superstitious fear of demons.[6]

To comment on these explanations briefly: In the first case,
accusations against sorcerers occur in precisely those areas and
classes which we know to have been the most effectively sheltered
from brutal dislocation— the senatorial aristocracy, for instance,
and the professors of the great Mediterranean cities. It was in just
such stable and well-oriented groups that certain forms of misfortune (see below, p. 134) were explained by pinning blame on individuals. Public and continuous misfortune, by contrast, was
habitually explained in this age of bitter confessional hatreds, by
the anger of the gods or of God at the existence of dissenting
religious groups—Christians, pagans, or heretics.[7]

---

[1] Cited by Beattie in Middleton & Winter (1963, p. 54, n. 1).
[2] See, most notably, Festugière (1944) and Abel (1957, pp. 291 ff.).
[3] Festugière (1944, pp. 1–18).
[4] Audollent (1904, pp. lxi and cxvii); Nock (1929, pp. 219 ff.); Nilsson (1948).
[5] Maurice (1927, pp. 108 ff.); MacMullen (1967, pp. 124–7).
[6] Notably Barb (1963, esp. pp. 105–8).
[7] The Christians, see de Ste Croix (1963, p. 37, n. 136) and Courcelle (1964,
pp. 67–77); Jews, Samaritans, pagans, and heretics, see Theodosius II, *Novella*
III (438), c. 8.

As for the last, it is an inverted anachronism common among historians of the Later Roman period to project an undifferentiated force of 'superstition' into the safe remoteness of the fourth century, and to endow this force with far greater potency in directing men's behaviour than can be observed among the *hommes moyens sensuels* of any contemporary society that still believes in suprahuman sanctions and dangers. Suffice to say that we have detailed descriptions of those emperors who followed up sorcery—accusations, from the pen of a pagan, Ammianus Marcellinus. Now, Ammianus describes the Christian emperor Constantius II as showing 'an old wives' superstition' only when discussing the *minutiae* of the Christian Trinity,[1] but, faced by sorcery and illicit divination, he is judged for the way he acted strictly as a politician, and not as a religious man—he was 'suspicious and over-precise'.[2] Taken altogether, the purges that followed accusations of sorcery and illicit divination point, not to any increase in a 'terror of magic', but to a more precise, if more prosaic, development—to an increase in the zeal and efficacy of the emperor's servants, and their greater ability to override the vested interests of the traditional aristocracies of the Empire, whether to collect taxes or to chastise the black arts.

Thus it is far from certain that there was any absolute increase in fear of sorcery or in sorcery practices in the Late Roman period. Nor is it certain that the religious and intellectual changes of Late Antiquity greatly changed the basic attitudes of ancient men to sorcery: in the first century A.D. for instance, Pliny the Elder had already taken for granted that 'there is no one who is not afraid of becoming the object of lethal spells' (*Historia Naturalis*, XXVIII, 4, 9). All that can be said is that, in the fourth century A.D., we happen to know more about sorcery because we are told more about it, in accounts of the politics of the Imperial court and in the careers of professors. We meet sorcery, therefore, in its *social* context.

My paper must take this fact as its starting-point. I shall have to ask the historian of the religious ideas of Late Antiquity to suspend belief for a moment. Sorcery accusations in Late Roman sources, I would suggest, need not be used exclusively to illustrate the regrettable ramifications of superstition in a 'post-classical' world: they point to social phenomena. My thesis, in the first part of this paper, is that a precise *malaise* in the structure of the governing classes of

[1] Ammianus Marcellinus, *Res gestae*, XXI, xvi, 18.
[2] Amm. Marc. XIX, xii, 5.

the Roman Empire (especially in its eastern, Greek-speaking half) forced the ubiquitous sorcery beliefs of ancient man to a flash-point of accusations in the mid-fourth century A.D. The incidence of these accusations synchronizes with changes within the structure of the governing class: thus they reach a peak at a time of maximum uncertainty and conflict in the 'new' society of the mid-fourth century: they are substantially reduced as occasions for conflict and uncertainty are progressively restricted, by a growth of political and social stability, whose results are best documented for the sixth century A.D.—the age of Justinian and of the first 'barbarian' kingdoms in the West.

The *malaise* to which I refer cannot be seized through the conventional catalogue of catastrophes attending the fall of the Roman Empire in the West, still less by laments on the decline of Greek rationalism, but by an analysis of the points of uncertainty and conflict in the structure of the governing classes of the Empire. These strong and weak points can be grasped most easily by contrasting the views of two schools of modern social historians, describing the society of the fourth, fifth, and sixth centuries A.D.[1] One school saw in this period an increase in 'vested' power and social rigidity: an oriental despotism; an emperor raised above his subjects by theocratic doctrines of divine right; his authority rendered impersonal by an elaborate court ceremonial; his person surrounded by eunuchs; Late Roman society, as a whole, stagnant and hierarchical —divided into rigid castes with little hope of personal advancement, its culture directed towards producing a 'mandarinate' of noblemen, 'reared above the common lot of men', by an archaic literary language. The other, more recent, view has stressed the fact that many individuals in this society enjoyed a remarkable degree of social fluidity; that the emperor was open to constant symbiosis with and impingement from a diffuse governing class, ranging from traditional great landowners to Christian bishops; that the educational system of this society was an area exceptionally favourable to social mobility; and that its dominant religion, Christianity, had seeped triumphantly upwards, at just this time, from the lower middle classes into a court aristocracy of *parvenus*.

I would suggest that, far from the one view replacing the other, we should work with both. Late Roman society was dominated by

[1] For a survey and discussion of all recent work, see Brown (1967a, esp. pp. 337–339 [see sup. 62 sq.].

the problem of the conflict between change and stability in a traditional society.

It is here that we find a situation which has been observed both to foster sorcery accusations and to offer scope for resort to sorcery. This is when *two systems of power* are sensed to clash within the one society. On the one hand, there is *articulate* power, power defined and agreed upon by everyone (and especially by its holders!): authority vested in precise persons; admiration and success gained by recognized channels. Running counter to this there may be other forms of influence less easy to pin down—*inarticulate* power: the disturbing intangibles of social life; the imponderable advantages of certain groups; personal skills that succeed in a way that is unacceptable or difficult to understand. Where these two systems overlap, we may expect to find the sorcerer.

In some areas, where competition is not easily resolved by normal means, we find actual resort to sorcery. Far more important, however, in a situation where articulate and inarticulate power clash, we find greater fear of sorcery, and the reprobation and huntingdown of the sorcerer. In this situation, the accuser is usually the man with the Single Image. For him, there is one, single, recognized way of making one's way in the world. In rejecting sorcery, such a man has rejected any *additional* source of power. He has left the hidden potentialities of the occult untouched. He is *castus*. The sorcerer, by contrast, is seen as the man invested with the Double Image. There is more to him than meets the eye. He has brought in the unseen to redress the balance of the seen. His achievements may be admired, but they are, essentially, illegitimate.

To fear and suppress the sorcerer is an extreme assertion of the Single Image. Many societies that have sorcery-beliefs do not go out of their way to iron out the sorcerer. The society, or the group within the society, that actually acts on its fears is usually the society that feels challenged, through conflict, to uphold an image of itself in which everything that happens, happens through *articulate* channels only—where power springs from vested authority, where admiration is gained by conforming to recognized norms of behaviour, where the gods are worshipped in public, and where wisdom is the exclusive preserve of the traditional educational machine.

The best-documented aspect of this problem is the conflict in the governing class of the Later Roman Empire between fixed vested roles, on the one hand, and the holders of ambiguous positions of personal power, on the other. This personal power was based largely on skills, such as rhetoric, which, in turn, associated the man of skill with the ill-defined, inherited prestige of the traditional aristocracies. Thus we find men whose positions in society were plainly delimited as servants of the emperor lodging accusations against men whose positions and whose successes were less easy to define, based as they were on the imponderable, almost numinous prestige of classical culture and aristocratic values in Late Roman society. This conflict passed through its most acute phase in the fourth century; and it is precisely in the areas marked out by it that we find the overwhelming majority of cases of sorcery.[1]

To take the governing class in its narrow sense and to view it from the hub outwards—that is, to analyse purges based largely on accusations of sorcery in the reigns of Constantius II, Valentinian I and Valens.[2] The scene is usually the inner ring of the court: it is played out among officials, ex-officials, local notables. All of these men would have had personal contact with the emperor as a man, and not only as a remote figure of authority.

To rationalize such accusations as 'smears' is only half the truth.[3] They certainly were not pretexts for suppressing political conspiracies. Ammianus is firm on this point: the emperor knew only too well what an assassination plot was, and suppressed it as such.[4] Rather, these accusations indicate very faithfully a situation where organized political opposition was increasingly unthinkable: the days of a 'senatorial opposition', able to make itself felt by assassination, were gone forever; the civilian governing class was overtly homogeneous, and stridently loyalist.[5] Thus, resentments and anomalous power on the edge of the court could be isolated only by the more intimate allegation—sorcery. Indeed, seen from the point of view of the emperor's image of himself, some sorcery was even a necessity: for to survive sorcery was to prove, in a manner

---

[1] For this perspective, I am particularly indebted to the fertile suggestions of Douglas (1966, esp. pp. 101–12).

[2] Amm. Marc. XVI, viii, 1 ff.; XIX, xii, 3 ff.; XXVIII, i, 1 ff.; XXIX, i, 5 ff. [Now see H. Funke, 'Majestäts- und Magieprozesse bei Ammianus Marcellinus', *Jahrbuch für Antike und Christentum*, 10, 1967, 145–175.]

[3] Amm. Marc. XXIX, i, 41; XXIX, ii. 3; Boethius, *De consolatione philosophiae*, I, iv, 37. (The statements of the victims or of supporters of the victims.)

[4] Amm. Marc. XXI, xvi, 10.

[5] Jones (1964, esp. pp. 321–65). See Rubin (1960, pp. 168–224) for the sixth century.

intelligible to all Late Roman men, that the vested power of the emperor, his *fatum*, was above powers of evil directed by mere human agents.[1] A sorcerer's attack, indeed, is an obligatory preliminary, in biographies of the time, to demonstrating the divine power that protected the hero, whether this be the divine *daemon* of the pagan philosopher, Plotinus, or the guardian archangel of St. Ambrose.[2] When we see them in this light, we can appreciate how the sorcery accusations of the fourth century mark a stage of conflict on the way to a greater definition of the secular governing class of the Eastern Empire as an aristocracy of service, formed under an emperor by divine right. In this way, as in so many others, Constantius II stands 'à la tête de la lignée des souverains de Byzance'.[3]

For these accusations are rarely made by the *parvenus* of the court among themselves: they are usually made by such groups against the holders of ill-defined, traditional status—to 'shake the pillars of the patrician class'.[4] In the fourth century, the boundary between the court and the traditional aristocracy coincided, generally, with a boundary between Christianity and paganism. It is often assumed that to accuse a pagan aristocrat of sorcery was a covert form of religious persecution. (To the Christian, who took for granted that a pagan *worshipped* demons, it was convenient to assume that he would also *manipulate* them, in sorcery;[5] and so the burning of books of magic, a traditional police action, is continued, in the Christian period, as a cover for the destruction of much of the religious literature of paganism.[6]) However, the boundary between

[1] Amm. Marc. XIX, xii, 16.

[2] Porphyry, Life of Plotinus, 10 (transl. MacKenna, *Plotinus, The Enneads*, 2nd edn. 1956, 8); Paulinus, *Vita Ambrosii*, 20.

[3] Piganiol (1947, pp. 107–9) is excellent on Constantius II.

[4] Amm. Marc. XXIX, ii, 9.

[5] Martroye (1930, pp. 669 ff.), an admirable study of the traditional anti-magic laws in the Christian period, underestimates the use to which these laws were put to victimize paganism in general. For a 'working misunderstanding' of the law, in the reverse direction, see John Beattie in Middleton & Winter (1963, p. 49): colonial laws directed against pagan 'impostures' used against sorcery, taken as 'real'.

[6] Valens: Amm. Marc. XXIX, i, 41 (burning of magic books); cf. XXIX, ii, 4 (libraries burnt to protect their owners from accusations). The destruction of magic books to justify the raiding of pagan houses: Marc le Diacre, *Vie de Porphyre*, c. 71, ed. Grégoire Kugener, 1930, p. 57 (Gaza); Barns (1964, pp. 153–154 and 157) (for Upper Egypt). A vivid description of a burning of magic books in sixth-century Beirut: Zachary the Scholastic, *Vie de Sévère,Patrologia orientalis*, II, pp. 69 ff.

court and aristocracy long survives the disappearance of the boundary between Christianity and paganism; in the sixth century, the falls of two great patricians, good Christians both—Boethius in Italy and Mummolus of Bordeaux in Gaul—are accompanied by charges of sorcery.[1]

We can appreciate the urgency of the problem if we look at it from the rim of the wheel, as it were, in the works of Libanius of Antioch.[2] Here we have a man identified with the traditional aristocracy, whose status was an *'achieved'* status, based on his skill in rhetoric. In general, professors of rhetoric and philosophy, and poets (and, on a local level, in their own communities, the Jewish *rabbis*)[3] were the supreme examples of men whose status was not fixed.[4] They could become the *éminences grises* of the court; as the spokesmen of their cities, they could exert indefinable pressures on the central government: they were indispensable to the emperor as propagandists.[5] Their position among their colleagues was dependent on the fluctuation of their talents, in cities that had great zeal for such 'stars' but very little money left to give them a proper position. Any study of the *rhetors*, at any period of Late Roman history, takes us into situations of intense and insoluble rivalry,[6] between men who had not absorbed Homer for nothing, for whom 'shame' was worse than death. Not surprisingly, therefore, the life of Libanius was punctuated by accusations of sorcery: accusations by him and against him.[7] Rivalry, however, was not all. More precisely, the accusations against Libanius are, all of them, accusations that explain his ill-defined *power*: a rival 'went around with the fairy-tale that he had been worsted by magic. I was intimate, so he said, with an astrologer who controlled the stars and through

---

[1] Boethius, *De consolatione philosophiae*, I, iv, 37. See, most recently, Wes (1967, p. 181) and Gregory of Tours, *Historia Francorum*, VI, 35. On the Merovingian governing class, see Sprandel (1961, pp. 33 ff.).

[2] Excellently translated and commented by Norman (1965). See Petit (1955).

[3] Neusner (1966, p. 147). [See now J. Neusner, *A History of the Jews in Babylonia*, vol. IV, 1969, 279–402.]

[4] See esp. Hopkins (1961, pp. 239 ff.).

[5] Cameron (1965, pp. 470 ff.).

[6] See Marwick (1952, p. 127) on such situations as bringing about accusations of sorcery.

[7] Norman, *Libanius' Autobiography*, §§. 43 ff. (pp. 30–31); §. 50 pp. 34–5); §. 62 (pp. 38–40); §. 71 (pp. 44–5); §. 98 (pp. 60–61); §. 162 (pp. 92–3); §§. 247–249 (pp. 128–9), and *oratio* xxxvi, *de veneficiis*, on which see Campbell-Bonner (1932, pp. 34 ff.).

them could bring help or harm to men—just like a tyrant with his bodyguard',[1] and, later still, he had to face 'allegations that I had cut off the heads of a couple of girls and kept them for use in magic, one against the Caesar Gallus, the other against his senior colleague (Contantius II)'.[2] Throughout these accusations, therefore, we have something more than the occult measures which men in a competitive situation undeniably did take to increase their success and crush their rivals:[3] there is an attempt to explain a theme that still puzzles the historian of the Later Empire, the *je ne sais quoi* of the predominance of an ill-defined aristocracy of culture and inherited prestige, constantly pressing in upon an autocracy whose servants derived their status from membership of a meticulously graded bureaucracy.[4]

Sorcery beliefs in the Later Empire, therefore, may be used like radio-active traces in an X-ray: where these assemble, we have a hint of pockets of uncertainty and competition in a society increasingly committed to a vested hierarchy in church and state.

Take the charioteer. He owed his position to a personal skill which was both increased[5] and frequently attacked[6] by magic. Furthermore, a chariot race in a Late Roman town owed its importance to the fact that, in these firmly governed communities, increasingly dominated by a single religious leader, the orthodox bishop, the rivalry of racing factions marked a welcome *détente* in unity, an opportunity for bitter confrontations among the local aristocracies and their supporters.[7] As long as the successes of the charioteers were bound up in the public imagination with the 'Fortune' of the city, this usually remote and stable figure (who would be easily assimilated to the unmoved majesty of a Christian archangel) was thrown on to the 'open market' by the talents of a star.[8] The

---

[1] Norman, *Libanius' Autobiography*, §. 41 (pp. 30–31).

[2] Norman, *Libanius' Autobiography*, §. 98 (pp. 60–61).

[3] See the material collected in Abt (1908, pp. 92 ff.) and Eitrem (1925, pp. 6, 35 ff.; 25, 35; 42–3). Given this literature, it cannot be said of Late Roman sorcery, as had been said of African, that such acts, 'although widely believed to be common, may in fact rarely, perhaps never, be performed' (Middleton & Winter, 1963, p. 4).

[4] See Brown (1967a, p. 339). [p. 66]

[5] Cassiodorus, *Variae*, III, 1.

[6] See Audollent (1904, cxxviii, and *Index*, V. *Defixionum genera et causae*, D, p. 473).

[7] Explicit in Jerome, *Vita Hilarionis* (*Patrologia Latina*, 23, 20).

[8] Libanius, *Oratio*, xxxvi, 15, 15.

charioteer himself was an undefined mediator in urban society: he was both the client of local aristocracies[1] and the leader of organized groups of lower-class fans—and so, at times, a potential figure-head in urban rioting, that nightmare of Late Roman government.[2] Along with athletes and actors, he belonged to the *demi-monde*— a very important class in the imaginations (and, one would suspect, also in the daily life) of the studiously aristocratic society of the Later Empire.[3] Accusations of sorcery frequently take us from upper-class families into a world where charioteer and sorcerer are intimately associated.[4]

For it is in this *demi-monde*, in the wide sense, that we find the professional sorcerer. The cultivated man, it was believed, drew his power from absorbing a traditional culture. His soul, in becoming transcendent through traditional disciplines, was above the material world, and so was above sorcery.[5] He did not need the occult. We meet the sorcerer pressing upwards against this rigid barrier, as a man of uncontrolled occult 'skill'. One such, Albicerius of Carthage, would help the young Augustine to find a silver spoon, and could even 'thought-read' verses of Vergil in the mind of a proconsul; but both educated men agreed—Albicerius could never be 'good' be-cause he could never be 'wise': for he lacked the only proper training of a classical education.[6]

It is in this *demi-monde*, of course, that we meet the Christian Church. Previously, the Church had been the greatest challenge from below to traditional beliefs and organization: the powers of its founders, Jesus and Peter, and of its clergy, were regularly ascribed to sorcery.[7] Moreover, in the fourth and fifth centuries, the Church was a group which had harnessed the forces of social mobi-lity to itself more effectively even than the teaching profession: its hierarchy was notably a *carrière ouverte aux talents*: and it played a decisive role in the 'democratization' of culture.[8]

Such a group pullulated saints and sorcerers. (In popular belief, the line between the two was very thin: St. Ambrose, to name only

[1] See, most recently, Picard (1964, pp. 101 ff.); Pietri (1966, pp. 123 ff.).
[2] See Macmullen (1967, p. 171, and nn. 10–12 at pp. 339–41).
[3] See Amm. Marc. XXVIII, i, 1 ff., and Norman (1965, §. 150, pp. 90–91).
[4] *Codex Theodosianus*, IX, xvi, 11 (389).
[5] Chadwick (1953, p. 356, n. 1).
[6] Augustine, *Contra Academicos*, I, vii, 19–21.
[7] See Barb (1963, p. 164, n. 2) and *Origen*, VI, in Chadwick (1953, p. 340).
[8] See Brown (1968a, p. 92 [p. 293]).

one saint, was associated with twelve deaths—more deaths than stand to the credit of any Late Roman *maleficus*.) To take only one example: as a Christian bishop, Athanasius of Alexandria was able to manipulate Late Roman public opinion, in his career as an ecclesiastical politician, with far greater *éclat* than a *rhetor* such as Libanius. It was through the insistent opposition of Athanasius to his religious policies, for instance, that the autocracy of the Emperor Constantius II 'received (in Gibbon's words) an invisible wound which he could neither heal nor revenge'. Athanasius reaped his due recognition from contemporaries in a reputation for sorcery.[1] The clergy followed their leaders. Sorcery was rife among the Syrian clergy of the fifth century.[2] This is, of course, partly a tribute to their 'book learning' and so to their reputation as guardians of the occult.[3] But knowledge of sorcery was more precisely associated with a fluid group. Clients turned to the clergy for the same reason as they had turned to Albicerius: to men in touch with ill-defined 'skills', on the penumbra of a dominant educated aristocracy.

We shall come, later, to the sequel (see below, p. 141). We should note, however, in confirmation of this suggestion, that, as Late Roman society grew more stable and defined, in the course of the sixth century, so sorcery accusations seem to have waned. The marked increase in the political violence of the racing factions of Constantinople, for instance, is not, to the best of my present knowledge, accompanied by any notable increase in sorcery.[4] Among many reasons, this may be because the 'Fortune' of the city was

[1] See Amm. Marc. XV, vii, 7.

[2] See the evidence amassed by Peterson (1959, pp. 333 ff.).

[3] See Barb (1963, p. 124) on the transmission of spells in clerical circles, and Kayser (1888, pp. 456 ff.). [William of Malmesbury, *Gesta Regum* (Monumenta *Germaniae Historica*, Scriptores X), p. 461, knew enough of this tradition to explain away the reputation for magic enjoyed by Pope Sylvester as due to his learning, citing Boethius as a parallel.]

[4] Apart from the reiteration of the law of 389 (cit. above, n. 44) in *Codex Justinianus* IX, xviii, 9, the reference to the magician Masades, patronized by sporting fans and local notables, is the only example known to me from the reign of Justinian: see John of Nikiou, *Chronique* § 96, ed. Zotenberg, 509. [Sorcery was still practised in the sixth century—in the Hippodrome: J. Deubner, *Kosmas und Damian*, 1901, no. 11, p. 123; and among courtiers—see P. Brown, 'The Rise and Function of the Holy Man in Late Roman society'. *Journal of Roman Studies* 61, 1971, footnote 119: but it was not made the subject of serious purges. Men in the same position as Libanius still enjoyed the same reputation for sorcery: L. Robert, *Hellenica*, 4, 1948, 115–126.]

more closely identified with suprahuman figures, and so, more clearly dissociated from human agents.[1] In the West, the triumph of the great landowners ensured that senatorial blood, episcopal office, and sanctity presented a formidable united front: any form of uncontrolled religious power received short shrift in the circle of Gregory of Tours.[2]

II

It was the particular merit of Professor Evans-Pritchard to have stressed the importance of witchcraft as an explanation of misfortune.[3] The historian of Late Antiquity must welcome this way of posing the problem. For he is acutely aware that the evidence for the political and social structure of the Empire will always remain fragmentary, while he finds himself the proud possessor of a body of religious literature of unparalleled richness and diversity, much of which deals directly with the problem of evil. So, he cannot avoid the challenge of the rise of Christianity in Late Antiquity, and its relation to sorcery beliefs.

In certain African tribes it has been noted that the rise of Christianity, by destroying many traditional explanations of misfortune (such as the anger of the ancestors), has led to an increased incidence in witchcraft accusations. Belief in human mystical agents of evil has had to take the full charge of explanations of misfortune that had, previously, been more widely distributed.[4] It could be argued that the opposite was true of the Late Roman period: Christianity mobilized a current drift, in the Late Antique world, towards explanations of misfortune through *suprahuman* agencies in such a way as to bypass the human agent.

For pagan and Christian alike, misfortune was unambiguously the work of suprahuman agents, the *daemones*. Whether these were the ambivalent 'spirits of the lower air' of much pagan belief, or actively hostile to the human race, as in Zoroastrianism, Christianity, and the Gnostic sects,[5] demons were the effective agents of all misfortune.[6] The sorcerer caused misfortune only by manipulating the

---

[1] See Baynes (1960).
[2] For instance, Gregory of Tours, *Hist. Franc.* VIII, 34; IX, 6; X, 25.
[3] Evans-Pritchard (1937, pp. 63–83, 99–106).
[4] Jean la Fontaine in Middleton & Winter (1953, p. 192).
[5] Dodds (1965, esp. p. 17).
[6] See Origen, *Contra Celsum* I, 31, in Chadwick (1953, pp. 30–31).

demons,[1] the curser, by 'delivering over' his victim to their hostility.[2] In Late Antique literature, the human agent is pushed into a corner by the demon-host: 'If we believe that the myriad bacilli about us were each and all inspired by a conscious will to injure man, we might then gain a realisation of the constant menace that broods over human life in the biographies of Byzantine saints'.[3]

It may well be the case that the Christian Church effected a *détente* in sorcery beliefs in this period. But it did not do this through its repeated and ineffective injunctions against 'superstitious' practices:[4] rather, the Christian Church offered an explanation of misfortune that both embraced all the phenomena previously ascribed to sorcery, and armed the individual with weapons of satisfying precision and efficacy against its suprahuman agents. I would suggest that this change in the explanation of misfortune coincides with social changes in just those milieux where Christianity became dominant.

To take explanations of misfortune first: When we read the later works of Augustine, written to rally public opinion and deeply in touch with the sentiments of the average Christian,[5] we realize that his doctrine of the punishment of the human race for the sin of Adam has been widened so as to embrace all misfortune. Misfortune, indeed, has eclipsed voluntary sin as the object of the old man's bleak meditations. Because of Adam's sin, God had permitted the demons to act as His 'public executioners'—to use the phrase of an earlier Christian writer.[6] The human race was the 'plaything of demons',[7] damage to crops, disease, possession, incongruous behaviour (such as the lapse of holy men), gratuitous accidents, and, as an insistent refrain, the untimely deaths of small children[8]— phenomena that might characterize a society in which the sorcerer had been given *carte blanche* to wreak his will—are ascribed by Augustine to the abiding anger of God: '*He has sent upon them the*

[1] See the speech of the demon serving Cyprian the magician, in Radermacher (1927, pp. 86–8), and Libanius, *Declamatio* 41, 29.

[2] Audollent (1904, l–lix).

[3] Dawes & Baynes (1948, p. xii).

[4] Barb (1963, pp. 106–7, 122–3).

[5] Brown (1967b, pp. 385–6).

[6] Origen, *Contra Celsum* VIII, 31, in Chadwick (1953, pp. 474–5).

[7] Augustine, *Contra Julianum*, VI, xxi, 67.

[8] See esp. Augustine, *de civitate Dei*, XXII, 22.

anger of His indignation, indignation and rage and tribulation, and possession by evil spirits'.[1]

So much for the formal statement of views which became more widespread in this period. What one must seize, however, are the deep reasons that would lead a man like Libanius, almost an exact contemporary of Augustine, to react to a bad dream as an omen of '(magical) medicines, spells and attacks on me by sorcerers',[2] while Augustine will say, of the terror of dreams, that they 'show clearly that, from our first root in Adam, the human race stands condemned to punishment'.[3]

I would suggest that part of the reason may lie in differing attitudes to one's identity. Libanius and his colleagues were men identified with their skill. Magical attacks were conceived of as the most intimate possible attack on such a skill as rhetoric—loss of memory invariably provoked accusations of sorcery among such men;[4] for loss of memory damaged a man's identity at just the point where he was most certain of himself—in his mastery of classical literature through having memorized it. We are dealing with incidents that are accompanied by shame, by discrepancies in performance, such as have been defined as 'when what is exposed is incongruous with, or glaringly inappropriate to, the situation, or to our previous image of ourselves in it'.[5] The misfortunes traditionally ascribed to sorcery in the ancient world relate, precisely, to such an experience of incongruity: a professor forgets his speech, a chaste and noble woman falls in love,[6] a lover is impotent.[7] Death by sorcery is also experienced as an incongruity between the victim's death and his 'natural' span.[8]

[1] Psalm 77, 49, in *Contra Julianum* V, iii, 8; also cited by Origen—Origen, *Contra Celsum* VIII, 32, in Chadwick (1953, p. 475). In general, see Brown (1967b, pp. 394–7).
[2] Norman, *Libanius' Autobiography*, §. 245 (pp. 128–9).
[3] Augustine, *de civitate Dei*, XXII, 22.
[4] Cicero, *Brutus* 60, 217; Norman, *Libanius' Autobiography*, §. 50 (pp. 34–5); §. 71 (pp. 44–5).
[5] Lynd (1958, p. 34).
[6] For this period alone, see Amm. Marc. XXVIII, i, 50; Jerome, *Vita Hilarionis* (*Patrol. Lat.* 23, 39–40); Theodoret, *Historia Religiosa*, xiii (*Patrol. Graeca* 82, 1406 ff); Amphilochius of Iconium, *Vita Basilii*, in Latin translation, *Patrologia Lat*, 73, 303 AB: Greek edition in Radermacher (1927, pp. 122–49); Gregory the Great, *Dialogues* I, 4 (*Patrol. Lat.* 77, 168 B).
[7] Ovid, *Am. III*, vii, 27–8.
[8] See esp. *Corpus Inscriptionum Latinarum* VIII, 2756. In comparison with

Now incongruity assumes a very fixed image of a man's identity. Augustine, by contrast, had a most acute sense of discrepancies in behaviour,[1] but, for him, they fitted into a view of man's identity which, unlike that of Libanius, has had the bottom knocked out of it: 'For noone is known to another so intimately as he is known to himself, and yet noone is so well known even to himself, that he can be sure as to his own conduct on the morrow'.[2]

The two reactions may allow us to glimpse two different worlds. Libanius lived most of his life among the well-oriented upper classes of Antioch. When subjected to a misfortune ascribed to sorcery, he knew on whom he might pin blame: he would be blamed by others; he and his colleagues drew their identity from skills common to a traditionalist society. When such professors and civic notables competed among themselves, they trod a narrow stage whose backdrop had changed little. In so stable, well-oriented a world, a man would expect to be certain of his identity: he knew what was expected of him, and he knew that he could live up to these expectations. When an incongruity suddenly appears in his performance, he defends his image of himself by treating it as an intrusive element, placed there, from the outside, by some hostile agent. 'Misfortune' of the kind we are discussing is experienced as an attempt, from the outside, to sabotage the 'good fortune' to which a man's conscious control of his environment entitles him. And, in the world of Libanius, it is possible to identify the saboteur in the precise human figure of one's jealous colleague.

By contrast, the Christian communities in the third and fourth centuries had grown up in precisely those classes of the great cities of the Mediterranean that were most exposed to fluidity and uncertainty.[3] For the lower classes of these cities continued to be recruited by the immigration of rootless peasants from the country.[4]

African material, death is rarely ascribed to sorcery, though it was believed to be possible and to have been committed even by Christians; see Council of Elvira (311) canon 8. On the ideas surrounding untimely death, see esp. Dölger (1930, pp. 21 ff.).

[1] See Brown (1967b, p. 405).

[2] Augustine, *Letter* 130, ii, 4.

[3] Clearly appreciated by Dodds (1965, p. 78, n. 1 and pp. 137-8). [For a vivid impression of the fluidity of wealth in Antioch, see W. Ceran, 'Stagnation and Fluctuation in Early Byzantine Society', *Byzantinoslavica*, 31, 2, 1970, 192-203.]

[4] See Mazzarino (1951, pp. 217-61).

In the fourth century, just those groups whose attachment to the government service made them most mobile were, also, predominantly Christian.[1] More important still, perhaps, was the inner exile imposed on leaders of the Christian Church, Augustine included, by the ascetic movement: the monastic life was 'the life of a stranger';[2] the Christian community was described, not without justification, as a 'race of strangers'.[3]

In the fourth and fifth centuries, therefore, the sense of a fixed identity in a stable and well-oriented world, that would encourage the blaming of sorcerers and would single out incongruities in public behaviour as *the* misfortune *par excellence*, was being eroded in both the social milieu and the religious ideas associated with the leaders of Christian opinion. This situation changed as Late Roman society became more fixed. The stabilization of the local Christian communities and the elaboration of a finely articulated penitential system placed boundaries on Augustine's sense of the unidentifiable guilt of a bottomless identity. The idea of ill-defined guilt hardened into a sense of exposure to misfortune through the neglect of prescribed actions. At the end of the sixth century, it was plain to Gregory the Great that a woman who slept with her husband before a religious procession would risk demonic possession, just as the nun who ate a lettuce without first making the sign of the Cross on it would swallow a demon perched on its leaves.[4]

In the earlier centuries, however, the Christian communities grew up through a belief in human 'vested' agents of good, endowed with inherent powers, as 'bearers of the Holy Spirit', to combat suprahuman agents of evil.[5] The confrontation of Saint and Devil stole the scene from the sorcerer. 'Our struggle', wrote St. Paul, 'is not *with flesh and blood*, but against . . . the World-Rulers of the darkness of this existence, against spiritual forces of evil in the heavenly regions'.[6] A belief which, as Origen remarked, 'has led the rank and file of Christian believers to think that all human sins are due to the powers of the upper air: so that, to put it another way, if

[1] See Jones (1963, esp. pp. 35-7).
[2] Leclercq (1960, pp. 212 ff.).
[3] Augustine, *Enarratio in Ps.* 136, 13: see Brown (1967b, pp.323-4, esp. p. 323, n. 7).
[4] Gregory the Great, *Dialogues*, I, 30 (*Patrol, Lat.* 77, 200-201) and I, 4 (*ibid.*, 169).
[5] See the abundant material collected by Tamborino (1909, pp. 27 ff.).
[6] *Ephesians* 6: 12.

the Devil did not exist, no man would sin'.[1] From the New Testament onwards, the Christian mission was a mission of 'driving out' demons. Martyrdom, and later asceticism, was a 'spiritual prize fight' with the demons.[2] The bishop's office was 'to tread down Satan under his feet'.[3] Full membership of the Christian Church, by baptism, was preceded by drastic exorcisms.[4] Once inside the Christian Church, the Christian enjoyed, if in a form that was being constantly qualified, the millennial sensations of a modern African anti-sorcery cult.[5] The Church was the community for whom Satan had been bound: his limitless powers had been bridled to permit the triumph of the Gospel;[6] more immediately, the practising Christian gained immunity from sorcery.[7]

Now it cannot be stressed often enough that the rise of Christianity in the third and fourth centuries was not merely the spread of certain doctrines in a society that already possessed its own principles of organization—as might well be the case in modern Africa:[8] it was an effort of, often, rootless men to create a society in miniature, a 'people of God'; its appeal lay in its exceptional degree of cohesion and, at a later time when this cohesion was diluted, at least in the greater precision with which a bishop or a holy man resolved the disputes of a community.[9] But a newly established group committed to mutual love, its leaders acutely sensitive to the 'worldly smoke' of rivalry, could hardly survive the interplay of blame and envy that accompanied a belief in human agents of misfortune. What we find instead is a 'humanizing' of the suprahuman agents of

---

[1] Origen, de principiis III, 2, 1 (Patrol. Graeca 11, 205).

[2] E.g. Brown (1967b. p. 244).

[3] Canones Hippolyti, xvii (ed. Achelis, Texte und Untersuchungen, VI, 4 1891).

[4] Vividly described for North Africa by Poque (1965, pp. 27–9). [See now 'Exorzismus' Reallexikon für Antike und Christentum, 7, 1969, 44–117.]

[5] See Douglas (1963, pp. 247 and 257).

[6] Augustine, de civitate Dei, XX, 8.

[7] Origen, Contra Celsum VI, 41, in Chadwick (1953, pp. 356–7). [See Palladius, Historia Lausiaca XVII, 9—a lady who neglected taking the Eucharist was turned into a horse by a magician.]

[8] This would apply less to the governing class, who adopted Christianity after the conversion of the emperors. See, for example, Brown (1961, pp. 1 ff.) and (1968b, p. 101). For analogous cases in Africa, where the chief was the agent of conversion, see Schapera (1958).

[9] See, for example, Brown (1967b, pp. 195–6). [And now P. Brown, 'The Rise and Function of the Holy Man', Journal of Roman Studies 61, 1971.]

evil. In all Christian literature, the ambivalent and somewhat faceless *daemones* of pagan belief are invested with the precise, unambiguous negative attributes and motives that Libanius still saw in a professional rival who resorted to sorcery. The Devil was the 'rival' of the saint; envy, hatred, and the deadly spleen of a defeated expert mark his reactions to the human race. On Christian amulets we may be sure that *Invide*, 'O Envious One', refers, not to the Christian's neighbour, but to the Devil.[1] Where the teachings of the Fathers of the Church clash with popular belief, it is invariably in the direction of denying the *human* links involved in sorcery (they will deny, for instance, that it is the souls of the dead that are the agents of misfortune),[2] in order to emphasize the purely *demonic* nature of the misfortunes that might afflict their congregations.

One incident illustrates this tendency very clearly. A girl had been bewitched by a love-spell. The saint, Macedonius, was brought in to exorcise her. When abjured, the demon excused itself. It could not come out so easily, for it had entered under duress; and it named the sorcerer who had constrained it. Straightway, the girl's father lodged an accusation against the sorcerer in the governor's court. For a moment it seems as if the testimony of a demon interrogated by a saint would solve a problem of blame-pinning that had previously been left to the clumsy Roman method of examining under torture the servants and intimates of the sorcerer.[3] Macedonius, significantly, refused this role. He chased away the demon before it could involve the sorcerer in a further string of misfortunes, and converted the sorcerer; and so, with the exception of the case of the girl, he left the role of the sorcerer in mid-air, as far as the human participants were concerned.[4]

It is interesting to note that this incident took place in Antioch, at almost exactly the same period as the life of Libanius. The girl's father and the governor plainly still thought of sorcery as Libanius did, in terms of blame-pinning, occasionally followed by a capital prosecution of the offender. The new holy man had refused to use his spiritual powers to relieve human uncertainties. His traditional enemy was the demon, not the sorcerer. *Exceptio probat regulam*:

[1] Diehl, *Inscriptiones latinae christianae veteres*, I, 1961, no. 2388 (pp. 462–3).

[2] Chrysostom, *Hom. 28 in Matthaeum* (*Patrologia Graeca* 57, 353).

[3] E.g. Amm. Marc. XXVIII, i, 7, and Norman, *Libanius' Autobiography*, §. 41 (p. 26).

[4] Theodoret, *Hist. religiosa*, xiii (*Patrol. Graeca* 82, 1405 ff.).

compared with the vast number of direct conflicts with demons in the popular literature of the Christian Church, cases of confrontation with demons in the service of sorcerers are notably few, and, of these few, in only two cases known to me does the abjuration of the demon lead back to relations with a human agent.[1] The usual attitude to a demon acting under a spell was 'I don't know how you got in, but I order you to get out . . .'[2]

In the fourth and fifth centuries, therefore, the rise of Christianity should be seen as the rise of a new grouping of Roman society and as an attempt to suspend certain forms of human relations within the fold of the 'people of God'. If there are sorcerers, they are usually seen to work outside the Christian community (hence the pervasive identification of paganism and magic in Christian sources); if there is misfortune, it is divorced from a human reference and the blame is pinned firmly on the 'spiritual powers of evil'. Hence, perhaps, the snowball effect of the rapid rise of Christianity. Men joined the new community to be delivered from the demons; and the new community, in turn, resolved its tensions by projecting them in the form of an even greater demonic menace from outside.

III

The period I have been discussing, from around A.D. 300 to 600, is a recognizable whole. I think that it is misleading to regard it, as many scholars have done, merely as a preview of the Middle Ages. Writing on an experience of Libanius, one has said: 'The incident heightens the impression made by all the other evidence, namely, that the fourth century was darkened by the most degrading superstitions in a manner that can only be compared to the benighted condition of Western Europe in the later Middle Ages'.[3] This reaction reflects the despair of the classical scholar: by falling away at all from the standards of an ideal ancient world, the Later Empire could hardly have fallen any *lower* than the Middle Ages! In fact, all recent research on the culture, the religion, and the institutions of the Later Empire has revealed it to be a period in which men

[1] Theodoret, cit. above p. 137, n. 4, and 'Life of Theodore of Sykeon', cc. 35 and 38, in Dawes & Baynes (1948, pp. 112 and 114–15).
[2] Jerome, *Vita Hilarionis*, 22 (*Patrol. Lat.* 23, 41).
[3] Campbell-Bonner (1932, p. 44).

worked (and most creatively) on an unbroken ancient legacy, and which is not to be reduced to a prelude of the Middle Ages.

This is particularly true of sorcery. For it is *sorcery* in the strict sense that I have been discussing throughout—an occult skill to which anyone can resort. Late Roman sorcery was an 'art'.[1] It was an art consigned to great books.[2] To possess or transcribe such books might jeopardize the owner,[3] but their destruction was accepted as sufficient guarantee of the change of heart of the sorcerer.[4] Knowledge of sorcery techniques could be widespread among the literate people that the historian meets;[5] but the knowledge tended to be specialized in professional practitioners.[6]

Now, as we have seen, the man accused of practising sorcery was a man of undefinable *power*. In extreme cases, the ideal type produced by the traditional 'vested' culture would wear this ambivalent halo: the philosopher Apollonius of Tyana was widely known as a *magus*;[7] many saints were spontaneously hailed as *magi*,[8] and it is, perhaps, not only a coincidence that, in popular Christian romances, the sorcerers should bear the same names as two of the greatest bishops in the Christian Church—Cyprian and Athanasius.[9] Therefore, when a Byzantine miniaturist wishes to portray a sorcerer, he shows an idealized portrait of a pagan philosopher.[10]

Above all, the sorcerer is a man who enjoys power *over* the demons, even over the gods. He can threaten the gods,[11] he works

[1] See Abt (1908, pp. 104–5).

[2] See Preisendanz (1950, pp. 226 ff.). See Zachary the Scholastic, *Vie de Sévère, Patrologia Orientalis* II, 58.

[3] See, for instance, Amm. Marc. XXVIII, i, 27; Chrysostom, *Hom. 38 in Act. Apostolorum (Patrol. Graeca,* 59, 273 ff.); *Vie de Sévère, Patrol. Orientalis* II, 65–6.

[4] *Codex Theodosianus* IX, xvi, 12 (409); *Vie de Sévère, Patrol. Orientalis* II, 61–2; *Life of Theodore of Sykeon,* 38, ed. Dawes & Baynes (1948, p. 115); Radermacher (1927), p. 104).

[5] E.g. *Vie de Sévère, Patrol. Orientalis* II, 37 (a book of invocations).

[6] For instance, Audollent (1904, xliv ff.), on the professional execution and uniformity of leaden cursing-tablets.

[7] See Chadwick (1953, p. 356, n. 3); MacMullen (1957, pp. 95–115); and, in general, Abt (1908, pp. 108–15) on the position of the magician as an ascetic and 'servant of God'.

[8] For instance, Jerome, *Vita Hilarionis,* 20 and 23 (*Patrol. Lat.* 23, 37 and 48).

[9] Radermacher (1927, p. 41).

[10] See the Byzantine miniature of the ninth century illustrating Cyprian the Magician, Radermacher (1927, facing p. 234).

[11] Now in Sodano (1958, pp. 61–3).

very largely by what the psychoanalyst would call 'introjective identification', that is, he *becomes* the god—'for Thou art I and I am
Thou: whatever I say must come to pass'.[1] In Christian sources, the
demons act as the servants of the sorcerer: he is the servant of the
Devil only in a very generalized sense, for he is free to abandon
him by destroying the books of his trade and by accepting Christian
baptism.[2] The contrast between the saint and the sorcerer is not
that the saint commands the demons while the sorcerer is their
agent: both can command; but the saint has an effective 'vested'
power, whereas the sorcerer works with a technique that is unreli-
able and, above all, cumbersome.

Such sorcery is very much a *carrière ouverte aux talents*. A man of
occult learning could placate, manipulate, even threaten suprahuman powers to his advantage. If a society gets the sorcery it deserves, then Late Antique sorcery is a tribute to the learned and
competitive spirit prevailing in the fluid areas of society in which it
was most rife.

This 'learned' sorcery, of course, will survive into the Middle
Ages, both in the West, in clerical circles,[3] and even more so in the
Eastern Mediterranean, among societies that had remained in touch
with their ancient roots—in Byzantium, Islam, and the Jewish
communities.[4] At the end of our period, however, it is joined by
another theme. We meet the *witch* in the full sense, a person who
either is born with or achieves an inherent character of evil. In this
case, it is not an unconscious mystical quality: it is gained by a
conscious act. But the power is gained by a binding compact with
the ultimate pole of evil—the Devil; and, once this quality is gained,
it is rare (outside pious stories) that the Christian authorities
accept the recantation of the new-style witch. The contents of this
new belief are well known. What matters is to seize the exact date
and milieu in which it comes to the fore.

It is a Mediterranean phenomenon. We meet witches after the
heart of the ethnographer in the law-codes of the Northern bar-

[1] See E. R. Dodds (1965, pp. 72–3) and Festugière (1944, pp. 290–8).

[2] See Radermacher (1927, p. 44): 'Denn dort ist der Zauberer Herr und
Gebieter über die Dämonen. Von einem Vertrag ist keine Rede . . . Die Rolle
Satans in der Historie ist kläglich.'

[3] See Barb (1963, pp. 122–4) and d'Alverny, 1 (1962, pp. 155 ff.).

[4] Kraus (1942); Ritter & Plessner (1962); and Golb (1967, pp. 12–15; 17, n. 26).
[See further, M. Margalioth, *Sefer ha-razim, Hū sefer keshāfim mitteqūfat-ha-
Talmūd*, Jerusalem 1967.]

barians.[1] But these witches are already glimpsed at a distance. They may not have long survived the process of rapid de-tribalization that coincided with Christianization, which marks the evolution of the barbarian ruling classes in Western Europe.[2] The idea of the 'servant of Satan', I would suggest, is a direct sequel of certain developments in Western and Byzantine society at the end of the sixth century.

By the end of the sixth century, we are dealing with a society which regards itself as totally Christian. The last occasions when notable cases of sorcery can be associated with the worship of the pagan gods belong to the Eastern Empire in the 570s.[3] From then on, there is only one possible outsider in a Christian world—the Jew. It is precisely at this time that we have the first widespread movements presenting the Jewish communities in Africa, Byzantium, Visigothic Spain, and, sporadically, Gaul, with the choice of baptism or exile.[4]

Most important of all, perhaps, a man's conscious identity was now deeply linked with his Christianity. In Christian popular opinion, the sorcerer could no longer be tolerated in the community on the condition that he recanted his *art*: for he was now considered to have abandoned his *identity*; he had denied his Christian baptism.[5] Accusations of sorcery now take us into entirely Christian circles: bishops were implicated;[6] and, in the new stories, the sorcerer is no longer the pagan outside the community—the man who delivers his soul to the Devil is a bishop *manqué*.[7] The power of sorcery is gained, not by skill, but by a compact, a sealed document

---

[1] E.g. *Edictum* of Rothari c. 376: 'Nullus praesumat haldiam alienam aut ancillam quasi strigam, quem dicunt mascam, occidere: quod christianis mentibus nullatenus credendum est, nec possibile ut mulier hominem vivum intrinsecus possit comedere.'

[2] See Thompson (1966, pp. 127–32) and Wallace-Hadrill (1962, p. 125). The cases of sorcery known to me at the Merovingian court, like so many other aspects of that society, strike me as quite definitely belonging to Late Antiquity, not to a 'barbarian' world.

[3] Evagrius, *Historia Ecclesiastica*, V, 18; John of Ephesus, *Hist. Eccles.* III, 29–30.

[4] See Blumencranz (1960, pp. 97–138) and Brown 1967a, p. 332). [See P. Brown, *The World of Late Antiquity*, 1971, pp. 172–174.]

[5] Theophylact Simocatta, *Historiae* I, 11 (ed. Bonn Corpus, 56, line 10): and John of Nikiou c. 98 (ed. Zotenberg, 534–5).

[6] Evagrius, *Hist. Eccles.* V, 18.

[7] The story of Theophilus, in Radermacher (1927, pp. 164 ff.).

delivered over to the Devil, renouncing Christ, His Mother, and one's baptism.[1] Significantly, the Jew plays a part in these stories, not only because he is an outsider, but, more particularly, because he had always denied Christ—he was the 'apostate' *par excellence*.[2] We have come to a world where the overt bonds are far more rigid. This can be seen more clearly, even, in Heaven than on earth. The correlation between Christian imagery and the social structure of the Later Empire is a fact almost too big to be seen: we meet it in every detail of the iconography of the Christian churches.[3] By the sixth century the image of the divine world had become exceedingly stable. Angels were the courtiers and bureaucrats of a remote Heavenly Emperor, and the saints, the *patroni*, the 'protectors', whose efficacious interventions at court channelled the benefits of a just autocrat to individuals and localities.[4] In the late sixth and early seventh century, sorcery is more often punished by the direct intervention of these divine governors: the sorcerer receives short shrift, as a traitor from a well-regimented celestial society.[5]

We have entered the tidy world of the Middle Ages. In Byzantium, an emperor conceived of as a 'servant of Christ', his person transparent to the image of Christ as King of Kings, will rule over a city where aristocracy and factions alike have been cowed.[6] At the other end of the Mediterranean, the Visigothic kings of Toledo are showing strident proof of their high level of 'civilization' by swearing oaths at their coronation to rid their land of the 'impiety of the Jews'.[7] And, at the far pole of men's minds, the Devil also has grown in majesty: he, also, is a great lord, a *patronos*,[8] he, also, can welcome his servants: 'Welcome, from this time forth, my own loyal friend.'[9]

---

[1] Radermacher (1927, p. 166).

[2] *ibid.*, p. 165.

[3] On this vast subject, see, for instance, Peterson (1935); Nordström (1953); Pietri (1961, pp. 275 ff.).

[4] See, for example, de Ste Croix (1954, esp. pp. 46 ff.) and Wallace-Hadrill (1962, p. 127).

[5] Moschus, *Pratum spirituale* c. 145 (Latin translation in *Patrol. Lat.* 74, 192); Evagrius, *Hist. Eccles.* V. 18—the Virgin appears in dreams, demanding vengeance against 'traitors' to Her Son.

[6] See esp. Breckenridge (1959).

[7] VI Council of Toledo (638), can. 3 in Hefele & Leclercq (1909, p. 279).

[8] Radermacher (1927, p. 168, line 17).

[9] *Ibid.*, p. 167.

REFERENCES

ABEL, A. 1957. La Place des sciences occultes dans la décadence. *Classicisme et déclin dans l'histoire de l'Islam*, Paris.

ABT, A. 1908. *Die Apologie des Apuleius von Madaura und die antike Zauberei.* Naumburg.

ALVERNY, M.-T. D'. 1962. La Survivance de la magie antique. *Antike und Orient im Mittalter, Miscellanea Medievalia I.* Berlin.

AUDOLLENT, A. 1904. *Defixionum Tabellae.* Paris.

BARB, A. 1963. The Survival of Magic Arts. A. D. Momigliano (ed.), *The Conflict between Paganism and Christianity in the Fourth Century.* London: Oxford University Press.

BARNS, J. 1964. Schenute as an Historical Source. *Actes du Xème Congrès International des Papyrologues.* Warsaw.

BAYNES, N. H. 1960. The Supernatural Defenders of Constantinople. *Byzantine Studies and other Essays.* London: Athlone Press (University of London).

BLUMENCRANZ, B. 1960. *Juifs et chrétiens dans le monde occidental, 430–1096.* Paris.

BRECKENRIDGE, J. D. 1959. *The Numismatic Iconography of Justinian II.* Numismatic Notes and Monographs 144. Harvard.

BROWN, PETER. 1961. Aspects of the Christianisation of the Roman Aristocracy. *Journal of Roman Studies* 51. London.

—— 1967a. The Later Roman Empire. Essays in Bibliography and Criticism LVI. *Economic History Review* (scr. 2) 20. London.

—— 1967b. *Augustine of Hippo.* London: Faber.

—— 1968a. Christianity and Local Culture in Late Roman Africa. *Journal of Roman Studies* 58. London.

—— 1968b. Pelagius and his Supporters: Aims and Environment. *Journal of Theological Studies* (n.s.) 19. Oxford.

CAMERON, A. 1965. Wandering Poets. A Literary Movement in Egypt. *Historia* 14. Wiesbaden.

CAMPBELL-BONNER, A. 1932. Witchcraft in the Lecture-room of Libanius. *Transactions of the American Philological Society* 63. Connecticutt.

CHADWICK, H. (ed.). 1953. *Origen; Contra Celsum.* Cambridge: Cambridge University Press.

COURCELLE, P. 1964. *Histoire littéraire des grandes invasions germaniques.* Paris.

DAWES, E. & BAYNES, N. H. 1948. *Three Byzantine Saints*. Oxford: Blackwell.

DODDS, E. R. 1965. *Pagan and Christian in an Age of Anxiety*. Cambridge: Cambridge University Press.

DÖLGER, F. 1930. Antike Parallelen zum leidenden Deinocrates. *Antike und Christentum* 2. Münster-in-Westfalen.

DOUGLAS, MARY. 1963. *The Lele of the Kasai*, London: Oxford University Press (for the International African Institute).

—— 1966. *Purity and Danger*. London: Routledge & Kegan Paul; New York: Praeger.

EITREM, S. 1925. *Papyri Osloenses, fasc. I. Magical Papyri*. Oslo.

EVANS-PRITCHARD, E. E. 1937. *Witchcraft, Oracles and Magic among the Azande*. Oxford: Clarendon Press.

FESTUGIÈRE, A. J. 1944. *La Révélation d'Hermès Trismégiste I; L'Astrologie et les sciences occultes*. Paris.

GOLB, N. 1967. Aspects of the Historical Background of Jewish Life in Medieval Egypt. In A. Altmann (ed.), *Jewish Medieval and Renaissance Studies*. Cambridge, Mass.: Harvard University Press; London: Oxford University Press.

GRÉGOIRE-KUGENER, 1930. *Marc le Diacre: Vie de Porphyre* (Editions Budé). Paris.

HEFELE, D. & LECLERCQ, J. 1909. *Histoire des Conciles*, Vol. III, 1. Paris.

HOPKINS, K. M. 1961. Social Mobility in the Later Empire: the Evidence of Ausonius. *Classical Quarterly* (n.s.) 11. Oxford.

JONES, A. H. M. 1963. The Social Background of the Struggle between Paganism and Christianity. A. D. Momigliano (ed.). *The Conflict between Paganism and Christianity in the Fourth Century*. London: Oxford University Press.

—— 1964. *The Later Empire*. 3 vols. Oxford: Blackwell.

KAYSER, G. 1888. Das Gebrauch von Psalmen zur Zauberei. *Zeitschrift der deutschen morgenländischen Gesellschaft* 42. Leipzig.

KRAUS, P. 1942. *Jābir ibn Hayyān*. Cairo.

LECLERCQ, J. 1960. Mönchtum und Peregrinatio im Frühmittelalter. *Romische Quartalschrift* 55. Rome.

LYND, H. M. 1958. *On Shame and the Search for Identity*. London: Routledge & Kegan Paul; New York: Harcourt, Brace.

MACMULLEN, R. 1967. *Enemies of the Roman Order*. Cambridge, Mass.: Harvard University Press; London: Oxford University Press.

MARTROYE, F. 1930. La Répression de la magie et le culte des gentils au IVe siècle. *Revue historique du droit français et étranger* (ser. iv) 9. Paris.

MARWICK, M. G. 1952. The Social Context of Cewa Witch Beliefs. *Africa* 22 (2): 120–35, (3): 215–33.

MAURICE, J. 1927. La Terreur de la magie au IVe siècle. *Revue historique du droit français et étranger* 6. Paris.

MAZZARINO, S. 1951. *Aspetti Sociali del quarto secolo.* Rome.

MIDDLETON, JOHN & WINTER, E. H. (eds.). 1963. *Witchcraft and Sorcery in East Africa.* London: Routledge & Kegan Paul.

NEUSNER, J. 1966. *A History of the Jews in Babylonia; II, The Early Sassanian Period.* Leiden.

NILSSON, M. P. 1948. Die Religion in der griechischen Zauberpapyri. *Bulletin de la Société de Lettres de Lund.* Lund.

NOCK, A. D. 1929. Greek Magical Papyri. *Journal of Egyptian Archaeology* 15. London.

NORDSTRÖM, E. 1953. *Ravennastudien.* Stockholm.

NORMAN, A. F. (ed.). 1965. *Libanius' Autobiography* (Oratio I). Hull.

PETERSON, E. 1935. *Monotheismus als politisches Problem.* Leipzig.

—— 1959. Die geheimen Praktiken eines syrischen Bischofs. *Frühkirche, Judentum und Gnosis.* Vienna.

PETIT, P. 1955. *Libanius et la vie municipale d'Antioche au IVe siècle.* Paris.

PICARD, G. C. 1964. Un Palais du IVe siècle à Carthage. *Comptes-Rendus de l'Académie des Inscriptions et Belles-Lettres.* Paris.

PIETRI, M. C. 1961. *Concordia apostolorum et renovatio urbis* (Culte de martyrs et propagande papale). *Mélanges d'archéologie et d'histoire* 73. Paris.

—— 1966. Le Sénat, le peuple chrétien et les factions de cirque à Rome. *Mélanges d'archéologie et d'histoire* 88. Paris.

PIGANIOL, A. 1947. *L'Empire chrétien.* Paris.

POQUE, SUZANNE. 1965. *Augustin d'Hippone; Sermons pour la Pâque.* Sources chrétiennes 116. Paris.

PREISENDANZ, K. 1928 and 1931. *Papyri Graeci Magici; Die griechischen Zauberpapyri.* 2 vols. Leipzig Berlin.

—— 1950. Zur Uberlieferungsgeschichte der spätantiker Magie. *Aus der Welt des Buches, Festgabe für G. Ley.* Leipzig.

RADERMACHER, L. 1927. Griechische Quellen zur Faustsage. *Sitzungs berichte der Wiener Akademie der Wissenschaften* 206 (4). Vienna.

RITTER, H. & PLESSNER, M. 1962. *Picatrix*. London: Warburg Institute (University of London).

RUBIN, B. 1960. *Das Zeitalter Justinians*, vol. I. Berlin.

STE CROIX, G. E. M. DE. 1954. Suffragium: from Vote to Patronage. *British Journal of Sociology* 5. London.

—— 1963. Why were the Early Christians Persecuted? *Past and Present* 26. Kendal.

SCHAPERA, I. 1958. Christianity and the Tswana. *Journal of the Royal Anthropological Institute* 88. London.

SODANO, A. 1958. *Porfirio, Lettera ad Anebo*. Naples.

SPRANDEL, R. 1961. Struktur und Geschichte des merowingischen Adels. *Historische Zeitschrift* 192. Munich.

TAMBORINO, J. 1909. *De antiquorum Daemonismo*. Naumburg.

THOMPSON, E. A. 1966. *The Visigoths in the Time of Ulfila*. London: Oxford University Press.

WALLACE-HADRILL, M. 1962. The Blood Feud of the Franks. In *The Long-Haired Kings*. London: Methuen.

WES, M. A. 1967. *Das Ende des Kaisertums im Westen des römischen Reiches*. The Hague.

WÜNSCH, R. 1912. *Antike Fluchtafeln* (Kleine Texte für Vorlesungen und Übungen, 20). Bonn.

Review of:
THE CONFLICT BETWEEN PAGANISM AND
CHRISTIANITY IN THE FOURTH CENTURY
Edited by A. Momigliano, Clarendon Press, 1963.*

These eight lectures, delivered at the Warburg Institute in 1958–9,
are the best possible kind of introduction to their subject. They do
nothing less than sum up a whole generation of Late Roman scholarship in the words of the scholars who have made this generation
what it is. Themes that had only appeared in passing in the great
continuous histories of the previous generation, often as no more
than humble 'factors' in a vast process of change, are here singled
out and treated with a newly-won certainty of touch. The dominant
impression of this book is freshness; in it, a new perspective has been
cast on the nature of the conflict between paganism and Christianity.

Thus, many inert ideas have been shifted in passing. There is no
comfort here for those who would like to see in the origins of the
Middle Ages a peaceful continuity of Roman and Christian, and,
in the end of paganism, an ineluctable 'evolution'. Nor is this tragic
tension presented as a melodrama. Instead, the conflict appears, in
this book, in the form of many brilliantly illuminated facets: the
hesitant evolution of Syncsius of Cyrene, by Professor Marrou; the
anxieties of the last pagan senators in Rome, by Professor Bloch;
the watershed of current religious ideas that separated pagans from
Christians, by Professor Courcelle; and, in a firm and differentiated
evocation of the gulf between Christian and pagan historical writing,
by Professor Momigliano, we have a timely reminder of the sinister
quality of the aftermath of the conversion of Constantine.

These lectures are concerned with the impact of religion upon
the public, rather than upon the private life of the time. They implicitly exclude certain depths: Dr. Barb's treatment of magic is
marked by such evident distaste that we are brought no closer
to understanding the dilemma of many late Roman pagans; and

* *The Oxford Magazine*, 16 May 1963, pp. 300–301.

the demons, another depth, appear only as a delightful comic relief.

Such a perspective, however, allows Momigliano to assert, in an introduction, the decisive role of religious factors in the fall of the Western Empire. Recent advances in the social and economic history of the Roman Empire have tended to exempt the modern historian from considering the role of Christianity as a factor in this decline. Yet, as Momigliano shows, the problem cannot be so easily avoided; and, in the light of the evidence collected in this book, the argument need not degenerate into a *Schuldfrage*.

Momigliano's interpretation is essentially 'aristocratic'. The leaders of the church were able to exercise power and create new forms of organized life in a demoralized society; but in so doing, they weakened certain necessary prejudices. In the West, they showed themselves only too ready to collaborate with other new rulers, untainted by the classical pagan past—that is, the barbarians.

As Professor Thompson shows, in the third lecture, the Christians in the Empire did not try to convert the barbarian tribes beyond the frontiers. It is a significant shortcoming. In his opinion, they were converted only when they entered the Empire and adopted Roman ways of life. Perhaps this conclusion makes too much of the social cleavage between the Roman and the barbarian worlds as the cause of this religious oversight. It may well be that the Christian church lacked the means to expand by missionary activity. The bishops were no more successful in converting the countryside of their own dioceses: their horizon was limited to their duties to their fellow-townsmen. Basil of Caesarea, whose priests were artisans, tied to their shops all day, would have envied the later opportunities of Gregory the Great, whose missionary activity assumed a team of monks to send to distant countries, and a firm administration, modelled on the Imperial bureaucracy, to take care of the 'dust of the world'. In such a way, the Christian church of the fourth century may well have contributed to the decline of the Roman Empire by encouraging that tendency of many small men to live in yet smaller worlds which is, perhaps, more dangerous for a society than the desertion of the world by the few. Its strength lay in the loyalty of small communities with narrow horizons; and when Augustine is in church, he can shrug off the sack of Rome, while telling his flock how the lapse of one converted heretic among them has really broken his heart.

The alliance of Church and State has, perhaps, blinded us to the shortcomings of the Christian church in this period. Thus, for Professor Jones, the conversion of Constantine is the decisive event in the diffusion of Christianity. In his opinion, the conversion of the Emperors coincided with a change in Roman society, by which the traditional governing classes were replaced by new men, dependent for their position on their relations with the Imperial bureaucracy. Such a society of new men was less prepared to resist the new religion of their benefactors. This view is only advanced as an hypothesis; but it carries conviction, and is destined to have a long and fruitful life. It may need to be qualified in some of its ramifications. The most explicit evidence reflects the perspective of one man only —of Libanius, the pagan sophist of Antioch. I doubt whether Libanius could have seen the changes around him in any other terms. The 'new' society of Constantinople, whose bizarre senators he describes, may well have appeared blatant only by contrast to more settled areas. Thus, in Africa, there is no evidence that the social pressures, which Jones describes so well for Constantinople, were operative, at this time, in the transition between paganism and Christianity. Nor is it possible to predict the religious effects of such fluidity. *Anomie* of this kind can often create its own braking-forces. In a fluid society, education plays a greater role as a mark of status; and this education was pagan in form and 'soundproof' to Christianity in effect. Many men wanted to stand still: a few barbarian generals even went out of their way to become classical pagans; and some of the spokesmen of Roman paganism may possibly have been more recent arrivals in the Senate than the Christian family of Paulinus of Nola. Late Roman history if full of such unpredictable oddies.

This excellent collection calls for some epilogue. The character of the fourth century emerges clearly. We are still in 'Late Antiquity'. Men like Synesius and Ammianus Marcellinus (the best-drawn portraits in the book) still share in the preoccupations of previous centuries: they had to decide to what extent they would expose themselves to the new religious ideas that had existed for a long time on the horizon of the classical tradition. By the end of the fourth century an entirely new element comes to predominate: the issue of authority. Religious coercion, the cloven foot of the religious history of the Later Empire, does not appear often in this book. The Roman pagans, described in the last lecture by Bloch, are the first to feel this issue. They had tried to ignore the conversion of Constantine. In themselves, they are not particularly heroic men; and in their dealings with an intolerant court, they had not avoided a large measure of appeasement, even of collusion. Even the strength of their 'Reaction', in 394, is magnified through appearing through Christian sources. It is, rather, the 'Catholic Reaction', of men such as Ambrose and Paulinus, which ensured that a complex and uneasy figure such as Nicomachus Flavianus and his pagan friends could no longer be taken for granted in the West. Thus the last pagan senators of Rome suddenly found themselves in an unaccustomed, heroic eminence:

> nec tibi nobilitas videatur libera, quam nunc
> sublimem attonita conspicis urbe vehi,
> quam cernis tanta sibi libertate videri,
> ut dedignetur flectere colla deo.

The proud words are those of Paulinus of Nola: no pagan senator would have brought himself to be so brutally frank.

Review of:
THE TRANSFORMATION OF THE ROMAN WORLD: GIBBON'S PROBLEM AFTER TWO CENTURIES
Edited by Lynn White, Jr. Berkeley: University of California Press, 1967.*

This collection of contributions is given to us as 'a prism of three faces': it aims to present a résumé of modern views on Late Antiquity and the Early Middle Ages; it seeks to understand Gibbon; it measures, in more general terms, the difference in perspective between Gibbon and a modern man. There is much in it of great interest to the historian both of the ideas of the Enlightenment and of the Later Empire (to take some examples, Andrew Lossky, 'Gibbon and the Enlightenment'; an excellent summary and bibliography of recent work on Byzantium by Speros Vryonis; an essay of unique quality by Miriam Lichtheim on the resurgence of vernacular cultures in the Christian East; and singularly stimulating remarks on the symbiosis of Christianity and Islam in the High Middle Ages by Lynn White). If this review is critical, let it be taken as a tribute to the firmly delineated standpoint of the contributors. For this Seminar seems to focus within a narrow span and in relaxed (even self-indulgent) prose, many of the vices, as well as the virtues, of some modern approaches both to Gibbon and to the Later Empire.

First of all, Gibbon is isolated: he is presented to us 'a magistral artifice of the eighteenth century'. What we miss are Gibbon's deep roots, not only in the erudition, but in the preoccupations of the seventeenth century. The 'Age of Enlightenment' cannot be treated as if it were a hothouse plant: its scholarship and its attitudes (Gibbon's attitude to religion, to take a highly-pertinent example) did not grow in a sheltered environment. Gibbon's problems, and

* *History* LIV, 1969, pp. 248–50.

the erudition that he brought to bear on them, had first forced themselves to the surface in the harsh climate of religious conflict in the seventeenth century. This explains why we still go back to Gibbon to understand the rise of the Christian Church in the Roman Empire: for the sharp smell of bitter prejudices and of ideological warfare still hung around him as he wrote the *Decline and Fall*.

If Gibbon is shorn of his past, he is also denied a future. For the cumulative impression of these essays is to deny Gibbon's relevance to the modern scholar. It is worthwhile grasping the difficult contribution of G. E. von Grünebaum, 'Islam: The Changing Perspective' to realize the extent to which a modern man is prepared to place the mountain-mass of German Romantic historicism between himself and the eighteenth century. We value the interest in the exotic in our modern culture, its 'affirmative faith in the pluralism of values'; we appreciate the art and are aware of the profundity of the thought-forms; we sympathize with the anxieties of the men of the Later Roman Empire; we would not wish to climb back over this barrier to Gibbon's studied indifference to vast areas of the culture of Late Antiquity. Unfortunately, history is not only the history of creativity: by identifying himself too closely with the creative achievements of a past age, the historian risks merging into the silver lining of a cloud; he forgets that he also has to face the problems of hatred, of statecraft, of demagoguery and (most difficult of all, perhaps) of mediocrity. The grandiloquent euphoria of Professor Ladner's 'The Impact of Christianity' fails to answer Gibbon, because it refuses to meet what Gibbon met. The balance of destructiveness and creativity in the rise of the Christian Church in the Roman Empire cannot be discussed in terms of a reassuring dichotomy between powerful ideas and frail men. For the powerful ideas placed power in the hands of men; and, as Gibbon knew only too well, from the immediate past of his own age, these men set about wielding it. Miriam Lichtheim comes closer to the ambivalent force of Christianity in the Near East, when she speaks of both 'a new identity' *and* 'a new intolerance'. To neglect the importance of the intolerance that went hand in hand with religious creativity, is to miss some of the most blatant landmarks of the period. Professor Warren Hollister, for instance, can sum up, in safely conventional terms, the debate on the 'continuity' between the Roman and the Germanic kingdoms, while overlooking the fact that the only form of 'continuity' between Roman and barbarian of which anyone was conscious in the Later Empire was a common adherence to Catholic orthodoxy, and that this was denied to some of the most effective Western Mediterranean states by a wall of dumb hatred: 'Happy the nose that cannot smell a barbarian' is the remark of a future Catholic bishop.

If a modern man is superior to Gibbon, it is not by floating above the ambivalent feelings which the Later Roman Empire still awakes in us—it is by having heightened his ambivalence. For we differ from Gibbon in having found much that is of direct value and concern to us within the Later Roman period. We have to face the fact that the creativity we admire happened in an age that was quite as desperate and ugly as Gibbon saw it to be—an age of absolutism and terror, that fostered timorous conformism and blind ideological and sectional prejudice. What is more, this creativity itself, by throwing up new religious groupings such as the Christian Church and its divisions, and by placing power in the hands of new men, such as bishops and barbarians, made this age even more desperate. Some of us who are most sympathetic to the cultural achievements of Late Antiquity would have left this society in the grips of a strange and rancorous creativity as precipitously as Gibbon himself intended to leave Lausanne during the French Revolution—'at the first stroke of a rebel drum'. *Pro nobis fabula narratur*. 'The classicist believes in the devil in history,' writes Andrew Lossky: the effect of these thought-provoking essays, on this reviewer, has been to turn to Gibbon again, to discover on what terms the modern historian must put him back in.

Review of:
THE GREAT CHURCH IN CAPTIVITY.
A STUDY OF THE PATRIARCHATE OF
CONSTANTINOPLE FROM THE EVE OF
THE TURKISH CONQUEST TO THE GREEK
WAR OF INDEPENDENCE
Steven Runciman. Cambridge University Press, 1968.*

This book has plainly been written as a labour of love: 'For the study of the orthodox faith of Eastern Christendom some intuitive gift is needed'. The 'Great Church' that is in captivity, one feels at every page, is not only the Greek church under Ottoman domination; it is, rather, the idea of a 'Great Church'—a Church where the hard lines of Western dogma are softened in the golden haze of an apophatic mysticism, where the tearing doubts of the Western believer are soothed away in the warm stream of a continuous tradition. This is the 'Great Church' that is languishing throughout the book: a religious tradition cut off in our own imagination, depleted yet tantalizing as a classical face glimpsed beneath the smokestains and the cluttering silverwork of an icon. It is this religious tradition which the author tries to set free for us, by reaching across a barrier in the Western mind—a barrier whose sad beginnings he has traced in *The Eastern Schism* and in the *History of the Crusades*.

The book conjures up the essence of the Greek orthodox tradition from the fourteenth to the nineteenth century, and tells of the tentative approaches of the post-Reformation churches to it. It has range, substantial erudition discreetly mobilized and—one must add —that brittle clarity of a narrative based almost exclusively on literary sources (and for the sixteenth and seventeenth centuries, mainly foreign ones at that) which continues both the achievements and the limitations of the *History of the Crusades*. We come away

* *Oxford Magazine*, 20 June 1969, pp. 380–81.

with an almost visual impression of vivid details, like the sharply-etched, cold Byzantine faces that look out among the mustachios and baggy trousers of a Moldavian fresco. We follow ecclesiastical mirages as they flicker from London to Aleppo, from Saxony to the orchards of Wallachia; we meet nimble *émigres* and opaque prelates; and we learn many facts deeply detrimental to human nature. But, on this occasion, a current of poignant feeling runs through the narrative. The obsessive theme of an alternative ordering of the Christian life in the Eastern Mediterranean gives a depth and unity that makes the *Great Church in Captivity* one of Runciman's best books.

The first part is the clearest account in English of the spirituality and culture of late medieval Byzantium: the author dwells lovingly on issues, on personalities who seem to garner in the richness of a thousand-year-old civilization. Nothing is more painful than the rapid depletion of that inheritance after the Turkish Conquest. One can always blame the Turks—and with good reason. But the terms on which a religion survives in a hostile environment depends, also, on what the religion itself can offer in the daily life of men in hard times. It strikes this reviewer that the Byzantine legacy to Greek orthodoxy was a heavy one to bear.

For this legacy was ideally suited to maintain the identity of a group, but at a high cost of inflexibility and passivity. The author states, proudly, that 'Byzantium was fundamentally a democracy' (p. 73), that the laity participated actively in ecclesiastical disputes, and that the Holy Spirit could speak through a layman. But this was largely because, in Byzantium, the Holy Spirit had become so thoroughly predictable. The author makes an invidious comparison with Russia 'where the populace was ignorant and usually inarticulate'. The problem is rather different. In Russia and in Western Europe, the laity was kept away from active participation not because they were uncultivated, but precisely because they had tended to participate too vigorously. [See, most recently, *Hérésies et sociétés dans l'Europe pré-industrielle. 11e au 18e siècles*, ed. Jacques Le Goff, 1968 and R. I. Moore, 'The Origins of Medieval Heresy', *History* LV, 1970, pp. 21–36.] The safely embedded 'democracy' of Byzantium never spilled over into an explosive proliferation of heresies and questionings. Distressing and crude though the popular movements of twelfth-century Europe or fifteenth-century Russia may have been, they were a sign that the disturbing 'charge' of the

Christian message had not been 'earthed' by centuries of tacit *consensus* in a great Empire. 'Happy is the nation without a history' does not apply to religion. In later centuries, change came to the Greek church from the outside only. The orthodox community had not been modified by internal tension. A Greek would have found it difficult to change within it: he must either break from it like a plastercast (as did the remarkable Calvinist patriarch, Lucaris), or keep it in a dusty corner, among other family-heirlooms (as did the later Phanariots when they annexed it to the 'Great Idea' of a Greek Revival).

Inflexibility, perhaps, is related to a split in Byzantine ethics. This split is the obverse of that apophatic tradition of mysticism which the author appreciates so highly, and understands so very well. Applied to dogma, the warm obscurity of a God of Whom little can be known is comforting and humane; but there is a harsher streak than this in the Byzantine tradition. For a God Who cannot be known may tend to become, for the average man, a God of unmodified dread; His mercy may appear merely as a spectacular suspension of the iron law of His retribution; and, among men, it is only by spectacular—and, so, infrequent—breaches in the iron law of a man's hard relations to his fellows that this retribution is turned aside. To love one's neighbour becomes a paradoxical gesture, inspired less by concern for one's fellowmen, as by the need to make part-payment of a debt to an unmeasured God for an unfathomable sin. Faced by such harsh, looming demands, a man can seek reassurance only by adhering to those ways of his ancestors that had swaddled the Unknowable in accustomed gestures, in the warmth of shared sentiments, in long memories. Only an exceptional man like Nicholas Carbasilas could see in the traditional liturgy a transformer that passed the raw charge of the Unknown God into daily life: more often, one feels, it was placed like an ornate screen between the frailties of the average man and the angry eyes of his Pantokrator.

The Byzantine tradition, with its vast history and geographical range, contained many more strands than these. But the historian, though he may use sympathy to evoke a religion, runs the risk of wishful thinking if he does not ask whether, in fact, one strand predominated to the detriment of others—and why. Here the author has not chosen the field where the historian may yet be able to give an answer. This is a book about the great. There is a sad connection

156

between the efflorescence of Byzantine culture and the extreme fragility of the aristocratic *élite* on which it depended. The Turkish conquest burst that rainbow-coloured bubble; with the Patriarchs and the Phanariots of later centuries we find ourselves in a vivid, but yet narrower field. To delineate the role of orthodox Christianity, the historian must go beneath history. He has to turn ethnographer and social anthropologist. He must collect folktales and immerse himself in the rhythms of village-life. The succession of recent monographs on Mediterranean peasant communities may bring us nearer than does this pageant of gifted *déracinés* to the early modern history of the Balkans.

For, strangely enough, this is a book without icons. These are the most touching clues to the continuity and quality of the orthodox tradition in early modern times. The traveller to Mistra cannot help feeling reassured as he passes from the flame-like, inviolable majesty of those aristocratic figures of the fourteenth and fifteenth centuries, into a side-chapel, to find, in a crude painting of Ottoman times, Christ portrayed—at last—as a beggar.

PART II

Rome

ASPECTS OF THE CHRISTIANIZATION
OF THE ROMAN ARISTOCRACY*

Perhaps the most significant feature of the end of paganism in Rome is that we do know about it; in the words of one of the earliest students of this death of a religion, Beugnot, 'L'histoire n'a daigné qu'assister aux funérailles du paganisme.'[1] That this is so is due largely to the central position occupied in the religious history of the late fourth and early fifth centuries, by the senatorial aristocracy of Rome. The direction of modern research has served to amplify our appreciation of their rôle. The 'Romans of Rome' continue to hold the centre of the stage. Ever since Beugnot, their paganism has been placed in a massive frame. Ample justice has been done to their claim to represent, in the cultural, the political and the social, as well as in the religious, life of the Later Roman Empire, the *pars melior generis humani*.[2] They can stand for the past; for the continuity of the Roman Senate[3] and for the preservation of Roman classical culture.[4] The careers and outlook of their religious leaders have come to be studied in great detail; Vettius Agorius Praetextatus, especially, now stands for the culmination of the most vital tendencies in Late Roman Paganism.[5] The archaeology of this period,

* *Journal of Roman Studies*, LI, 1961, 1–11. [On this subject, water has flowed more swiftly under academic bridges than is usual. I have attempted to make good some of my own deficiencies in more recent articles, and to do justice in these, to the most significant recent literature.]

[1] A. Beugnot, *Histoire de la destruction du paganisme en Occident*, Paris 1835, Vol. 1, 2.

[2] Symmachus, *Ep.* 1, 52.

[3] See, generally, Lécrivain, *Le Sénat Romain depuis Dioclétien*, Paris 1888; and P. de Francisci, 'Per la storia del senato Romano e della curia nei secoli V e VI,' *Atti Pont. Acc.* ser. iii, XVII, 1964-47, 275-317. [See p. 66.]

[4] Especially F. Klingner, *Vom Geistesleben Roms des ausgehenden Altertums*, Halle, 1941. [See p. 188.]

[5] He has received two detailed monographs in Dutch and Flemish respectively: Nicolaas, *Praetextatus*, Nijmwegen, 1940 and P. Lambrechts, *Op de*

in Rome and Ostia, has revealed both their style of life and the tenacity and consistency of their devotion to those Roman and 'oriental' cults which are discussed in the *Saturnalia* of Macrobius.[1] Quite apart from the religious situation of these men, we have come to appreciate that their gigantic wealth and unchallenged prestige had made it possible for them to influence decisively the political and social, as well as the religious, future of the Western Empire;[2] and it is this awareness of the position of the senatorial class in the society of the Later Roman Empire which promises to add a new dimension to their official rôle as members of the Roman Senate, Prefects of the City and priests of the public Roman religion.[3] Inevitably, since Seeck's monumental introduction to his works, Symmachus has remained at the centre of our picture, hardly through any renewed appreciation of his style, but just because his correspondence shows him at the centre of what had remained to him a small and, seemingly, unchallenged world.[4] Perhaps the most interesting feature for an historian of this circle, in the recently-discovered poems of his friend, Naucellius, is that they have nothing new to contribute; they mirror exactly this quiet world, dominated, in its literary expression, by the traditional forms of the 'good life':

---

grens van Heidendom en Christendom, het grafschrift van Vettius Agorius Prae-
textatus en Fabia Aconia Paulina, Med. Kon. Vlaamse Ak. XVII, 3, 1955. For a convenient summary of the career and reputation of Nicomachus Flavianus, see J. Guey, *Rev. Ét Anc.* 52, 1950, 77–89. For a general survey: A. Piganiol, *L'Empire chrétien*, Paris, 1947, 234–9 and K. Latte, *Römische Religionsgeschichte*[2], Munich, 1960, 366–71.

[1] H. Bloch, 'A new document of the Last Pagan Revival in the West, A.D. 393–4'. *Harvard Theol. Rev.* 38, 1945, 199–244 and table of priesthoods. [Now in *The Conflict between Paganism and Christianity in the 4th Century*, ed. A. D. Momigliano, 1963, pp. 193–218.] R. Meiggs, *Roman Ostia*, Oxford, 1960, esp. 211–13 and 388–403.

[2] See especially S. Mazzarino, *Aspetti sociali del quarto secolo*, Rome, 1951; and A. H. M. Jones, 'The Decline and Fall of the Roman Empire', *History* 40, 1955, 209–62. [See pp. 165 sq. and 232 sq.]

[3] L. Harmand, *Le Patronat sur les collectivités publiques*, Paris. 1957. Note the analysis of the 'imponderable' elements in the authority of the Prefects of Rome, in A. Chastagnol, *La Préfecture urbaine à Rome sous le Bas-Empire*, Paris, 1960, 459–462.

[4] O. Seeck, *Q. Aurelii Symmachi quae supersunt* (*Monumenta Germaniae Historica, Auctores Antiquissimi* VI, 1), Berlin, 1883; J. A. McGeachy, *Quintus Aurelius Symmachus and the Senatorial Aristocracy of the West.* Dissertation, Chicago, 1942 (Typescript); D. Romano, *Simmaco*, Palermo, 1955.

Parcus amator opum, blandorum victor honorum
hic studia et Musis otia amica colo
Iunius Ausoniae notus testudinis ales,
quodque voluptati est, hinc capio atque fruor:
rura, domus, rigui genuinis fontibus horti
dulciaque imparium marmora Pieridum.
Vivere sic placidamque iuvat proferre senectam,
docta revolventem scripta virum veterum.[1]

The upshot of this research has been a vivid cross-section of the pagan, senatorial class, extending roughly in time over the period covered by the active life of Symmachus—that is from 375 to 402. Like most cross-sections, however, it suffers from an inherent disadvantage; almost inevitably, and especially when it is taken across a class as ostensibly self-confident as the late Roman Senate, it is static. Yet Symmachus and his fellow-pagans lived in an age of rapid religious change, gleefully described by their Christian contemporaries as the fulfilment of the prophecies of the Old Testament. In the next century, their descendants continued to represent the *pars melior generis humani*—but as Christians. Thus a question has been posed acutely by the state of our present knowledge; what we have reconstructed is the coherence of the conservative elements in the Late Roman aristocracy; what we still need to explain is their gradual transformation in the *tempora Christiana*.

This article cannot claim to offer a complete explanation of the Christianization of the Roman pagans. Its main purpose is to approach, from a limited viewpoint, a problem in the interpretation of the religious history of the Later Roman Empire.

It had been believed, by many Christians since Constantine, that the Christianization of the Empire had come to depend on the authority of an emperor *militans pro Deo* (Ambrose, *Ep.* 17). Inevitably, the disestablishment of the official pagan cults of Rome, by Gratian in 382, and, finally, by Theodosius, took the form of a definitive act of public authority. Indeed, this exercise of authority by the Emperor was held by contemporaries to be so important that Prudentius, in his *Contra Symmachum* of 402, could represent the

---

[1] No. 5, *Epigrammata Bobiensia*, II, ed. F. Munari, Rome, 1955, p. 55. See W. Speyer, 'Naucellius u. sein Kreis. Studien zu den Epigrammata Bobiensia,' *Zetemata*, Heft, 21, Munich, 1959. [See P. Brown, *The World of Late Antiquity*, 1971, pp. 115–118.]

end of paganism in Rome as having taken place in an atmosphere of impeccable legality, according to the traditional Roman forms: in a meeting of the Senate, presided over by the Emperor Theodosius, Jupiter was defeated by Christ in a division of the house![1]

Needless to say, this explanation by Prudentius is a poetic fiction; the exercise of his authority in so blunt a manner by a Christian Emperor could never, in itself, explain the religious transformation of Rome. For this reason, it has seemed important to place the emphasis, in this study, upon those factors which affected the diffusion of Christianity within the senatorial families themselves—to examine the working of the common ties of marriage and culture as they affected the religious transformation of this class.

There has been a tendency to neglect the *Histoire des Moeurs* of the Later Roman Empire, in Rome;[2] the main sources, such as the writings of Jerome, are Christian, and, in consulting these, the historian may feel that he has been led from the unambiguous 'realities' of Imperial legislation and senatorial politics into a hot-house world of piety. But, to appreciate a change as profound, and far-reaching in its consequences, as the spread of Christianity in the most influential class of the Western Empire, due attention must be paid to such 'internal' factors; they ensured that the change in the official religion of Rome took the form, not of a brutal rejection of the past by an authoritarian régime, but of a transformation in which much of the Roman secular tradition was preserved.

Such an approach must, also, attempt to define the position of the emperor in the religious life of the age. It is, therefore, hoped that this article may contribute, in its narrow field, to the solution of the problem posed in the recent book of Dr. André Chastagnol, by his reconstruction of the manner in which the Christian policy of the emperors impinged on the political life of the leading Roman families;[3] that is, that, of the many problems of later Roman History, the greatest is that created by the conversion of Constantine and illustrated by the fate of paganism in Rome—the interaction of

[1] *Prudentius, Contra Symm*, II, 608 ff. [On the Imperial initiative, see now A. Cameron, 'Gratian's Repudiation of the Pontifical Robe', *Journal of Roman Studies*, LVIII, 1968, pp. 96–102.]

[2] An exception, of course, is Sir Samuel Dill, *Roman Society in the Last Century of the Western Empire*, 1898, esp. Book I, chapter I, 'The pagan aristocracy and the confusion of parties'.

[3] Chastagnol, o.c. [p. 162, n. 3] part iii, 'Les Préfets', 1–457, and *Les Fastes de la Préfecture urbaine*, 1962.

public authority and private belief in an age of dramatic political and religious change.

Before we study the conversion of the Roman families in terms of the *Histoire des Moeurs*, we must consider a view which offers a simple way to the understanding of this change in terms of a conflict of authority. It has been suggested that the struggle between Christianity and paganism can be understood in terms of the continuation of a pre-existing tension—that is, as a struggle, on various levels, between the pagan Roman Senate and the Christian Roman Emperor. Such a view, which invokes the impressive continuity of Roman history, has much to recommend it. The disestablishment of paganism by Gratian, in 382, was, unambiguously, a unilateral act on the part of a Christian emperor, enforced to the detriment of the Senate, which Symmachus claimed to represent. The defeat and suicide of Flavianus, in the civil war waged against Theodosius, in 394, is a similar, dramatic, turning-point; it has earned for this last pagan leader a comparison with Cato of Utica.[1]

The hope of understanding the position and aims of the pagan senators in these terms has led to great ingenuity. Above all, we have tried to isolate a specifically 'senatorial' attitude to the Christian Emperors; and we have only been able to find it in some of the least obvious sources—such as in the *Scriptores Historiae Augustae*[2] or in the 'ideological' content of tokens such as the *contorniati*.[3] Such interpretations, with similar efforts to explain the pagan resistance in terms of a defence of their threatened social position,[4] have been treated with a certain amount of scepticism. They do, however, open up a royal road to explaining why the paganism of these men did not continue. In asserting their religion, the senators of Rome were led to flout the authority of their emperor; and, in failing, they

---

[1] C. Julian, *Hist. de la Gaule* VII, 1926, 317.

[2] For instance E. Demougeot, 'Flavius Vopiscus est-il Nicomaque Flavien?' *Antiquité Classique* 22, 1952, 361–82. [The game continues, see p. 48, n. 4.]

[3] Esp. A. Alföldi, *Die Kontorniaten; ein verkanntes Propagandamittel d. stadtröm, heidnischen Aristocratie in ihrem Kampf gegen das christl. Kaisertum*, Budapest, 1943. See the criticisms of J. M. C. Toynbee, *JRS* XXXV, 1945, 115–21 and the wider remarks in S. Mazzarino, *Doxa* 4, 1951, 121–48.

[4] An interpretation suggested by L. Malunowicz, *De Ara Victoriae quomodo certatum sit*, Wilno, 1937, 108–19, fully developed by McGeachy, o.c. [p. 162, n. 4], 129–52, and criticized by Baynes, *JRS* XXXVI, 1946, 173–7 = *Byzantine Studies*, 361–6. It has been revived by F. Paschoud, 'Réflexions sur l'idéal religieux de Symmaque', *Historia* XIV, 1965, pp. 215–35; I remain unconvinced: see inf. p. 187.

revealed not so much the weakness of their religion, as of their political position. In the words of André Piganiol:

> Seulement ils se trompaient, car ce n'est point Accius et Virgile, Auguste ou même Antonin, qu'il fallait prendre pour modèle, mais bien Scipion et Marius. C'est en abandonnant le commandement des armées que cette aristocratie s'est condamnée, et ainsi s'explique le caractère archaïsant et désuet de son impuissante propagande.[1]

Inevitably, such an emphasis has concentrated attention on the public crises in the relations between Roman paganism and the Christian court. The end of paganism is seen, in concrete terms, as a tragedy of distinct acts: it includes the removal of the Altar of Victory and the disendowment of the Roman cults by Gratian in 382, the abortive appeal of Symmachus in 384, the *peripateia* of the elevation of Eugenius in 392, and the tragic dénouement of the defeat and suicide of Flavianus at the battle of the Frigidus, in 394. The remaining evidence for acute tension between Christians and pagans has been grouped, almost instinctively, around these 'turning-points'. Thus the most detailed and least squeamish of the anti-pagan lampoons—the 'contra paganos' (Cod. Paris, 8084)—is usually taken to refer to the reaction of 392-4 and has, so, been called 'Adversus Flavianum'.[2]

The principal difficulty of this interpretation is that it provides no sufficient explanation of the aftermath of the religious struggle between Senate and Emperor. After the débâcle of the battle of the Frigidus, the prestige of the 'Romans of Rome' continued unaffected by the outcome of the civil war, throughout the fifth century. The most striking evidence of this is the letter of the Emperor Valentinian III to the Roman Senate, in 431; it is inscribed on the base of an honorary statue erected to Flavianus, of all people. Here the Emperor shows an ability to forget the tensions of the immediate past which would be incredible in any other age. The paganism

[1] A. Piganiol, *Journ. des Savants*, 1945, 28.

[2] On the authority of Mommsen, *Hermes*, 1870, 350–63. This has been challenged by G. Manganaro, 'La reazione pagana a Roma nel 408–9 d.c. e il poemetto anomino "contra paganos",' *Giorn. it. filol.*, anno XIII, no. 3, 1960, 210–224. [J. F. Matthews, 'The Historical Setting of the *Carmen contra paganos*', *Historia* XIX, 1970, pp. 464–79 has made the best case for the identification of Flavianus, which I would now accept—while remaining unconvinced that the history of paganism in Rome can be reduced to a few dramatic moments of 'Revival.']

of Flavianus, and his rôle in the usurpation of Eugenius, are passed over in silence; instead, the eclipse of so great a name is ascribed to 'blind misrepresentation'. Valentinian, a pious Christian, is prepared to greet the sons of this pagan rebel, and the Senate, as politely as his grandfather Theodosius had always done; Flavianus, as a learned historian and dutiful servant was to receive a statue worthy of the 'more wealthy commonwealth' in which he had shone.[1]

This paradoxical rehabilitation was by no means exceptional. In the events of the appeal for the Altar of Victory, in 384, the same pattern of respect for the 'Romans of Rome' appears. The opportunist court at that time, anxious to maintain an 'Italian front' against two zealous new men—Maximus in Gaul, and Theodosius in the East—had no hesitation in employing eminent pagans and keeping them in office for a long time after the resounding snub to their paganism engineered by S. Ambrose in his letters 17 and 18, to the boy-Emperor, Valentinian II. When Praetextatus died, only an extremist like Jerome could indulge in indecent glee (Jerome, *Ep.* 23, 2, 1); the court behaved handsomely. The Senate's petition for honorary statues was immediately granted. Symmachus was sufficiently moved by this public demonstration of respect. He rounded on the extremists of his own party, who had intended, in defiance of religious protocol, to allow the Vestal Virgins to erect a statue of their own to Praetextatus;[2] in his view, the court, whatever their religious beliefs, had both done what was expected of them and all that needed to be done: 'inlustrior enim laus est de caelesti profecta iudicio' (Symm. *Rel.* 12, 4).

These incidents show an interrelation between court and senatorial aristocracy which cannot be explained in terms of a sharp dichotomy terminated with the failure of Flavianus. The 'Romans of Rome' remained indispensable. Carefully managed under Stilicho, they were still able, in the political chaos caused by the arrival of Alaric and the usurpation of Attalus—in 408-9—to express their views and to adopt their own religious measures for the safety of their City.[3] In the next century, the surface of their secular traditions

---

[1] *CIL* VI, 1783. See esp. Solari, *Philologus* 91, 1936, 357 sq.

[2] Symm. *Ep.* II, 36 to Flavian. See Bloch, art. cit. [p. 162, n. 1], 217–18, who interprets this issue as illustrative of a difference in spiritual outlook between the two currents in Roman paganism.

[3] Esp. S. Mazzarino, *Stilicone*, Rome, 1942, 231–49. Generally, E. Demougeot, *De l'unité à la division de l'Empire Romain*, Paris, 1951, 448–87, and G. Manganaro, art. cit. [p. 166, n. 2], 219–23. [See pp. 189–90.]

remained intact. Aëtius could pose for them as the 'Restorer of Liberty';[1] and even when there is no emperor left to woo them, the barbarian adventurers continue this tradition of respect. In the reigns of Odoacer and Theodoric, the senatorial mint resumed its activities, with a series of coins which showed Romulus and Remus, with the Wolf on the reverse and 'Roma Invicta' on the obverse.[2] Behind these courtesies lay the fact, emphasized in the early studies of Sundwall and Stein, of the unchecked preponderance of these Italians over a bankrupt and hamstrung court.[3] It was no less difficult than before to separate this tradition of perennial respectability from its pagan roots. It is hardly surprising that the Lupercalia should have continued to be celebrated, under the patronage of senators, until the end of the fifth century.

Yet this façade of continuity only masks an important change. When Pope Gelasius turned his attention to the Lupercalia, he could condemn them as a superfluous relic.[4] His opponent, Andromachus, was a Christian (§ 7); the Pope's answer had been provoked by a notoriously Christian criticism—an anti-clerical attack on the morals of one of his clergy (§ 2). In his argument he can appeal, conclusively, to the past; he points out that the ancestors of Andromachus had already decided to break with the traditions of Roman paganism (§ 28). It is, therefore, plain that the Pope is writing in a city whose upper-class had, at some time in the past, conformed to the *tempora christiana*; although it is hardly surprising that, as the Senate of Roma Invicta, they should have conformed on their own terms.

This, broadly speaking, poses the problem which needs to be answered. At some time—or, more precisely, over a certain period— the secular traditions of the senatorial class, traditions which one might have assumed to be intimately bound up with the fate of their pagan beliefs, came to be continued by a Christian aristocracy.[5] To

---

[1] As in a recently-discovered inscription: *Ann. Épig.* 1950 no. 30; see A. Degrassi, *Bull. Comm. Arch.* 72, 1946, 33–44. [See now B. L. Twynan, 'Aetius and the Aristocracy', *Historia* XIX, 1970, pp. 480–503.]

[2] See Stein, *Hist. du Bas-Empire* II, 44.

[3] Sundwall, *Weströmische Studien*, 1915, 150–61. Stein, *Histoire du Bas-Empire* I, 337–47. [But see p. 233.]

[4] 'Ep. adversus Andromachum', ed. G. Pomarès, 'Gélase Ier, Lettre contre les Lupercales et dix-huit Messes du Sacramentaire Léonien', *Sources Chrétiennes*, no. 65, 1959.

[5] [The impression is now confirmed, most notably by Alan Cameron, 'The

understand this 'sea change', it is necessary to consider the 'Romans of Rome' in themselves, apart from the public crises which they had weathered so effectively; and to see whether the Christianization of their class was not part of a long-term development, as elusive but, ultimately, as decisive as any change of taste.

The greatest difficulty in sketching this evolution lies in the highly-specialized nature of the literary evidence. It is hardly surprising that this evidence is exclusively Christian; but it is important, also, to remember that it reflects the preoccupations of a peculiar current in Christianity. As revealed in the correspondence, above all of Jerome and, to a lesser extent, in the works of Paulinus, Augustine, Pelagius and Palladius, the history of the conversion of the Roman families is part of the history of the impact of an extreme 'oriental' form of asceticism on the religious life of Rome. This ascetic movement represented a radical departure from the previous Christian traditions of Rome; its leaders were not Romans themselves; its ideals involved a rejection of the social life of the City and almost inevitably, the abandonment of Rome for the centres of the new devotion—the Holy Places and Egypt.[1]

Thus, the correspondence of Jerome throws a vivid, but exceedingly erratic, light on the Roman scene.[2] Since 385, he had had no first-hand acquaintance of the events which he describes; his most instructive letters, indeed, are cast in the *ex post facto* form of encomiums of the dead.[3] His intervention against Jovinian in 393 is typical of his eccentric position; written from a safe distance, his defence of virginity was so violent that his Roman friend, Pammachius, thought it best to suppress it.[4] His lively pictures of the

---

Date and Identity of Macrobius', *Journal of Roman Studies*, LVI, 1966, pp. 25–38; and by J. F. Matthews, 'Continuity in a Roman Family: the Rufii Festi, of Volsinii', *Historia* XVI, 1967, pp. 484–509.]

[1] For a full analysis of the ideals and chronology of this movement as it affected Rome: D. Gordini, 'Origine e sviluppo del monachesimo a Roma', *Gregorianum* 37, 1956, 220–60. [See pp. 221–6.]

[2] See F. de Cavallera, *S. Jérôme, sa vie et son œuvre*, Louvain, 1922, esp. I, 1, 84–120. [D. S. Wiesen, *Jerome as a Satirist*, 1964, is disappointing: see p. 210–213.]

[3] e.g. *Ep.* 108 to Eustochium on the death of Paula (404); *Ep.* 127 to Principia on the death of Marcella (413).

[4] Jerome, *Ep.* 49, 12, *CSEL*, 54, 367–9, with a characteristic complaint: 'Delicata doctrina est pugnanti ictus dictare de muro et, cum ipse unguentis delibatus sis, cruentum militem accusare formidinis'!

Roman families among whom he found support are deeply flawed with theological rancour: thus, Melania the Elder, one of the founders of the ascetic movement to the Holy Land, was condemned out of hand for her loyalty to Rufinus, as the woman: 'cuius nomen nigredinis testatur perfidiae tenebrae';[1] although a leading *dévot*, and a near relation-by-marriage of a branch of the Caeionian family which Jerome describes in great detail, she is passed over in silence.[2]

The general effect on our evidence of this narrow sympathy is most apparent, less in its occasional unreliability, than in the implicit delimitation of the range of our knowledge. It is limited in time to little more than a generation.[3] It is equally drastically limited in extent: Jerome, for instance, is content to describe the circle Pammachius in terms of the four philosophical virtues or the four-horsed chariot by which the prophet Elijah ascended into Heaven![4]

There might be a way out of this dilemma posed by the literary sources. The recent epigraphic evidence for the Roman nobility has greatly increased our knowledge of their paganism; it might add to our understanding of their Christianization. This has certainly been true of the family of the Anicii—a family which had stood aloof, throughout the fourth century, from the ascetic movement: the funeral inscription of the head of the family and the doyen of Roman society, Sextus Petronius Probus, shows a very different type of aristocratic piety;[5] and, among the most surprising discoveries in recent years, has been that of the inscription, known hitherto from a literary tradition, written by a representative of the other branch of that family—Anicius Bassus—for Monica, the mother of S. Augustine who had died, in 387, in Ostia[6]. In many cases, however, this 'indirect' evidence has outstripped our knowledge from the literary sources to an embarrassing extent. An interesting example of this is shown in attempts to identify a leading Christian lady: Italica. The Italica to whom Augustine wrote in 409

[1] Jerome, *Ep.* 133, 3, *CSEL* 56, 246. For these significant omissions see F. X. Murphy, 'Melania the Elder: a biographical note,' *Traditio* v, 1947, 59–77 at pp. 59–60. [Now see pp. 208–214.]

[2] In Jerome, *Ep.* 107 'ad Laetam'.

[3] An excellent guide to the chronological distribution of Jerome's letters is in Cavallera, o.c. (n. 28), 1, 2, 153–65, *Regesta Hieronymiana*.

[4] Jerome, *Ep.* 66, 2–3, *CSEL* 54, 648–9.

[5] *CIL* vi, 1756.

[6] See Meiggs, o.c. [p. 162, n. 1], p. 400.

seems to have played an important part in Roman religious life; Augustine can canvass her views in a theological debate.[1] The Italica to whom John Chrysostom wrote, in 406, may be the same; she is in a position to intervene with the Pope, and, perhaps, also with the Emperor, on behalf of Chrysostom at a crucial moment of his career.[2] Symmachus, also, refers politely to 'his sister' Italica.[3] The recent epigraphic evidence, however, has made it unwise to see in these Italicas the same person. There is now the Anicia Italica of an Ostian drainpipe, who is presumably the wife of a hitherto unknown man, Valerius Faltonius Adelphius;[4] and the Italica of an altar-support in the Lateran, presumably, again, the wife of an unnamed man.[5] Until we know more of either the new Valerius Faltonius Adelphius or the mysterious 'Prefect of the City, Patrician and Consul Ordinary', we can only assume that there may be more than one Italica, and that to create a single person out of the welter of Late Roman family names is to attempt to draw the net too tight. It is a sobering reminder of the fact that the homogeneity of the Roman 'patrician' families of this time is a pious hope—expressing a laudable intention of belonging to the traditionally recognized core of the *pars melior generis humani*;[6] it cannot be assumed by the prosopographer.

We are, therefore, left with the 'tone' of the religious transformation, as shown in the literary evidence and the few inscriptions, rather than with any independent, statistical, solution of the problem.

---

[1] Augustine, *Epp.* 92 and 99, *CSEL* 34, 436–44; 533–5, where she is a widow, with sons, interested in the property of the 'clarissimus et egregius iuvenis' Julianus, adjacent to the church in Hippo. He may be the Julianus who died without issue mentioned in *Sermo* 355, 4. For his house in Hippo, Marec, *Libyca*, I, 1953, 95–108.

[2] John Chrys. *Ep.* 170: *PG* 52, 709 sq. This letter is significantly placed between letters to two known members of the Anicii, Proba and Iuliana, at a time when their close relative, Anicius Probus, was consul.

[3] Symm. *Ep.* IX, 40.

[4] 'Valeri Faltoni Adelfi v c et in et Aniciae Italicae'. *N.S.* 1953, p. 170 n. 32. See Meiggs, o.c. (n. 6.), 212–13.

[5] [17 letters?] 's. v.c. et inl. p.u. pat. cons ord et Italica inl. f.' *Riv. arch. crist.* 33, 1957, 95–8, *Ann. Épig.* 1959, n. 237. [*The Prosopography of the Later Roman Empire*, I, 1971, pp. 465–466 judiciously divides the Italicas.]

[6] See the attempt of the Emperor Alexander Severus to trace his descent from the Metelli, SHA *Vita Alex. Sev.* c. 44: cf. the caustic comments of Jerome, *Ep.* 130, 3, *CSEL* 56, p. 177 'ut ramorum sterilitatem radix fecunda compenset, quod in fructu non teneas, mireris in trunco'.

There is one obvious feature in the *histoire des moeurs* of the fourth century as it affected religion; that is, mixed marriages. Christian opinion seems to have changed considerably on this issue; Augustine could say that a mixed marriage, regarded by S. Cyprian as a sin, was now no longer avoided as such.[1] The most striking example, from a family of which we know more than usual, is the position of the Caeionii at the end of the century.[2] Of the four sons born of pagan parents around the middle of the century, two are known; the daughters of both—Albina and Laeta respectively—were pagans: Caeionius Rufius Albinus was an intimate contemporary of Symmachus;[3] Pubilius Caeionius Caecina Albinus was known to Jerome as a Pontifex.[4] The results of their choice of wives are well known; the daughters of both—Albina and Laeta respectively—were devout Christians; their granddaughters, Melania the Younger and Paula, were the objects of solicitous attention from Christian contemporaries. In his letter to Laeta, Jerome could paint an idyllic picture of the gradual evolution of this mixed family; the old pagan pontiff seemed doomed by the solidarity of his Christian kinsfolk:

candidatus est fidei, quem filiorum et nepotum credens turba circumdat. Ego puto etiam ipsum Iovem, si habuisset talem cognationem, potuisse in Christum credere.[5]

In fact, such a picture—borne out in a more fragmentary manner for the other families—poses many problems. A mixed marriage might often be a *mariage de convenance* between unequal partners; thus, the Christian heiress, Proiecta, of the Esquiline casket in the British Museum, may have married, at the age of 16, an elderly pagan of over 60.[6] What is remarkable, then, is either the tolerance of the husband or—what one might suspect but cannot show—the strength of the Christian families in ensuring that the religion of the bride was respected. Only Praetextatus seems to have taken in hand the religious education of his wife;[7] the rest seem to have ignored

[1] Aug. *De Fide et Operibus* 21, 37 *CSEL* 41, p. 80.

[2] See the excellent study of A. Chastagnol, 'Le sénateur Volusien', *Rev. Ét Anc.* 58, 1956, 241–53, with a revised stemma on p. 249, and 'La famille de Caecina Lolliana, grande dame païenne du IVème siècle, *Latomus* xx, 1961, pp. 752–758.

[3] Macrobius, *Saturnalia* III, 4, 12; VI, I, 1.

[4] Jerome, *Ep.* 107, 1: *CSEL* 55, p. 291.

[5] ibid.

[6] As supposed by Weigand, *Jahrb. deutsch. archäol. Inst.* 52, 1937, 128–9.

[7] See *CIL* VI, 1779.

the advice of Plutarch, that husbands should make their wives conform to their choice of gods as of friends. Indeed, the formidable circle of patrician ladies gathered around Jerome needs to be explained in general terms of the position of women in the aristocracy of the late Roman Empire.[1] In this respect, the contrast with Antioch is suggestive; in this city, intermarriage, Christianity in the women's quarters and the ascetic propaganda of John Chrysostom were equally prominent features of fourth-century society without producing such high-spirited ladies.[2]

It is the wives, themselves, that are often an insoluble problem. We do not know when they became Christian. With the doubtful exception of a Vestal Virgin,[3] there are no spectacular conversions among them; the 'conversions' of a Melania the Elder or of the heroines of Jerome are from the 'world' not from paganism. They do, in fact, add a new dimension of time to the problem. The cases of Marcella and Melania suggest that the heiresses of important families were already Christian in the age of Constantine and Constantius II.[4] We would like to know to what extent these influential Christians could be defined as belonging to 'provincial' or 'new' families, from the more Christianized parts of the Empire—Melania the Elder, we know, was a Spaniard;[5] at the moment, however, we do not know enough of the recruitment of the later Roman aristocracy to answer the question in these terms.[6]

[1] See some acute remarks on the position of these *clarissimae feminae* in S. Mazzarino, *La fine del mondo antico*, Milan, 1959, 135–43. But it must be remembered that the most obvious feature of this emancipation, the relaxation of the divorce-laws, shocked Christian sentiment: see *Ps. Aug. Quaestiones*, cxv, 12 and 16, *CSEL* 50, 322 and 323. Yet Jerome can get over even this stumbling-block in the character of his heroine, the divorcée, Fabiola: *Ep.* 77, 3, *CSEL* 55, pp. 38–9: 'aliud Papinianus aliud Paulus noster praecepit'!

[2] See P. Petit, *Libanius et la vie municipale d'Antioche au IVe siècle*, Paris, 1955, 191–216; P. Canivet, *L'histoire d'une entreprise apologétique au Ve siècle*, 1957, esp. 21–41; and A. J. Festugière, *Antioche païenne et chrétienne*, Paris, 1959.

[3] Prudentius, *Peristephanon* II, 524 ff. *CSEL* 61, 315: O. Marucchi, 'La vestale cristiana', *Nuovo boll. di arch. crist.* 1899, 207.

[4] See Theodoret, *Hist. Eccl.* II, 16, on the negotiations between Constantius II and Liberius, in which Liberius is accused of having snubbed the Emperor 'to please the Senate'.

[5] See Murphy, art. cit. [p. 170, n. 1], p. 60 and *stemma* p. 63.

[6] For Italian connections equally distributed between pagans and Christians at the end of the fourth century, see the list of '*Patroni ex origine*' of Italian towns in Harmand, o.c. [p. 162, n. 3], 204–5. [But see p. 67, n. 1.]

Despite Jerome's optimism, mere intermarriage remained an in-conclusive means of Christianization. To emphasize this aspect would mean ignoring the immense *esprit de corps* of a Roman *gens*, with its pagan roots. In the case of the Ceionii the most striking feature is not the factors contributing to the religious disintegration of the family—by mixed marriages or asceticism; it is the solidarity of the male members in an ancestral paganism. The son of Rufius Albinus, Rufus Antonius Agrypnius Volusianus, remained a pagan up to his death-bed in 437; the son of Caecina Albinus, Caeionius Contucius Gregorious, was regarded, more ambiguously, in 400, as a 'veteris sanctitatis exemplar'.[1]

The paganism of Volusianus seems to have been taken for granted. He appears with his father in the ostensibly self-confident circle of pagans to which Rutilius Namatianus expressed his belief in the permanence of Rome—after the Gothic sack of 410.[2] And yet, he belongs to a completely new generation: he was, perhaps, born in the early 380's—that is, after the official suppression of paganism. He is treated by Augustine, in 412, with great tact and esteem; on the surface, he belongs to a Christian family consisting of his mother, sister and niece; the exchange of letters contains only what the intermediary could regard as 'threadbare arguments'[3]—argu-ments such as could be made from within Christianity itself; the correspondence is later referred to by Augustine as 'my letters on the virginity of Mary to the illustrious Volusianus, whom I mention with esteem and affection',[4] and yet, despite his caution, Volusianus seems to have remained loyal to a tradition which may have begun with his father. He had stickled at the Incarnation, and the closely related problem of the Virgin Birth; but so, also, had his father before him.[5] Thus we see two generations of Roman pagans pro-

[1] *CIL* VI, 1706.

[2] Rut. Namat, *De Reditu suo* I, 415 ff.

[3] Marcellinus to Augustine, *Ep.* 136, 1: *CSEL* 44, p. 94. But Volusianus was hardly in a position to push his objections to Christianity to extremes at that time; his criticism of the political relevance of Christian morality is notably subdued, see *Ep.* 136, 2, *CSEL*, XLIV, 95.

[4] Augustine, *Enchiridion* 34, 10. [See now p. 206, n. 2, and P. Brown, *Augustine of Hippo*, 1967, pp. 300–2.]

[5] Photius, cod. 230 ed. Becker, p. 271, B. 29. This has been taken by Seeck, o.c. [p. 162, n. 4], p. CLXXXI to imply that Rufius Albinus was a Christian. E. Liénard, 'Un courtisan de Théodose', *Rev. belge de philol.* 13, 1934, 73 ff. has built upon this assumption the ingenious theory of a politic conversion, in 389, as a sequel to the defeat of Maximus by Theodosius.

voking from the greatest Christian thinkers of their time—Ambrose and Augustine respectively—impeccable statements of the central doctrine of the new religion.[1]

Yet if we are to believe the *Vita Melaniae Iunioris*, Volusianus was eventually converted on his deathbed by his niece, Melania the Younger, when on an official mission to Constantinople in 437.[2] He died, murmuring benignly to his niece, that 'If Rome had had three such priests as the patriarch Proclos, the word "pagan" would have vanished from the city'.[3] It is a touching family reunion. It may, however, have been no more than that: the *Vita* implies that Volusianus had been more afraid of being forcibly baptized by the Emperor Theodosius II;[4] and Melania, despite the close relation with her uncle on his deathbed, had arrived in Constantinople, in the first instance, not to convert her relative but to help him in the negotiations for a political marriage.[5]

Indeed, with the reasonable hope before them that the pagan tradition of the family would be continued in their sons, the heads of such families could well afford to be indiscriminating. The elder sister of Volusianus, for instance—Albina—was married to a Christian member of a largely Christian family—Valerius Publicola. Publicola was a moderate: educated in Rome while his mother Melania the Elder was in the Holy Land, he had grown up as a Christian, but as a thorough aristocrat. He cuts a tragic figure; caught in the spiritual currents of his age, he only became reconciled on his deathbed to the asceticism of his 21-year-old daughter, Melania, whose personal austerities, encouraged by her mother and grandmother, had, despite his anxious attentions, already led to a stillbirth and whose charitable intentions threatened to dissolve the enormous wealth of both families.[6]

---

[1] For the fate of Augustine's answers to Volusianus, see, P. Courcelle, *Rev. de l'Hist. des Religions* 146, 1954, 174–93.

[2] The Latin *Vita* in *Analecta Bollandiana*, 8, 1889, 19–63 [L]; the Greek in ibid. 22, 1903, 7–49 [G]. [Now in D. Gorce, *Vie de sainte Mélanie* (Sources chrétiennes 90), 1962: the Greek text.]

[3] *Vita L.* II, 22, p. 53. *G.* c. 53 p. 37. [Gorce, p. 232.]

[4] *Vita L.* II, 23, p. 53 p. 37. [Gorce, p. 232.]

[5] *Vita L.* II, 19, p. 51. *G.* c. 50, p. 35. [Gorce, p. 232.]

[6] *Vita L.* I, 12, p. 29. *G.* c. 7, p. 12. [Gorce, pp. 138 and 140.] On his death, see the reassuring opinion of Augustine: *Ep.* 94, 3, *CSEL*, 34, 2, p. 499 'maternae humilitatis nobilitatem, si veste non gesserit, mente praetulerit'. In his relations with Augustine he had shown himself nothing if not scrupulous, *Epp.* 46 and 47, *CSEL* 34, 123–36.

It should be realized, however, that the generation of Volusianus was, in many ways, exceptional. It saw both the height of the ascetic movement and the disaster of the sack of Rome [see now 'Pelagius and his Supporters', inf. p. 189–192]. The headstrong behaviour of Melania and her husband, Pinianus, in selling out the family property for charity, had involved both moderate Christians and pagans in a scandal, where domestic tensions were swept into a wider current of violence. The truculent intervention of Serena, the wife of Stilicho, on the side of the young couple, at a time of mounting tension, threatened to turn the affair into a political issue.[1] The incident ended with the execution for high treason of Serena, a punishment which, though carried out at the instance of the Christian Galla Placidia, was regarded by the pagans as a punishment for her sacrilege;[2] and with the lynching of a pagan Prefect of the City in the act of confiscating what remained of the property of the Christian couple.[3] Following close on this, the Gothic siege, the pagan reaction of Attalus in 409 and the sack of the City, ensured that the internal divisions between pagan and Christian were crystallized as seldom previously. To a Christian, such as Pelagius, the horrors of the siege were a timely reminder of the Last Judgement.[4] It is hardly surprising, after such an experience, that the Anician family, as refugees in Africa, should have, at last, countenanced the new devotion by consecrating Demetrias, the grand-niece of Petronius Probus, as a nun: 'invenisse eam, quod praestaret generi, quod Romanae urbis

---

[1] *Vita L.* I, 11–13, pp. 28–31 and *G.* c. 11–13, pp. 14–16. [Gorce, pp. 146–154.] The date of this interview with Serena, 404, does not coincide with the evidence for the death of Publicola, mentioned there, but ascribed to 407–8 on the basis of the correspondence of Augustine with Paulinus. Courcelle, *Rev. Ét. Anc.* 53, 1951, 276, n. 1, has therefore, rejected the account given in the *Vita Latina*. The date of the interview is taken as resting on other evidence—on the ages of the couple and the coincidence of their marriage with the return of Melania the Elder to Rome, in 397. [See Gorce, p. 137 n. 2.]

[2] Zosimus v, 38. Only the *Vita G.* (c. 14, p. 17) mentions the good relations between Pinianus and Serena. [Gorce, pp. 154–156.]

[3] *Vita L.* II, 1, p. 42. *G.* c. 19, p. 19–20. [Gorce, p. 166.]

[4] Pelagius, *Ep. ad Demetriadem*, c. 30, pl. 30, 45. 'Recens factum est, et quod ipsa audisti, cum ad stridulae buccinae sonum Gothorumque clamorem, lugubri oppressa metu domina orbis Roma contremuit. Vbi tunc nobilitatis ordo? ubi certi et distincti illius dignitatis gradus? Permista omnia et timore confusa, omni domui planctus et aequalis fuit per cunctos pavor. Vnum erat servus et nobilis. Eadem omnibus imago mortis.'

cineres mitigaret.'[1] We can only guess at the effect of the same events on a young man such as Volusianus; they, at least, stirred up sufficient resentment to provoke Augustine's 'City of God'.[2]

Many less fully-documented cases, before these years of crisis, however, show the strength of the movement towards a respectable, aristocratic Christianity. By far the most important of these is the conversion of the Anician family, and, especially, the late baptism of the *doyen* of Roman society, Petronius Probus, celebrated in a grandiose epitaph, and acclaimed by Christian writers as the 'first' conversion among the Roman aristocracy.[3] Despite the courtesy of these Christian admirers, this spectacular 'conversion' had been long-prepared. There is no evidence that Probus had ever been a pagan; early in his official career, he was known as the patron of S. Ambrose;[4] Proba, the grandmother of his wife, had already written a Vergilian canto on the 'Creation and the Life of Christ'.[5] Indeed, the baptism of Probus only marks the culmination of a long career dedicated to the aggrandisement of his family and to the founding of a tradition of self-interested loyalty to the powers-that-be;[6] as the inscription implies, he had now exchanged the intimacy of the Emperor for that of Christ. Typically, the ivory diptych, presented by his son to the Emperor Honorius, in 406, is the best-produced example of a specifically Christian ideology of the empire; the Emperor holds in his left-hand an orb surmounted by the traditional winged Victory, but in his right he carries the standard of Constantine—the Labarum—with 'in nomine Xpi vincas semper'.[7]

---

[1] Jerome, *Ep.* 130, 6, *CSEL*, 56, p. 181.

[2] See Courcelle, 'Propos antichrétiens rapportés par S. Augustin', *Rech. augustiniennes* I, 1958, 149–95. Only later was Gelasius, l.c. [p. 168, n. 4] 31 able to place the pagan argument on its head by saying that the decay of Rome was due to the survival of pagan practices. [See p. 190 and P. Brown, *Augustine of Hippo*, pp. 199 and 292.]

[3] *CIL* VI, 1756; Prudentius, *Contra Symm.* I, 552 ff.

[4] Paulinus, *Vita Ambrosii*, cc. 5 and 8 (see c. 25 for evidence of the inordinate respect of the author for the *potentia Probi*).

[5] Edited Schenkl, *CSEL*, 16, 1888, 569–609.

[6] See Amm. Marc. XXVII, 11 and esp. XXX. 5, 4: 'non ut prosapiae suae claritudo monebat, plus adulationi quam verecundiae dedit'; and A. Momigliano, 'Gli Anicii e la storiografia del VI° secolo d.C.', *Atti Accad. Lincei, Rendiconti, cl. mor. stor. e filol.*, ser. 8, 11, 1956, 279–280, for the same pattern of intimacy with semi-barbarian politicians such as Aëtius.

[7] E. Delbrueck, *Die Consulardiptychen*, Berlin, 1929, n. 1, 84–7, where he calls himself the 'famulus' of the Emperor.

In the case of the Anicii, also, it is possible to appreciate a change which cannot be shown on a family-tree. For Christians and pagans to live together, and, eventually, to accept whole-heartedly the *tempora Christiana*, a common ground had to be found in the classical culture of the age. The Vergilian cento of Proba is a symptom of this profound change.[1] It is a type of 'salonfähig' Christian literature which brought out the most waspish in Jerome;[2] yet, in the eyes of Isidore of Seville, it gave Proba a place as the only woman ecclesiastical writer.[3] The final address to her husband Adelphius strikes an impeccably classical note of self-confidence which the subsequent history of the family did nothing to belie:

> i decus, i, nostrum, tantarum gloria rerum,
> et nos et tua dexter adi pede sacra secundo
> annua, quae differre nefas. celebrate faventes
> hunc, socii, morem sacrorum: hunc ipse teneto,
> o dulcis coniunx, et si pietate meremur,
> hac casti maneant in religione nepotes.[4]

This impression of an unexplored border-line between the pagan and Christian culture of Rome is increased by the rare examples of a frank syncretism: for instance, by the frescoes discovered in 1956, in a catacomb on the Via Latina, where scenes from the Bible and from pagan mythology are juxtaposed.[5]

It is this drift into a respectable Christianity—a drift which may have begun as early as the reign of Constantius II—which explains how a Christianized Roman aristocracy was able to maintain, in Italy, up to the end of the sixth century, the secular traditions of the City of Rome. These traditions had survived effectively into the fifth century; they had not been seriously damaged either by the

---

[1] F. Ermini, *Il centone di Proba e la poesia centonaria latina*, 1909. [It was not even very orthodox, see I. Opelt, 'Der zürnende Christus im Cento der Proba', *Jahrbuch für Antike und Christentum*, VII, 1964, pp. 106–116.]

[2] Jerome, *Ep.* 53, 7, *CSEL* 54, 453–4.

[3] Isidore of Seville, *De vir. illustr.*, c. 18, *PL* 83, 1093: 'cuius quidem non miramur studium, sed laudamus ingenium'!

[4] ll. 689–94.

[5] See H. I. Marrou, 'Une catacombe pagano-chrétienne découverte à Rome', *Bull. Soc. Art.* 1956 [1958], 77–81. [See now A. Ferrua, *Le pitture della nuova catacomba di Via Latina*, 1960 and H. I. Marrou, 'Sur une peinture de la nouvelle catacombe de la *Via Latina*', *C. R. Acad. Inscript. et Belles Lettres*, May 1969, pp. 250–256.]

defeat of the pagan leaders who had rallied to the cult of Rome, nor by the flood-tide of the ascetic movement. That this was so is due, in part, to the slow transformation of whole families, such as the Anicii, the Valerii and, eventually, even of the Caeionii; a transformation which continued beneath the surface of the spectacular crises. It led to a blurring of the sharp division between a pagan past and a Christian present which is noticeable in the poems even of so austere a critic as Paulinus; faced by a whole clan of Roman senatorial Christians—the Valerii—he can even go as far as to raise and accept a problem which Augustine had raised only to reject— the problem of pagan virtue:

> miramur opera conditoris ardui
> et praeparatos a vetustis saeculis
> successionum mysticarum lineis
> pios stupemus inpiorum filios;
> tamen in tenebris inpiarum mentium
> lucis videmus emicasse semina
> in tempore ipso noctis antiquae sitis,
> quibus probata quamlibet gentilibus
> mens et voluntas lege naturae fuit.[1]

This survival of secular traditions was aided by the Imperial government, which, in the fifth century, insisted on accepting the 'Romans of Rome' on their own valuation—even to the extent of being buried in Rome, their 'capital', as their colleagues had been buried in Constantinople in the past century[2]—and, paradoxically, by Pope Leo. From the very beginning of his pontificate, Leo ensured that the 'Romans of Rome' should have a say in the religious life of the City: acting together, the Senate and the Pope had cleansed the City of Manichaeans.[3]

This gesture, in fact, is symptomatic of a significant change. At the end of the fourth century, it would be possible to write of the Christianization of the Roman aristocracy with only a passing mention of the Roman church itself. Pammachius stands almost alone

---

[1] Paulinus, *Carm.* XXI, 230–8, *CSEL* 30, 165–6.
[2] See H. Koethe, 'Zum Mausoleum d. weström. Dynastie bei Alt-Sankt-Peter', *Röm. Mitt.* 46, 1931, 9–26.
[3] Leo, *Epp.* VII and VIII (*Constituto Valentiniani* III), *PL* 54, 620–4. See Chastagnol, o.c. (n. 8), 177–8 on the previous reduction of the religious jurisdiction of the Prefect of the City in favour of the Pope.

in having stayed at Rome, and dedicated himself to the normal religious life of the City.[1] By the time of Leo, however, the Roman *dévots* of the age of Jerome, Augustine and Pelagius, had returned to the public life of Rome. Demetrias, for instance, had been advised, by Pelagius, in 413, to live a life of complete self-effacement, avoiding even charitable works;[2] at the persuasion of Leo, however, she founded a church on her estate in the Via Latina dedicated to S. Stephen—a memory of her retirement in Africa, almost a generation before, when the newly found relics of the saint had first made their appearance.[3] In the inscription, the advice of Pelagius is forgotten; she retains the illustrious name of her family.[4] It is probable, also, that the family-church founded in his palace by Pammachius received, at last, its due recognition.[5]

The success of the work of integration begun immediately by Leo shows clearly the importance of this 'sea-change' in the religion of Rome for the later development of medieval Christendom. Both traditions—the Christian and the secular—contributed to the position of Rome in the early middle ages. Contemporary opinions on the career of Aëtius illustrate this fusion: to the Senate he could remain the 'restorer of Liberty'; to Gallic writers he was campaigning under the aegis of S. Peter.[6] It is not impossible that the sermons of Leo, carefully-prepared, monumental statements as they are of the claims of S. Peter and the privileged position of his Roman congregation, were regarded as a final reassurance of the direct descendants of the anxious pagan leaders of the fourth century. Symmachus had invoked the figure of Rome to defend the altar of Victory and had made it his constant concern to ensure that Roman religion should continue to be celebrated in Rome; his descendants could be made to feel that their own, considerably more precarious, world still depended upon a similar religious hegemony, admirably upheld by Leo in the name of Peter and Paul:

[1] See esp. Paulinus, *Ep.* 13, 15, *CSEL* 29, 96: which emphasizes his isolation 'Poteras, Roma, illas intentas in apocalypsi minas non timere, si talia semper ederent munera senatores tui'.

[2] Pelagius, *Ep. ad Demetriadem*, c. 22, *PL* 30, 38.

[3] *Liber Pontificalis*, ed. Duchesne, Paris, 1886, 1, 238. See Antonelli, *Riv. arch. crist.* 1935, 173–5.

[4] *Liber Pont.*, I, p. 531: 'Demetrias Amnia virgo'.

[5] A. Prandi, *Il complesso monumentale della basilica celimontana dei SS. Giovanni e Paolo*, Rome, 1955, p. 475–7.

[6] See Greg. Turon, *Hist. Franc.* II, 7 (MGH Script, rer. Merov. 1, 69–70).

Isti sunt qui te ad hanc gloriam provexerunt, ut gens sancta, populus electus, civitas sacerdotalis et regia, per sacram beati Petri sedem caput orbis effecta, latius praesideres religione divina quam dominatione terrena.[1]

In such a study the defects of the evidence combine with the nature of the subject to give weight to Harnack's warning, that religious history runs on narrow lines. The picture which emerges, however, is significantly different from that of Ambrose and Prudentius, who attributed an overwhelming importance to the intervention of the Christian successors of Constantine. Due emphasis must, also, be placed on those commonplace links of culture and marriage which expressed the formidable solidarity of the 'Romans of Rome' in the face of the religious tensions of the age. The spectacular interventions of the emperors in the interests of Christianity, under Gratian and, to a lesser extent, under Theodosius and Honorius, not only solved nothing; they might even be said to have prejudiced the spread of their own religion by more peaceful means. When religion became involved with political issues affecting the authority of the emperors, whether this happened directly, as in 382, or indirectly, in the relations of Serena with the younger Melania and in the crushing moral defeat of the sack of Rome, the process of adaptation to the new official religion was brutally halted; parties became crystallized around leaders, and men such as Symmachus, Flavianus and Volusianus were forced to bring their religious grievances into the open.

Such a disastrous situation had been avoided, on the whole, before 382. The results of such tactful handling can be seen in the position enjoyed by Christian heiresses, such as Marcella and Melania the Elder, as early as the reign of Constantius II, and in the politic conformity of a great figure such as Petronius Probus under Valentinian I. Despite the complaint of Symmachus—'nunc aris deesse Romanos genus est ambiendi' (*Ep.* 1, 51)—the Roman aristocracy had already found a modus vivendi with those who adhered to the religion of the court; Publicola, the son of Melania, was brought up, evidently as a Christian, under the care of the Prefect of the City. The process of accommodation started in that early generation was less spectacular, and so less documented, than the

[1] Leo, *Sermo* 82, 1, *PL* 54, 422–3.

blatant renunciations later encouraged by Jerome; but in the long run, it would prove decisive.

After 410, the Imperial court could no longer offer any provocation: its effective control of Italy had been weakened by the barbarian invasions, and its control of the religious life of Rome had been abandoned to the popes. This state of affairs is reflected in the religious evolution of the later Caeionii. After 410, the ancestral paganism of a Volusianus seems to lack not so much conviction as an issue on which to fight. It is hardly surprising, then, that men who came from families in which Christianity had been, for generations, acceptable to their wives and relatives, should have, at last, adopted this official religion of an Empire which had no power left to hurt, but which, with themselves, continued to guarantee that a minimum of Roman civilization would survive in a dangerous world.

PELAGIUS AND HIS SUPPORTERS:
AIMS AND ENVIRONMENT*

The Pelagian controversy has long been the joy of historians of dogma: 'There has never, perhaps, been another crisis of equal importance in Church history', wrote Harnack, 'in which the opponents have expressed the principles at issue so clearly and abstractly' (*Dogmengeschichte*,[4] iii. p. 167 = *History of Dogma*, v, Dover edition, p. 169). More recently, the isolation of a large body of Pelagian literature concerned less with abstract principles than with exhorting and castigating Christian members of the aristocracy of the Western Empire, have tempted historians of Late Roman society to take an interest in Pelagius and his supporters. The Pelagian controversy has come to be interpreted as, in some way, throwing light on the social and political tensions of the declining Roman Empire.

Despite these attempts to place Pelagius in a secular context, one cannot resist the impression that the 'vast zone of silence', which stretches between the pagan and the Christian writers of the fourth century,[1] intervenes also between the Christian writers and the preoccupations of the Late Roman man in the street. A crevasse still separates the passion and creativity with which educated men conducted theological disagreements and the secular problems of the age. To attempt to throw ropes across this crevasse remains a risky business. The integration of ecclesiastical and secular history is frequently acclaimed as desirable. But when it is conducted with too strenuous a determination to reduce phenomena to a single explanation, with too great an anxiety to cut down to manageable proportions the intricacies of thinking men, this integration will take place on terms that can only impoverish both: the theologian will

Journal of Theological Studies, N.S., Vol. XIX, Pt. 1, April 1968, pp. 93–114.
[1] A. Momigliano in *The Conflict between Christianity and Paganism in the Fourth Century* (1963), p. 96.

see the complex and passionate concern of an Augustine or a Julian of Eclanum drained of life, by being presented as no more than an ideological superstructure; while the historian of the Later Empire will be equally dismayed by the reduction of the subtle functioning of Roman society to a stereotyped pattern of conflict between rich and poor, administration and provincials.

This paper, therefore, will not produce any single 'explanation' of the Pelagian movement. Still less will it attempt to relate Pelagianism in its initial phases (that is, from around 394 to 420) to any single series of political events—and, least of all, to the obscure revolutions of fifth-century Britain.[1] For, to attempt to relate Pelagius' ideas to political events in such a way is implicitly to limit the field of the social historian of the Later Empire. There is room, in the social history of this period, for more than the study of the most spectacular developments, for more than the analysis of the overthrow of governments and of the tensions of classes: there is room for a more intangible but equally important subject—for the forms taken by the struggle of the individual to define himself within or against society, for the efforts of groups of men and women to live a life, to create values for themselves, different from the conventional, the second rate, the unthinking life of their fellows. This is a more intimate, a more fragile theme: but I would suggest that it is essential for the understanding of the rise of Christianity in the Western Empire.

My method, therefore, will be more like that of the military historian, who, when given a sketch of a battle, will seek to transfer the

---

[1] J. N. L. Myres, 'Pelagius and the End of Roman Rule in Britain', *J.R.S.* 1 (1960), pp. 21–36 and J. Morris, 'Pelagian Literature', *J.T.S.* N.S. xvi (1965), pp. 26–60.

Scholars better equipped than I can take issue with the points raised in these articles. W. Liebeschuetz, 'Did the Pelagian Movement have Social Aims?', *Historia*, xii (1963), pp. 227–41, and Claude Moussy, *Gratia et sa famille* (1966), seem to me to have shown that the idea of *gratia* had more complex associations in the social life and linguistic usage of the Later Empire than those suggested by the texts cited by Myres, art. cit., pp. 24–6. It is a complexity of which Augustine himself was well aware: *Ep. ad Rom. incoh. expos.* 8–9.

W. Liebeschuetz, 'Pelagian Evidence on the Last Period of Roman Britain?', *Latomus*, xxvi (1967), pp. 436–47 and A. Cameron, *J.T.S.*, N.S. xix (1968), pp. 213–15, have removed many of the supports of Dr. Morris's hypothesis.

While it is impossible to veil my disagreement with these two scholars, it would be ungrateful not to record how much my own interest in the Pelagian controversy owes to their erudition and freshness of approach.

neat coloured squares of the conflicting regiments on to a map of the physical features of the area: he can, at least, point out the significance of some of the positions taken up by the opposing forces, in relation to the contours of the landscape over which they fought.

Pelagius lived in Rome until 410.[1] In Rome, he wrote his *Commentary on the Epistles of St. Paul*;[2] it was 'to a Roman' that he addressed his exhortations.[3] His most considered manifesto—his letter to Demetrias—was written at the invitation of leading members of the *Anicii*, the doyens of the Christian aristocracy of Rome.[4] His acquaintances included Paulinus of Nola, a man intimately connected with Roman Christian society;[5] his patrons, a Roman priest, Sixtus—who later became pope.[6] Pelagian ideas had an immediate resonance in just those areas of Italy that had always been overshadowed by Rome and its aristocratic residents; in Campania[7] and, most notably, in Sicily, an island of senatorial estates, noted, in the Later Empire, for the delights and the eccentricities of the senatorial life of *otium*.[8]

It is against this background that we must first attempt to place Pelagius.

[1] On the Roman residence of Pelagius, see G. de Plinval, *Pélage, ses écrits, sa vie et sa réforme* (1943), pp. 47–71—on this, as on every other aspect of Pelagius, fundamental but far from definitive.

[2] Ed. A. Souter, *Pelagius' Expositions of 13 Epistles of St. Paul*. Texts and Studies, 9, 1 (1923), (cited as Souter) now reprinted by A. Hamman, *Patrologia Latina, Supplementum I* (1958), coll. 1110–1374 (cited as *P.L. Suppl.*).

[3] The *Testimonia*: Aug. *C. ii Epp. Pelag.*, IV, viii. 21. Liebeschuetz, *Latomus*, xvi (1967), pp. 444–6.

[4] Pelag., *Ep. ad Demetriadem* (*P.L.*, 30. 15–45); de Plinval, *Pélage*, pp. 214–16.

[5] See, generally, P. Courcelle, *Les Confessions de S. Augustin* (1963), pp. 590–5 and Peter Brown, *Augustine of Hippo* (1967), pp. 342, 383, and 384.

[6] Aug. *Ep.* 191, 1.

[7] Ibid. 186, viii, 29; Quodvultdeus, *Liber Promissionum: dimidium temporis*, vi. 12, ed. R. Braun, *Sources chrétiennes*, 102 (1964), pp. 610–12.

[8] *Ep.* 'Honorificentiae tuae', 5th ed. Caspari, *Briefe, Abhandlungen und Predigten* (1894), p. 12 (cited as Caspari) = *P.L. Suppl.*, 1692, a *clarissima femina*; Aug. *Ep.* 156—at Syracuse. Julian of Eclanum ended his career in a Sicilian *vicus*: Fulgentius in *P.L.* 45, 1041–2. Many would have been refugees from Rome after 408, for whom see Rufinus, *Prol. ad Ursacium*, *P.G.* 12, 583–6; and *Vie de sainte Mélanie*, ed. D. Gorce, *Sources chrétiennes*, 90 (1962), ch. 19, 166–8. The evidence for philosophical and literary pursuits associated with the ideal of *otium* in Sicily has been collected by S. Mazzarino, *Rend. Acc. Lincei*, ser. 8, viii (1954), pp. 417–21 and A. Ragona, *Il proprietario della villa romana di Piazza Armerina* (1962).

For there is one feature of the Roman aristocracy of the late fourth and early fifth centuries which, I would suggest, throws some light on the circumstances of the rise and fall of Pelagianism in Rome.

This aristocracy was, as always, a heterogeneous and, in part, a nondescript body of men. We should not be misled by the impression created by the letters of Symmachus or by the inscriptions that show the *cursus honorum* of leading senators.[1] Many more senatorial residents of Rome have escaped our knowledge, simply by having escaped distinction.[2] They passed their life in the manner of many an ineffective and affluent nobility:[3] they ate too much;[4] they read light literature;[5] they gambled;[6] they fell in love with actresses;[7] the more enterprising risked their necks at adultery and the black arts.[8]

Yet the most striking feature of the age is the success with which contemporaries disguised this fact from themselves and, so, largely, from posterity. There is hardly a writer from this environment who does not give the impression of moving among an *élite*. Symmachus, the great pagan orator, is a notable example. He was a senator of moderate means and of middling political success. He is far from being the patrician figure of the imagination of some later historians. He is much more interesting. Here we have a man who has defined himself. He has studied to cut himself out, among his con-

[1] For whom see A. Chastagnol, *Les Fastes de la Préfecture urbaine sous le Bas-Empire* (1962). A. H. M. Jones, *The Later Roman Empire*, ii (1964), p. 550, rightly stresses the diversity of the Senate.

[2] For instance, Naucellius of Spoleto: W. Speyer, *Naucellius und sein Kreis. Studien zu den Epigrammata Bobiensia*, Zetemata 21 (1959). Unfortunately, it is just such senators, who lived outside the limelight of the traditional *cursus honorum*, who played a decisive role in the intellectual and religious life of the age; the majority of the Roman addressees of Augustine, Jerome, and Paulinus are equally obscure by traditional standards.

[3] Clearly perceived by Ammianus Marcellinus: see the most important treatment of A. Cameron, 'The Roman Friends of Ammianus', *J.R.S.* liv (1964), pp. 15–28.

[4] Amm. Marc. *Res gestae*, xiv. 6, 14: xxvii. 4, 34: Jerome, *Ep.* 33, 3.

[5] Amm. Marc. xxviii. 4, 14. [A suspicion delightfully confirmed by Sir Ronald Syme, *Ammianus and the Historica Augusta*, 1968.]

[6] Id. xiv. 6, 14.

[7] Ambrose, *de obitu Valentiniani*, 17. (It is interesting that the senatorial bishop—like the senatorial youths—expected the Emperor to be indulgent in such cases.)

[8] Amm Marc. xxviii. 1, 26–56

temporaries, by a passionate identification with the Senate and its pagan traditions. Overshadowed, as a political and social influence, by the Christian families connected with the court, constantly thwarted by the inertia and the opportunism of his colleagues, he punctiliously upheld, in the solemn protocol of the Senate-house and in the immemorial ceremonies of Rome, a rallying-point for an *élite* of men like himself, for a *pars melior generis humani*.[1]

Symmachus' position of strenuous conservatism is characteristic of a fluid and ill-defined society. The late fourth century saw a proliferation, even a confusion, of the ways in which a group could display its status.[2] For, beside the pagan Senate of a Symmachus, there was the 'Christian Senate' of a Jerome: here was another acutely self-conscious *élite*: 'Learn from me a holy arrogance: you are different from them.'[3]

Such groups were prepared to practise what they preached. One is not surprised to learn that Symmachus expected young men to bathe with senatorial gravity—no splashing, no diving.[4] But, at the age of 17, also, the younger Melania, when embarked on the ascetic life, found it easy to forgo the use of wine: 'For, even in the world, she had never touched it; because that is the way the children of senators are brought up in Rome.'[5] 'Look at how the daughters of noblemen behave', a Pelagian writer will exclaim: 'look at how they carry themselves; look at their careful education. . . . Inspired by their sense of high birth, they rise above the ordinary behaviour of

[1] This aspect of Symmachus has recently been described, with little sympathy or understanding, by F. Paschoud, 'Réflexions sur l'idéal religieux de Symmaque', *Historia*, xiv (1965), pp. 215–35.

[2] The proliferation of spurious genealogies is one feature of this confusion: see Brown, *J.R.S.* li (1961), p. 6, n. 42, p. 171, n. 6. It was a fashion shared by members of the Roman clergy: Jerome, *In Ionam*, iv, ad v. 6 (*P.L.* 25, 1147) A more profound symptom of confusion is the emergence of the women of senatorial families as leaders of the ascetic movement. All ecclesiastical writers state, quite frankly, that their heroines eclipsed the traditional honours of their menfolk: Aug. *Ep.* 150, Pelagius, *Ep. ad Dem*, 14 (*P.L.* 30. 30 B), Jerome, *Ep.* 130, 3. At a time when the consulship was thought to be in danger of falling out of the control of traditional families, pious exhortation played on genuine anxieties. The temptation to shine on behalf of, or at the expense of, the exclusively male tradition of public eminence was great, and constantly preferred—witness Jerome, *Ep.* 130, 6: 'quam sponsam hominis una tantum provincia noverat, virginem Christi totus orbis audivit.'

[3] Jerome, *Ep.* 22, 16.

[4] Symm., *Ep.* viii. 23.

[5] *Vie de sainte Mélanie*, ch. 22, p. 174 (ed. Gorce).

mankind . . . by habitual discipline, they have created in themselves a nature different from the common run of men.'[1]

Groups of men and women determined to live according to such distinctive standards of excellence were in constant need of mentors —from teachers of literature to father-confessors. They took these from the intelligentsia of the provinces. Pelagius, surrounded by his admirers in the Rome of the 390s and 400s would have been no more than the last figure in a long series, beginning, in the Late Roman period, with Plotinus, continuing through Marius Victorinus, Jerome, and the orator Magnus—a line of educators of senatorial families that included for a short time the biggest fish of all (the one, that is, that got away), the young *rhetor*, Augustine.[2] [We only know of the last eccentric needs and choices; but Nestorius, a Platonic philosopher of Athens travelled to Rome to heal a noble lady 'poisoned' by the memory of her previous reincarnations in the bodies of animals—Proclus in *Rempublicam*, II, pp. 324–325; the hermit Sarapion, clad in nothing but a loin-cloth, came to persuade a noble nun that, if she were truly above passion, she should walk naked through the streets—Palladius, *Historia Lausiaca*, xxxvii, 15; and Macarius, in Egypt, was constantly 'troubled by vainglorious thoughts . . . that he should visit the city of the Romans to cure the sick'—Palladius, ibid xviii, 23. Given such candidates for spiritual guidance, fourth-century Rome manage to remain inexplicably sober.] And there is no doubt that Pelagius' writings, and those of his followers, are by far the most accomplished reflections, in Late Roman literature, of this widespread striving to create an aristocratic *élite*. Behind the counsels of perfection of Pelagius, we can sense the high demands of *noblesse oblige* and the iron discipline of a patrician household. The ideal

---

[1] Pseudo-Jerome, *de virginitate*, 12 (*P.L.* 30. 178A).

[2] On Plotinus, see Porphyry, *Vita Plotini*, 7 and R. Harder, *Kleine Schriften* (1960), pp. 257–95. On Marius Victorinus, see Aug. *Conf.* viii and Diehl, *Inscript. lat. christ. vet.* i. 104 (the epitaph of his granddaughter); with P. Hadot, Introduction to Marius Victorinus, *Traités théologiques sur la Trinité, Sources chrétiennes*, 68 (1960), pp. 7–76 [and now, *Marius Victorinus, Recherches sur sa vie et ses œuvres* (1971)] and Courcelle, *Les Confessions*, pp. 69–74. On Flavius Magnus, see Diehl, *Inscript. lat. christ. vet.* i. 102 and Jerome, *Ep.* 70. On Augustine, see Brown, *Augustine of Hippo*, pp. 70–71. A Chastagnol, *La Préfecture urbaine sous le Bas-Empire* (1960), p. 453, n. 2 provides an impressive list of the intellectual interests of the Prefects of Rome; but Cameron, *J.R.S.* liv (1964), pp. 25–7, is a timely reminder that the senators did not always live up to their pretensions.

Christian of Pelagian literature was a *prudens*, carefully reared in conformity to the divine law, to be different from 'the ignorant crowd'.[1]

Pelagianism in its hey-day, therefore, between 390 and 410, had appealed directly to a powerful centrifugal tendency in the aristocracy of Rome—a tendency to scatter, to form a pattern of little groups, each striving to be an *élite*, each anxious to rise above their neighbours and rivals—the average upper-class residents of Rome.

And it is precisely this tendency that will be formally condemned in Pelagianism in Rome. The followers of Pelagius and Caelestius are the only religious group in Rome that will be condemned not only for being heretical, not only for being disturbers of the peace, but, also, for claiming to be superior to everybody else: in the words of the Imperial Rescript of 30 April 418: 'They consider that it is a sure sign of being low-born and commonplace, to think the same as everybody else; and a token of exceptional expertise— *singularis prudentiae palmam*—to undermine what is unanimously agreed.'[2]

To understand the exceptionally shrill note of this decree, we must bear in mind the dilemma of the Roman aristocracy in the previous twenty years, especially as it impinged on the Imperial court.

This aristocracy had been aimless and deeply divided. In the late 390s, feelings had run high, even among Christian families, over ascetic renunciations; that of the young couple, Pinianus and Melania, being the best known to us.[3] Such incidents had already driven a wedge into the Senate. With the approach of the Gothic army, late in 408, the old division between pagans and Christians in the Senate had come out into the open: we can glimpse the rancours of those terrible years in the accusations of collaboration with the barbarians that, later, surrounded the Christian family of the *Anicii*,[4] and in the smug account, in the *Life of St. Melania*, of the vengeance of God in the lynching of a pagan Prefect of the City during a food-riot.[5]

The years after 410 are marked by a reaction. Rome—its population shrunk, its shops empty, its landscape marred by the burnt-out

[1] *de malis doctoribus*, xviii. 3, Caspari, p. 104: *P.L. Suppl.* 1450.
[2] *P.L.* 48. 379–86.
[3] *Vie de sainte Mélanie*, chs. 8–14, pp. 141–57.
[4] Zosimus, *Historia Nova*, vi. 7 and Procopius, *de bellis*, iii. ii. 27.
[5] *Vie de sainte Mélanie*, ch. 19, p. 166.

shells of great palaces[1]—could no longer afford the luxury of harbouring conflicting groups. By 417, most of the old wounds had healed: the city itself had been repaired,[2] its public services got back to normal;[3] a studied optimism prevailed among pagan and Christian members of the governing-class;[4] the Emperor Honorius could celebrate his triumph in the City: and, in the procession of prisoners, there walked a tangible reminder of the result of religious division in the Roman Senate—the puppet-usurper, Attalus, who had been thrown up by a clique of romantic pagan senators in the crisis of 409–10.[5] These years, indeed, saw a strong *centripetal* movement. The need for solidarity is shown, above all, in the final welding together of Christian and pagan in a homogeneous Christianized aristocracy. This homogeneity had been prepared, in the Christian Church in Rome, by an emphasis on *concordia*, on 'unanimity', summed up in the carefully elaborated papal ideology of the *Concordia Apostolorum*, the agreement, on all matters, of Saints Peter and Paul.[6] This alliance would be visibly sealed, in the next decades, by the building and decoration of vast churches, whose size and impressive iconography would have asserted the privileged position of the Roman people and its bishop, after the catastrophe of 410, in as palpable a fashion as the great Baroque churches of the City would do, some 1,100 years later, after the Sack of Rome of 1527.[7] The newly achieved solidarity of the upper-class residents of Rome would not be allowed to be challenged. For there was a real danger, in such a situation, that in this nominally Christian aristo-

[1] See E. Demougeot, *De l'unité à la division de l'empire romain, 395–410* (1951), pp. 470–85, and S. Mazzarino, *Aspetti sociali del quarto secolo* (1951), pp. 239 f.

[2] *C.I.L.* vi. 37128 (of 412).

[3] Olympiodorus, *fr.* 25: (*F.H.G.* iv. 62) for 414 and *Cod. Theod.* xiv. 4, 10 (of 419).

[4] See P. Courcelle, *Histoire littéraire des grandes invasions germaniques*, 3rd ed. (1964), pp. 104–11. [See now J. F. Matthews, 'Olympiodorus of Thebes and the History of the West (A.D. 407–425)', *Journal of Roman Studies*, LXI (1970), pp. 79–97.]

[5] Prosper, *Chron.* ad ann. 417 (*P.L.* 51. 592A): on Attalus, see Demougeot, op. cit. (sup. n. 1), p. 449.

[6] M. Ch. Pietri, '*Concordia apostolorum et renovatio urbis* (Culte de martyrs et propagande papale)', *Mél. d'archéol. et d'hist.* lxxiii (1961), pp. 275–322.

[7] R. Krautheimer, 'The Architecture of Sixtus III: a fifth-century Renaissance?', *Essays in honour of Erwin Panofsky. De artibus opuscula*, 40 (1961), pp. 291–302.

cracy the old crevasses might open again, this time around a *Christian* heresy. And, after all, this is precisely what the ideas of Pelagius had threatened to do in Rome: in 417 and early in 418, the city was again divided between the supporters and the opponents of Pelagius; riots had even taken place.[1] In the circumstances of the time this was unpardonable; in Rome, Pelagius and Caelestius did not fall victims to the doctrinal exigencies of Augustine and his African colleagues; they were, rather, a minority whose tendency to create yet another separate *élite* was jettisoned by the leading residents of the city in their new bid for solidarity.

Seen in this light, the condemnation of the Pelagians in 418 is the symptom of an irreversible change. For it coincided, significantly, with the official Christianization of the Roman Senate. From this time on, the Senate would collapse inwards, around the Roman Church. By the time of Pope Leo, for instance, it will appear as a united Christian body, led by its bishop against recognized outsiders —against the Manichees.[2] The relations of the resident aristocracy of Rome and their clergy will not change from henceforth throughout the Middle Ages: the senators will back rival candidates for the papacy; they will squabble for the control of the lands of the Church;[3] but, after 418, they will never, at least until the time of Arnold of Brescia, again attempt to differ from their bishop in matters of doctrine.

Alaric, therefore, unwittingly sealed the fate of the Pelagian movement.

The Sack of Rome immediately depleted the Roman Christian community by provoking a *diaspora* of influential laymen and ascetics—Pelagius and many of his protectors among them.[4] The fortunes of Pelagianism in Italy, therefore, were left in the hands of a rump of priests and provincial bishops.

As for the great families who returned to their palaces in Rome, they would move with the times—towards uniformity. The ladies of the Anician family, for instance, had commissioned Pelagius to write to Demetrias; Demetrias' mother, Juliana, had sheltered him,

---

[1] Prosper, *Chron.* ad ann. 418 (*P.L.* 51. 592A).

[2] Brown, *J.R.S.* li (1961), pp. 10–11 [pp. 179–181].

[3] M. Ch. Pietri, 'Le Sénat, le peuple chrétien et les partis de cirque à Rome sous le pape Symmaque (498–514),' *Mél. d'archéol. et d'hist.* lxxviii (1966), pp. 123–39.

[4] For an interesting example of such an emigration, see Courcelle, *Histoire littéraire des grandes invasions germaniques*, pp. 60–63.

for a moment, from the scruples of Augustine and Alypius.[1] Now they will behave in character, as descendants of the great Petronius Probus, a grandee whose political career was more marked by the qualities of the flexible willow than of the sturdy oak.[2] Juliana remained 'an outstanding limb' of the Roman Church;[3] Demetrias will be associated with Pope Leo;[4] and so we may catch a glimpse of this typical family of the resident aristocracy of fifth-century Rome through the last embittered Pelagian tract—*de malis doctoribus*—in an unexpected position, quaking with fear and shame before the Judgement Seat of Christ, while the saints exclaim: 'Was it not *they* who, in this life, were known as more Christian than anybody else . . . they, whose fame was wafted through almost all the world?'[5]

To see Pelagianism, in this way, in terms of the general tendencies of its Roman environment may help us a little towards understanding both the momentum of the movement, in its opening phases, and the immediate circumstances of its suppression. We must now look closer, however, at Pelagius and the Pelagians, if we are to understand the aims they set themselves in this environment, and if we are to enter into the appeal of their ideas, and to assess the significance of their defeat.

There is only one definition of a Pelagian by Pelagius: he was a *Christianus*;[6] his followers strove to be *integri Christiani*—'authentic Christians'.[7] The behaviour of these *integri Christiani* was always thought of as being a reaction, an act of self-definition, the establishment of a discontinuity between the 'authentic' Christian and the rank-and-file of Christians in name only.

The problem of what *was* Christian behaviour, indeed, had

[1] *Ep.* 188, i. 3.

[2] See Amm. Marc. xxvii. 11, 2.

[3] Innocent, *Ep.* 15 (*P.L.* 20. 518).

[4] *Liber Pontificalis*, ed. Duchesne, i (1886), p. 238: see Brown, *J.R.S.* li (1961), p. 10. [p. 180].

[5] *de malis doctoribus*, xxiv. 3, Caspari, p. 112: *P.L. Suppl.* 1456.

[6] This is the point of the famous remark, in *de divina lege*, 9 (*P.L.* 30. 119): 'ego te christianum volo esse, non monachum dici'; cf. *Fragmenta Pelagiana Vindobonensia*, ed. Dold, *Rev. bénéd.* li (1939), p. 128: *P.L. Suppl.* 1561; *Ep.* '*Humanae referunt litterae*', 3, Caspari, p. 17: *P.L. Suppl.* 1377; *de vita christiana*, 1 and 6 (*P.L.* 40. 1033 and 1036). The idea is far more radically developed than in Augustine—see E. Lamirande, 'La signification de "christianus" dans la théologie de S. Augustin et la tradition ancienne', *Revue des études augustin.*, ix (1963), pp. 221–34.

[7] *Ep.* '*Humanae referunt litterae*', 3, Caspari, p. 18: *P.L. Suppl.* 1378.

reached a crisis in late fourth-century Rome. Too many leading families had lapsed into Christianity—by mixed marriages, by political conformity.[1] Among such people, no discontinuity existed between the pagan past and the Christian present. The conventional good man of pagan Rome had imperceptibly become the conventional good Christian 'believer'. Aristocratic habits of conspicuous waste, for instance, had merely continued unchanged as Christian almsgiving. Everybody agreed that it was 'better to give than to receive': it appears on an inscription, for instance, at Nola.[2] But, as a Pelagian pointed out, like all biblical tags used to ease the conscience nobody quite knew where it came from: and nobody wanted to know that Christ had also said: 'If you would be perfect: sell all you have and give to the poor.'[3]

'When I lived at home', wrote one convert to the message of Pelagius, 'I thought that I was being a worshipper of God. . . . Now, for the first time, I have begun to know how I can be a true Christian. . . .'[4]

Now one of the difficulties in interpreting the message of Pelagius is that it is only too easy to keep on the circumference of his thought and to miss its centre. What strikes the modern reader in the Pelagian writings are the extreme positions: we see Pelagianism, therefore, in terms of its radical emphasis on the independence of the individual, for instance, or on the equity of God's law;[5] or in its extreme views on the redistribution of wealth.[6] What we forget, often, is that these extreme positions are only *arcs on a circle*; they point to a centre—a centre which, as is often the case, is usually taken for granted by Pelagius and his followers. Yet we would be wrong to ignore this centre just because it does not strike us so forcibly; for movements gather strength, not only through their explicit

[1] Brown, *J.R.S.* li (1961), pp. 6–9 [pp. 172–177]

[2] Diehl, *Inscript. lat. christ. vet.* 1, 2474.

[3] *Ep.* 'Honorificentiae tuae', 4, Caspari, p. 10: *P.L. Suppl.* 1691–2.

[4] *Ep.* 'Honorificentiae tuae', 2, Caspari, p. 8: *P.L. Suppl.* 1690–1.

[5] As with Myres, *J.R.S.* l. (1960), pp. 27–9. The danger lies in the notorious 'timelag' between disciplines. Often the historian's interpretation of the function of a doctrine merely canonizes a description of a doctrine that is already out of date for the theologian. The Pelagius of Dr. Myres is the Pelagius of *Dogmengeschichte* and of the heresiologists, not necessarily the real Pelagius. On the limitations and persistence of the traditional image of Pelagius, see T. Bohlin, op. cit. (p. 195 inf., n. 2), p. 6.

[6] Morris, *J.T.S.*, N.S. xvi (1965), pp. 44 f.

programmes and their more *outré* slogans but through claiming to give effect to what the average supporter had always taken for granted.

This is particularly so in the case of Pelagius. He had the genius to harness his message to the most ancient and potent theme in Western Christian thought—to the idea of the Church. The Pelagian's sense of the free will enjoyed by the Christian, his promises of perfection, his inexorable insistence on obedience to the just law of God —all this is firmly based on a distinctive idea of the Church. For Pelagius and the Pelagian the aim always remained not to produce only the perfect individual, but, above all, the perfect religious group: *Sanctum esse populum suum Deus voluit. . . . 'Beata gens, cuius est Dominus Deus eius, populus, quem elegit in haereditatem sibi.'*[1]

Thus the most marked feature of the Pelagian movement is far from being its individualism: it is its insistence that the full code of Christian behaviour, the Christian *Lex*, should be imposed, in all its rigours, on every baptised member of the Catholic Church: 'There is *one* law for all. . . .'[2] 'Surely it is not true that the Law of Christian behaviour has not been given to everyone who is called a Christian? . . . There can be no double-standard in one and the same people.'[3] This insistence meant, in practice, that the standards of perfection, evolved in the past generation by the leading representatives of the ascetic movement, will be prescribed as the basis of the morality of the average Christian: the stream of perfectionism which, in a Jerome, a Paulinus, an Augustine, had flowed in a concentrated jet, will be widened, by Pelagius and his followers, into a flood, into whose icy puritanism they would immerse the whole Christian community. The exposure of the whole community to ideals held to be binding, previously, only on the few is the hallmark of the Pelagian literature: little wonder that it created

---

[1] *de vita christiana*, 9 (*P.L.* 40. 1038).

[2] Pelagius, *Ep. ad Dem.* 10 (*P.L.* 30. 26B).

[3] *de divitiis*, vi. 3, Caspari, pp. 32–3: *P.L. Suppl.* 1387. It is typical of the ecclesiological concerns of the author, and his audience, that the traditional 'naturalistic' argument for equality of ownership, from the common benefits of nature, is treated as less important than a new argument from the equal participation of all baptised Christians in the Sacraments, *de divitiis*, viii. 3. Caspari, pp. 35–6: *P.L. Suppl.* 1389–90: 'videamus si alia lex divitibus, alia est lata pauperibus, si alio illi, alio isti baptismate renascuntur, si non eandem peccatorum veniam santificationemque iustitiae consequuntur, si non uno omnes spiritu munerantur, si non eiusdem altaris communione vescuntur. . . .'

a crisis in the Catholic Church such as would not recur, to the best of my knowledge, until the spiritual turmoil of the twelfth century.[1]

This Christian community is defined by baptism. The *Christianus* of the Pelagian writings is the baptized Christian. It has been the singular merit of Dr. Torgny Bohlin, in his essay *Die Theologie des Pelagius und ihre Genesis*, of 1957,[2] to draw attention to this, the central position of baptism in the theology of Pelagius.

The implications of his study deserve to be stressed most forcibly. In the first place, there is little room for the caricature of Pelagianism first sketched by Augustine and often repeated by modern scholars: there is no out-and-out 'naturalism' in Pelagius, for the simple reason that the man who has recovered his natural capacity to act, inside the Christian Church, is discontinuous with any 'natural' man outside the Church. The rite of baptism, coinciding, more often than not, with the subjective experience of conversion, has placed a glass wall between the past and the present. The 'natural' man, of course, existed for Pelagius: Abel and Job, for instance, had achieved holiness by merely following the dictates of the natural law, engraved on their conscience; the heroes of classical antiquity, also, had achieved some more piecemeal 'sanctity'. But these naturally just men lived a long, long time ago, and Pelagius was very much a Late Roman man. The passing of time, for him, could only bring about decline:[3] the history of man was marked by the ineluctable onset of the forgetfulness of innocence, by the corroding rust of habit, as evil actions and examples had piled up as slowly and as

---

[1] H. Grundmann, *Religiöse Bewegungen im Mittelalter* (1935) esp. pp. 13–69, and M. D. Chenu, 'Moines, clercs, laïcs au carrefour de la vie évangelique (XIIème siècle)', *Rev. d'hist. ecclés. xlix* (1954), 59–89.

[2] T. Bohlin, *Die Theologie des Pelagius und ihre Genesis*, Uppsala Universitets Årsskrift, 9 (1957), pp. 29–43.

[3] e.g. Pelagius, *Ep. ad Dem.* 8 (*P.L.* 30. 24C); cf. Pelagius, *Expos. Ep. ad Rom.*, Souter, p. 24: *P.L. Suppl.* 1123. Ambrose, *Ep.* 45, 14–15, is typical of this mentality, which admits the existence of a 'natural' innocence, while relegating it to the distant past. Traditional doctrines on the original community of goods are similar: see Norman Cohen, *The Pursuit of the Millennium* (1957), Mercury Books (1962), p. 200: 'But—and this was central to his whole argument—Seneca was convinced that the old egalitarian order was not only lost but necessarily lost. As time passed, men had become vicious; . . .' This pessimistic attitude to history is a distinguishing feature of Latin Christianity: see A. Luneau, *Histoire du salut chez les Pères de l'Église. La doctrine des âges du monde*, (1964), p. 260, on Ambrose.

massively as a coral reef.[1] 'O wretched man that I am, who shall deliver me from this body of death?' For Pelagius it was axiomatic that this was the cry of the sinner on the eve of baptism.[2]

In this emphasis on the nature of the constricting force of habit, we have a subtle parting of the ways between Pelagius and Augustine. Pelagius was undoubtedly influenced by the early anti-Manichaean works of Augustine; like Augustine, he used the force of habit, a force, that is, created by previous acts of the free will, as a way of rejecting determinism while facing the observed fact that men do find it difficult to control their actions.[3] But, with Augustine, this force of habit became increasingly internal, deeply insidious. It established itself permanently in profound, unconscious layers of the personality: it worked, he thought, like the tendencies of the reformed drunkard towards alcoholism:[4] it betrayed itself—as later it would betray itself for Freud—even by so innocent a phenomenon as a slip of the tongue.[5]

For Pelagius, by contrast, habit remained essentially external to the personality:[6] it was a rust, a rust that could be rubbed off. Hence, the great emphasis placed by Pelagius on baptism and on the experience of conversion. For in such an act, habit could be broken; the past of a man could be sloughed off; from that time onwards, the exhortations of Pelagius would be devoted to creating—by a highly judicious ascetic discipline—the good habits that would perpetuate a state of regained innocence—the innocence that came from abandoning the past.[7] Characteristically, the innocence that Pelagius was

---

[1] Pelag., *Ep. ad Dem.* 8 (*P.L.*, 30. 24C).

[2] Jerome, *Dial. c. Pelag.* ii. 2–3 (*P.L.* 23. 560–1); Augustine, *de gratia Christi*, xxix, 43; *c. Julianum*, II. iii. 5 and VI. XXII. 73; *Op. Imp.* i. 67.

[3] For this dilemma in Augustine, see Brown, *Augustine of Hippo*, pp. 148–9; in Pelagius, see *Expos. Ep. ad Rom.*, Souter, pp. 58–9; *P.L. Suppl.* 1144. The example of swearing may have been taken directly from Augustine, *c. Fortunatum*, 22—a work that may have been made available to Roman readers through the library of Paulinus of Nola.

[4] Augustine, *Sermo*, 151, 4.

[5] Id., *de perfect. iust.* xxi. 44.

[6] Pelagius, *Expos. Ep. ad Rom.*, Souter, p. 59; *P.L. Suppl.* 1144: 'Habitat quasi hospes et quasi aliut in alio, non quasi unum, ut accidens scilicet, non naturale.'

[7] See esp. Pelagius, *Expos. Ep. ad Rom.*, Souter, p. 49: *P.L. Suppl.* 1138–9— 'ut ne signa quidem veteris hominis agnoscantur in nobis, nec enim aliquit velle aut cupere debemus, quod volunt aut cupiunt qui nondum sunt baptizati', and *Ep. Honorificentiae tuae*, 1, Caspari, p. 5: *P.L. Suppl.* 1689 'Christianus est

concerned to defend was not the innocence of babies: it was the *innocence of the post-conversion state*—of the adult who had 'turned away from his sins'.[1] His criticism of the doctrine of original sin, therefore, was determined by the fear that once a sin was regarded as 'natural' rather than 'voluntary', it would be allowed to survive the geological fault between a man's past and his present that Pelagius associated with conversion and with the rite of baptism.[2]

A man's sinful behaviour, therefore, could be reversed: he was constricted by past habits that he could disown and, beyond himself, by the habits of a society which he could reform. Such ideas determined the attitude of the radical Pelagians to Roman society as a whole: plainly, Pelagian groups in Sicily regarded accumulated wealth as yet another bad habit, piled up from the evil actions of the pagan past that could be shrugged off by the Christian on baptism.[3] There is even a charming strain of primitivism in a man such as Julian of Eclanum. Adam, 'the harmless tenant of a pleasant plot', with God as his affable landlord, is one of a long series of idealized

---

. . . ut breviter multa concludam, qui post baptismi ablutionem alienus est a peccato.'
On the creation of good habits in the ascetic discipline of Pelagius, see. *Ep. ad Dem.* 13 (*P.L.* 30. 29B).

The ascetic discipline and aims of Pelagianism are the least original aspect of the movement: they form part of the general reception of oriental monastic traditions in the late fourth century, made available in the translations of Rufinus: W. Jaeger, *Two Rediscovered Works of Ancient Christian Literature: Gregory of Nyssa and Macarius*, Harvard Institute for Classical Studies (1954), pp. 89–98, esp. p. 91, and R. Lorenz, 'Die Anfänge des abendländischen Mönchtums im 4. Jh.', *Zeitschrift für Kirchengeschichte*, lxxvii (1966), pp. 35–8.

Such traditions admitted a high degree of human freedom and the possibility of reaching a state of Christian perfection; but they are concerned with the training of the monk, for whom perfection is a goal *in the future*. The distinguishing feature of Pelagianism is that Christian perfection follows, or should follow, from the fact of baptism—from an event, that is, in the *past* experience of many full Christians—and, so, that it might involve whole congregations. This *ecclesiological* bias may explain why a movement which originated *a quibusdam monachis* (Augustine, *de gest. Pelag.* xxxv. 61), eventually commanded the support of 18 bishops in Italy alone. [Now see L. W. Barnard, 'Pelagius and Early Syriac Christianity', *Recherches de Théologie ancienne et médiévale* xxxv (1968), pp. 193–196.]

[1] Augustine, *de gest. Pelag.* vi. 16; cf. *de natura et gratia*, iii. 60–liv. 64.
[2] Ibid. lii. 60.
[3] Id., *de gest. Pelag.* xi. 23; xxxii. 57.

pictures of peasant life: appropriate perhaps in a young man who had grown up near the landscape that had inspired the *Georgics* of Virgil. He had also read his Juvenal: and, as a Pelagian, he could firmly believe that no irreversible Fall of man—only a thin wall of 'corrupt manners'—stood between the true Christian and the delightful innocence of man's first state.[1] It was an idea widespread among sophisticated people in the Later Empire. When young Julian married, Paulinus of Nola would bless this simple clerical occasion: by shunning the vulgarity of a fashionable wedding, he said, the young people had recaptured the *simplicitas*, the unaffected innocence, of Adam and Eve.[2]

But I think that it would be wrong to reduce Pelagius' emphasis on the essentially external nature of the force of habit to an annexe of his denial of original sin. His approach had deeper roots in the attitude of early Christians to the world around them. From the time of Tertullian onwards, habit—*consuetudo*—had always been thought of as an external, social force, and the Christian as being exposed, not only to his own 'bad habits', but to being suffocated and contaminated by the way of life of the pagan society around him.[3]

Indeed, the need to break the hold of the past was one of the deepest currents in Western Christian attitudes to membership of the Church. It had meant that Christians had always tended to look at their own past from across the chasm of baptism. Cyprian's *Letter to Donatus* is a typical document. He was a man who could still hardly believe that 'such a volte-face' could have taken place in himself; who was anxious to point out, to his friend, that sins that had seemed so deeply rooted in him as to appear part and

---

[1] Brown, *Augustine of Hippo*, p. 382.

[2] Paulinus of Nola, *Carmen*, xxv, esp. line 102. *Simplicitas* was a favourite virtue with the Pelagians, as it was with Tertullian and Ambrose: by contrast, it is notably absent in Jerome, see P. Antin, *Rev. bénédictine*, lxxi (1961), pp. 371–81. That the baptized recovered the childhood innocence of Adam and Eve was a common idea: e.g. pseudo-Cyprian, *De singularitate clericorum*, 14 (*C.C.E.L.* iii. appendix, p. 189). It is asserted, also, in the upright stance of the baptized at prayer: see A. Wlosok, *Laktanz und die philosophische Gnosis*. Abhandl. Heidelberger Akad. Wiss. (1960), pp. 176–7. (This excellent study is a salutary reminder to the exclusive student of the classical tradition of the strange currents that flow beneath the apparently placid surface of a 'Christian Cicero'.)

[3] '*Beneath the encrusting prejudices imposed by the customs and habits of society*, the soul is anima naturaliter christiana', H. Chadwick, *Early Christian Thought and the Classical Tradition* (1966), pp. 2–3, on Tertullian (my italics).

parcel of human nature itself could vanish 'in a single, drastic instant'.[1]

If we want to know what it was like for an adult Western Christian of the age of Pelagius to commit himself specifically to baptism, we would not be naïve to read Book viii of the *Confessions* of Augustine: Pelagius assumed that just such a moral earthquake would precede the resolve of his ideal Christian. If we want to catch something of the sudden relief of tension, the happy unclouded sense of serious purpose which Pelagius expected to follow from such a decision, we need only read the early works of Augustine, those written after his conversion and after his baptism. The little coteries of Pelagian enthusiasts that had collected in Rome, Campania, and Sicily around 410 might not have been so very different from the group that had followed Augustine from Milan to Ostia to Africa, in the late 380s. When Augustine wrote to Paulinus of Nola, in 417, to warn him that to tolerate the supporters of Pelagius would be to favour men who, like the pagan philosophers, held out the hope of achieving a 'blessed life'—a *beata vita*—in this world, we can see how Augustine, himself once the author of a book *de beata vita*, 'On the Blessed Life', written under the influence of pagan neo-Platonic philosophers, had understood, from his own experience as a young convert in Milan (now thirty years past), the great hope of the Pelagian movement: 'Behold, all things have become new'.[2]

For Augustine, all things had not become new. To the classic, even somewhat conventional, account of a dramatic conversion, in Books viii and ix of the *Confessions*, Augustine, the middle-aged bishop, would add the amazing Book x. When this Book x was read in Rome, Pelagius was 'highly indignant'.[3] He was right. This one book of the *Confessions* marks the parting of the ways. Augustine,

[1] Cyprian, *Ad Donatum*, 3–4 (*C.S.E.L.* iii, pp. 5–6). Lactantius is equally emphatic: *Divinae Institutiones*, iii. 26, 9 f. 'Uno enim lavacro malitia omnis abolebitur. Tanta divinae sapientiae vis est, ut in hominis pectus infusa, matrem delictorum stultitiam uno semel impetu expellat.' This is an implicit refutation of Seneca, *Ep.* 31, 5: 'nos multa alligant, multa debilitant, diu in istis vitiis iacuimus, elui difficile est, non enim inquinati sumus, sed infecti . . .' (see Wlosok, *Laktanz*, p. 43, n. 135). Pelagius knew both authors (see de Plinval, *Pélage*, pp. 75–80). His attitude is the same: the experience of conversion to Christianity refutes the idea that evil is inevitable; the idea that evil is inevitable is refuted in order to provoke conversion.

[2] Augustine, *Ep.* 186, xi. 37. On Augustine's own great hopes after his conversion, see Brown, *Augustine of Hippo*, pp. 110–14, 121–2, and 146–7.

[3] Augustine, *de dono perseverantiae*, xx. 53.

in a scrupulous examination of his abiding weaknesses, in his evocation of the life-long convalescence of the converted Christian, had
tacitly denied that it was ever possible for a man to slough off his
past: neither baptism nor the experience of conversion could break
the monotonous continuity of a life that was 'one long temptation'.[1]
In so doing, Augustine had abandoned a great tradition of Western
Christianity. It is Pelagius who had seized the logical conclusions
of this tradition: he is the last, the most radical, and the most paradoxical exponent of the ancient Christianity—the Christianity of
discontinuity.[2]

In judging the success of Pelagian ideas, we should remember
that, in the Italy of the late fourth century, there was still room for a
Christianity of discontinuity. For the Christian Church envisaged
by the Pelagians was still the Church of a minority. It was a missionary group: it was recruited by the conversion of adults, for
whom baptism was still a meaningful step; it could define itself
over against a pagan majority by distinctive behaviour. This is the
atmosphere of the Pelagian cells in Sicily. As we have seen, the baptized rich man would be expected to abandon his family property;
but he would have joined a minority. He knew that the radical
standards of its members would not be shared by the world at large;
Sicilian society, as a whole, would have remained unaffected, safely

---

[1] Brown, *Augustine of Hippo*, pp. 177–80.

[2] Brilliantly characterized in Cyprian by W. H. C. Frend, *Martyrdom and Persecution in the Early Church* (1964), p. 402. 'Discontinuity', the idea that conversion and initiation could make a total break in the personality, is most closely associated with Gnostic circles, where it is fundamental to their attitude to the world in general (see H. C. Puech, 'La gnose et le temps', *Eranos Jahrbuch*, XX (1951), pp. 57–113, esp. p. 87), as is a 'mystique of baptism' based on St. Paul (see *de resurrectione* (Codex Jung), ed. Malinine, Puech, and Quispel (1963), p. xiii): see E. R. Dodds, *Pagan and Christian in an Age of Anxiety* (1965), pp. 76–7. But the attitude was widespread in the Early Church; see K. E. Kirk, *The Vision of God* (1931), pp. 229–34.

Western aristocratic Christianity had remained very close to these primitive roots: the world of *petites églises* survived up to the end of the fourth century— see E. Ch. Babut, *Priscillien et le priscillianisme* (1900), pp. 57–60. The sup-
porters of Priscillian in Spain are typical of such *côteries* formed by the newly baptized: 'peractis omnibus humanae vitae experimentis et malorum nostrorum conversationibus repudiatis, tamquam in portum securae quietis intravimus'— Priscillian, *Liber apologeticus*, 2 (*C.S.E.L.* xviii, p. 4). See also *Praedestinatus*, i. 86 (*P.L.* 53. 616), for an astonishing case of noble patronage for a group of followers of Tertullian in Rome. The Novatianists remained important in Rome throughout the period of Pelagian activity: Socrates, *Hist. Eccles.* vii. 9 and 11.

cushioned against the revolutionary demands made on the core of baptized Christians by a substantial buffer-state of catechumens.[1]

But in many areas of Italy Christianity had only just emerged from the situation reflected in Pelagian writings. Ambrose was admired by the Pelagians, partly because he had found himself in a position similar to their own. He had been able to provide recently established Christian bishoprics with nothing less than ethical charters that regulated the social behaviour of the Christian minority in many North Italian towns—how to respect grazing-rights around Imola;[2] how to avoid usury in Trent (where agricultural debt, then as now, weighed heavily on the peasants of the foot-hills of the Alps).[3]

The debate between Augustine and the Pelagian bishops of Italy, on the authority of St. Ambrose, makes us realize that there were two Ambroses. There is the ascete: the man with a sensitive revulsion from the human condition, 'swaddled in passion'; the Platonist, for whom any earthly perfection was vanity.[4] But there is also Ambrose the great missionary bishop: the man, that is, who devoted himself to instructing candidates for baptism, whose most eloquent appeals were those in which he urged his congregation to pass through this drastic rite, whose baptistery of St. Thecla, with its octagonal shape, conveyed, through the symbolism of the Eternal Sabbath of the Saints, the hope that the baptized, Christian *populus* that emerged from it might really form a church *sine macula et ruga* 'without spot or wrinkle'.[5] This is the Ambrose who rightly inspired the Pelagian bishops; and, one suspects that, without this strain in him, Ambrose would not have converted Augustine.

Ambrose's disciples show this tradition at work in small towns. The sermons of Maximus of Turin, for instance, gravitate insistently around the rite of baptism: he earned his reputation as the author of

---

[1] *de divitiis*, xii. 5, Caspari, pp. 58–49: *P.L. Suppl.* 1401–2.

[2] Ambrose, *Ep.* 2. 30.

[3] Id., *Ep.* 19. 5.

[4] Apud Aug. *de gratia Christi*, xliv. 48–xlix. 54.

[5] Ambrose, *in Luc.* i. 17 apud Aug. *de natura et gratia*, liii. 75. On the importance of Ambrose in the Pelagian controversy, see, most recently, de Plinval, *Essai sur le style et la langue de Pélage* (1947), p. 118 and A. Paredi, 'Paulinus of Milan', *Sacris Erudiri*, xiv (1963), p. 212.

It is to Ambrose the preacher that Julian of Eclanum appealed: *Op. Imp.* iv. 119. 'Imitemus sane eorum illud studium, quo populos aedificaverunt exhortando obsecrando, coarguendo'; to which Augustine replied, drily: 'Et nos pro modulo nostro populos aedificamus . . quod fecit Ambrosius.'

sermons *de speciali gratia baptismi*—'on the exceptional grace of baptism'.[1]

Only a decade later such provincial bishops would have to choose between Pelagius and Augustine. Eighteen bishops chose Pelagius. We can see why, in the brilliant journalism of Julian of Eclanum: to accept the ideas of Augustine, Julian argued, would be to encourage whole congregations, who had only recently nerved themselves to enter upon the drastic commitment of Christian, baptism, to settle back into the moral torpor of confirmed invalids.[2] Julian accused Augustine of being a Manichee, of preaching fatalism—these were merely conventional bogeys.[3] But what really hurt, before such an audience, was the remark that, as Augustine presented it, the great rite of baptism was no more than a superficial 'shaving' of sin: it left the Christian with roots and stubble that would only too soon grow again.[4]

In Rome itself, in the 390s, all the material lay to hand for a radical interpretation of the rite of baptism. Adult baptism, for instance, had been forced to the fore by the wave of aristocratic conversions to Christianity at the end of the fourth century.[5] The crucial idea, in Pelagian literature, that Christianity was a 'Law' merely echoed the widespread attitude that Christ delivered his Law to the Christian at baptism, an idea that had already been expressed, with all the majesty of Imperial art, in scenes such as the *Dominus Legem Dat* of Santa Costanza.[6] Later, the most eloquent verses on the meaning of baptism—that it involved the creation of an undivided, holy people—would be placed in the Lateran baptistery by none other than Pope Sixtus III, the man, that is, who, as a priest, had been regarded as a patron of Pelagius.[7] Perhaps, it was

---

[1] Gennadius, *de script. eccles.* 40 (*P.L.* 58, 1082).

[2] Apud Aug. *Op. Imp.* ii. 8 and iv. 114.

[3] Brown, *Augustine of Hippo*, pp. 369–71.

[4] Augustine, *c. II Epp. Pelag.* I. xiii. 26: cf. *Praedestinatus*, ii (*P.L.* 53. 626).

[5] See, generally, J. Jeremias, *Infant Baptism in the first four centuries*, transl. Cairns (1960), pp. 88 f.

[6] See W. N. Schumacher, 'Dominus Legem Dat', *Röm. Quartalschr.* liv (1959), pp. 1–39.

[7] Diehl, *Inscript. lat. christ. vet.* i. 1513, esp. *c*
   Nulla renascentum est distantia, quos facit unum
   unus fons, unus spiritus, una fides.
Cf. *de divitiis*, viii. 3 cit. sup. p. 102, n. 5, and Ps.-Jerome, *Ep.* (148) *ad Celantiam*, 21 (*C.S.E.L.* lvi, p. 347): 'nec interest, qua quis condicione natus sit, cum omnes in Christo aequaliter renascamur'.

just this 'baptismal' view of the Church that he had shared with the reformer. The heresy of Jovinian shows that a crisis in the associations surrounding baptism was imminent.[1] Jovinian would argue that the sanctity conferred by baptism was sufficient to keep the Christian, thereafter, safe from sin; above all, that this rite fused the Christian community into a single group, in such a way as to make unnecessary the distinction between a 'perfect' ascetic life and a less perfect life of the married laity. Pelagian enthusiasts will merely stand Jovinian's views on their head—by making the ascetic life obligatory for all baptized Christians, in a similar, drastic *reductio ad unum*.[2]

After 410, Augustine will be faced, in Carthage, with congregations that included nuns, *continentes*, noble refugees who, in Rome, had been influenced by the teachings of Pelagius. He quickly summed up his audience. By far the most perceptive and closely reasoned of his sermons on Pelagianism will be his sermons on the meaning of baptism—not the demagoguery of his performance on infant baptism, but those that really came to grips with the implications of the baptismal theology of Pelagius. In these sermons he will point out, with considerable courtesy to his audience, that the baptism of an adult did not necessarily mean a new start to his life: that the convert should think of himself, not as a healed man, but like the man found wounded on the road from Jerusalem to Jericho—saved from certain death by the ointment of baptism, he must, nevertheless, be resigned to spending a lifetime of precarious convalescence in the Inn of the Catholic Church.[3]

The watershed between the Pelagians and their opponents, therefore, passed directly through the idea of the Church. As a Sicilian observer wrote of the Pelagian 'cells' in his town: their activities posed the problem of 'the state of the Church in this world'.[4] And Augustine was the last man not to give an answer to such a problem. It is a symbolic coincidence that Augustine first glimpsed the face of Pelagius at a distance, when he was at Carthage at a meeting of his episcopal colleagues, during the great days of the

---

[1] Jerome, predictably, would labour the similarity: *Dialog. c. Pelag.* iii. 1 (*P.L.* 23. 595B).

[2] See S. Prete, 'Lo scritto pelagiano "De castitate" è di Pelagio?', *Aevum*, xxxv (1961), pp. 315–22, esp. 318.

[3] e.g. Augustine, *Sermo* 131, 6 (of 23 Sept. 417); cf. *de natura et gratia*, lii. 60.

[4] Id., *Ep.* 257, iv. 40.

Conference with the Donatists of 411.[1] He would approach Pelagianism with the momentum of twenty years of controversy with the Donatists precisely on this issue—'the state of the Church in this world'.

I think it would be wrong to limit the appeal of the Augustinian idea of the Church as presented against the Pelagians. Some scholars have emphasized the sacramental powers, the hierarchical structure, the authoritarian *ethos* of the Catholic Church as presented by Augustine, and so have presented Pelagianism, by contrast, as an appeal to individual initiative, as a manifestation of 'liberal temper'.[2]

The Pelagians were Late Roman men, to a depressing extent. For them, as for everyone else in that age of absolutism, reform meant only one thing: reform from the top; yet more laws, sanctioned by yet more horrific punishments. The Pelagians would have reformed the Catholic Church exactly as Vegetius proposed to reform the Roman army—by re-imposing the old discipline: 'Corruption and its antidote, Terrorism', a just summary of the reforming policy of the Emperor Valentinian I, could be the sub-title of any Pelagian tract.[3] Adam, they said, had suffered the death-penalty for breaking one single prohibition; and even he was less to blame than us, for he did not have the great benefit of the previous execution of a human being to deter him.[4] To be a reformer in the Later Roman Empire meant to be an authoritarian—and the Pelagians are no exception.[5]

The weakness of the Pelagian position, over against that of Augustine, was rather that, as we have seen, the reformed Pelagian Church

[1] Id., *de gest. Pelag.* xxii. 46.

[2] Morris, *J.T.S.*, N.S. xvi (1965), p. 59.

[3] From A. Alföldi, *A Conflict of Ideas in the Later Roman Empire* (1952). See F. Vittinghoff, 'Zum geschichtlichen Selbstverständnis der Spätantike', *Historische Zeitschr.* cxciv (1964), p. 566, for hopes of reform through a return to the old ways. *De malis doctoribus*, iv. 2, Caspari, p. 71: *P.L. Suppl.* 1422, is typical of the Pelagian belief in Hellfire: 'nescio quomodo Christus Dominus non venit solvere legem sed adinplere, si per eius credulitatem disciplina non aucta est, sed minuta. Minuta enim est, si timoris causa sublata est, timoris autem causa sublata est, si poena dimota est.' The Emperor would have agreed, in seeing *perdita et soluta disciplina* as the root of all evils: *Paneg. lat.* vi (vii), 2, 2.

[4] *Ep. 'Honorificentiae tuae'*, 1, Caspari, p. 7: *P.L. Suppl.* 1689.

[5] The frequency of the word *censura* was sufficient to betray Julian of Eclanum as the author of an anonymous commentary: G. Morin, *Rev. bénédictine*, xxx (1913), p. 11.

was assumed to be a minority: the 'sacrifice of praise' envisaged by
the Pelagian, was to be the praise of pagan public opinion for the
small, compact, and perfect group in its midst.[1] In his dealings with
the Donatists, Augustine's thought had already taken him beyond
this position. He assumed that Catholicism could be a majority
religion. The sacraments of the *Catholica* had already cast strong,
invisible tentacles throughout the largely Christianized society of
Africa—binding the saint, the sinner, even the schismatic.[2] The
development of his views on religious coercion merely meant that
the Catholic Church had room, also, for forced adherents, bound to
her only by the normal pressures of secular society.[3] Now, as Augustine presented it against the Pelagians, this Church was also a
church of convalescents. The rite of baptism was essential; but its
immediate effects would remain largely invisible. Pelagius, with his
emphasis on man's natural capacities, might seem to blur the
boundary between the Christian believer inside the Church and the
good pagan outside it: in fact, he only argued from pagan virtue
to establish, *a fortiori*, an austere perfectionism as the sole law of the
Christian community. His reformed church would have stuck out,
in the midst of Roman society, like an uneroded outcrop of ancient
rock. Augustine, for all his harsh emphasis on the necessity of
baptism for those outside the Church, appears, paradoxically, by
contrast to Pelagius, as the great exponent of moral tolerance inside
it. For, once within this exclusive fold, Augustine could accept with
ease the slow and erratic processes of spiritual healing—by which the
flaking image of the average man's soul was constantly 'touched up'
with the 'little brush' of prayer.[4] Augustine would find room in the
Catholic Church for the ordinary Christian layman of the Later
Empire: a man, that is, with a few good works to his name, who slept
with his wife *faute de mieux*—and often, just for the pleasure of it; a
man prickly on points of honour, given to the vendetta; not a land-
grabber, but capable of fighting to keep hold of his own property—

---

[1] *de vita christiana*, 9 (*P.L.* 40. 1038).

[2] Brown, *Augustine of Hippo*, pp. 223-5.

[3] Brown *JRS.* liv, (1964), 107-16 [pp. 260-78] and *Augustine of Hippo*,
pp. 237-40. The Augustinian tradition of forcible adhesion to the Catholic
Church will be applied, a decade after Augustine's death, against the Pelagians
in Campania: Quodvultdeus, *Liber promissionum*, II, vi, 11, ed. Braun, p. 320—
'Colligit sane etiam illa nolente quos ad unitatis suae membra pertingere
cognoscit quoniam "novit dominus qui sunt eius".'

[4] Augustine, *Sermo* 111, vi, 8.

though in the bishop's court; and, for all that, a good Christian in Augustine's senses, 'looking on himself as a disgrace and giving the glory to God'[1].

And one should not forget that, in Rome and in Italy, the problem of assimilating the average, upper class layman was, if anything, even more acute than in Africa. In the Roman Senate, many representatives of old families lived, uncomfortably, in a 'post-pagan' world—men like Volusianus, of the Caeionii, were the servants of Christian emperors, they were surrounded by Christian womenfolk, they would be courteously besieged by Christian bishops; perhaps, even, they had become officially *catechumens* of the Roman Church.[2] One wonders whether the jettisoning of the harsh ideals of Pelagianism in Rome, its former centre, was not the price the Roman Church was prepared to pay to hasten the absorption of such men.

As for Augustine, the Pelagian controversy, is, in many ways, the diptych of his campaign against the Donatists; together, they gave the Catholic Church *carte blanche* to swallow Roman society whole.[3] Whether it ever managed to digest the beast is a question I must leave to the historian of the Middle Ages.

The significance of the defeat of Pelagianism, therefore, lies in the idea of the Church in Western society. Some scholars have suggested that Pelagian plans for reform might have affected the whole structure of the Western Empire.[4] This view, I think, misunderstands the position of Christianity in Roman society: the most active and creative Christians were not interested in the unwieldy fabric of

[1] Augustine, *c. II Epp. Pelag.* III, v, 14.

[2] Brown *JRS* li (1961), pp. 6–11 [pp. 172–82]. Volusianus of the Caeionii (on whom see Brown *JRS* li (1961), pp. 6–8 [pp. 174–5] and *Augustine of Hippo*, p. 300), may have been a catechumen up to his death-bed, in 437: *Vie de sainte Mélanie*, c54 fin, p. 234, his niece, Melania, is anxious ὅτι κινδυνεύει τελευτῆσαι κατηχούμενος. A Cameron, 'The Date and Identity of Macrobius', *JRS* lvi (1966), pp. 25–38, in dating the *Saturnalia* to the 430s, shows how much of their pagan past the new members of the Roman Church could take with them.

[3] Augustine, *Sermo*, 4, 19.
Augustine would have agreed wholeheartedly with Mephistopheles,

> Die Kirche hat einen guten Magen
> Hat ganze Länder aufgefressen
> Und doch nie sich übergegessen,
> *Faust*, 1.

[4] Myres, *J.R.S.* l (1960), pp. 21–36.

Roman society as a whole; yet many were convinced that they could reform the world in miniature—that they could, at least, create a *sanctus populus* within a religious group. The momentum of reform, therefore, already pointed away from the world at large and inwards to the core of the Church. But in Pelagianism this core was wider than it would be in any future period of the early Middle Ages Church: what concerned Pelagius was the *populus Christianus* in the widest sense—all baptized Christians, laity and clergy alike. Only a generation later the laity had sunk into the background. The reforming literature of fifth-century Gaul is already a predominantly clerical literature: the author of the *De Septem Gradibus Ecclesiae* would lament that avarice, having raged in the Roman Empire, had now entered the Church, but all he means is that the metropolitan of Arles was docking the salaries of his minor clergy.[1]

The defeat of Pelagianism is yet one more stage in the end of the ancient world and the beginning of the Middle Ages. But the 'ancient world' that was abandoned with Pelagius was less the ancient world of classical dignity, of individualism, of 'self-salvation', and liberal values that some have mourned in the passing of the first British heretic: it was the 'Ancient World' of the early Christian Church—of a group that had spread across the Mediterranean precisely because it had been small, separate, ferociously self-sufficient: *Sancti estote, quoniam ego sanctus sum, Dominus Deus vester.* 'Be ye holy, for I, the Lord your God am Holy'.[2]

---

[1] *de vii ordinibus ecclesiae*, 5 (*P.L.* 30. 159A).
[2] *de vita christiana*, 9 (*P.L.* 40. 1038) and *de possibilitate non peccandi*, iv. 2, Caspari, p. 119: *P.L. Suppl.* 1461.

THE PATRONS OF PELAGIUS: THE ROMAN ARISTOCRACY BETWEEN EAST AND WEST*[1]

The writings of the Pelagians are notoriously anonymous;[2] and so are their supporters. Most of the participants in the Pelagian controversy, indeed, are no more than names to us. The historian must content himself with the few well-known figures connected with Pelagius and Julian of Eclanum, knowing that he is able to see only the tips of icebergs.[3] But, given the pyramidal structure of Late Roman society, a tip invariably betrays an iceberg. When approached by Augustine and Alypius, Juliana Anicia will speak not only for herself, but also for *domus nostra*;[4] Jerome and Augustine will approach their addressees in exactly the same spirit—throughout the Pelagian controversy, it was the support of whole *domus* that was at stake.[5]

The division of Roman society between its aristocratic families is a fact of Late Roman life.[6] Their influence is a constant feature of

* *Journal of Theological Studies*, N.S., Vol. XXI, Pt. 1, April 1970, pp. 56–72.

[1] I have been grateful to Dr. Gerald Bonner, of Durham University, for encouragement and much helpful comment; and I am heartened to find that something of what I had already written in draft (in 1966) was confirmed, as well as much corrected, by R. F. Evans, *Pelagius: Inquiries and Reappraisals* (1968).

[2] See the evidence collected in *P.L.* xlviii. 419–23. [See also, H.-I Marrou–J. R. Palanque, *Prosopographie du Bas-Empire, Fascicules provisoires* L, *Prosopographie pélagienne* (1967).]

[3] See G. de Plinval, *Pélage, ses écrits, sa vie et sa réforme* (1943), pp. 211–16. In my opinion, de Plinval is wrong to place his main emphasis on the relation between Pelagius and the *gens Anicia* (pp. 214–16). Everybody had to approach the Anici: approaches to this leading Christian family in Rome, in the form of letters of address, of exhortation, of consolation, were *de rigueur* [and, one should add, profitable, see Jerome, *Ep.* 130, 7]. One was free to pick and choose patrons only among the lesser nobility.

[4] Augustine, *Ep.* 188. i. 3.

[5] Jerome, *Ep.* 133, 13 and Augustine, *Ep.* 200. 2.

[6] On the general forms of the intellectual life of the Roman aristocracy in the late fourth century, see Peter Brown, 'Pelagius and his Supporters: Aims and

the theological life of Rome, up to the sixth century;[1] but it reached a peak in the late fourth century. For, in Rome, the ascetic movement had been limited to individual families; its protagonists lived in their own palaces or on estates near the city (in a manner associated as much with the traditional deportment of an aristocrat *in otio*, as with any new monastic organization);[2] and so, the most turbulent areas in the theological activity of the City would have been located quite literally under the roofs of the great. (The impersonality and independent *esprit de corps* of the great urban monasteries of Constantinople in later centuries, for instance, would have been notably lacking in these *sancta conciliabula*.) Divisions of opinion, therefore, would tend to take on a momentum of their own, due to the solidarity of each Christian *domus* in the City and its alliances: antipathies, once generated, might be passed from generation to generation; *ententes*, once sealed, might afford protection to a variety of newcomers. This certainly happened in contemporary Constantinople: there we find the widows of conflicting generals at the time of the Gothic wars of Theodosius predictably ranged on opposing sides for and against John Chrysostom.[3] I would suggest that it is possible to invoke one such grouping of parties among the

---

Environment', *J.T.S.*, N.S. xix. 1 (1968), pp. 93–114 at pp. 96–7 [pp. 186–189]. Such rivalries of aristocratic houses may be betrayed by the genealogical claims for different families in the *Scriptores Historiae Augustae*: see the suggestions of Santo Mazzarino, *Il pensiero storico classico* (1967), pp. 219–22. Rival rhetors had long been supported by rival factions: Philostratus, *Lives of the Sophists*, p. 490; see Santo Mazzarino, '*Prima Cathedra*', *Mélanges A. Piganiol*, iii (1966), pp. 1653–65, at pp. 1661 ff. and G. W. Bowersock, *Greek Sophists in the Roman Empire* (1969), p. 91: 'Neither sophist could have had the slightest doubt but that the quarrel increased the reputations of both.' It is a precedent of which Jerome was only too well aware in his rival Rufinus. Jerome, *Apologia c. Rufinum*, iii. 30.

[1] Ch. Pietri, 'Le Sénat, le peuple chrétien et les partis de cirque à Rome sous le pape Symmaque', *Mélanges d'archéologie et d'histoire*, lxxviii (1966), pp. 123–139; M. Wes, *Das Ende des Kaisertums im Westen des römischen Reichs* (1967), pp. 101 and 145–7, on the relations between Eugippius, the library of Anicia Proba and the circle at the *Castellum Lucullanum*; and Ennodius, op. vi, cdlii, 23 (*M.G.H.*, A.A., vii, p. 315), on the *Salon* of Barbara.

[2] R. Lorenz, 'Die Anfänge des abendländischen Mönchtums im 4. Jht.', *Zeitschrift für Kirchengeschichte*, lxxvii (1966), p. 6.

[3] Namely, Pentadia, widow of Timasius, supported John against Castricia, widow of Saturninus: Palladius, *Dialogus de vita S. Johannis Chrysostomi*, chs. iv and x. Saturninus had been judge on the tribunal that had exiled Timasius in 396: Zosimus, *Historia Nova*, v. 8 ff. (details kindly supplied by J. F. Matthews).

Christian aristocracy of Rome, in order to discover a little more
about the milieu in which Pelagius rose to eminence in Rome, and,
even, perhaps, to catch a glimpse of some of the forces at work
during the Pelagian controversy.

The quarrel between Rufinus and Jerome over the diffusion of the
ideas of Origen, which culminated in A.D. 400, is a watershed in the
allegiances of some of the most active members of the Christian
aristocracy of Rome. Jerome's supporters in Rome had been closer
to clerical circles: Marcella was a widow of the Roman church,[1] and
Pammachius, a priest *manqué*, whose lavish donations to the poor
were studiously associated with the cult of St. Peter.[2] They could
secure the condemnation of Origenism from Pope Anastasius. To
the orthodox, the matter appeared closed: compared with Jerome,
wrote a Renaissance scholar, the writings of Rufinus were 'as the
strumming of a flea to the trumpeting of the Indian elephant'.[3] At
the time, however, it was almost exactly the reverse. Marcella and
Pammachius were quite outclassed. The great Melania the Elder
had arrived from the Holy Land, in 399. She was greeted by a vast
cortège of senators. She was well able to protect her father-con-
fessor, Rufinus. Paulinus, her relative and one of the very few 'true-
blue' aristocrats in the Christian Senate, rallied to her.[4] Jerome
might trumpet: at Rome it was a very distant noise, indeed, with the
mass of Paulinus and the Elder Melania placed between him and
Rufinus. When Rufinus returned to Rome from Aquileia, he would
settle down, unmolested, in the entourage of Melania the Elder.

Therefore, whatever their relations with Rufinus might be, newcomers would find themselves on a watershed, one side of which
very definitely sloped *away* from Jerome. Augustine immediately
found himself on that side. His own breach with Jerome is notorious
—and it was hardly healed before 408.[5] He would soon eclipse
Jerome for good as the intellectual mentor of Paulinus.[6] It is

[1] Jerome, *Ep.* 127, 9: Lorenz, 'Die Anfänge . . .', p. 5.

[2] Jerome, *Ep.* 48, 4.

[3] Cited in *P.L.* 21, 175A.

[4] Clearly demonstrated by P. Courcelle, 'Paulin de Nole et Saint Jérôme',
Revue des études latines, xxv (1947), pp. 250–80.

[5] See most recently, Y. M. Duval, 'S. Augustin et le *Commentaire sur Jonas*
de Saint Jérôme', *Revue des études augustiniennes*, xii (1966), pp. 9–40.

[6] Suggested by J. Doignon, 'Nos bons hommes de foi: Cyprien, Lactance,
Victorin, Optat, Hilaire (*de doctrina christiana*, II, 40, 61)', *Latomus*, xxii (1963),
pp. 795–805.

through Paulinus that he had most contact with Italy:[1] his one letter to Jerome's friend, Pammachius, by contrast, is hesitant and purely formal.[2] By 409, he will be joining with Paulinus in praising Melania the Elder[3]—whose name Jerome had already erased from his *Chronicle*.[4]

One might even suggest that Augustine had implicated himself with the faction of Rufinus by challenging Jerome over his translation of the Scriptures from the Hebrew. His first rebuke found its way to Rome—one wonders how—and was there published as an anonymous pamphlet against Jerome—one wonders by whom.[5] In his *Apologia*, Rufinus canvassed for conservative support against Jerome's 'modernist' translation of the Bible.[6] At one time his propaganda had been discussed at 'a meeting of African bishops which had been called for certain ecclesiastical affairs'.[7] Now Augustine very frequently found himself voicing less his own opinion than that which he shared with his intensely tradition-minded colleagues.[8] I would suspect that it was Rufinus' remarks to the African bishops that mobilized Augustine's appeal to tradition.

I would suggest that Pelagius, also, gravitated to this side of the watershed, and that, living as he did in Rome, he had far greater opportunity than did Augustine to benefit from the protection and to share in the interests of a circle that we could define as consisting of the friends of Rufinus and the friends of the friends of Rufinus.

For instance, the relations of Paulinus with Pelagius are notorious. Pelagius probably came to know of Augustine's works through Paulinus: it may have been in the company of Paulinus that he had reacted so indignantly to a reading of Augustine's *Confessions*;[9] it

---

[1] See the evidence collected by P. Courcelle, 'Les Lacunes dans la correspondance entre saint Augustin et Paulin de Nole', *Revue des études anciennes*, liii (1951), 253–300 and *Les Confessions de saint Augustine* (1963), pp. 559–607.

[2] Augustine, *Ep.* 55.

[3] Augustine, *Ep.* 94, 3.

[4] Rufinus, *Apologia*, ii. 26.

[5] Jerome in Augustine, *Ep.* 72, 2. The letter followed the same route as did the defences of Rufinus—Rome to Dalmatia: Jerome, *Apol. c. Ruf.* iii. 7.

[6] Rufinus, *Apologia*, ii. 32–5.

[7] Jerome, *Apol. c. Ruf.* ii. 24.

[8] Excellently demonstrated by G. Bonner, 'Les Origines africaines de la doctrine augustinienne sur la chute et le péché originel', *Augustinus*, xii (1967), pp. 97–111.

[9] Augustine, *De dono perseverantiae*, xx. 53; see Courcelle, *Les Confessions*, p. 580.

may have been in Paulinus' library that Pelagius and, later, Julian of Eclanum had studied the anti-Manichaean works of Augustine to their great profit. (It is not irrelevant to the anti-Manichaean posture of both men, that Augustine seems to have used Paulinus especially as a depository for anti-Manichaean works, aiming, perhaps, at the respectable and influential Manichaean community in Rome and Campania.)[1] Pelagius' long letter to Paulinus of Nola of about 404[2] coincided with a particularly crucial moment in Paulinus' career—during the months of terror and indecision of the invasion of Radagaisus; and it may have been occasioned by that notable 'gathering of the clans'—the visit of the Elder Melania and her relatives, known recipients of the works of Rufinus, to the shrine of St. Felix at Nola.[3]

Paulinus's relations with Julian of Eclanum are equally well attested: he wrote a poem for the young man's marriage.[4] In 417 he had to be warned against the supporters of Pelagius.[5] On his deathbed he allowed Pelagians go take communion in his church[6] (a crucial concession in that time of suppression).[7] His intimate friend, Sulpicius Severus, 'sinned by speaking' in favour of Pelagianism.[8] The strength of such links is interesting in a man whose own writings betray no tendency towards Pelagius' doctrine.

It was not only the circle of Paulinus, the close ally of Melania the Elder and the friend of Rufinus, that was open to Pelagius. The descendants of Melania the Elder, her granddaughter, Melania the Younger and her husband Pinianus, seem to have continued this

---

[1] e.g. Augustine, *Contra Secundinum*, xi, tells Secundinus the Manichee that he can consult the *De libero arbitrio* (used also by Pelagius) in the possession of Paulinus. See Courcelle, *Recherches sur les 'Confessions' de saint Augustin* (1950), p. 29 n. 3, on the anti-Manichaean 'Pentateuch' sent by Augustine to Paulinus, in A.D. 395. It seems possible to me that Pelagius also knew of the *Contra Fortunatum*: compare *Contra Fortunatum*, 22 with Pelagius, *Expositio in Ep. Pauli ad Rom.*, Souter, pp. 58–9 (*P.L.* Suppl. i. 1144) on compulsive swearing as evidence of the power of habit.

[2] Mentioned in Augustine, *De gratia Christi*, xxxv. 38. (The recipients of the *De gratia Christi*, Pinianus and Melania, were closely connected with Paulinus.)

[3] Paulinus, *Carmen*, xxi; and *Ep.* 46, urging Rufinus to join them.

[4] Paulinus, *Carmen*, xxv.

[5] Augustine, *Ep.* 186, viii. 29.

[6] Uranius, *De obitu sancti Paulini* (*P.L.* liii. 859).

[7] See especially Praedestinatus, 88 (*P.L.* liii. 618) 'catholicae plebi permixti sunt, quia ecclesiam aliam non habent . . . de quaestione [inquiunt] non de communione discernimur'.

[8] Gennadius, *De viris illustribus*, 19 (*P.L.* lviii. 1073).

friendship. We find Timasius, the disciple of Pelagius, as a close companion of Pinianus.[1]

Nor did this grouping escape the notice of Jerome. He will insist on bracketing the doctrines of Pelagius with the ideas first spread by Rufinus.[2] It is the singular merit of Dr. Robert Evans's recent treatment to have emphasized the dominant role of Jerome, rather than of Augustine, in the beginnings of the Pelagian controversy. As he shows so well, the Origenist quarrel provided both men with material for their confrontation. Jerome will identify Pelagius' exhortations to perfection with Origenist spiritual teaching on the 'passionless' state; while, as Dr. Evans suggests, Pelagius' statements on original sin in his *De natura* were not aimed at Augustine's views on the effects of the sin of Adam, but rather against an Origenist 'sin of existing', whose black stain he sensed in the ascetic piety of Jerome and of his Roman followers. Two years before Melania the Younger arrived in the Holy Land, Jerome was still associating the doctrines of Pelagius with 'the mad old woman', Melania the Elder. It is hardly surprising that Pelagius should make his last appearance in history, in the company of the daughter-in-law and the grand-daughter of Melania, 'black by name and black by nature'[3]— Albina and Melania the Younger.[4]

Last of all, it was the uncle of Melania the Younger, Volusianus, who, as the Urban Prefect for 419, needed to be reminded to be conscientious in unearthing the supporters of Pelagius and Caelestius in Rome.[5] Volusianus was a pagan—or, at least, not a baptized Christian:[6] but he was also a Roman aristocrat, from a family whose sense of solidarity had embraced the religious differences of its individual members for generations;[7] a 'man of great

[1] Augustine, *Ep.* 126, 6.
[2] For what follows see R. F. Evans, *Pelagius: Inquiries and Reappraisals*, ch. 2 'Pelagius and the Revival of the Origenist Controversy' (1968), pp. 6–25. [See now Y.-M. Duval, 'Sur les insinuations de Jérôme contre Jean de Jérusalem: de l'Arianisme à l'Origénisme; *Revue d'Histoire Ecclésiastique* LXV (1970), pp. 353–374.]
[3] Jerome, *Ep.* 133.
[4] Augustine, *De gratia Christi*, I. i. 1.
[5] In *P.L.* xlv. 1750–1: see A. Chastagnol, *La Préfecture urbaine sous le Bas-Empire* (1961), pp. 170–1.
[6] *Vie de sainte Mélanie*, ed. D. Gorce, *Sources chrétiennes*, 90 (1962), 54 (p. 234).
[7] P. R. L. Brown, 'Aspects of the Christianisation of the Roman Aristocracy', *J.R.S.* li. (1961), pp. 7–8 [pp. 174–175.]

perception',[1] he would later not hesitate to mobilize his eccentric niece, Melania, to help him to bring off a diplomatic *coup*.[2] Had he decided that, in a Christian world, it would be unwise to use his official position as Urban Prefect, charged with persecuting the Pelagians, to upset the traditional pattern of friendships among the Christians of his family?

The family and circle of Melania the Elder is closely associated with another fold in the landscape of Italian Christianity that would influence the strategy of Julian of Eclanum, and that helped him in his quest for supporters in the Italian episcopate: that is, the *cause célèbre* of John Chrysostom. The desperate mission of the supporters of John had lodged with Melania the Younger, in 404.[3] The leader of the mission of Italian bishops, Aemilius, was the Bishop of Beneventum, a town of which the son of Melania the Elder, Publicola, was *patronus ex origine*.[4] Aemilius, the friend of Paulinus of Nola, became the father-in-law of Julian of Eclanum.[5] In a world of clerical dynasties, with pretensions to noble birth,[6] the local bishops may well have achieved a high degree of aristocratic solidarity, warmed by shared memories and loyalties, consolidated by intermarriage.

If any event was calculated to provoke such solidarity, it was the deposition and brutal exile of John Chrysostom. For this incident coincided with a period of tension and strident propaganda between the Eastern and the Western parts of the Empire.[7] It confirmed the worst suspicions of right-thinking Italians: the court at Constantinople had elevated a eunuch to the consulship;[8] now, it had got rid of a holy bishop. Italian opinion was skilfully mobilized: John wrote to the Anician aunts of the Western consul of the

---

[1] *Vie de sainte Mélanie*, 53 (p. 235).

[2] *Vie de sainte Mélanie*, 50 (p. 255).

[3] Palladius, *Hist. Laus.* 61 (Butler, p. 157).

[4] *Corpus Inscriptionum Latinarum*, ix. 1591.

[5] Paulinus, *Carmen*, xxv.

[6] Witness the effort of Fulgentius to present Julian as unworthy of the *fasces Aemiliorum*, and the suggestion that he was a 'bed-pan baby' (*P.L.* xlv. 1040–2).

[7] See E. Demougeot, *De l'unité à la division de l'empire romain* (1951), pp. 335 and 345 ff.

[8] A situation brilliantly exploited in the poems of Claudian, and well understood by A. Cameron, 'Wandering poets', *Historia* xiv (1965), pp. 503–4 [and A. Cameron, *Claudian, Poetry and Propaganda at the Court of Honorius* (1970), pp. 124–55].

year;[1] bishops returned with hair-raising tales of the sort of treatment given to ambassadors at Constantinople.[2] Constantinopolitan opinion remained divided over John Chrysostom for the next decade. When the second generation of the family of Melania the Elder came to the eastern Mediterranean, they took up their positions, as if on a barely expunged palimpsest, in relation to alignments formed both by the Origenist controversy and by the closely related issue of the fall of John Chrysostom.[3] Such alignments determined their choice of company at a surprisingly late time: when Melania the Younger visited Constantinople in 436, it was by the chamberlain Lausus, the recipient of Palladius' *Lausiac History* and a patron of the supporters of John, that she was welcomed and entertained.[4]

In Italy, memories of the incident created a bond of shared indignation that would last many a provincial bishop for a lifetime. To write, as one of them did, in praise of John Chrysostom, that he 'was not a destroyer of the churches, but had built them up',[5] was to show that you were *engagé* on the right side. Julian of Eclanum and his supporters promptly exploited this grouping of Italian opinion. The translations of the sermons of John Chrysostom were the work of a Pelagian cleric.[6] They were addressed to resolute Pelagian bishops; and the translator was careful to point out that, in John, they had an illustrious precedent in being deposed and exiled without fair trial. (Certainly, Alypius, distributing eighty stallions at the Imperial court, was doing his best, as far as the means of the church of Africa allowed, to live down to the diplomatic methods used by Theophilus of Alexandria against John.)[7] If the Pelagian manifesto of 418 was addressed, as is usually thought, to the Bishop of Aquileia, then we can appreciate how, in Northern Italy as around Beneventum, the Pelagians felt that they had most chance of

[1] John Chrysostom, *Ep.* 167 to Proba; *Ep.* 171 to Juliana.
[2] Palladius, *Dialogus*, iv. 15; Sozomen, *Hist. Eccles.* viii. 28.
[3] See the suggestions of H. Grégoire–B. Kugener, *Marc le Diacre: Vie de Porphyre* (1930), pp. lxxxiv–lxxxvi.
[4] *Vie de sainte Mélanie*, 53 (p. 231).
[5] Pelagian appeal to Augustine of Aquileia, x (*P.L.* xlviii. 525).
[6] Anianus of Celeda: see his Preface in *P.L.* xlviii. 626–30, and B. Altaner, 'Altlateinische Übersetzungen von Chrysostomusschriften', *Kleine patristische Schriften*, T. U. 83 (1967), pp. 416–36. [For other translations of Chrysostom, now see J. P. Bouhot, 'Version inédite du sermon "Ad neophytas" de Jean Chrysostome utilisée par S. Augustin', *Revue des études augustiniennes*, XVII (1971), pp. 27–41.]
[7] Augustine, *Op. Imp.* i. 42.

touching the sympathies of the clergy that had the most direct
memories of the incident of Chrysostom.

Can any conclusions be drawn from these ramifications, other
than that they happened? This in itself is a banal enough fact, given
the conditions of Late Roman aristocratic Christianity; but it is one
which is too often overlooked in dealing with Pelagius.

First, certain problems concerning the pace and quality of the
Pelagian controversy might be explained:

The most marked feature of this controversy seems to be the
extreme reluctance of all parties to fire the first shot. One may
suggest that many influential Roman Christians were 'once bit
twice shy'. They had had their witch-hunt. The measures of the
Bishop of Rome and the Emperors against Origenism had been
severe: they included the first attempt by the State to prevent
people from reading condemned books.[1] But this witch-hunt had
been stalemated by the great lay-patrons of Rufinus. A Roman com-
promise was reached, that will be carried into the papal attitude
over the Pelagian controversy: the pope would agree that, while
terrible thoughts were going around, nobody in particular was
thinking them. This sound attitude was based on a fusion of Roman
and Jewish legal safeguards against false accusation.[2] But it also
reflects a precise situation in the intellectual life of Christian
Romans: in order to enjoy a high standard of Christian culture, influential laymen were prepared, in Rome, to tolerate the occasional
doctrinal *faux pas* of their *protégés*. Both Rufinus and Pelagius bene-
fited from this permissive state of mind: Rufinus claimed 'Suppose
it to be superfluous; this does not make it criminous'; he was
followed by Pelagius, who claimed to have erred '*non criminaliter sed
quasi civiliter*'.[3]

Seen in this perspective, the fact that the Pelagian controversy got
under way at all and that it was terminated by such a massive ecclesiastical intervention is, in itself, a landmark in the cultural history
of Latin Christianity. It represents the climax of a generation of exuberant creativity—a Renaissance of Latin Christian culture, running
beside (and, in the case of Jerome, plainly interweaving with) one

---

[1] Anastasius, *Ep.* i. 5; *P.L.* xx. 72B.

[2] Anastasius, *Ep.* 1, esp. ch. 6: *P.L.* xx. 73A; Zosimus, *Ep.* '*Postquam a nobis*',
esp. ch. 3 (in *P.L.* xlv. 1722).

[3] Rufinus, *Apologia*, i. 18: Pelagius, apud Augustine, *De pecc. origin.* xxxiii.
26; cf. Pelagius, apud Augustine, *De gestis Pelagii*, vi. 16.

of the 'Three great epochs' of Latin secular literature.[1] It put the Latin Christians in the flattering position of both having actually, at last, produced a heresy, and then of being able to condemn it. The sense of identity which this double process gave to the Catholic Church in the West should not be underestimated. For it coincides with the self-conscious rallying of secular sentiment around the tradition of *Roma Aeterna*.[2] Both movements—the further definition of Catholic orthodoxy against Pelagianism and the final hardening of Roman aristocratic patriotism—reassured thinking men in the West that, although they could do little about either barbarians or heretics, at least such clearly identifiable 'outsiders' provided a *raison d'être* for their own brittle sense of identity.

More particularly, the existence of influential patrons of Pelagius explains why Augustine showed himself remarkably hesitant before coming to grips with Pelagius by name.[3] His hesitation contrasts markedly with the rapidity with which he would decide, despite misgivings, to commit himself to the 'great and arduous work' of the *City of God*.[4] Even more puzzling is the lack of any previous contact with the ideas of Pelagius, while Pelagius was still at Rome. Augustine, of course, had been drawn in on the Donatist controversy: but, throughout that period, he had somehow found time to elaborate great books—the *De doctrina christiana*, the *De Trinitate*, the *De Genesi ad Litteram*—which betray no small *Auseinandersetzung* with ideas outside Africa. Nor did he lack contact with the Roman aristocracy. A convert of St. Ambrose, he seems to have known the family of Ambrose's protectors, the Anicii.[5] In 409, he could write a blunt enough pamphlet to an Anicia, Italica, and to other eminent Romans on the issue of the Vision of God.[6] It may well be that, up to 410, Augustine knew Roman society only through circles well disposed to Pelagius—through Paulinus of Nola. Augustine depended for much of his knowledge of contemporary events outside Africa on none other than the *Historia Ecclesiastica* of

---

[1] Sir Ronald Syme, *Ammianus and the Historia Augusta* (1968), p. 210.

[2] See M. A. Wes, *Das Ende des Kaistertums im Westen des römischen Reichs* (1967) and F. Paschoud, *Roma Aeterna* (1968).

[3] Evans, *Pelagius . . .*, esp. pp. 70–80. [But not so Pelagius, see the interesting suggestions of G. Martinetto, 'Les premières réactions antiaugustiniennes de Pélage', *Revue des études augustiniennes*, XVII (1971), pp. 83–117.]

[4] Peter Brown, *Augustine of Hippo* (1967), pp. 299–304.

[5] See the evidence in Brown, *Augustine . . .*, p. 128.

[6] Augustine, *Epp.* 92, 147, 148.

Rufinus.[1] (Significantly, Orosius will deviate from Augustine partly because he drew his information from the other camp: it is Jerome and a circle of Western refugees gathered at Bethlehem—avid, as refugees would be, for any reassurance—who provided much of the material for Orosius' treatment of contemporary events in the *Historia adversus paganos*.[2] In this case, we may suspect the hand of Jerome and the influence of a sojourn in the solid and self-confident Eastern Empire in many of those historical attitudes of Orosius in which he departs from Augustine.) It was from such a circle that Augustine may have heard nothing but good of Pelagius.

After 410, the situation had become extremely delicate in Africa itself: the noble refugees from Rome had to be handled with care. Augustine and Alypius had great hopes from a couple such as the Younger Melania and Pinianus. Their arrival caused quite sufficient difficulties, without adding the additional embarrassment of a heresy-hunt among the Pelagian intimates of Pinianus.[3] Only when the family left Africa, in 415, did Augustine feel free to answer Pelagius by name, without ruffling his potential protectors.

Secondly, it may help us to appreciate the acute embarrassments caused by the emergence of Caelestius. For Pelagius' position had been protected by the momentum of an old and largely unthinking alliance. By the time that Caelestius appeared in the scene, Melania the Elder and Rufinus were already dead. Many hatchets were already buried (notably between Augustine and Jerome). Old loyalties continued, if with diminished momentum, among those with any close memories of Melania the Elder. But any alliance that had to include Caelestius could no longer be unthinking. In the contrast between the cautious Pelagius and the 'prodigious'[4] Caelestius, we can sense the contrast between the teacher, who developed his ideas in the protecting but restraining environment of a patron-protégé relationship, and the eccentric aristocrat; Caelestius, *nobilis natu*,[5] could afford to look after himself.

[1] See the important studies of Y. M. Duval, 'L'Éloge de Théodose dans la "Cité de Dieu" (v. 26, 1). Sa place, son sens et ses sources', *Recherches augustiniennes*, iv (1966) pp. 135–79 and 'Saint Augustin et les persécutions de la dernière moitié du ive. siècle (Cité de Dieu, XVIII. 52)', *Mélanges de science religieuse*, xxiii (1966), pp. 175–91.

[2] e.g. Orosius, *Historia adversus paganos*, vii, 43.

[3] See Brown, *Augustine . . .*, p. 294.

[4] Vincent of Lérins, *Commonitorium*, 24.

[5] Marius Mercator, *Liber subnotationum*, 2.

Thirdly, the contrast between Pelagius and Caelestius raises the problem of the precise intellectual milieu in which Pelagius developed his ideas. For the proximity of Rufinus can be sensed in both men, though their reactions to Origenism were very different. Pelagius drew cautiously on the more acceptable aspects of Origen, as made available by Rufinus. The influence of Origen's commentaries on St. Paul is evident in Pelagius' *Expositiones*.[1] More generally, the body of Greek monastic literature which Rufinus had brought with him from the East would have added vast prestige to Pelagius' own speculations; for Rufinus' translation of the '*Rule*' of St. Basil, for instance, would have revealed to Latin readers an *anima naturaliter pelagiana*, who had long expected his monks to practise what Pelagius was now preaching.[2]

Moreover the anti-fatalist arguments, which Rufinus had circulated, drew on a philosophical tradition whose power in shaping the Pelagian dialectic of freedom has recently been recognized: *Mathematicorum venerat solvere quaestiones et soluit fidem christianorum*, Jerome's tag on Rufinus,[3] could well summarize Father Refoulé's brilliant contentions on the intellectual formation of Julian of Eclanum.[4] Intellectual sympathies, along these lines, have often been invoked to account for the appearance of Pelagian supporters in those areas which had previously had most contact with Rufinus and his friends—Aquileia, Rome, and Sicily.[5]

The relation of Caelestius to the circle around Rufinus was more idiosyncratic. I would suggest that the ideas of Caelestius on original sin betray a direct reaction against Origenist ideas circulating in Rome. We meet Caelestius at the palace of the 'leader of the opposition' in Rome, Pammachius, at a discussion in which Rufinus, a Syrian, refuted traducianism and its implications.[6] Such a dis-

[1] See now Evans, *Pelagius . . .*, esp. pp. 19–21.

[2] See esp. W. Jaeger, *Two rediscovered Works of Ancient Christian Literature: Gregory of Nyssa and Macarius* (1954), pp. 89–98, and Lorenz, 'Die Anfänge . . .,' *Zeitschrift für Kirchengeschichte*, lxxvii (1966), pp. 35–8.

[3] Jerome, *Apol. c. Ruf.* iii. 32.

[4] F. Refoulé, 'Julien d'Éclane, théologien et philosophe', *Recherches de science religieuse*, lii (1964), pp. 42–84 and 233–47, esp. p. 241.

[5] As by H. von Schubert, *Der sogenannte Praedestinatus* (*Texte und Untersuchungen*, 24, 4, 1903), pp. 80–1.

[6] Augustine, *De peccato originali*, iii. 3. But now see H.-I. Marrou, 'Les attaches orientales du Pélagianisme', *Comptes rendus de l'Acad. des Inscr.* (1968), pp. 459–72. [See now G. Bonner, 'Rufinus of Syria and African Pelagianism', *Augustinian Studies* (1970), pp. 31–48.]

cussion was inseparable from any criticism of Origenist ideas on the previous fall of the soul into the body. If this Syrian, Rufinus, was acting at that time as the agent of Jerome and if, somewhat later, he became the author of a *libellus fidei* denying any original taint in infants, one can appreciate how easily a reaction to Origenist ideas of a previous fall of the soul into the body might 'escalate' into a denial of *any* previous fall, whether of the soul or of Adam.[1]

It is not surprising that *quaestiones* on the origin of the soul should have been the forcing-ground of extreme assertions and denials of the idea of original sin.[2] It is almost impossible to imagine a meeting of intellectuals in the Late Antique world where the subject of the fall of the soul would not be raised: Porphyry interrogated Plotinus on the issue for three days on end.[3] The long letters which Augustine found himself forced to write to Roman Christians and to Jerome on the origin of the soul, show how the Pelagian controversy originated in an atmosphere already clouded by doubts on this issue.[4] Above all, the practice of infant baptism had been invoked to support Origenist speculations on a pre-existent 'taint' in the soul.[5] In singling out this rite for criticism, Caelestius betrays most clearly a direct acquaintance with circles that took the ideas of Origen as a serious challenge.

Altogether, the intellectual events of the last decade of the fourth century are a reminder that controversies emerge not only when people have new ideas, but also when they suddenly wake up to realize that they no longer have the old ones. In understanding Paul's deep sayings on 'election' *ante constitutionem mundi* (Eph. i. 4), for instance, Late Roman Christians were encouraged, by the whole climate of their philosophical culture, to keep something like an Origenist idea of the pre-existent 'fall' of the soul into a materially created body at the back of their minds, as a convenient safety exit. Origenist ideas had been especially pervasive in Latin ascetic circles. This is hardly surprising, for we are dealing with a very

[1] See F. Refoulé, 'La Datation du premier concile de Carthage contre les Pélagiens et du *Libellus fidei* de Rufin', *Revue des études augustiniennes*, xi (1963), pp. 41–9.

[2] For which see Jerome, *Ep.* 130. 16.

[3] Porphyry, *Vita Plotini*, 13: compare the same problem discussed by the circle of the pagan lady Sosipatra, in Eunapius, *Vitae Sophistarum*, 470. See A. J. Festugière, *La Révélation d'Hermès Trismégiste*, iii (1953), pp. 63–96.

[4] Augustine, *Ep.* 143. 5–6; *Ep.* 166, to Jerome; and *Ep.* 180. 5.

[5] N. P. Williams, *The Ideas of the Fall and Original Sin* (1927), pp. 223–6.

close-knit world of North Spanish and Aquitanian aristocrats, one of whose *foci* was the circle of Melania the Elder. Even Martin of Tours—too often dismissed as a simple soul, interested only in the local issue of Priscillianism—felt their troubling presence.[1] Suddenly in the 390s, Origen's solution became at once both topical and unacceptable: for Pelagius, the solution of the fall of the soul was 'what certain heretics have dreamt up'.[2] Men would have to decide how much of the baby of 'election' would have to go out with the bath-water of Origenism. Why, then, *did* God hate Esau before he was born? Paulinus writes to Jerome; a Pelagian sets to meditating on the hardening of the heart of Pharaoh; Simplicianus appeals to his former pupil, Augustine . . .[3]

Pelagius, therefore, gravitated towards the circle around Rufinus, partly through intellectual sympathy, partly perhaps because—if we believe de Plinval[4]—he may have already crossed swords with Jerome. Common dislike of Jerome is an entirely credible motive. Yet, the reasons for so formidable and influential a grouping of Roman opinion may not have been entirely conscious. In opting for Rufinus, one suspects, members of a newly Christianized aristocracy were opting against a *farouche* expatriate, in favour of a man whose work of translation gave them back their classical past in Christian guise—and introduced their Christian past in classical guise. Apronianus was a typical new convert: his Christian instruction was undertaken by Melania the Elder.[5] He received impeccable

[1] B. Studer, 'Zu einer Teufelerscheinung in der "Vita Martini" des Sulpicius Severus', *Oikumene* (1964), pp. 351–404, esp. 374 f.; and 'Zur Frage des westlichen Origenismus', *Texte u. Untersuchungen*, 94 (1966), pp. 270–87.

[2] Pelagius, *Expos. in Ep. ad Ephes.* 1. 4 (*P.L.* Suppl. i. 1289 = Souter, 345).

[3] Origen, περὶ ἀρχῶν, ii. 8, 3 (*G.C.S.* 5, p. 128) on Esau: 'Quod et de anima scrutantes possumus invenire, propter antiqua peccata cum in deteriori vita esse damnatum.' Jerome, *Ep.* 85. 2 (see Courcelle, 'Paulin et Jerome . . .'); the Pelagian *De induratione cordis Pharaonis*, ed. de Plinval *Essai sur le style et la langue de Pélage* (1947), ch. 13, p. 151 (= *P.L.* Suppl. i. 1512/13), with de Plinval's comments on pp. 125–34; and Augustine, *De diversis quaestionibus ad Simplicianum*, quaestio ii, esp. ch. 8. (See Brown, *Augustine . . .*, pp. 153–4). R. J. O'Connell, 'The Plotinian Fall of the Soul in St. Augustine', *Traditio*, xix 1963), pp. 1–35, shows how close to the wind Augustine himself had once sailed on this issue. [See now the preface of Almut Mutzenbecher to her edition of *De Diversis Quaestionibus*, Corpus Christianorum, ser. lat. XLIV (1970), pp. IX–XXXIII.]

[4] de Plinval, *Pélage . . .*, pp. 50–5, and now Evans, *Pelagius . . .*, pp. 26–42 (who makes a somewhat stronger case).

[5] Palladius, *Historia Lausiaca*, 54 (Butler, pp. 146–7).

Pythagorean maxims, under the name of the martyr—Pope Sixtus.[1] Gaudentius, Bishop of Brescia, got Clement of Rome, 'come home at last—as a Roman'.[2] The importance of this translating activity should not be underestimated.[3] We are in a world where Seneca writes letters to St. Paul;[4] and where Pope Zosimus may have chosen the *titulus sancti Clementis* as the *venue* for his crucial examination of Pelagius and Caelestius,[5] not only because its ample forecourt would hold a large crowd, but, also, because of the memory of a predecessor recently 'made Roman' by Rufinus.

Jerome was out of date: 'and as for Rome', wrote Rufinus, 'Rome, which with the favour of God is the head of Christians, look at how he is saying the sort of things about the City, that used to be said when it was pagan and the residence of persecuting Emperors.'[6] This criticism hurt. The Rome of the 400s was a Rome recently endowed, by the Emperor Theodosius, with a vast new basilica of St. Paul.[7] It had become something of a Holy City, to which a Christian governor, such as Prudentius, could retire with a clean conscience.[8] Its Senate dutifully attended the vigils of St. Lawrence.[9]

[1] See H. Chadwick, *The Sentences of Sextus* (*Texts and Studies*, N.S. v (1959); G. Delling, 'Zur Hellenisierung des Christentums in den "Sprüchen des Sextus" ' (*Texte und Untersuchungen*, 77 (1961)), pp. 208–41; and the excellent remarks of Evans, *Pelagius* . . ., pp. 43–65, on their influence on Pelagius.

[2] Rufinus, Praef, 4, ed. B. Rehm, *Die Pseudoklementinen, II* Rekognitionen (*G.C.S.* 1965), p. 3.

[3] F. Winkelmann, 'Spätantike lateinische Übersetzungen christlicher griechischer Literatur', *Theologische Literaturzeitung*, xcv (1967), pp. 229–40 and, on a revealing point of detail, Basile Studer, 'A propos des traductions d'Origène par Jérôme et Rufin', *Vetera Christianorum*, v (1968), pp. 137–55.

[4] A. D. Momigliano, 'Note sulla leggenda del Cristianesimo di Seneca: La corrispondenza tra Seneca e San Paolo', *Rivista storica italiana*, lxii (1950), pp. 325 ff. = *Contributo alla Storia degli Studi classici* (1955), esp. pp. 13–16.

[5] Zosimus, *Ep.* ii. 2 (*P.L.* xx. 650A).

[6] Rufinus, *Apologia*, ii. 23.

[7] See A. Chastagnol, 'Sur quelques documents relatifs à la basilique Saint Paul-hors-les-Murs', *Bull. soc. nat. des Antiquaires de France* (1954–5), pp. 125–7, and, generally, J. Kollwitz, 'Probleme der theodosianischen Kunst Roms', *Rivista di archeologia cristiana*, xxxix (1963), pp. 191–233.

[8] On Prudentius and his outlook, see the many recent studies: for instance, Italo Lana, *Due capitoli prudenziani*, Verba Seniorum, N.S. ii (1962); J. Fontaine, 'Le Pèlèrinage de Prudence à S.-Pierre et la spiritualité des "eaux-vives",' *Orpheus*, xi (1964), pp. 99–122; Reinhart Herzog, *Die allegorische Dichtkunst des Prudentius* (Zetemata, 42 (1966)).

[9] *Vie de sainte Mélanie*, 5 (p. 135) and Prudentius, *Peristephanon*, ii, esp. ll. 517–28.

Pelagius, also, though studiously impersonal, had tacitly opted against Jerome. He had read his Pope(!) Sixtus; he admired St. Ambrose;[1] he wanted his church to be 'without spot or blemish', according to the high standards of the ascetic movement—but he was careful not to say that the Roman clergy looked more like bride-grooms than clerics.[2]

It is a sign of the times. Reform has replaced satire. Satire assumes the absence of a viable alternative. At best, the satirist can threaten to opt out of the society he describes but cannot change. This Jerome and his circle had done.[3] The reformer stays with a society, to over-haul it. Pelagius' thought is harnessed to the idea of the church;[4] in practice, the Pelagian movement was tied to the existing Catholic congregations. Pelagius would write to priests and bishops;[5] the Pelagians would insist on remaining Catholics.[6]

The reform of Catholic congregations assumed a stable environment. For only a stable environment would make possible the slow colonization of the clergy and episcopate of Rome and Italy by Pelagian idealists. For a decade, from 398 to 408, this had seemed possible. The 'brain drain' of ascetic emigrants to the Holy Land came to a halt. Western clergymen came to think twice about pour-ing money into the Holy Places.[7] The energies of the ascetic move-ment flowed directly into the Roman environment. Melania the Elder returned to Rome; the younger generation, Melania the Younger and Pinianus, intended to stay in Rome. Their piety was satisfied by the cult of St. Lawrence; their constant presence in the great basilicas of Rome may have left its traces on the early monastic liturgies.[8]

---

[1] de Plinval, *Essai* . . ., p. 118, on the stylistic influence of Ambrose; see Pelagius, apud Augustine, *De gratia Christi*, i. 46. It was a respect which, as Rufinus pointed out, was notably lacking in Jerome: *Apologia*, ii 24–5.

[2] Jerome, *Ep.* 22. 28, predictably cited by Rufinus, *Apologia*, ii. 5.

[3] Notably Jerome, *Ep.* 46. 12: see P. Antin, 'La ville chez S. Jérôme', *Latomus*, xx (1961), pp. 298–311.

[4] See Brown, 'Pelagius and his Supporters', *J.T.S.*, N.S. xix (1968), esp. pp. 102 ff. [pp. 194 ff.]

[5] To Bishop Constantius: Augustine, *De gratia Christi*, xxxvi. 39. To a priest: Augustine, *De gestis Pelagii*, xxx, 54.

[6] Pelagius in Augustine, *De gestis Pelagii* xxx. 54: ne per eius occasionem se aliquis a corpore Ecclesiae separet' and Praedestinatus, 88 (*P.L.* liii. 618); see above p. 212 n. 7.

[7] Vigilantius, in Jerome, *Contra Vigilantium*, 13.

[8] See D. Gorce, Introduction, ch. vi, to *Vie de sainte Mélanie*, pp. 79–85.

It was in this atmosphere that a Pelagian lady in Sicily could persuade a wandering enthusiast, that God need not be sought, as he had thought, 'in the East'.[1]

The Gothic invasion of 408 to 410 was a crushing blow to these hopes. Physical insecurity and the virulent re-awakening of confessional hatreds provoked another avalanche of ascetics to the East.[2] Pelagius was among them. This was a fatal blow. The Pelagians who stayed behind might have found an opportunity for direct Christian action, to which their writers had urged them.[3] Julian of Eclanum sold his estates to relieve the famine that followed in the wake of the Gothic army.[4] He would have had his equivalents among the rich and popular Pelagian bishops of a beleaguered Britain.[5] But, with the material basis of the Roman way of life crumbling around them, bishops did not need to be told by the Pelagians that they needed to impose a minimum of order and Christian decency. Aristocratic Roman society in the West, before 410, had contained an overlarge proportion of otiose *rentiers*, who needed to be reminded, by the Pelagians, of elementary social duties.[6] The barbarian invasions marked the end of the indecent affluence of the absentee-landownership of the previous century. In the poorer, dislocated world of after 410, local ties and, often, local responsibilities became stronger.[7] In Rome, the growing influence of the Church in the life of the city ensured that Christianity did not only exist but was seen to exist—the aim of Pelagian exhortations: generous and opulent priests and vast new basilicas gave the Romans a sense of being a 'holy people' in a way far more

[1] *Ep. Honorificentiae tuae*, 4: Caspari, *Briefe und Abhandlungen*, p. 12 = *P.L.* Suppl. i. 1693.

[2] See Brown, 'Pelagius and his Supporters', *J.T.S.*, n.s. xix (1968), pp. 98–100 [pp. 189–191].

[3] See esp. *De vita Christiana*, viii (*P.L.* xl. 1037).

[4] Gennadius, *De viris illustribus*, 45 (*P.L.* lviii. 1084).

[5] See esp. J. N. L. Myres, 'Pelagius and the End of Roman Rule in Britain', *J.R.S.* l (1960), pp. 21–36.

[6] See A. H. M. Jones, *The Later Roman Empire*, ii (1964), p. 784, for such widespread estates. The phenomenon of absentee landlordism accounts for the ease with which these rootless senators abandoned their locality in the face of the barbarian invasions: see Jones, *Later Roman Empire*, ii, p. 1059.

[7] See Peter Brown, 'The Later Roman Empire' (Essays in Bibliography and Criticism, lvi), *Economic History Review*, ser. 2, xx (1967), p. 340 [p. 68] [and P. Brown, *The World of Late Antiquity* (1971), pp. 126–31].

concrete—and far less exacting—than the abstract demands of a Pelagius.[1]

This last point deserves emphasis.[2] The defeat of Pelagianism forced the Roman clergy to the fore. The great lay patrons of the late fourth and early fifty centuries cautiously stepped aside:[3] the condemnation of Pelagius and the contestation of Julian of Eclanum were fought out among clergymen. Superficially obscured by a generation of *déraciné* eccentrics, the deeply rooted oligarchy of clerical Rome will come into its own after 418. It was the Roman church which had decided against Origenism; it was they who decided against Pelagianism.[4] As pope, they would choose Boniface, a leading figure of the *corps diplomatique* of Pope Innocent.[5] Boniface knew Jerome: with Jerome, he had been mentor to Eustochium.[6] For Jerome was a priest. Behind the satirist's dazzling artifice of alienation there lurked (thinly veiled, but surprisingly little noticed by modern scholars) the cautious *esprit de corps* of the Latin clergyman. Paulinus, deacon of Milan, Jerome, Orosius, Augustine, and Boniface: in varying ways, every one of the men against whom Pelagius and Caelestius stumbled, were concerned with the interests of a group tied to the destinies of great churches. It is they who, by the way in which they condemned Pelagius and the reasons for which they expected others to condemn him, brought to a close the spring of a Christian lay culture in the Latin West.[7]

As for Pelagius and the circle among which he had moved, very many found themselves in Palestine, quite as much refugees as pilgrims. They were disillusioned with the West: Sicily was unsafe, Africa unsympathetic. Their presence in the Holy Land is a symptom of the sudden, ominous widening of the gap between the standards of culture and stability prevailing in the Eastern and the Western parts of the Mediterranean.

For the circles we have been describing have one thing in com-

---

[1] See the inscription of the priest Petrus in Santa Sabina: Diehl, *Inscript. lat. christ. vet.* i. 1778a.

[2] I owe this emphasis, in part, to an invaluable letter of criticism on the subject of my paper 'Pelagius and his supporters . . .', from Professor Y. M. Duval.

[3] See Brown, 'Pelagius and his Supporters', *J.T.S.*, N.S. xix (1968), p. 110. [p. 192.]

[4] Julian's appeal to Rufus of Thessalonica: *P.L.* xlviii. 534.

[5] E. Caspar, *Geschichte des Papsttums*, i (1930), p. 325.

[6] Jerome, *Ep.* 153.

[7] de Plinval, *Pélage . . .*, pp. 210–16.

mon. They had been formed by events that had happened in the eastern parts of the Empire. Though they had been content, even proud, to live in Italy, they still had dreams of ships sailing in from the East.[1] After 410, the Eastern Empire and its theological issues sank further towards the horizon. By 418, Julian had realized that 'the West' had closed against him;[2] Augustine would confirm his fears with gusto.[3] Julian had to wage a 'Punic War' of the mind;[4] he realized that the theatre of war would be confined to the Western Mediterranean. Seen in terms of the previous opinions and alliances of Roman aristocratic Christianity, Pelagianism appears, once again, as an incident in the relations between the Latin and the Greek worlds.

[1] Rufinus, *Apologia*, i. 11.

[2] Appeal to Rufus of Thessalonica: in *P.L.* xlviii. 536.

[3] Augustine, *C. Jul.* I. iv. 13; 'Quid ergo faciemus, cum illi Graeci sunt, nos Latini? Puto tibi eam partem orbis sufficere debere, in qua primum Apostolorum suorum voluit Dominus gloriosissimo martyrio coronare.'

[4] See Brown, *Augustine . . .*, pp. 383–7.

Review of:

M. A. WES, DAS ENDE DES KAISERTUMS IM WESTEN DES RÖMISCHEN REICHS

's-Gravenhage, Staatsdruckerei 1967 (Archeologische Studien van het Nederlands Historisch Instituut te Rome, Deel III).*

In this learned and perceptive book, Dr. Wes, a young Dutch scholar, has made a fundamental contribution to our understanding of the history of Italy in the fifth and sixth centuries. He has thrown light on the meaning to contemporaries of the deposition of Romulus Augustulus, the last Roman Emperor, in 476.

Dr. Wes has adopted an approach that has already yielded rich results in the hands of A. D. Momigliano, in 'Cassiodorus and the Italian Culture of his Time', *Proceedings of the British Academy* XLI, 1955, pp. 207–45, now in *Studies in Historiography*, 1966, pp. 181–210, and 'Gli Anicii e la storiografia latina del sesto secolo', *Rendiconti, Accademia dei Lincei, cl. di scienze morali, storiche e filologiche*, ser. VIII, vol. XI, 1956, pp. 279–97, now in *Secondo Contributo alla storia degli studi classici*, 1960. Through a minute scrutiny of the conflicting opinions of sixth-century historical writers, he takes us into the social and cultural situation of Italy in the last century of the Western Empire and under barbarian rule.

Wes makes a convincing case. Briefly, it is this: He follows through more consistently and in greater detail a suggestion first made by Ensslin ('Des Symmachus Historia Romana als Quelle für Jordanes', *Sitzungsberichte der bayerischen Akademie der Wissenschaften*, phil.-hist. Abt. 1948, 3). He has shown that behind the view that the 'Western Empire of the Romans' definitely came to an end in 476—a view which occurs in both the 'Roman History' of Jordanes and in the *Chronicon* of Count Marcellinus—there lies the historical work, the *Historia Romana*, of Quintus Aurelius Memmius Symmachus, the father-in-law of Boethius.

* *Rivista storica italiana*, LXXX, 1968, pp. 1018-22, which I have translated freely from my original Italian.

The fateful date—476—has tended to be dismissed as a school-master's convention, and not a real turning-point in the Decline and Fall of the Roman Empire. Dr. Wes shows that it was a 'mental fact' of some importance: 476 plainly meant a lot to a proud and intransigent representative of Roman tradition such as Symmachus.

Wes has not only brought to life the pale shade of Symmachus, he has conjured up a whole world—the 'Romans of Rome' of the age of Theodoric, fervent Catholics, good haters of barbarians, convinced that *their* Empire (the Western Empire as it had been moulded to fit their traditional ideals in the previous century) had fallen beyond recall with Romulus Augustulus. Only men of such tenacious traditions could maintain that the world had come to an end thirty years previously. Wes' scrupulously objective exploration of these men enables us to understand (far better, for instance, than does Stein in his cold pages on the fall of Boethius—*Histoire du Bas-Empire*, 2, 1949, pp. 130–2) the true measure of their tragedy: Boethius and Symmachus were such very lonely figures.

This is a deeply learned book. Its bibliography covers all the vast literature on the subject. Better still, it is a well-conceived book. Wes has realized that, to understand the situation of sixth-century Rome, we must go right back to the fourth. He is right to begin with the reign of Constantius II, and to stress the fissure that had already begun to open in the first half of the fourth century between the eastern and western parts of the Empire.

For Wes, the evident drifting apart of the two halves of the Empire counts for more than its juridical unity. By 476, the Western Empire had ceased to be merely an administrative division of a united Roman state. It could not be said in the West that the Empire 'survived', just because an Imperial capital still survived at Constantinople. For the Western Empire had become something very specific and irreplaceable: it was a state governed by a *princeps* of the senatorial tradition, in direct contrast to the early Byzantine autocracy of the *Basileus* of Constantinople.

Dr. Wes' insistence on the contrast between East and West is of far-reaching importance for our understanding of the sixth century. According to him, men like Boethius and Symmachus never dreamt of restoring any other Empire than a 'Western' Empire, dominated by the Senate, as in the *belle époque* of the fifth century. Constantinople hardly entered into their calculations. The autocratic *Basileus* of the Eastern Empire lay outside the narrow horizon of their sympathies and political experience. Dr. Wes confirms, for the politics and historical perspective of Boethius and his circle, an impression of basic self-sufficiency, that we had already begun to suspect in his philosophical culture: despite the view canvassed by P. Courcelle, *Les lettres grecques en Occident*, 1948, 257–312 [now in English translation as *Late Latin Writers and their Greek Sources*, transl. H. E. Wedeck, Cambridge, Mass., 1969] that the philosophical culture of Boethius derived from the contemporary schools of the Eastern Empire, this culture, like the political attitudes of Boethius, was distinctly 'home-grown'.

What criticisms we have of Wes are best made in terms of his own felicitous image of an algebraic equation. Let us define some of his terms more closely, in order to make his interpretation of Italian history a little more dynamic.

First: To contrast East and West has been both fruitful and fashionable in recent literature on the Later Empire (two important recent books are dominated by this concern: W. H. C. Frend, *Martyrdom and Persecution in the Early Church*, 1965, and F. Dvornik, *Early Christian and Byzantine Political Philosophy*, 1966). Yet the distinction has been invoked so often of late, that it has become a little rigid. It is not enough to blur the contrasts between East and West, even though one could realize how slowly and how erratically a great cosmopolitan capital such as Constantinople found its identity in the fifth and sixth centuries: at least up to the mid-sixth century no one living there would have felt that he was unambiguously in an 'Eastern' Empire. (On this process and its vicissitudes, see H. G. Beck, 'Senat und Volk von Konstantinopel', *Bayerische Akademie der Wissenschaften*, 1956, no. 6, B. Hemmerdinger, 'Les lettres latines à Constantinople', *Byzantinische Forschungen*, I, 1966, pp. 174–8, and G. Dagron, 'Aux origines de la civilisation byzantine: langue de culture et langue d'État', *Revue historique*, CCXLI, 1969, pp. 23–56, [and P. Brown, *The World of Late Antiquity*, 1971, pp. 137–143].)

What we should look for, in the Roman Empire of the fourth century, are those linking factors, those groups interested in unity and the creation of a common culture, that enabled the Emperors to rule a united Empire in the face of the growing alienation of the cultivated classes of both parts of the Mediterranean world.

In this connection, I would suggest that we pay more attention to the cultural role of the Roman army. The fourth-century army provided a *milieu* that was exceptionally favourable to unity and to the transmission of ideas. The army, for instance, was most notably free of the intolerance that bulked large in the imagination of the civilian townsmen of the Later Empire. As a soldier, Ammianus Marcellinus moved in a world with a distinctively tolerant *ethos* on matters of religion, as shown recently by P. M. Camus, *Ammien Marcellin*, 1967, pp. 133–56: he was unaffected by prejudice against Romanized Germans, see A. Demandt, *Zeitkritik und Geschichtsbild im Werk des Ammianus*, 1965, pp. 31 sq.

In the life of the court—also an institution closely bound to the army—it is possible to find areas where East and West could meet in a free exchange of ideas. Though an enthusiastic 'Hellene', Julian the Apostate knew his Roman history far better than any of his civilian Greek contemporaries. I do not agree that we should see Julian's veneration for the consulship as merely the attempt of Julian, an autocrat in the Eastern tradition, to conciliate the Roman Senate, as Wes does; still less was it due to a 'reactionary' Romanticism on Julian's part (as Dvornik, *op. cit.* maintains: on which see a penetrating critique by Oswyn Murray, *Journal of Theological Studies*, n.s., XIX, 1968, esp. p. 677). Whole-hearted reverence for a Roman institution such as the consulship already appears in Julian's early *Panegyric on Eusebia*, as if it were the most natural thing in the world. For Julian, it was part and parcel of his average culture as a 'Roman' prince in the family of Constantine.

Wherever there was an effective Imperial court established in the West, a 'Latin Byzantinism' (the term was coined by H. I. Marrou, *Saint Augustin et la fin de la culture antique: Retractatio*, 1949, pp. 696–7), sprang up quite spontaneously around it. In Milan, the Emperor was always treated as a *Basileus* (see Claudian, *In IV. consul. Honorii*, l. 565–75 to which add Ambrose, *Expos. in ps.* cxviii, 8, 19). Ambrose, in his frequent confrontations with the Emperors at Milan, did not find himself dealing with a *princeps* in a senatorial tradition: he was up against a *Basileus*; and his encounters took place in a framework created by a court-protocol that was common to any Imperial residence, in East and West alike.

The young Augustine, also, when he was writing at Milan in 387, betrays traces of a Platonizing political thought, that is a distant but clear echo of what Themistius had propounded at Constantinople as a characteristically 'Byzantine' theory of kingship and society.

(See E. Cranz, 'The Development of Augustine's Ideas on Society before the Donatist Controversy', *Harvard Theological Review*, XLVII, 1954, pp. 255–316.) Augustine's later evolution, therefore, can be said to reflect a change in environment: outside the court-life of Milan, a philosophical orator would have found no resonance for Platonic enthusiasms on the state. To move south to Africa, was to lose touch with the artery that had pumped the blood of the Greek world into the West, as the Emperor and his court moved along the military highroads, linking Antioch and Constantinople to Milan and Trier.

The collapse of the Roman army in the West, therefore, was a double catastrophe. It spelt both military defeat and cultural disintegration. For the growing predominance of the civilian aristocracy in the West, at the expense of the Roman army, involved the erosion of the one group in Roman society which had an interest in transcending the narrow horizons and the virulent intolerances, that Wes describes so well in the Western senators and bishops of the fifth and sixth centuries.

Second: In his characterization of the senatorial tradition of the Later Empire, Dr. Wes seems to attribute to the aristocratic culture of the late fourth century a degree of homogeneity which, in my opinion, it did not achieve until some generations later. The senatorial 'nexus' that was once thought to connect Ammianus Marcellinus and the author of the *Historia Augusta* with the circle of Symmachus, seems to me to have been definitely dissolved, as a result of the work of Sir Ronald Syme (*Ammianus and the Historia Augusta*, 1968) and of Alan Cameron ('The Roman Friends of Ammianus', *Journal of Roman Studies*, LIV, 1964, 15–28).

The cultural life of late fourth-century Rome was far too prolific to be caught in a single net. We are not dealing with a single, monolithic senatorial group, but with a notoriously diffuse and fluid *Geistesadel*, an aristocracy of talent whose activities and interests ranged from the exuberant fraudulence of the *Historia Augusta* to the high seriousness of the Pelagian movement (see P. Brown, 'Pelagius and his supporters: aims and environment, *Journal of Theological Studies*, n.s., XIX, 1, 1968, 93–114—in this volume, sup. pp. 183–207). The 'circle of Symmachus' is a myth: but it is a myth that throws much light on the conditions of the following century. If we accept the persuasive arguments of Alan Cameron, who would place the *Saturnalia* of Macrobius in 430 (*Journal of Roman Studies*, LVI, 1966, 25–38), we can put our finger on a typical development in the aristocracy of the period that followed the Sack of Rome in 410: the surviving aristocracy of that 'post-war' generation tended to project backwards into the still prolific and turbulent age of Symmachus and Praetextatus, the social structure and intellectual life of their own days. This has become more rigid and more oligarchic. Despite the undeniable continuity of the senatorial tradition in Rome, we should not neglect this change towards a more restricted, more oligarchical social and cultural life among the 'Romans of Rome' of the fifth and early sixth centuries. Rome had become a city overshadowed by a double oligarchy of senators and clergymen.

Third: If there is something lacking in his shrewd reconstruction of the obscure vicissitudes of the latter half of the fifth century, it is that Wes fails to explain the tendency that ended in the tragic isolation of Boethius.

As many new problems have been raised as have been solved by recent work on the continuity and recruitment of the Roman aristocracy of the fifth and sixth centuries (see the exemplary studies of A. Chastagnol, *Le sénat romain sous le règne d'Odoacre*, 1966, and J. F. Matthews, 'Continuity in a Roman Family: the Rufii Festi of Volsinii', *Historia* XVI, 1967, 484–509). It seems to me that, when Wes deals with the social and economic position of the Roman aristocracy, his interpretation has suffered from being too dependent on the conclusions of J. Sundwall, *Weströmische Studien*, 1915, pp. 150–61 and E. Stein, *Histoire du Bas-Empire*, 1 (French edition), 1959, pp. 342–50. (It is puzzling that the revolutionary book by Lellia Ruggini, *Economia e società nell' Italia annonaria*, 1961, does not seem to be mentioned.)

The whole problem of the economic position of the Roman senatorial nobility in the fifth century needs re-examining. The importance of the landed wealth of the Senate, at that time, cannot be denied. Yet I doubt whether it is now possible to speak *tout court* of an outright economic 'preponderance' of the Senate over the Court. We should not forget the extreme fragility of the landed wealth even of the most wealthy families: such fortunes could be jeopardized by a succession of consuls—or of holy women! The enormous fortunes of the fourth century depended on conditions that no longer prevailed in the fifth. The senatorial revenue had come from properties scattered all over the Empire. They were at the mercy of communications and of the efficiency of the local estate-managers (the power of these agents and even of the slaves themselves is shown, for example, in the *Vita Melaniae*, c. 11, ed. D. Gorce, Sources Chrétiennes 90, 1962, p. 146).

The barbarian invasions hit the 'Romans of Rome' quite as hard as they hit their Emperors. The political preponderance of the fifth-century Roman aristocracy, their evident determination to control the machinery of government, was not the consequence of an economic preponderance: it betrays, rather, the need to seek in political dominance, an insurance against the ever-present threat of financial ruin.

Even in the fourth century, the most traditionalist Romans were not always the richest. (Against the common opinion on the wealth of Symmachus the Orator, I would prefer the sober anlysis of J. Rougé, in the *Revue des études anciennes* LXIII, 1963, pp. 59–77, that shows the precarious nature of his finances.) We may suspect the same for the aristocracy of a century later. The disappearance of 'their' traditionalist Empire, in 476, was a very hard blow indeed for that narrow group. Wes is right to stress the importance of the appropriation of one third of the estates—the *tritomorion tôn agrôn*—that sparked off the final usurpation of Odoacer.

More important still, perhaps, than these confiscations, was the disappearance of the Imperial court itself. This destroyed the last dyke that had protected the 'Romans of Rome' against an upsurge of social fluidity; for a Germanic court was more open to *novi homines* from the petty nobility of the provinces. A 'Roman' like Liberius was never on the same footing as a Symmachus or a Boethius. It is difficult to think of Boethius, a *consul sine Marte*, galloping into Arles, gravely wounded, as did the warlike Liberius. (The sixth century in the West saw an inarticulate, and so ill-documented, change in the style of life of the Roman provincials: more frequent opportunities for indulging in warfare came the way of a *déclassé* nobility, whose aggressive urges had, up till then, found outlet only in hunting.)

Against the bustling, prosperous world of Northern Italy, that was loyal to the *regimen Italiae* of Theodoric the Ostrogoth, the 'Romans of Rome' stood out in growing isolation. Political influence cost money. It meant a lot to a careerist like bishop Ennodius, that Boethius could, perhaps, no longer afford to give him an *hôtel de ville* in Milan as part of the 'goodwill presents' of a consul to his supporters. '*Symmachus war Römer*', writes Dr. Wes. In Late Roman Italy, it was never enough to be just 'a Roman'; in the kingdom of Theodoric, it was downright dangerous.

PART III

Africa

RELIGIOUS DISSENT IN THE LATER
ROMAN EMPIRE: THE CASE OF
NORTH AFRICA*

Modern students of the Roman Empire have come a long way from the enthusiasm of Petrarch—'For what is all history but the praise of Rome?' A simple reason for this change in opinion is that we have added to our knowledge of the rise of Rome the sad picture of its decline. We have listened to the Christian writers of the fifth century, to many of whom the disasters of the Roman Empire were but the nemesis of a 'lust for domination'. To Augustine, the Roman Empire was the result of conquest; and the Roman state had been based upon the exploitation of the conquered. Although he might be prepared to see the will of God in this expansion, he would admit to the sober reflection that: 'In this little world of a man's body, is it not better to have a mean stature with an unmoved health, than a huge bigness with intolerable sickness?'[1] We know how some men reacted to the 'intolerable sickness' of this bulk. For fifth-century Gaul, we have Salvian; for Africa, we have Commodian. It is hardly surprising that many modern scholars should wish to see, in this mysterious poet, the gloating reaction of a Christian provincial to the Gothic sack of Eternal Rome;

Haec quidem gaudebat, sed tota terra gemebat;
vix tamen adinvenit illi retributio digna.
Luget in aeternum, quae se iactabat aeterna.[2]

---

* *History* XLVI, 1961, pp. 83–101.
[1] Augustine, *de civ. Dei*, III. 10, transl. John Healey, *Everyman's Library*, 982, p. 83.
[2] Commodian, *Carmen de duobus populis*, 921 ff., ed. J. Martin, *Corpus Christianorum*, ser. latina, cxxviii, 1960, p. 107. 'She, indeed, used to rejoice, but the whole earth was groaning. None the less, vengeance has devised for her such disasters, small enough as they are. She who bragged of her eternity, weeps to eternity.'

In North Africa, the decline of the Roman Empire has come to be connected with the rise of a dissenting form of Christianity. In 312, the Christian Church in Africa was divided on what seemed a technical point—the treatment of those who had lapsed in the last Great Persecution of Diocletian. Such divisions had occurred before, but, on this occasion, the schism became permanent, and remained permanent, in some areas, until Christianity itself disappeared from Africa. The rise of such a vocal schismatic church, organized in a masterful fashion by Donatus, the schismatic bishop of Carthage, who gave his name to the movement, has ensured that the history of North Africa in the fourth and fifth centuries should be treated as one of the most dramatic periods of ancient history. We have long known one of the actors in this drama: S. Augustine, as bishop of Hippo from 396 to 430, devoted much of his time to the attempt to stamp out this schism. More recently we have become aware of the significance of a parallel movement of dissent in Egypt; after the Council of Chalcedon in 451, the Coptic population of Egypt are held to have rejected a form of orthodoxy imposed upon them by the Eastern Emperor, and to have clung tenaciously to their own Monophysite view of the relation between the divine and the human natures in Christ. Again, it appears that a technical point, visible in Gibbon's phrase only to the 'theological microscope', had led to the alienation of a whole province.

The tragedy of this situation was felt, and forcibly expressed, by the Roman Emperors. Since the conversion of Constantine in 312 they had thought of themselves as the one authority which could ensure the unity of the Christian Church within their Christian Empire. It was a claim which few of them refrained from attempting to put into practice; and it was a claim which was ostentatiously rejected by both the Donatist Church in Africa and by the Coptic Church in Egypt. As the Emperor Honorius wrote to the bishops assembled at the conference of Carthage in 411: 'The Donatists . . . discolour Africa, that is, the greatest portion of our kingdom and faithfully adhering to us in all its secular obligations, by a vain error and a superfluous dissension.' It has been suggested, however, in recent studies of Roman Africa, that the phenomenon of Donatism cannot be explained in purely religious terms as a 'superfluous dissension'; that a schism which began, ostensibly, as a quarrel between bishops on the application of a traditional penitential discipline to the see of Carthage, grew into a nucleus of social and political discontent. The foundation in Africa of a church overtly dedicated to upholding a strict 'purity' and appealing above all to the cult of the martyrs, has come to be appreciated no longer as a religious freak—in Augustine's pungent phrase, as frogs sitting in a pond and croaking 'We are the only Christians!'—but as a 'Movement of Protest in Roman North Africa'. So it becomes part of our attempt to understand the Decline and Fall of the Roman Empire.

The choice of Africa for such exhaustive studies as those of Dr. Frend, Professor Courtois and Professor Brisson is hardly fortuitous.[1] It is due in part to the fact that this province, which was the centre of Christian Latin literature and the home of Augustine, has also been the scene of the most recent and impressive advances of the 'archaeological revolution'. What Collingwood had said of the early days of Roman archaeology in other provinces—'It was a recently established and exciting fact that by excavation you could reconstruct the history of Roman sites not mentioned in any authority and of events in Roman history not mentioned in any book'[2] has been shown to be particularly true of Roman North Africa. The archaeologists have done nothing less than discover another Africa: the Africa of the inland plateau, stretching to the Aures Mountains and the Sahara—a new world which had hitherto been obscured by the Africa of literature, dominated by Carthage and by the Roman cities of the Mediterranean seaboard. The archaeological evidence for the strength and persistence of Donatism in Southern Numidia has made possible Dr. Frend's book; and the discovery of the remains of a sub-Roman civilization in Mauretania has ensured that the centre of interest in Professor Courtois' treatment of the Vandals in Africa should lie no longer exclusively in the 'Fourth Punic War', waged by the fleets of Genseric from Carthage, but in this hinterland, which might be called the 'Forgotten Africa'.

The Roman Empire is 'on trial' in these books on its African provinces; and our interest in its shortcomings is greatly increased by our knowledge of the impending 'judgement of history'—the conquest of Africa by the Muslims, and its consequent loss, not only to Rome, but to Christianity and Europe. In no other province is the

[1] W. H. C. Frend, *The Donatist Church, a movement of protest in Roman North Africa*, 1952. Chr. Courtois, *Les Vandales et l'Afrique*, 1955. J. P. Brisson, *Autonomisme et christianisme dans l'Afrique romaine de Septime Sévère à l'invasion vandale*, 1958.

[2] R. G. Collingwood, *An Autobiography*, 1939 (Pelican Books, 1944, p. 58).

drama of the 'end of the ancient world' both so well documented and, to most of us, so conclusively terminated as by the loss of Roman, Christian Africa to Islam.

All three books lend weight to the paradox sensed by Hilaire Belloc as a visitor to modern Algeria: 'It is thoroughly our own. The race that has inhabited it from its origin and still inhabits it is our race; its climate and situation are ours; it is at the furthest limit from Asia; it is an opposing shore of our inland sea; it links Sicily to Spain . . .: yet even in the few centuries of written history foreign gods have twice been worshipped there and foreign rulers have twice held it for such long spaces of time that twice its nature has been forgotten.'[1]

In *The Donatist Church*, Dr. Frend makes this problem clear, and goes into its implications thoroughly. The fact that North Africa no longer belongs, as Hilaire Belloc thought it should, to the Catholic Mediterranean is, perhaps, the central theme of his book. The way in which he treats this theme is a tribute to our growing awareness of the continuity between ancient and medieval history: arbitrary divisions between the two periods can only prevent us from understanding a process as profound as this loss of the southern Mediterranean. His book is a tribute, also, to the continued relevance of the problems raised by the two greatest scholars of the social and economic history of the two ages—by Pirenne in his *Mohammed and Charlemagne*, and by Rostovtzeff in his *Social and Economic History of the Roman Empire*.[2]

The fact that Dr. Frend should have turned to two social and economic historians to explain the rise of a church and the loss of a Roman province is an indication of the progress of our attitude to history since Gibbon. Both modern writers have shown, brilliantly and conclusively, that the painful reconstruction of social and economic change is not mere 'talk of the stock of bulls', but is, perhaps, the key to the 'style' of two whole civilizations—of the ancient world and of the Middle Ages.

Pirenne taught us to look to the Mediterranean. As long as the unity of this inland sea was preserved, the wealth and culture of the ancient world survived; when this unity was broken, and when the

---

[1] Hilaire Belloc, *Esto Perpetua: Algerian studies and impressions*, 1906, p. 4.

[2] Henri Pirenne, *Mohammed and Charlemagne*, transl. by B. Miall, ed. by J. Pirenne, 1939; M. I. Rostovtzeff, *The Social and Economic History of the Roman Empire*, 1926: 2nd ed. revised by P. M. Fraser, 1957.

Mediterranean ceased to belong to the Christian rulers of Europe, the Middle Ages had come. Thus, it was the rise of Islam as a hostile and exclusive power along the southern shores of this Christian Roman lake, which destroyed the unity of the ancient world. Mohammed had done what the northern barbarians had not wished to do; and Charlemagne, forced by the Islamic blockade of the South to turn to the land-locked, agrarian economy of the Frankish North, became, *malgré lui*, the 'founder of the Middle Ages'.

Rostovtzeff reached a very different conclusion. He looked to the Graeco-Roman cities, which, in the case of Africa, depended upon the Mediterranean. These were the guardians of ancient civilization; when they were victimized and deserted, this ancient civilization could no longer subsist. This collapse of the cities took place as early as the third century A.D. It was the dénouement of the relations between the parasitic guardians of an upper-class urban culture and the under-Romanized and dangerously under-privileged countryside on which these cities had depended. In describing this 'silent and brutal revolution', Rostovtzeff, an emigré from Soviet Russia, claimed to have seen more clearly than Trotsky and the city-bound Marxist orthodoxy: far from being content to be the 'packhorses of civilization', the peasantry of the third century were the destroyers of this urban world. As soldiers in the Roman army, they took advantage of the military anarchy of that age to victimize the upper classes of the towns—by looting, executions and by a system of arbitrary levies which crippled the finely-balanced economy on which the civilization of the Roman towns had depended. A wealthy and cultivated 'commonwealth of cities' had been replaced, by the end of that century, by a military despotism whose oriental trappings pandered to the tastes of the lower classes of the provinces.

In Africa, the revolution had been particularly drastic. In A.D. 238, a Numidian legion had suppressed with extraordinary savagery a revolt of the upper classes of Africa Proconsularis. This was only the beginning of the rise of the hinterland—and especially of Numidia—at the expense of the Roman cities of the coast. According to Dr. Frend, the legacy of this revolution was the resistance of the Numidian Church of Donatus to the Catholic Christianity of the Emperor and of the Romanized governing-class of the towns.

Thus Dr. Frend and Rostovtzeff had offered an explanation for the problem of the fate of the Mediterranean, posed acutely by

Pirenne. In Africa, at least, the hinterland of the Mediterranean had been lost to Roman civilization, and the hold of this civilization on the seaboard had been tragically weakened, as early as the third century. Far from being a sudden and violent rupture, the rise of Islam only made irreversible this shift of the balance of power to the South—away from the Roman Mediterranean. By the eighth century the process is completed: the maritime world of Carthage and Alexandria has given way to a world whose power was exercised from inland cities—from Kairouan, Cairo and Damascus—and whose religion was orientated away from Rome and Constantinople to Mecca.

The novelty of Dr. Frend's approach is his insistence on linking this social revolution with the rise of Christianity. For him, the most obvious symptom of this 'end of the ancient world' in North Africa is not a political but a religious movement. Such an interpretation sees in the diffusion of Christianity more than a random and uncertain process; in Africa and Egypt the rise of Christianity is intimately connected with a concrete event—the crisis of the pagan towns. The result of this change is the growth of schismatic churches in each province—the Donatist Church in Africa and the Coptic Church of Egypt. Thus the rise of Islam is only the culmination of a process started as early as the fourth century; and Mohammed only made final the religious separation of the Catholic and the schismatic shores of the Mediterranean.

This interpretation represents a revolution in our attitude to the rôle of Christianity in the Later Roman Empire; and in a recent article Dr. Frend has put forward a thoroughgoing statement of this view, which connects the problem of the rise of Christianity with an interpretation of the social crisis of the third century.[1] Thus, the rise of Christianity has come to be regarded as one of the symptoms of that profound revolution which, in the third and fourth centuries, had sapped not only the religious, but the social and political foundations of the ancient world.

The wish to connect the rise of Christianity in some way with an increased tension between the central government of the Roman Empire and the local traditions of its provinces is not of recent origin; Dr. Frend has attempted only to explain the roots of this situation in the crucial years at the end of the third and the begin-

[1] W. H. C. Frend, 'The Failure of the Persecutions in the Roman Empire', *Past and Present*, No. 16, Nov. 1959, pp. 10–29.

ning of the fourth centuries. Many years ago Sir Llewellyn Woodward, in his *Christianity and Nationalism in the Later Roman
Empire*,[1] had argued that the stubborn attachment of whole populations to heresy and schism could not be explained merely in religious terms. His acute sense of the mingling of religious and extra-
religious factors in the mentality of the Late Roman Christians led
him to suggest that heresies such as Monophysitism in Egypt were
an expression of the prejudices of the Coptic-speaking Egyptian
provincials against the orthodoxy of their Greek administrators.
The Copts got a Christianity they had made themselves; they set up
a church ruled from Alexandria and using a language different from
that of the Greeks; and anathematized 'the tyrant of Byzantium and
the orthodox who are his slaves'. They were prepared to welcome
the small Arab force of 'Amr rather than sacrifice their 'national'
Christianity to the Greeks.

In a certain sense, there is nothing new in this emphasis on extra-
religious factors in the rise of the great heresies. It springs, ultimately, from discontent with a purely theological interpretation of
ecclesiastical history: the boundaries between 'orthodoxy' and
'heresy' had seemed fixed, as a matter of dogma; they were not to
be explored—much less blurred—by the historian. The first scholar
to set out to form his own opinion on the factors underlying these
sectarian alignments between 'heresy' and 'orthodoxy' deserves
to be called the 'Father of Later Roman History': he is neither the
Jansenist scholar, Tillemont, nor the philosophic historian, Gibbon
—he is the German pietist, Gottfrid Arnold. His *Impartial Historical
Examination of Churches and Heretics*, published in 1699, is, in many
ways, a very modern book.[2] His dislike of all established ecclesiastical bodies led him to ask of the fourth century questions which are
still acutely relevant: above all, how was it that, in the centuries after
Constantine, more Christians were persecuted under Christian
Emperors as 'heretics' than had been persecuted as Christians by
the pagans? He finds the answer in a striking fashion: 'orthodoxy' is
not a dogma, it is an ecclesiastical vested interest—the *Cleresei*—
whose power, prepared since post-Apostolic times, was fully recognized and increased, in return for empty flattery, by Constantine.

[1] E. L. Woodward, *Christianity and Nationalism in the Later Roman Empire*,
1916.
[2] Gottfrid Arnold, *Unparteyische Kirchen- und Ketzer-Historie von Anfang des
Neuen Testaments bis auf das Jahr Christi* 1688. Frankfurt am Mayn, 1699, I.

With such a perspective, a completely new ecclesiastical history is possible. What is at stake is no longer a doctrine (a finespun rationalization) but something more concrete and more readily apprehended by an historian—a system, the *Cleresei*, and the movements of protest which this system provoked, the so-called 'heresies'. The high-road of ecclesiastical history is secularized: the orthodox leaders appear no longer as the defenders of truth, but as the creators of a tyrannous system which outlives them; only the 'heretics' are pure.

We have at last done justice to this important insight, but in a way which Arnold would have repudiated. Instead of starting at the top, as he did, we have filled in the bottom: the 'heresies', prized by Arnold as the last resort of religious purity, are now being regarded as extra-religious systems. Indeed, we are even tempted to regard the local dissenting churches as the expression *par excellence*, in a Christianized Empire, of secular grievances—whether 'social' or 'nationalistic'.

What we have lost in our search for 'pure religion' in the Later Roman Empire, we have gained in the widening of our historical sympathies. We like to believe, with Pascal, that '*à mesure qu'on a plus d'esprit on trouve plus des hommes originaux*'. Indeed, we have rescued half of the ecclesiastical history of the period—the origin and development of the great heretical churches—from the grotesque obscurity to which it had been condemned by the ecclesiastical Billingsgate of a none too fastidious age of controversy. We no longer seek to interpret the careers of the great heresiarchs—Donatus of Carthage and the Monophysite Patriarchs of Alexandria—in terms of personal ambition. For Africa, scholars have agreed to see in the Donatist Church of the 'just who suffer persecution and do not persecute', something more than the pungent caricature sketched with such art by Augustine; it can be accepted, and welcomed, as standing for some principle of protest against the shortcomings of an Empire whose demands were arbitrary and whose vaunted order was maintained by a penal code of quite appalling brutality.[1]

---

[1] See Augustine, *Contra epistulam Parmeniani*, i, 8, 13: CSEL li, p. 34: alioquin si, quisquis ab imperatore vel a iudicibus ab eo missis poenas luit, continuo martyr est, omnes carceres martyribus pleni sunt, omnes catenae iudiciariae martyres trahunt, in omnibus metallis martyres aerumnosi sunt, in omnes insulas martyres deportantur, in omnibus poenalibus locis iuridico

Such a view also carries with it a positive judgement on the cultural history of the Later Roman provinces such as Gibbon could not have arrived at. Quoting Longinus, he had regretted the stultifying uniformity which resulted from the constant imposition on the citizens of the Roman world of a shallow classical culture: it is the nearest he came to the nineteenth-century idea of cultural 'decadence'.[1] Today, however, we are able to see the cultural history of the end of the Roman Empire in terms of local revivals; we have learnt in this country to appreciate the most beautiful of these—the revival of Celtic art; and in the southern and eastern Mediterranean similar cultural revivals are being associated with the rise of local forms of Christianity. The Monophysite Church in Egypt adopted a native liturgy and produced a native literature; and in Africa the rise of the Donatist Church is held to have coincided with a revival of Berber art.[2]

This view can, of course, be appreciated in widely different ways. Not every scholar has shown the same enthusiasm for the 'national-social' revolt of the schismatic churches. Thus Ernst Stein, an émigré from the National-Socialist régime in Germany, could regard the Monophysite Church in Egypt as an entirely negative, disruptive force. He criticized an Emperor such as Zeno (474–91) for having adopted a policy of appeasement in his relations with this 'nationalist' movement, whose manipulation of social grievances and development of the techniques of religious terrorism were a challenge to the civilization of a universal, Catholic Empire.[3]

In the case of North Africa, the result of the acceptance of this interpretation has been that two views of the rôle of Christianity in

---

gladio martyres feriuntur, omnes ad bestias martyres subriguntur aut inssionibus iudicum vivi ignibus concremantur.

A similar attempt has been made to see in the Pelagian heresy the inspiration of a movement of political reform which precipitated the end of Roman rule in Britain—see J. N. L. Myres, 'Pelagius and the End of Roman Rule in Britain', *Journal of Roman Studies*, 50, 1960, pp. 21–36. This ingenious, though fanciful, interpretation assumes that Pelagius' attack on the Augustinian system, which emphasized the unlimited 'grace'—*gratia*—of an omnipotent God, can be regarded as the reflection—or, perhaps, as the focusing-point—of criticisms of the uncontrolled 'graft'—*gratia*—of the totalitarian Roman Empire. [See p. 184.]

[1] Gibbon, *Decline and Fall*, Ch. ii, ed. Bury, 1896, I, p. 58.

[2] W. H. C. Frend, 'The Revival of Berber Art', *Antiquity*, December, 1942, pp. 342–52. [See p. 279 n.]

[3] See esp. Ernst Stein, *Histoire du Bas-Empire*, II, 1949, pp. 34–6.

the Later Roman Empire have come to coexist where previously there had been one. There is the view of Eusebius, Optatus of Milevis and Augustine. The Emperors had given their sanction to the universal mission of the Catholic Church; in the fourth century, both Church and Empire stand for values held to be universal throughout the Mediterranean; in the Middle Ages, the Catholic Church is the continuator of this universal Roman civilization. To this view has been added a growing awareness of the strength and originality of another form of Christianity: the religion of Donatus, who had asked 'What has the Emperor to do with the Church?' This religion is held to express the aspirations of a local Christian church, representing the resistance of one group to an alien civilization; it formulated its resistance in rejecting as impure the universal Catholic Church and in maintaining all that was most intransigent in the Early Church—the cult of the martyrs, martyrs who could be made under both a pagan and a Christian Roman government.

These appear as two very different forms of Christianity; and it will long remain the task of the historian to decide to what extent they were mutually exclusive in the fourth century. To what extent did Donatism really represent an exclusive, local tradition of resistance, and so can be treated as a symptom of the break-up of the parasitic bulk of the Roman Empire; and to what extent has this emphasis on what was local and exclusive in Donatism obscured its links with the Christian Church as a whole? It may perhaps be shown that Donatism—for all its local power—was part of a wider revolution, provoked by the rise of Christianity, in the Latin world; and that the history of this African schism is relevant not only to the rise of Islam in the south, but to the development of medieval Latin Catholicism in the north.

In its enthusiastic reconstruction of the local roots of Donatism, Dr. Frend's book is a reminder of the progress made, over the past century, by French scholarship in Algeria. For the historian, the most striking contribution of this tradition of regional scholarship has been the tendency to treat North African history as a continuous process which admits no sharp and arbitrary division between the ancient world and the Islamic Middle Ages. Thus Dr. Frend not only makes use of our knowledge, derived from archaeology, of what was local and continuous—the churches, gravestones, olive-presses and martyrs' shrines of Numidia; he has arranged this knowledge around a permanent theme in African history—Donatism is only a phase in the religious history of that impermeable bedrock of African particularism, the Berber people. 'Is Donatism', he asks, 'part of a continuous native tradition as fundamentally unchanged as the Berbers in the outline of their daily life?'[1]

Seen in such a light, those features of Donatism which so shocked Augustine are made to form part of an impressive continuum of Berber history. The Circumcellions are the precursors of the *marabouts*; and their leader, the notorious Optatus of Timgad—to Augustine, the 'ten-year groan of Africa'—foreshadows the Kharedjite ruler of the tenth century, Abu Aziz. This first wakening of the religious fervour of the Maghreb showed that 'North Africa' could become 'Berbery'.

But while recognizing the attraction of this theory, it is important to draw attention to a bias implicit in the search for continuity in every period of African history. Our greatest advances have been made, of late, under the guiding-star of an appreciation of the continuous strength of particular, local traditions; and what is continuous we like to regard as being what is peculiar to Africa. Such an emphasis is one-sided. It fails to do justice to the other factor in North African history. In both the Later Roman and the Islamic periods, the province was part of a Mediterranean-wide Empire, claiming official allegiance to a universal and exclusive religion. Thus the 'universal' and the 'particular' have had to coexist in Africa; they can also be seen to interact. Modern Algerian sociology has, on the whole, failed to analyse this interaction. Early, it discovered the Berbers, and has continued to treat them as the 'real', because permanent, Africans. It has studied most fully the non-Islamic or sub-Islamic elements in Berber law and religion; and it has assumed, too readily, that Islam is the 'façade' and that the Berbers, least affected by this universal and, superficially, exclusive faith, are the 'reality' in North African life.[2] There is little wonder that so convincing a model should have been adopted and applied, somewhat ruthlessly, by scholars wishing to understand the religious dislocation of Roman Africa: thus, the 'Roman' Catholicism of Augustine was the 'façade' and Donatism the 'reality' in the Berber province of Numidia.

[1] Frend, *op. cit.* p. xvi.
[2] J. Berque, 'Cent vingt-cinq ans de sociologie maghrébine', *Annales*, 11e année, No. 3, 1956, pp. 296–324. [See p. 282, n. 2.]

But, if such an emphasis is incomplete for modern Algeria, it is all the more so for Roman North Africa. We are not faced with the choice between 'façade' and 'reality'. It is the combination of great local power with a 'universal' Latin culture and a Christian religion of 'universal' validity which is the most striking feature of the Donatist predominance in Africa. Take the position of Optatus of Timgad, the dictator of the Numidian Donatist movement. The city from which he ruled is far from being a Berber holy place, with Optatus himself representing an exclusively native element. His control of Numidian Donatism cannot be ascribed solely to his alliance with the Circumcellions and to the sinister toadyism which marks his relations with the Moorish count Gildo; it could have been derived in part from the fact that Timgad was a Roman city. This ensured that the see in which he had planted his enormous cathedral, dedicated, in Latin, to his own glory, had enjoyed the incalculable prestige of being a centre of Roman civilization in an under-urbanized area, sharing a long tradition of Roman culture and municipal life, whose resilience is shown not only by many inscriptions of the third century but by the famous municipal *Album* of 364, with its list of patrons, civic officers, pagan priests and officials.[1]

The danger of a one-sided emphasis on the local roots of Donatism among the Berbers is that, in interpreting the ecclesiastical history of the fourth century, we may be led to look in the wrong direction. By insisting on seeing in concrete terms the religious tensions between a Christian Church and a Christian Emperor, we may forget that this tension was, in the first instance, a tension common to much of the Christian Church, and so required no local model of discontent to explain its appearance and persistence in the Latin world.

The conversion of Constantine had led to sufficient confusion, and the demands of the Imperial government continued to be sufficiently unpopular in other provinces, to provoke reactions reminiscent of extreme Donatism. We should not think, for instance, of looking in the works of the pagan Ammianus Marcellinus for examples of the cult of the martyrs as an expression of popular discontent; but it is there, of all places, that we learn that, in Milan, three leading

[1] See M. Leglay, 'La vie intellectuelle d'une cité africaine des confins de l'Aurès, *Hommages à Léon Hermann*, Collection Latomus, xliv, 1960, pp. 485–91. [See p. 294.]

officials, unjustly executed by the Emperor Valentinian, were revered as martyrs at a spot called *Ad Innocentes*, and that this Emperor had been deterred from ordering the execution of whole town-councils in Pannonia for fear of provoking a similar reaction.[1] Nor should this surprise us; if we are surprised, it is because we live in a very law-abiding country, and assume, too readily, that only an exceptional degree of social or ethnic tension could provoke the violent religious protests which we associate with these episodes as with Donatism.

An attitude to the Emperor as intransigent as that of the Donatists is by no means peculiar to Africa. The attempt of Constantius II to impose his brand of orthodoxy on men such as Hilary of Poitiers and Lucifer of Cagliari led to protests which, in their proclaimed allegiance to the integrity of the 'church of the martyrs', and, also, in the remarkable vehemence of their language, outdid the most swingeing manifestos of the Donatists. Hilary could write to the Emperor:

I proclaim to you, Constantius, what I would have spoken to Nero, what Decius and Maximian would have heard from me: you are fighting against God, you vent your wrath against the Church, you persecute the saints, you hate the preachers of Christ, you take away religion; you are a usurper, not only of things human, but of things divine;[2]

and the intransigence of Lucifer of Cagliari led to the foundation of small schismatic communities in Sardinia, Rome and in many other towns of the Empire.[3]

Such protests cannot be compared, in their results, with Donatism; but neither protest should be treated in isolation from the other. The 'foreign policy' of the Donatists, as analysed by Professor Brisson, does not add up to much;[4] but this need not mean that the Donatist leaders were unaware of sharing with elements of Christianity outside Africa a similar attitude to the State and to the integrity of the Church. We know that a cultured Donatist had read the letters of Hilary castigating the tame collaboration of the Eastern

[1] Ammianus Marcellinus, *Res gestae*, xxvii, 7, 5, 6 ed. Clark, pp. 433–4.
[2] Hilary, *Liber contra Constantium*, 7: PL 10, 583.
[3] G. Krüger, *Lucifer Bischof von Calaris u. das Schisma d. Luciferianer*, 1886.
[4] Brisson, *op. cit.*, esp. pp. 205–18.

churches under Constantius II;[1] and a man such as Tyconius, for what little we know of him, may be the representative of a frame of mind which saw the place of Africa in the Christian world not in terms of a dichotomy between 'separatism' and 'universalism', but as a microcosm whose views would, sooner or later, be shared by the macrocosm—'What has been done in Africa', he wrote, 'must appear to the whole world.'[2]

Perhaps the search for a concrete basis of local discontent has been carried too far. To look for 'nationalism' of any sort in the Later Roman Empire would seem an anachronism. It involves a judgement on the thought-world of the Late Roman Christians which, however necessary and desirable it is to recover this world, is far from certain. Anachronism, however, is an easy ghost with which to frighten historians; and most treatments of North Africa have been singularly free from the temptation to import modern notions into a history which is so continuous and, apparently, self-explanatory. A more sophisticated danger lies in the adoption of 'models' of the social and ethnic structure of a province; models which are, in themselves, too simple to explain the vagaries of religious dissent.

In a recent article, Professor A. H. M. Jones has come to an entirely negative conclusion on the evidence presented by Sir Llewellyn Woodward, Dr. Frend and Ernst Stein, among others, for the assumed 'social' and 'national' basis of the great heresies and schisms.[3] His attack on the simplicity of this thesis is the most interesting part in his treatment. The emphasis on monolithic cleavages cannot find room for the oddities of religious dissent. Augustine, for instance, found in his own diocese—in a countryside noted for its aggressive Donatism—a Berber village occupied by a sect which had succeeded for a long time in imitating the continence of Abel.[4] Nor were the towns any more homogeneous; in Carthage, a sect dedicated to the memory of Tertullian survived into the fifth century.[5] But these are trifles; what matters most is that those who look for a social basis of discontent have to face the fact that, of all the subjects studied by an historian, the relation of the parts of a

[1] Augustine, *Ep.* 93, vi, 21, to Vincentius of Cartennae, CSEL xxxiv, p. 467.

[2] T. Hahn, *Tyconius—Studien*, 1900, p. 85. [See pp. 294–6.]

[3] A. H M. Jones, 'Were the ancient heresies national or social movements in disguise?' *Journal of Theological Studies*, new series, x, 2, October 1959, pp. 280–95.

[4] Augustine, *De haeresibus*, 87: PL 42, 47.

[5] *Ibid.* 86, PL, 42, 46.

society—whether of classes or areas—to each other is the subject in which certainty is least possible, and a false certainty most misleading.

Thus our knowledge of the urbanization of the Later Roman Empire has led to a modification and, for certain areas, to a rejection of Rostovtzeff's interpretation of the crisis of the third century, and of the state of the towns resulting from this crisis.[1] The evidence varies from province to province. In Italy, urbanization seems to continue at the expense of the smaller towns: the population of Rome remained at a high level;[2] while the structure of a town such as Ostia may have changed rather than the town itself decayed.[3] In Africa, the collection of a surprising number of inscriptions which proclaim the continued resilience of many Roman towns has been regarded as 'one of the most interesting facts revealed by the epigraphy of North Africa'.[4]

Such evidence is, inevitably, fragmentary and ambiguous. It should be noted, however, that the most recent studies of the life of the towns in this period have emphasized not so much their economic as their cultural position in Later Roman society.[5] The balance between towns and countryside cannot be seen in purely quantitative terms of wealth and population; in the culture of the period, the towns are still separated from the countryside by the immeasurable, qualitative, gap between civilization and its absence.

A Christianity which rejected the towns is improbable; and the fact that the Donatist movement continued, throughout the fourth century, to be led from Roman centres such as Carthage, Cirta and Timgad seems to suggest that such a conscious rejection did not take place. In Egypt, however, it has been customary to regard monasticism as an entirely non-urban movement: the hermits are said to have shunned both the subtleties of the urban theologians

---

[1] See esp. Santo Mazzarino, *Aspetti sociali del quarto secolo*, 1951, ch. v, pp. 217–69. [See p. 57, n. 1.]

[2] A. Chastagnol, 'Le ravaitaillement de Rome en viande au ive siècle', *Revue historique*, 210, 1953, pp. 13–22.

[3] A. P. Fevrier, 'Ostie et Porto à la fin de l'Antiquité: topographie religieuse et vic sociale', *Mél. d'Archéologie et d'Histoire*, lxx, 1957–8, pp. 295–330; but cf. Russell Meiggs, *Roman Ostia*, 1960.

[4] B. H. Warmington, *The North African Provinces from Diocletian to the Vandal Conquest*, 1954, p. 37.

[5] E.g. P. Petit, *Libanius et la vie municipale d'Antioche au ive siècle*, 1951. [See p. 90.]

and the ecclesiastical hierarchy of the urban bishops.[1] This may not be the case. There are many examples of close relations between these monastic communities and the ecclesiastical hierarchy of the Egyptian Church; and the monastic movement was so effective, in the ecclesiastical politics of the East, because it was so well led by the ecclesiastical leaders—that is, by the bishops in the towns, of whom the patriarch of Alexandria was the greatest.[2]

Indeed, a view which sees in the survival of a great schismatic church the expression of inevitable loyalties does not do sufficient justice to the rôle of leadership and to the commonplaces of ecclesiastical administration. What is particularly true of the 'Empire' of the patriarch of Alexandria is true also of the organization of the African Church. The most striking feature of this is the combination of an extraordinarily high number of bishops—at the Conference of 411 the Donatists had 284 bishops and the Catholics 286—with the unchallenged hegemony of a single leader—for instance, of the successive primates of Carthage, both Catholic and Donatist— Cyprian, Donatus 'Prince of Tyre', Primian and Aurelius. This is not surprising: as bishops of small townships and villages, the majority of the rank and file had no wish to quarrel with such leaders. Such massive acquiescence gives an impression of solidarity which could be interpreted as the expression of some more forceful loyalty. In fact, the local bishops had already got what they most appreciated; they were the masters of their small worlds and so virtually irremovable. Their position is a tribute to the cohesion of the African villages,[3] but hardly to their animus against the religion of the towns. Both sides experienced the limited anarchism of these little men. The Catholic Council regretted that, once a priest had installed himself as the bishop of a village, there was no getting rid of him—'they lord it, like a usurper in his fortress'.[4] And the co-

---

[1] Frend, *art. cit.* p. 23: For this view see esp. Reitzenstein, *Historia monachorum u. Historia Lausiaca*, 1916; K. Heussi, *Der Ursprung des Mönchtums*, 1936.

[2] H. Bacht, 'Die Rolle d. orientalischen Mönchtums in d. kirchenpolitischen Auseinandersetzungen um Chalkedon (431–519)', *Das Konzil von Chalkedon*, II, 1953, pp. 193–314.

[3] For the good effects on the morale of a village of the establishment of a church and a priest, see John Chrysostom, *Hom. in Act. Apost.*, 18, 4 and 5: PG 60, 147. [See p. 295, n. 3].

[4] *Concilium Carthaginiense*, III, c. 42: now in C. G. Goldaraz, *Los concilios de Cartago de un codice Soriense: Reconstrucción*, 1960, p. 84.

hesion of these small communities could cut either way. The Catholics found that Donatist villages were quite prepared to remain loyal to their new masters as long as they were provided with a bishop: this happened at Tucca, a small town in the Donatist diocese of Milevis, which hitherto had had to be content with a priest.[1]

By pointing to such a mundane problem as the passivity of a country clergy—a phenomenon too easily mistaken for a deeply-motivated tenacity—we do not intend to replace one unduly simple model by another. It is sufficient to have drawn attention to some of the weak points of a view which sees in the rise and persistence of a schismatic church such as Donatism, the expression of deeper forces of disintegration. Such a view forms part of an emphasis which has affected deeply our approach to the Later Roman Empire in general. We talk of the 'break up' of the Later Roman Empire; and in recent years we have increased our knowledge of this period by our insistence on dissecting the sinister process of fragmentation which we choose to see in every aspect of Later Roman life. At the top, we see conflicts between a Christian Imperial administration and the selfish isolationism of a predominantly pagan senatorial class of landowners;[2] at the bottom, in Salvian's Gaul of the fifth century, social discontent prepared even to welcome the barbarians;[3] and in Egypt, the uncomprehending localism of the Coptic peasants, expressed in a charming fairy-tale which saw in the battle of Adrianople and the Gothic invasions, nothing more than a distant single combat: 'When the Emperor Theodosius saw a great and powerful barbarian bearing down upon him, he was afraid, and fled; and we have been told that the barbarian ran through all the Roman people, running hither and thither, seeking the Emperor with great violence!'[4] The most obvious example of the working of these centrifugal forces—the lasting division between East and West—has been treated not merely as the result of a political division of the Empire

---

[1] *Gesta Collationis Carthaginiensis* 1, 65 and 130: PL 11, 1274–5 and 1298.

[2] J. A. McGeachy, Jr., 'Quintus Aurelius Symmachus and the Senatorial Aristocracy of the West', Dissertation of the University of Chicago, 1942. A. Alföldi, *A Conflict of Ideas in the Later Roman Empire, the clash between the Senate and Valentinian I*, transl. H. Mattingly, 1952.

[3] E. A. Thompson, 'Peasant Revolts in Later Roman Gaul and Spain', *Past and Present*, No. 2, 1952, pp. 11–21.

[4] R. Rémondon, 'Problèmes militaires en Egypte et dans l'Empire romain à la fin du ive siècle', *Revue historique*, 213, 1955, pp. 21–38 quoted on p. 33.

between the sons of Theodosius I, but as the symptom of this process of social and cultural fragmentation.[1]

In this picture dominated by centrifugal forces, we have left very little room for a centripetal reaction. Yet this same period saw not only the Imperial reconquest of Justinian, but the growth in Gaul and Italy of a universal Catholic Church, whose bishops remained conscious of the universal links of Latin culture and senatorial rank. These men, or their predecessors, did not live—and live well—in a disintegrating world without some reaction. Thus the only trace of 'nationalism' in the incident of the rebellion of Count Gildo in Africa is not to be found in the limited aspirations of that military adventurer, but in the tirade of Claudian, the poet of the Roman Senate, who poured scorn on the *regnum Bocchi*—the petty native principality—which had dared to oppose the universal mission of Rome.[2] At least this senatorial class, the continued influence and cohesion of which we are beginning to appreciate more fully,[3] was aware that the values of a universal civilization were at stake. The reflection of this concern found its way into the prayers of the Roman Church. The Church was to enjoy its 'liberty' not only in the strictly Christian sense of asserting its freedom from servitude to the Devil, but in a Roman sense—in the freedom to enjoy a stable order: hence the prayer of the Gelasian Sacramentary, that *'ut superatis pacis inimicis, secura tibi serviat Romana libertas'*.[4]

But whether we interpret the origins of religious dissent in terms of other centrifugal tendencies or not, it remains, in itself, an ominous sign. It shows that a large proportion of the Christians subject to the rule of an emphatically orthodox emperor took very little notice of his frequent exhortations that there should be 'One Catholic Veneration, One Salvation'. In Africa, and elsewhere, such dissent had remained normal and virtually unchallenged for

[1] E. Demougeot, *De l'unité à la division de l'Empire romain*, Paris, 1951.

[2] Claudian, *de bello Gildonico*, 1. 94, ed. M. Platnauer, Loeb I, p. 104.

[3] For Gaul: K. Stroheker, *Der senatorische Adel im spätantiken Gallien*, 1948.
For Italy: A. D. Momigliano, 'Cassiodorus and the Italian Culture of his Time', *Proc. Brit. Acad.* xli, 1955, pp. 207–45; and 'Gli *Anicii* e la storiografia latina del vi. secolo d.c.', *Acc. Lincei*, anno cccliii, 1956, viii, *Rendiconti*, vol. xi, fasc. 11–12, pp. 279–97 [pp. 64–6].

[4] G. Tellenbach, *Church, State and Christian Society at the Time of the Investiture Contest*, transl. R. F. Bennett (*Studies in Medieval History*, 3); 1940, p. 14, n. 2. 'That, having overcome the enemies of peace, the Roman Liberty might serve Thee in security.'

generations. The Imperial administration, which continued to show its strength by disastrously over-taxing its subjects,[1] seems to have done very little to reduce to order the many brands of Christianity established throughout its provinces. The remark of the ecclesiastical historian, Sozomenos, on the effect of the decrees of the Emperors against the Montanists in Phrygia, reveals a strange situation: 'The Phrygians suffered the same treatment as the other heretics, in all the Roman provinces except Phrygia and its neighbouring regions, for here they had, since the time of Montanus, existed in great numbers, and do so to the present day.'[2]

Africa is the most notorious example of this failure of a Christian Empire, conscious of its unity and still able in other matters to impose its will. In this province the union of the two centripetal forces in fourth-century society—the Imperial authority and the Catholic Church—was effectively challenged. The drama of the situation is increased if we believe, with some scholars, that this alliance had been a calculated act of policy. The alliance had been made by Constantine and was tested immediately by the outbreak of the Donatist schism in 312. Were it not for the avidity with which the Catholic party collected a dossier of the official pronouncements of Constantine on the notorious 'case of Caecilian', we should know immeasurably less about his attitude to the Christian Church immediately after his mysterious conversion at the Milvian Bridge. It is important that we should know. The 'Constantinian problem' lies at the root of Later Roman history; and it is the great merit of Professor Brisson's book that the problem of Constantine's relations with the Christian Church has been placed in the forefront of his treatment of Donatism. The conversion of Constantine is, in his view, the centripetal reaction *par excellence*. The issue at stake is not the protest of a particularist group, but the autonomy of a provincial tradition of Christianity in a universal and parasitic Empire. It was Constantine who provoked this struggle by allying the Empire with the universal Catholic Church.

Gibbon had already sensed the importance of such an alliance: 'The passive and unresisting obedience', he remarked, 'which bows under the yoke of authority, or even of oppression, must have

---

[1] A. H. M. Jones, 'Over-Taxation and the Decline of the Roman Empire', *Antiquity*, xxxiii, 1959, pp. 39–43.

[2] Sozomen, *Hist. eccles.* II, 32, 6, ed. J. Bidez, *Die griechischen christl. Schriftsteller der ersten Jahrhte.*, 1960, p. 98. [See pp. 301–331.]

appeared in the eyes of an absolute monarch the most conspicuous and useful of the evangelic virtues.'[1] But Gibbon had not been prepared to embark upon the difficult, and unpopular, task of deciding whether this Erastian vision of the passivity of the only unified religious body in his Empire was, in fact, the consideration which prompted Constantine in his conversion. Modern scholarship has forced many of us to make this decision. In England we have been protected by the works of Norman Baynes and A. H. M. Jones from doubts as to the somewhat inept sincerity of Constantine in his relations with the Christian Church.[2] This is not so in M. Brisson's France. The legendary nexus of Constantine's conversion and, especially, the *Life of Constantine* by Eusebius, have been discredited as later falsifications. With them goes the picture of Constantine as a sincere Christian Emperor, swearing that he had been converted by a sign. We are left with what is very much the Constantine of the African Catholic dossier: a formidable patron of the Catholic religion, whose sincerity is unknown, but whose insistence, from the earliest years of his reign, on the peace and unanimity of both the Christian Church and his newly-conquered Empire, is so marked a feature of his public utterances that we are left to suspect that this craving for the unity of his own Empire under one god is the clue to his constant alliance with the one Church.

The conversion of Constantine has come to be regarded as a unilateral act of patronage by the Roman state to such an extent that it has even been suggested that the position of the Catholic bishops was equated to that of the more privileged officials of the Empire; and that their insignia, in the coming centuries, were a visible sign of the incorporation of the Church into the all-powerful bureaucratic machine.[3] In the words of Professor Grégoire, whose dissection of the evidence for the conversion of Constantine has done most to provoke such a conclusion on the policy of the first Christian Emperor: 'J'ai dit et je répète que de la grande

[1] Gibbon, Ch. xx, ed. Bury, II, p. 294.

[2] N. H. Baynes, 'Constantine the Great and the Christian Church', *Proc. Brit. Acad*, xv, 1929, pp. 341–442. A. H. M. Jones, *Constantine and the Conversion of Europe*, 1948.

[3] Th. Klauser, *Der Ursprung der bischöflichen Insignien u. Ehrenrechte* (Bonner akad. Reden, 1), 1948, which argues that the bishops had enjoyed the honorary rank of *viri illustres*, and that Papal insignia, such as the *pallium*, the *stola* and the shoes, were bestowed by the Emperor in recognition of the official rank of the Popes.

révolution religieuse du ive siècle, il est non le Dumouriez, mais le Napoléon.'[1]

To M. Brisson, the foresight of Constantine is amply justified by the vigorous loyalty of the African Catholics—represented by Optatus and Augustine—who clamoured to the Emperor to impose religious 'Unity' on a divided province, by force if needs be. The problem of religious coercion raised its ugly head; and in a form destined to have a long history. M. Brisson sees the justification, by Augustine, of the coercive powers of the Emperor in a new and interesting light. Such a justification, he believes, should not be treated as merely an expedient reaction to immediate political necessity and local interests. It was—as one would only expect from Augustine—something both deeper and more thoroughly developed than this: it was the reflection of a whole view of society, authoritarian and patriarchal. And in thus enunciating, in its most thorough form, the Catholic Ethic, Augustine appears as the theorist of the Constantinian revolution: 'Cette coincidence de la morale chrétienne et d'un ordre social déterminé, qui justifiait pour Augustin le recours au pouvoir civil en matière religieuse, Constantin en avait eu l'intention au moins confuse.'[2]

Whatever we are prepared to think about the intentions of Constantine, the fact remains that the unilateral act which marked the alliance of Church and State, and whose effects are so obvious in the Byzantine Empire, was a revolution which failed most notably to reach fulfilment in the West. It would be wrong, in concentrating too closely on the local roots of a schism, to ignore the extent of this failure and the spiritual revolution which made such a failure inevitable.

Passive obedience was not the only virtue of the Christian; his crowning virtue had, for three centuries, been martyrdom. No matter how much we may, as historians of law, follow Gibbon in devaluing the number of the victims, the physical horrors and the political repercussions of the Roman persecutions, we have still to explain the fact that martyrdom was regarded as an integral part of the relations between Christians and the 'world', and that the Persecutions of the Church were regarded as being nothing less

---

[1] H. Grégoire, 'Les persécutions dans l'Empire romain', Académie royale de Belgique, classe des lettres et des sciences morales et politiques, mémoires, 2e série, tom. 46, 1950, p. 89.

[2] Brisson, op. cit., p. 288 [pp. 260–278].

than the central issue in the history of the Roman Empire as written by Christian historians. This question has been raised and answered most cogently by Dr. Frend, and, on a more purely intellectual plane, by Professor Ehrhardt.[1] Dr. Frend's contribution is most rewarding: with his gift for the concrete in religious history, he has traced the Christian attitude to martyrdom from the previous history of religious tension between Greeks and Jews in Palestine and in the cities of the Hellenistic world. The Christian tradition of martyrdom reached back to the Maccabees; its immediate background is provided by the vicious outburst of anti-semitism in Alexandria and elsewhere, beside whose victims, numbered in their thousands, the list of Christian martyrs pales into insignificance.

Seen in this light, the origins of religious dissent in the Later Roman Empire reach back to the rise of Christianity itself on the fringes of the Jewish diaspora. It succeeded Judaism as the spearhead of a revolution. On the religious plane, the rise of Christianity marked the end of the 'Ancient City', whose values are so clearly summed up by Fustel de Coulanges: 'L'État et la religion étaient si complètement confondus ensemble qu'il était impossible nonseulement d'avoir l'idée d'un conflit entre eux, mais même de les distinguer l'un de l'autre.'[2]

Such a view had never been imposed on Christianity; and in the West the newly established church was still raw from this conflict. To Christian contemporaries, Nebuchadnezzar, King of Babylon, was the symbol of the newly established Christian Empire. He was a significant and ambiguous symbol. As Nebuchadnezzar had cast the Three Children of Israel into the fiery furnace, so the Roman Emperors had persecuted the Just; like Nebuchadnezzar, again, they had been converted, and were expected to persecute the Unjust— the pagans and heretics. But neither Catholics nor heretics showed any hesitation in reminding the Emperors of their unconverted past. Pope Liberius implied that Constantius II was his Nebuchadnezzar; and it is Augustine, not a Donatist writer, who said that, when the Feast of the Three Children of Israel—a feast celebrated with especial fervour in all the churches—came round each year, the

---

[1] W. H. C. Frend, 'The Persecutions: some links between Judaism and the Early Church', *Journal of Ecclesiastical History*, ix, 1958, pp. 141–58; Arnold A. T. Ehrhardt, *Politische Metaphysik von Solon bis Augustin*, Bd. II, 'Die christliche Revolution', 1959 [pp. 337–8].

[2] Fustel de Coulanges, *La Cité antique*, livr. III, c. vii, 4, 5th ed. p. 197.

Christian Emperor should remember his past and contemplate with profit the 'pious liberty' of these archetypes of the Christian martyrs.[1] Such advice was kept by the Catholics of the West. In Latin Christianity, Constantine did not become a saint, as he did in the Greek Church.[2] It was a significant and undeniable difference: however much it might be regretted by some contemporaries—and later by Dante—this 'desertion of the West' by Constantine was the hallmark of the papal Middle Ages:

> sotto buona intenzion che fè mal frutto
> per cedere al pastor si fece greco.[3]

Thus the battle for the freedom of the church in a pagan state was too recent to be easily forgotten. It is not surprising that Lucifer of Cagliari, in his most vehement tract against an heretical Christian Emperor—'*On dying for the Son of God*'—should have copied out those passages in the *Divine Institutes* of Lactantius in which this 'Christian Cicero', himself an African, had defended in a magnificent appeal against the conservative autocracy of the pagan Emperor Diocletian, the rights of the individual conscience in religion.[4] The failure of the Great Persecution of Diocletian was regarded as the confirmation of a long process of religious self-assertion against the conformism of a pagan Empire. Freedom to assert a belief not recognized by the State was won and held. 'However much Christian Churches and States may have sinned, in later times, by their religious coercion, the martyrdoms of the Roman Persecutions belong to the history of freedom.'[5] And in this revolution, which affected so deeply the North African provinces of the fourth and fifth centuries, the issues at stake were not merely the local grievances of a province; they were nothing less than the place of religion in society.

[1] Augustine, *contra litteras Petiliani*, II, xcii, 211, CSEL lii, p. 136. For an example of the scene of Nebuchadnezzar and the three Children of Israel in fourth-century art, see the painting in the catacomb of SS. Mark and Marcellianus, illustrated in the *Rivista di Archeologica Cristiana*, 25, 1949, p. 13.

[2] W. Kaegi, 'Vom Nachleben Konstantins', *Schweizerische Zeitschrift f. Geschichte*, 8, 1958, 289–326.

[3] Dante, *Paradiso*, xx, 56 f.

[4] Lactantius, *Divin. Inst.*, v, 18–21, CSEL, xix, pp. 458–72. See N. H. Baynes, 'The Great Persecution', *Cambridge Ancient History*, vol. XII, 1939, pp. 646–77.

[5] J. Vogt. s.v. 'Christenverfolgung' (historisch) I, *Reallexikon f. Antike u. Christentum*, 2, Lieferung 16, 1954, col. 1207.

ST. AUGUSTINE'S ATTITUDE TO RELIGIOUS COERCION*†

Augustine had to face the issue of religious coercion throughout his episcopate, and especially in his dealings with the Donatist schism. As far as I know, he is the only writer in the Early Church to discuss the subject at length. He even changed his mind on the issue, and he has told us of this 'conversion' with characteristic disarming frankness. It is a change which cannot fail to interest us, for whom the problem remains acutely relevant. He went on to justify religious coercion with a thoroughness and coherence which is quite as much part of his character as is his candour: and so Augustine has appeared to generations of religious liberals as 'le prince et patriarche des persécuteurs'.[1]

Augustine's attitude to coercion is typical of the general quality of his thought. This thought never appears as a 'doctrine' in a state of rest: it is marked by a painful and protracted attempt to embrace and resolve tensions. As a result of this quality, Augustine's thought on coercion, like many of his other opinions, has been regarded, throughout the centuries, with profound ambivalence. The historian who wishes to understand Augustine's evolution on this issue must resign himself, as best he can, to living with this ambivalence. It will

* *Journal of Roman Studies*, LIV, 1964, pp. 107–16.

† This paper was given at the Fourth International Congress on Patristic Studies, in September, 1963. I owe a particular debt to the challenging treatments of W. H. C. Frend, *The Donatist Church* (Oxford 1952) and R. Joly, 'S. Augustin et l'intolérance religieuse,' *Rev. belge de philol. et d'histoire* XXXIII (1955), 263–94; and to the helpful remarks of Dr. Frend and le R. P. M. F. Berrouard, O.P. at the time of the Congress.

[1] E. Lamirande, 'Un siècle et demi d'études sur l'ecclésiologie de S. Augustin: Essai bibliographique', *Rev. des études aug.* VIII (1962), 1–124, contains extensive references to the literature on this subject. All references accompanied simply by volume number and page are from the *Corpus Scriptorum Ecclesiae Latinorum* of Vienna.

not help his understanding if he cuts the Gordian knot. He cannot simply erect Augustine's 'attitude' into a 'doctrine'—a fleshless abstraction that may be demolished, modified or justified (as has been done since the Reformation).[1] Nor can he avoid this ambivalence by following the more recent historical fashion, by dismissing Augustine's attitude as a mere *ex post facto* rationalization of inevitable circumstances: as the expression of an 'age of intolerance',[2] or as the natural reaction of a Roman bishop to movements which, it is said, had threatened to disrupt the social order with which he was identified.[3]

For this reason, I should like to abandon the word 'doctrine' and substitute the word 'attitude'. We may make some progress in understanding Augustine's ideas if we treat them as an 'attitude'— that is, as placed a little lower than the angels of pure Augustinian theology, and a little higher than the beasts of the social and political necessities of the North African provinces.

In the later Roman Empire, religious coercion, in some form, was one of the 'facts of life' for a provincial bishop. Even if contemporaries did not wish to deplore or justify what was going on around them, they had to take up some attitude towards it: and this attitude would, at least, allow them to impose shape and meaning on the events in which they were so deeply implicated. The ecclesiastical sources of the Latin Empire contain many fragments of just such attitudes to the problem of coercion. One need expect very little from these in terms of intellectual content: attitudes are moulded less by abstract thought than by the unconscious and unreflective selection of certain prejudices. But it is possible to trace in them the rudiments of what—to adapt, and limit, the excellent term of Lucien

[1] v. J. Lecler, *Histoire de la Tolérance au siècle de la Réforme*, vols. I, II (1955) (transl. Weston, *Toleration and the Reformation*, 1960). P. Bayle, *Commentaire philosophique* . . . (revised ed. Amsterdam, 1713), remains the classic demolition of Augustine's argument.

[2] v. references and criticisms in Joly, art. cit. [p. 260, n.†], 263–6.

[3] For reserves on such an interpretation of the problem of coercion in the Later Empire v. P. R. L. Brown, 'Religious Coercion in the Later Roman Empire: the case of North Africa', *History* XLVIII (1963), 283–306 [pp. 237–259]. The best exponents of this view, Frend, o.c. [p. 260, n.†], 227–43, and J.-P. Brisson, *Autonomisme et christianisme dans l'Afrique romaine* (1958), 269–88, contain shrewd judgements on Augustine's final attitude to coercion, but pay insufficient attention to its sources and evolution. [See now R. Joly, 'L'intolérance de Saint Augustin, doctrine ou attitude?', *Hommages à Marcel Renard*, I (Collection Latomus, 101), 1969, pp. 493–500.]

Febvre[1]—we might call an 'outillage moral', a 'moral equipment'. Each writer has a slightly different 'outillage moral'. He draws upon a wide, yet distinctive, field of thought and experience: and we can see how it is the nature and source of his 'outillage' that moulds his attitude. We can appreciate that he is arguing under different stars from Augustine, that he reflects a different climate of opinion, and, in certain cases, that his assumptions would lead him to very different conclusions from those of the Bishop of Hippo. Thus, when Bishop Porphyry of Gaza is confronted, in 402, with a situation similar to that which will confront Augustine after the suppression of the Donatist church in 405—that is, with a whole new congregation converted by coercive measures—he will turn instinctively to a different world of experience from that of Augustine. He can justify his reception of such men by appealing to the fact that there are sorts of virtues that come from circumstances—that is, περιστατικαὶ ἀρεταί.[2] This term takes us into what is distinctive in Porphyry's world, and unknown in Augustine's: the problem of monks who had been forced to flee the world, not through religious impulse, but merely by the force of overwhelming circumstances. Such a monk was Macarius, the Murderer, who had originally become a hermit because he had committed a murder and, so, had been forced to flee to the desert. Palladius had told this story in his 'Lausiac History' to show that there could be such things as περιστατικαὶ ἀρεταί;[3] and for Porphyry and the readers of his biography, such a little anecdote of the devious ways of human beings in the Egyptian desert would provide a reassuring analogy to grapple with the more sinister problems of religious coercion.

So, when we study Augustine, we must go behind the somewhat threadbare arguments contained in his justification of the coercion of the Donatists, and attempt to reconstruct, on a deeper level, the sources and shape of his own, distinctive, 'outillage moral'. This can be a rash undertaking. It must involve speculating about the possible relation of different planes of thought and experience; and it is in danger of appearing, perhaps, too sophisticated an instrument of research when applied to the blunt and unambiguous language of

---

[1] L. Febvre, *Le problème de l'incroyance au XVIe siècle: La religion de Rabelais* (Évolution de l'Humanité, 1942), 157.

[2] Marc le Diacre, *Vie de Porphyre*, c. 73, ed. Grégoire-Kugener (Association G. Budé, 1930), 57–9.

[3] Palladius. *Historia Lausiaca*, c. xv.

Augustine's pamphlets against the Donatists. But, just as the modern psychologist can perceive significant patterns and relations in the apparently unrelated and somewhat trite remarks of a patient, so the historian must use refined tools to seize the full implication of Augustine's explicit statements; and so we may use these pamphlets as a door into the moral climate of this crucial age, which saw the final establishment of Christianity as the official religion of the Roman Empire.

Another danger to be avoided, at all costs, is the temptation to impose an academic consistency on Augustine, a man of mysterious discontinuities, wielding authority in a complex and violent situation. But it is one thing to see a man's thought as a whole; and quite another to attempt to make it seem consistent. The historian must risk a task of integration if he is to understand any attitude, and especially an attitude to a subject such as this. For example: when Augustine wrote his *Retractationes*, he modified a quite innocuous remark in his *De Vera Religione*, in which he had said of Christ that: 'He did nothing by force, but all things by persuading and admonishing'. He felt obliged to add another dimension: he now adds that Christ had driven the money-changers from the Temple, and that demons are exorcised by the 'force of his power'.[1] A remark such as this shows the extent to which issues of constraint and, even, of violence, that are usually extrapolated in isolation as a 'doctrine' of religious coercion, principally directed against the Donatists, had continued, throughout his life, to exercise Augustine on very many levels.

It has become usual to isolate Augustine's attitude to coercion by treating it purely in terms of his 'conversion' to such a policy—a conversion which, it is sometimes said, was largely forced upon him by the violence of the Donatists. It is said that, until 405, Augustine had expressed purely 'liberal' principles, by advocating a solution of the schism through free discussion; that he was disillusioned by the unwillingness of the Donatists to listen to reason; and that the unexpected success of the severe Imperial 'Edict of Unity' of 405, had caused him to change his mind.[2] This interpretation is

---

[1] *De Vera Religione* XVI, 31; *Retract.* I, 12, 6.
[2] A well-known summary of this view is G. O. Willis, *St. Augustine and the Donatist Controversy* (1950), 127–35, which seems to be accepted in A. H. M. Jones, *The Later Roman Empire* (1964) II, 935. For the wider aspects of the problem (the supposed anti-social nature of the Donatist movement, v. p. 261,

insufficient for many reasons. It throws no light on the nature and sources of Augustine's attitude. In the hands of less differentiated exponents, this aspect of Augustine's life is reduced to a trite catena of citations, designed to show the essential reasonableness of Augustine's views on the repression of religious error.[1] Above all, such an interpretation claims to be able to impose a simple and schematic explanation on this notoriously complex man. We may be dealing less with a *volte-face* provoked by external circumstances, than with a phenomenon common to many aspects of the thought of Augustine—that is, with a sudden precipitation, under external pressures, of ideas which, previously, had evolved slowly and imperceptibly over a long time.[2]

I doubt whether the essentially diplomatic letters which Augustine addressed to neighbouring Donatist bishops, and local notables, between 392 and 402, can bear the interpretation usually put upon them.[3] In his early years in Hippo, Augustine was confronted with a situation similar to a Cold War. He wished to take the initiative in this situation without incurring the odium of appearing as an aggressor. So his early letters to individual Donatist bishops are marked by all the ponderous courtesy of Great Powers in a Cold War. They follow a fixed form: Augustine waits until provoked by

---

n. 3. Two points should be noted. First, that the violence of the Donatists, alone, cannot explain Augustine's change of attitude. The Rogatist sect had no record of violence, yet Augustine would not exempt them from the laws against heretics: *Ep* 93, iii, 11 (34, 2, p. 455): 'sed nulla bestia, si neminem vulneret, propterea mansueta dicitur.' Second, that Augustine's statements cannot be treated as being all of equal value, or as reflecting a single viewpoint. Thus, in his later works, the violence of the Donatists comes to predominate, to the exclusion of other elements: *Contra Julianum* III, 5 (421): *Retractationes* II, 5 (426/7); *C. Julianum op. imperf.* 1, 10 (420/30), and Possidius, *Vita Augustini* cc. IX and X. This later perspective unduly simplifies the more differentiated account in *Ep*. 93 of 408 (34, 2, 445 f.).

[1] Most recently: H. Jans, 'De Verantwoording van geloofsdwang tegenover Ketters volgens Augustinus' correspondentie', *Bijdragen* XXII, 2 (1961), 133–63.

[2] e.g. the evolution of the central ideas of the '*City of God*': v. J.-C. Guy, *Unité et structure logique de la 'Cité de Dieu'* (1961), 5–10.

[3] These are: *Epp.* 23 (34, 2, 63 sq.)—Maximin bishop of Sinitum: 33 (34, 2, 18 f.)—Proculeianus bishop of Hippo; 34 and 35 (34, 2, 23 f.)—on the same subject: 43 and 44 (34, 2 85 f.)—debate with Fortunius bishop of Tubursicubure: 49 (34, 2, 140 f.)—bishop Honoratus: 51 (32, 2, 144 f.) and 66 (34, 2, 235 f.—Crispinus of Calama. [See now P. Brown, *Augustine of Hippo* (1967), 226–230.]

some incident committed against his own flock; setting this grievance aside, he offers to meet the bishop responsible in a pacific conference; and he goes on to imply that, if his offer is refused, he will feel justified in letting the world know of his side of the case. In such small negotiations, explosive issues would, inevitably, be shelved; and, for the Donatists, the most explosive issue of all had been the use of force by the Catholics. Such attempts at local conferences plainly suited Augustine's temperament, as well as his circumstances. He had been intimately involved with the Manichees, and the Manichees seem to have used the public religious debate as a usual means of propagating their ideas[1] (a fact which would have made Augustine's application of such tactics to the Donatists seem, perhaps, more revolutionary than we now appreciate). But such letters cannot be expected to exhaust Augustine's attitude to coercion. Indeed, if we are to see this attitude forming rapidly, we should look outside the immediate problem of the Donatist schism altogether.

The historian of the Later Roman church is in constant danger of taking the end of paganism for granted. Yet the fate of paganism filled the imagination of the Christian congregations; and the place of a bishop in Roman society, indeed, the whole sense of direction of his church, was intimately linked with the fortunes of his traditional enemies—the pagan gods.

The period between 399 and 401 marks one of the climaxes of the official suppression of paganism in Africa. In 399, a special mission had arrived in Carthage to close temples.[2] Religious riots, leading to at least sixty deaths, may have broken out in the same year.[3] By 401, the Catholic Council of Carthage, in one of its busiest sessions, had sent a legation to appeal for yet more legislation against the 'remnants of idolatry'.[4] It is hardly surprising, therefore, that Augustine may have first taken up a firm stand on the issue of coercion, not

---

[1] v. Andreas-Henning, 'Mitteliranische Manichaica,' M. 2. *S.P.A.W. Phil.-Hist. Kl.* VII (1933), 301 (Mission of Addas): Philostorgius III, 15, ed. Bidez, 461 (Challenge to debate by Apthonius to Aetius of Antioch); Marc le Diacre, *Vie de Porphyre* c. 85 f., ed. cit. (n. 6), 66 f. (debate of Julia with Porphyry); *Contra Fortunatum* and *Contra Felicem* (25, 81 f. and 801 f.)—debates with Augustine in Hippo; *De Duabus Animabus* IX, 16 (25, 65)—Augustine's debates as a Manichee. [See p. 112 n. 2.]

[2] *De Civ. Dei.* XVIII, 54.

[3] *Ep.* 50 (34, 2, 143).

[4] *Conc. Carth.* V, can. 15.

in the local politics of Hippo, but in his visits to Carthage in these exciting years.

Indeed, if it is possible to date Augustine's sermons, especially his sermons 24 and 62, to the years 399 to 401,[1] we can see in them nothing less than a dress-rehearsal of his justification of the coercion of the Donatists after 405. In one sermon of great charm, he had even defended the politic conformity of one leading pagan by referring to the forcible conversion of St. Paul—Paul, also, had been converted *ex necessitate*, by being knocked down and blinded on the road to Damascus.[2] This scene of divine violence had begun to exercise Augustine:[3] he would later use it extensively in his writings after 405, both *ad hominem*[4] and applied to the Donatists in general.[5] Thus, in Augustine's first public work against the Donatists—the *Contra Epistolam Parmeniani*, which appeared in late 400—half of his attitude to coercion is already fully formed. The Christian Roman Emperors have an unquestioned right of *cohercitio*, in the strict legal sense, to punish, restrain and repress, those impious cults over which God's providence had given them dominion.[6] This is a deliberately provocative work, written 'pour épater les bourgeois'. In it the storm-cloud of the Imperial severity may still be distant; but its outline, in principle, is quite distinct.

What had enabled Augustine to take up so firm an attitude? Perhaps the most profound reason is that he and his colleagues were in the enviable position of knowing why history was happening. In his *Trattato di storia romana*, Professor Mazzarino has recently characterized the Later Roman period in terms of attitudes to authority current at the time: he has headed his chapter on the fourth and fifth centuries, 'La prospettiva carismatica', 'The Charismatic viewpoint'. We might enter even deeper into the outlook of the Christian bishops if we substituted the title: 'La pros-

---

[1] *Sermo* 24: 16th June, 401: v. *Sermones de Vetere Testamento*, ed. Lambot, *Corpus Christianorum*, 41, 1961, 234. *Sermo* 62: 399 or later: O. Perler, *Rech. augustin.* 1 (1958), 12. For an earlier dating—398–9, v. Tillemont, *Mémoires Ecclésiastiques*, vol. XIII, 318–20.

[2] Morin I, c. 1. *Sermones post Maurinos Reperti*, Miscellanea Agostiniana, 1930, 590; 23rd June, 401.

[3] *Serm.* 24, 7; 169, 10; 279, 4. All in reference to *Deut.* XXXII, 39: 'Ego percutiam et ego sanabo: ego occidam et ego vivere faciam'.

[4] *Ep.* 173, 3 (44, 641).

[5] e.g. *inter multa, Ep.* 93, ii, 5 (1, 342, 449).

[6] esp. *Contra Epistulam Parmeniani* VIII, 15 (51, 35).

pettiva profetica', 'The Prophetic viewpoint'. What was happening around them happened *secundum propheticam veritatem.*[1] It was a prophetic truth that the Church should be diffused among all nations: this was Augustine's main contention against the Donatists. But it was a prophetic truth on exactly the same level that the Kings of the Earth should serve Christ in fear and trembling; that the gods of the nations should be uprooted from the face of the earth,[2] and that what had been sung, centuries before by King David, should now become manifest, as a public command,[3] in the repression of pagans, Jews and heretics throughout the Roman Empire.

It is difficult for a historian who is accustomed to seeing the Later Roman Empire in terms of a slow evolution, over a long period of time, to enter into the 'mirages' of one generation within it, the generation of Augustine. But, in these early works of Augustine we can still sense the mood of heady optimism which the sudden collapse of paganism had induced, for a moment, before the disasters of the next decade: it had all happened, as Augustine said, in a sermon, 'valde velociter'.[4]

For this reason, I think that it is not unimportant that these events should have coincided with the culmination of Augustine's attempts to unravel the prophetic truths of Biblical history. We see this in all the levels of his work at this time: from the *De Consensu Evangelistarum*[5] to the simple historical 'narratio' which he regarded as essential for his model catechism, in the *De Cathecizandis Rudibus.*[6] Thus, Augustine's reaction to the suppression of paganism and to the possibility of suppressing other forms of religious dissent, is, in part, determined by the deeper change which had led him from the purely allegorical exegesis of ten years previously to a concrete vision of the fulfilment of prophecy in history.[7]

---

[1] e.g. *Contra Cresconium* III, xlvii, 51 (52, 458).
[2] See the references and remarks of A. Mandouze, 'S. Augustin et la religion romaine', *Rech. augustin.* I (1958), 218–22.
[3] *Con. Ep. Parm.* VIII, 15 (51, 35).
[4] *Enn. in Ps.* VI, c. 13.
[5] *De Cons. Evang.* I, XXVI, 40 f. (43, 39 f.).
[6] *De Cath. Rud.* XXVII, 53.
[7] v. B. Lohse, 'Augustins Wandlung i. seiner Beurteilung d. Staates', Studia, Patristica VI, *Texte u. Unters.* LXXXI (1962), 447–75, for the reflection of this attitude in his early evaluation of the State, and his later change of view. [See further, R. A. Markus, *Saeculum, History and Society in the Thought of Saint Augustine* (1970).]

But we have still to understand the final phase of Augustine's attitude: that is, the way in which his conviction that the Emperors could punish impieties shifted to a belief that such punishment could be coercive in the full sense of the word—that external pressures could provoke changes of allegiance in whole congregations. We will gain nothing by setting aside Augustine's frequent admissions that, at a crucial stage in the Catholic campaign against the Donatists, between 403 and 405, he had been unwilling to impose such full coercive measures against the Donatists.[1]

This was a genuine inhibition. It concentrated effectively on one point: the problem of the *ficti*—of the landslide of feigned conversions which such a measure would have provoked.[2] Indeed, similar concerns remained as a constant braking-force on religious coercion throughout the Later Roman period. When the Christian church was still only one religious group among many in an 'open' society, responsible bishops felt that they could not absorb too great an influx of bad Christians.[3] Augustine's early letters and sermons on the rowdy celebrations of the *Parentalia* in Africa and of the *Laetitia* of S. Leontius in Hippo show how he regarded the low standards of his own congregation as having arisen, largely, from the 'hypocrisy' of pagans who had joined the church in masses after its official establishment by the Emperors.[4] So, we would be going against the evidence of Augustine's pastoral experience if we suggested that he regarded with anything less than genuine reluctance, the prospect of seeing the steady trickle of semi-pagans turned into a flood of resentful Donatists, used to being solemnly drunk on the feast of St. Leontius.

Yet Augustine seems to have accepted the new situation with surprising ease. This confidence in the absorptive powers of the

[1] v. esp. *Ep.* 93, v, 17 (34, 2, 461/2).

[2] v. esp. *Ep.* 93, v, 17 (34, 2, 461). This anxiety is confirmed by the *Commonitorium* of the Council of 404. The laws affecting the testamentary powers of heretics were to be applied: 'His sane exceptis, qui lite pulsati putaverint ad Catholicam transeundum, quia de talibus credibile est, non metu coelestis judicii potius quam terreni commodi aviditate unitatem catholicam praeoptasse.'

[3] e.g. Jean de Nikiou, *Chronique*, c. XCIX, ed. Zotenberg, *Extraits des manuscrits de la Bibliothèque Nationale* XXIV, 1, 535, on Domitian of Mitylene: 'Domitien . . . ordonna que l'on forçât, par contrainte, les Juifs et les Samaritains à recevoir le baptême et à devenir chrétiens. Mais ce furent de faux chrétiens. . . .'

[4] *Enn. in Ps.* VII, c. 7. *Ep.* 29, 9 (34, 1, 120). [P. Brown, *Augustine of Hippo* (1967), 206–207.]

Catholic Church calls for some explanation. Part of this explanation would, of course, take us into the details of Augustine's pastoral activity. Unfortunately, the measures which Augustine and his colleagues took to absorb the congregations that had rallied to the Catholic Church are insufficiently documented.[1] But, for Augustine, this work of absorption may well have been a landmark in a long and subtle process of symbiosis with the common, popular religion of African Christians: the congregations which Augustine had to take over, after 405, may no longer have appeared so alien and, hence, so 'indigestible', as they had first appeared to him when he had returned to Africa as a Catholic.

But we must not forget another reason for this confidence: the development of Augustine's doctrine of grace and predestination. This doctrine, after all, was posed in terms of the disparity between the bewildering discontinuity of human actions and circumstances, and the invincible purposes of an omnipotent God. Briefly, such a deeply-ingrained attitude would lead Augustine to leave the crucial problem of the *ficti* to God. To object to the Catholic policy because it produced such feigned conversions came to appear as tantamount to denying the 'Virtus Dei'—the Power of God, Who could seek out His own among the multitude who had conformed with a bad grace to the Catholic Church.[2]

Augustine's reaction to the problem of the *ficti* reveals a distinctive feature of his attitude to coercion as a whole: his tendency to think in terms of processes rather than of isolated acts. Seen in this perspective, the individual act of free self-determination—the *liberum arbitrium*—is not denied: but it is mysteriously incorporated in an order which lies outside the range of such self-determination. This preoccupation had led Augustine to circumvent the previous tradition of thought available to Christians on the subject of coercion. It had appeared self-evident that freedom of choice—*voluntas* or *liberum arbitrium*—was the essence of religion; that adherence to a religion could be obtained only by such free choice; and that a religious institution which resorted to force must be a *figmentum*,[3] a merely human 'artifice', since only an institution resting on human custom could resort to such all-too-human means of securing obedience. This tradition was articulate and respectable in the

---

[1] v. P. R. L. Brown, art. cit. (n. 4), 293 [p. 314].
[2] e.g. *Contra Gaudentium* xxv, 28 (53, 226).
[3] *Contra Gaudentium* xxxiii, 42 (53, 241).

Latin world: it was shared in various ways by Christian apologists, Tertullian and Lactantius, and by Donatist writers, Petilian[1] and Gaudentius.[2]

But it would be a brave man who could challenge Augustine on the *liberum arbitrium*. He made his own position clear in an answer to Petilian. Petilian had said 'For the Lord Christ says, "No man can come to me except the Father draw him". But why do you not permit each several person to follow his free will, since the Lord God Himself has given free will to men, showing to them, however, the way of righteousness, lest any one by chance perish from ignorance of it.' And Augustine answered: 'If I were to propose to you the question how God the Father draws men to the Son, when He has left them to themselves in freedom of action, you would perhaps find it difficult of solution. For how does He draw them to Him if He leaves them to themselves, so that each should choose as he pleases? And yet both these facts are true; but it is a truth which few have intellect enough to penetrate. So, therefore, it is possible that those warnings which you have been given by the correction of the laws do not take away free will.'[3]

An answer such as this cannot be divorced from the main body of Augustine's thought. In this thought, the final, spontaneous act of the will could be preceded by a long process—of *eruditio* and *admonitio*—in which elements of fear, of constaint, of external inconvenience are never, at any time, excluded. This attitude is epitomized by two words which recur constantly in Augustine's writings on coercion: *disciplina* and *occasio*. The meaning of both words are moulded by Biblical usage. *Disciplina* is always used to describe a process of divinely-ordained impingements, *per molestias eruditio*, such as had marked the relations of God with the people of Israel.[4] *Occasio* derives from the Book of Proverbs: 'Da sapienti occasionem et sapentior erit.' Thus it is used to communicate the pressures of the Imperial laws as no more than one indirect im-

[1] *Contra Litteras Petiliani* II, lxxxiv, 185 (52, 115), cf. II, lxxxiii, 183 (52, 112), and *Gesta Collationis Carthag.* iii die. no. 258 (*Patrol. Latina* XI, 1413C), that the Catholics were distinguished in their policy of forcing men to believe against their wills.

[2] *Contra Gaudentium* XIX, 20 (53, 215).

[3] *Contra Lit. Pet.* II, lxxxiv, 185 (52, 115), transl. Dods, *The Works of Aurelius Augustine*, vol. iii (1872), 354–5.

[4] v. H. I. Marrou, '*Doctrina* et *disciplina* dans la langue des Pères de l'Eglise', *Bull. du Cange* IX (1934), esp. XII, 21–5.

pingement among many in the *eruditio* of the wise religious man.[1]

The acceptance of external impingement as a factor in moral evolution is particularly associated with Augustine's analysis of the force of habit, of the *vis consuetudinis*, an analysis which is one of his most profound and original contributions to ethical thought. From his earliest works, morally neutral impingements, such as the fear of death or the inconveniences of the life of the senses, are accepted as part of the 'pulchritudo justitiae' of a universe in which this force of habit may be broken in men.[2] And from his works against the Donatists, one can see how it is this precise area of Augustine's thought—the force of habit and its sharp remedies—which overlaps with his judgement on the 'wall of hard habit' which, in his opinion, had protected the schismatic congregations.[3] Therefore, what is common to Augustine's attitude to coercion and his thought in general is the acceptance of moral processes which admit an acute polarity—a polarity of external impingement and inner evolution, of fear and love, of constraint and freedom. It is summed up in the last sentence of the only surviving sermon which Augustine preached on the notorious text 'Compelle eos intrare' of the Gospel of St. Luke: 'Foris inveniatur necessitas, nascitur intus voluntas'.[4]

Yet, it is undeniable that, in order to make religious coercion merge unobtrusively into this wider background, Augustine has applied a certain amount of intellectual camouflage. A coercive policy, in imposing a series of direct physical restraints and penalties on the individual, would seem to lead to a sudden debasement of motives: purely physical fear would come to predominate stripped of the religious implications which usually surround Augustine's concept of 'fear and trembling'.[5]

Therefore, it is difficult to enter fully into Augustine's acceptance of this polarity if we do not consider some of the nuances of his

---

[1] e.g., *inter multa*, *Ep.* 93, v, 17 (34, 2, 462-8). It is used for the indirect pressure to adopt Christianity brought to bear on the sons of the pagan rebel, Nicomachus Flavianus: *De Civ. Dei.* v, 26, 36 (*Corpus Christianorum* 47, 162). For the nature of these pressures on the individual—which did in fact include the use of direct force against *coloni*—v. Brown, art. cit. (n. 4), 286 [pp. 306 and 310-13].

[2] e.g. *De Genesi contra Manichaeos* II, c. 42, and *De Vera Religione*, c. 29.

[3] e.g., *inter multa*, *Ep.* 89, 7 (34, 2, 424).

[4] *Sermo*, 112, 8.

[5] For a formal analysis of Augustine's general doctrine v. R. Rimml, 'Das Furchtproblem i.d. Lehre d. Hl. Augustins', *Zeitschr. f. kath. Theol.* XLV (1921), 43-65, 229-59.

attitude to the Old Testament. The concrete events of the Old Testament were very much alive to Augustine and his contemporaries, and the attitude which they adopted to the present was, in large part, moulded and defined by their attitude to this distant past. It is noticeable that many of the *exempla* which Augustine uses in his arguments with the Donatists—Elias, Nebuchadnezzar, Paul— are not cited merely as precedents for severity: they are deliberately chosen as symbols of the polarity we have just mentioned. They are, in fact, crucial examples of the deeper polarity which marked the Christian scriptures as a whole: a polarity of severity and mildness, of fear and love, which approximated to, without ever coinciding with, the division of the Old and New Testament. They were thought of as the 'duae voces' of the Scriptures of the one God. Now, it is revealing that Optatus of Milevis, when discussing the coercion of the Donatists by Count Macarius,[1] and Augustine, in his early sermons against the pagans[2] should both see the coercive measures of their time against the background of these 'duae voces'. The issue is, also, taken up by the Donatists: they wished to 'Separate the Times',[3] to claim that coercive measures were suited only to the severity of the Old Testament, and, so, were inapplicable in the *tempora Christiana*, a time marked by *mansuetudo*.[4]

On this subject, Augustine had, yet again, by-passed the attitude of his opponents. He had been a Manichee, and had developed his early Catholicism in opposition to the Manichees. Thus, for ten years before the problem of the coercion of the Donatists had arisen, Augustine had been defending the polarity of the Scriptures against Manichaean criticisms. As a result, all the examples of legitimate severity cited by Augustine against the Donatists occur in his earlier works whenever it is necessary to deal with prevalent Manichaean criticisms: they are handled in detail and justified *con brio* in works as different in tone as the *De Sermone Domini in Monte*,[5] the *Contra Adimantum*[6] and the *Contra Faustum*.[7] This is a good example of

[1] Optatus, *De Schismate Donatistarum* III, 5 (P.L. XI, 1013B): 'Unus Deus et duae diversae voces'.

[2] *Sermo* 24, 4.

[3] Optatus, *De Schism, Don.* III, 7 (P. L. XI, 1017A): 'Sed video vos hoc loco tempora separantes'.

[4] Implied in *Contra Cresconium* IV, xlvi, 56 (52, 553-4).

[5] *De Sermone Domini in Monte* I, cc. 63-5.

[6] *Contra Adimantum*, c. 17 f. (25, 166 f.).

[7] *Contra Faustum* XXII, 20 (25, 608 f.).

the way in which subjects which, if seen in isolation in Augustine's anti-Donatist writings, appear as mere debating-points, have, in fact, a considerable previous history as part of the genuine preoccupations of Augustine in his early years.

It is tempting to risk a further speculation. In justifying the Old Testament to the Manichees, Augustine was well aware that he had to justify a coercive situation: the profoundly meaningful institutions of Israel had been imposed on the majority of Israelites frankly by fear; the Law was a *paedagogus*—it had acted, coercively, by threats.[1] So, in dealing with the concrete institutions of Israel, Augustine could not avoid dealing with the wider problem of the *utilitas timoris*[2]—the rôle of fear as a necessary element in enforcing a religious establishment.

Augustine's justification of the Old Testament against the Manichees is one of his most ingenious excursions into the field of concrete historical reconstruction. The extent to which he had accepted as necessary this régime of fear is often effaced by his emphasis on the antithesis of Law and Grace in the anti-Pelagian writings.[3] But, far from abandoning this concrete view of the Old Testament, certain changes in Augustine's historical perspective may even have brought it a stage closer to his own times. He had ceased to think of the Old Testament as a distinct 'stage' in the moral development of the human race—valuable and inevitable in its own time, but a stage that had now been transcended.[4] His later perspective of history did not admit such an irreversible moral ascent. Because of this, perhaps, Augustine could see the *utilitas timoris* of the Old Law, not as a remote 'period', reflecting an alien '*gradus morum*',[5] so much as a continuous and necessary complement of the grace of the New dispensation. The Old Law, with its coercive qualities, was, of course, always doomed to remain incomplete, and it was certainly less predominant than in the time of Moses: but in an incomplete existence, its permanent utility could not be denied. And so, the concrete example of the people of Israel, with their

---

[1] e.g. *De Utilitate Credendi* c. 9 (25, 12); cf. *Sermo* 62, 8, where the image of a *Paedagogus* is used of the Imperial legislation against Jews, heretics and pagans.

[2] *Contra Faustum* XXII, 21 (25, 611, 7).

[3] e.g. B. Blumencranz, *Die Judenpredigt Augustins* (1946), 144–5.

[4] v. Edw. Cranz, 'The development of Augustine's ideas on Society before the Donatist controversy', *Harv. Theol. Rev.* XLVII (1954), esp. 273–6 and 271–81, for Augustine's early 'periodisation' of history, and its gradual abandonment.

[5] e.g. *Contra Faustum* XXII, 23 (25, 618).

enforced laws, could come very close indeed to the ecclesiastical realities of Augustine's North Africa.

This nuance in Augustine's attitude to the Law had coincided with a profound change in the imagination of his contemporaries. For the first time, the events of the Old Testament had become the true *gesta maiorum* of a large body of the Roman governing class. The Emperor Theodosius might claim to be descended from Trajan; but he was more aware of his resemblance to King David. The contemporary relations of Church and State were only fully comprehensible in terms of the relations of Kings and Prophets, relations for which no precedent could be found in the actions of the Apostles.[1] And with this, there came the inevitable undertone of harshness: it is perhaps no coincidence that the 'Zeal of Phineas', that grisly incident of righteous violence, is mentioned by Optatus in connection with the coercive measures of Count Macarius[2] and also appears, in an almost contemporary fresco, of the newly discovered catacombs of the *Via Latina*.[3] It is in such subtle changes as these that we can trace the beginning of a Double Image of the Old Testament—at one and the same time the symbol of an outmoded dispensation and the ever-present precedent for an established religion, enforced by law. It is a Double Image which, from the time of Augustine to that of Spinoza,[4] will be very near the root of every controversy on religious tolerance.

In practice, however, there is no question, with Augustine, of a reversion to the harshness of the Old Testament. Instead, one cannot help but be struck by the way in which his view of the coercive process seems to have been deliberately modelled upon the disciplinary processes of the church. Even his usual term for 'coercion' is not *cohercitio*—root of our own word—which had retained its purely negative, legal meaning of 'restraint' and 'punishment': it is *correptio*—'rebuke'—defined by its aim, *correctio*, 'setting right'. *Correptio*—*Correctio*: this is a doublet of deep meaning in Augustine's

[1] v. esp. *Ep.* 93, III, 9 (34, 2, 453).

[2] Optatus, *De Schism. Don* III, 5 (*P.L.* XI, 1013–14). cf. Jerome, *Ep.* 109, 2–3, with remarks of H. Silvestre, *Rev. d'Hist. éccles.* LVIII (1963), 532–6.

[3] A. Ferrua, *Le pitture della nuova catacomba di Via Latina* (1960), tav. XCII, and 48–9. [It is revealing that only in the late 4th century do scenes of the *collective* history of the people of Israel appear in Christian art: A. Grabar, *Christian Iconography. A Study of its Origins* (1969), pp. 95–96.]

[4] v. H. Liebeschutz, 'Die politische Interpretation d. Alten Testaments bei Thomas v. Aquino u. Spinoza', *Antike u. Abendland* IX (1960), 39–62.

ecclesiastical vocabulary: and it may be that the words are chosen, here, to ensure that his attitude to coercion should not be construed as purely punitive, but that it should appear as a positive process of corrective treatment—a treatment, therefore, subjected to the same inner checks and inspired by the same spirit, by the same *modus dilectionis*, as formal ecclesiastical sanctions.

Augustine's choice of language may have been partly determined by his position as a bishop, writing to justify his position to other bishops. In this context one should remember that the Donatists had claimed complete spiritual and disciplinary autonomy for their church: 'that . . . in the church alone should the commands of the Law to the people of God be taught'.[1] Thus, for Augustine's Donatist readers, his extension of such disciplinary powers to the Emperor was the measure of his departure from the previous Christian tradition. One may hazard that Augustine's choice of language was dictated, in part, by a need to allay the misgivings of such readers by assimilating the exercise of the Imperial authority as much as possible to the traditional authority of a Christian bishop. In any case, it is a choice of language of momentous importance in the evolution of ideas in a Christian society.

As a bishop, Augustine was, also, in a strong position to impose his concept of authority on the execution of the Imperial laws.[2] In his many letters to lay officials, we can see how he was determined to ensure that the work of suppressing the Donatist church should be carried out according to the norms of corrective discipline current in the Catholic Church, and, hence, according to norms which he, himself, was in the habit of exercising with such scrupulous care.[3]

---

[1] *Contra Cresconium* I, x, 13 (52, 335). cf. the most illuminating reconstruction of part of this attitude by W. H. C. Frend, 'The Roman Empire in the eyes of Western Schismatics during the 4th century', *Miscellanea Historiae Ecclesiasticae*, Stockholm, 1960 (1961), 9–22. [See P. Brown, *Augustine of Hippo*, pp. 239–240.]

[2] The administrative circumstances of North Africa gave a bishop extensive powers to intervene in the application of the laws on religious dissent: v. Brown, art. cit. [p. 261, n. 3] [pp. 324–31]. Augustine's interventions by letter, therefore, should be treated as exceptions to the usual routine of suppression: they reflect circumstances where the application of the laws had passed beyond his immediate control and, so, called for correspondence.

[3] v. esp. the correspondence between Augustine and Macedonius, *Epp.* 152–5 (44, 393 f.), where the doctrinal basis of Augustine's attitude is made explicit. I regret that I have been unable to consult G. Keating, *The Moral problems of fraternal, paternal and judicial correction*, Diss. fac. theol. Pontif. Univ. Gregor. (Rome, 1958).

This last aspect of Augustine's attitude should not be taken for granted. Anyone who has followed modern debates on penal reform will realize the extent to which the issues which Augustine had to handle, the infliction of punishment and the exercise of power, tend to conjure up attitudes in a particularly incoherent, semi-conscious and primitive form. It is only too true, in this field, that 'he goes farthest who knows not whither he is going'.

Augustine lived in a violent and authoritarian age. The death penalty and brutal tortures were imposed indiscriminately. At least it can be said of Augustine that, in this situation, he kept his head. In justifying religious coercion, he also thought about it: he had reflected on why he was advocating such a policy, and, so, he knew to what extent he was prepared to go in putting it into effect. Plainly, the Spanish bishops who had hounded Priscillian to his death in 386, had not been as certain as Augustine as to when they should have stopped. It would be naïve to maintain that in the Latin Empire Augustine's *mansuetudo Christiana* was a Christian monopoly. Ambrose speaks of pagan governors who were proud of never having inflicted the death penalty during their administration.[1] But the most effective guarantee of the quality of authority is not only that those who wield it should be sensitive and scrupulous men; but that they should be in the habit of wielding it. Here the long record of the undisturbed exercise of authority which a Christian bishop such as Augustine could enjoy is a most impressive guarantee of quality.

We have seen how much of the attitude to coercion which Augustine finally took up after 405 can be traced back for a decade, at least; and so we can conclude that this harsh policy was grafted on to a living and mature organism, so that its application was subjected to a whole series of inner checks and balances which more hurried or less experienced men might not have been able to take into account. Seen in this perspective, the months which Augustine spent in his first year as a priest in Hippo, reading his Bible for *saluberrima consilia*[2] that would enable him to adapt himself to a new life as a public figure, are quite as important, for his biographer, as are his readings in the *Libri Platonicorum*. For this reading laid the foundations of an ideal of authority which would dominate Augustine for the rest of his life. We should never underestimate the

[1] Ambrose, *Ep.* 25, 3.
[2] *Ep.* 21, 6 (34, 1; 54, 5).

extent of the reorientation which this change of ideal had involved, nor the exacting standards of self-examination on which this ideal rested. Phrases which seem to drop tritely enough from Augustine as an old man are often built upon massive foundations: the notorious epigram by which he justifies the coercion of the Donatists in a sermon of 413—'Dilige et quod vis fac'[1]—is first formed, twenty years earlier, in his *Expositio epistulae ad Galatas*, in a passage in which Augustine had turned over the general problem of administering a sharp rebuke with scrupulous sensitivity and honesty.[2]

But remove the foundation of honesty for one moment from this attitude, and Augustine's phrases become fallacious, horrible and insidious. In the excuses which the members of the congregation of Caesarius of Arles gave their bishop for having robbed the Jews, we can see a grim caricature of the subject we have just been discussing:

'Et tamen hic forte respondebis: Ego non ex aliquo odio poenam ingero, sed de dilectione potius disciplinam; ideo exspolio judaeum, ut per hanc asperam et salubrem disciplinam faciam Christianum'.[3]

The historian must face this challenge honestly. He cannot merely circumvent it by defining, justifying or palliating a 'doctrine' which he reads of in the pages of Augustine. He must undertake the long and exacting task of assessing the quality of the man who wrote these pages. Augustine does not emerge from such an examination as an entirely simple figure. His charity seems to vary greatly with the degree to which he was personally involved in the suppression of a powerful rival. He is a sensitive and conscientious pastor up to his victory over the Donatists; but, in 420, he can appear, for an instant, as a harsh and cold victor. The whole weight of his doctrine of predestination is turned, with horrible emphasis, on the broken remnants of a great church: the Donatist bishop of Timgad had threatened to burn himself with his flock in his basilica. Augustine can write:

sed quoniam deus occulta satis dispositione sed tamen iusta

---

[1] In *I Ep. Joh.* VII, 8. v. J. Gallay, '*Dilige et quod vis fac*: Notes d'éxegèse augustinienne,' *Rech. de sc. relig.* XLIII (1955), 545-55.

[2] *Ep. ad Gal. Expos.* c. 57. [See P. Brown, *Augustine of Hippo*, pp. 208-209.]

[3] *Caes. Arelat. Sermo* 183, 6 (*Corpus Christianorum* 104, 748) derived from Augustine, *Sermo*, 178, 5.

nonnullos eorum poenis praedestinavit extremis, procul dubio melius incomparabili numerositate plurimis ab illa pestifera divisione et dispersione redintegratis atque collectis, quidam suis ignibus pereunt . . .[1]

Yet in a letter which he wrote to Paulinus of Nola, in 408, at a time when the bearer, Possidius, was on his way to the court to ask for more laws against heretics and pagans, we can glimpse the paradox by which Augustine can appear both as 'le prince et patriarche des persécuteurs', and, at the same time, as an eloquent exponent of the ideal of corrective punishment, an ideal whose realization is still so painfully incomplete in our own 'civilized' societies:

'What shall I say as to the infliction and remission of punishment in cases in which we only desire to forward the spiritual welfare of those we are deciding whether or not to punish? . . . What trembling we feel in these things, my brother Paulinus, O holy man of God! What trembling, what a darkness! May we not think that with reference to these things it was said: "Fearfulness and trembling are come upon me, and horror hath overwhelmed me. And I said, O that I had wings like a dove, for then I should fly away and be at rest." '[2]

[I have expanded some of the views given in this article, in *Augustine of Hippo*, 1967, pp. 236–40. I would accept the point raised by A. C. de Veer, in his perceptive notice in *Revue des études augustiniennes*, XII, 1966, p. 295, that, while pagans, though deprived of the right to worship, were not forced to join the Catholic Church the Donatists were forced to join.

The difference between a pagan and a Donatist was that, as a schismatic, the Donatist was being compelled to *return* to the Catholic Church: he was being forcibly reminded of an obligation previously entered into. Reminders of previous obligations, by a god, could be very forcible indeed—sickness might ensue from a broken oath (see *P. Oxy.* 1381, in A. D. Nock, *Conversion*, 1933, pp. 86–8). Augustine also envisaged 'dreams' as among the pressures that 'reminded' Donatists of their duty to make good their obligation to the Catholic Church: *Ep.* 105, iv, 13 (34, 2, 604).]

---

[1] *Ep.* 204, 2 (57, 318).
[2] *Ep.* 95, 3 (34, 2, 508–9).

CHRISTIANITY AND LOCAL CULTURE
IN LATE ROMAN AFRICA*†

I

The task of this paper is, in part, an invidious one: for I shall have to begin by looking a gift-horse in the mouth. I shall have to question a group of opinions that link the rise of Christianity in Africa with a resurgence of the local culture of the area. This resurgence, it is said, explains not only the rapid collapse of Roman rule at the time of the Vandal invasion of 429, but the disappearance of Roman civilization and of Christianity itself in Africa in the early Middle Ages.[1]

Discussion of this suggestion, however, tends to be jeopardized from the start because claims for the honour of being the resurgent local culture of Late Roman Africa have been enthusiastically advanced on behalf of *two* distinct and mutually-exclusive local cultures, associated with the *two* native languages—with Punic, on

* *Journal of Roman Studies* LVIII, 1968, pp. 85–95.

† This paper was delivered at a Graduate Class on the Local Cultures of the Roman Empire, organized by Dr. Fergus Millar at The Queen's College, Oxford. I am grateful to Dr. Millar both for his erudition and good sense, and, particularly, for the enterprise that gathered contributors from an unprecedented range of interests upon a sadly neglected theme of great importance for the Roman historian.

[1] For a discussion of the literature on this problem, see P. R. L. Brown, 'Religious Dissent in the Later Roman Empire: the case of North Africa', *History* XLVI, 1961, 83–101 [p. 237–259]. More recently, see S. Mazzarino, 'La democratizzazione della cultura nel Basso Impero', *Rapports du XIe congrès international des sciences historiques* II, 1960, 35–54; R. MacMullen, 'Provincial Languages in the Roman Empire', *American Journal of Philology* LXXXVII, 1966, 1–14 (esp. 12–13, on Africa) and *Enemies of the Roman Order* (1967), 202–41. [See now Fergus Millar, 'Local Cultures in the Roman Empire: Libyan, Punic and Latin in Roman Africa'; *Journal of Roman Studies* LVIII (1968), pp. 126–134 and 'Paul of Samosata, Zenobia and Aurelian: the Church, Local Culture and Political Allegiance in the Third Century';*Journal of Roman Studies* LXI (1971).]

the one hand, and with 'Libyan' (which is often described by a convenient if perilous anachronism as 'Berber'), on the other. What is more, these claims have been advanced by two equally distinct groups of scholars, handling different evidence. The evidence for the survival of Punic—or, so as not to prejudge the issue, of a *lingua Punica*—is literary: Augustine of Hippo[1] and Procopius[2] are the sole authorities for the period. The evidence for 'Berber', by contrast, is largely confined to the interpretation of Libyan inscriptions[3] and of traces of unchanging habits of worship and craftsmanship allegedly betrayed in the remains of the Christian Churches of Central Numidia.[4]

The rival claimants, therefore, overlap neither in area nor in subject matter. If Punic survived in Late Roman Africa, it survived in a limited area, in the traditional areas of Carthaginian settlement, in certain Punicized towns of Numidia, and, perhaps, in the countryside, as an ill-defined fringe of 'Punicized' Libyan *patois*, for which some evidence had been adduced in Tripolitania.[5] The area of known Libyan inscriptions does not coincide with this; still less do the modern islands of Berber speech. These are associated with the High Plains of Numidia and the mountainous hinterland of the coast. So little do these areas overlap, indeed, that Dr. Frend and Dr. Courtois[6] have argued that the *lingua Punica* to which Augustine refers (when he writes in Thagaste and Hippo) is not even 'Punic', but the entirely non-Semitic Libyan dialect of Numidia: an educated Latin, Augustine merely used 'Punic' as the undifferentiated, Latin term for *any* native language in Africa, much as the modern

---

[1] Collected and commented by W. M. Green, 'Augustine's Use of Punic', *Semitic and Oriental Studies presented to W. Popper* (Univ. of California Publications in Semitic Philology, XI), 1951, 179–90: see inf. pp. 285–87.

[2] Procopius, *de bello Vandalico* II, 10.

[3] See esp. J. B. Chabot, *Recueil des inscriptions libyques* (1940–1); Galand-Février-Vajda, *Inscriptions antiques du Maroc* (1966): Galand, 'Inscriptions libyques,' nos. 1–27; J. F. Février, 'Que savons-nous du libyque?', *Revue asiatique* c (1956), 263.

[4] See esp. W. H. C. Frend, 'The Revival of Berber Art', *Antiquity* XVI (1942), 342–52.

[5] G. Levi della Vida, 'Sulle iscrizioni "Latino-libiche" della Tripolitania', *Oriens Antiquus* II (1960), 65–94, and 'Frustuli neo-punici tripolitani', *Acc. Lincei, Rend. sci. mor. stor. e filol.* ser. 8, XVIII (1966), 463–82.

[6] W. H. C. Frend, 'A Note on the Berber background in the life of Augustine', *Journal of Theological Studies* XLIII, 1942, 188–91; Chr. Courtois, 'S. Augustin et la survivance de la Punique', *Revue africaine* 94, 1950, 239–82.

European tends to lump together Berber- and Arabic-speakers as 'Arabs'.

But this difference between 'Berber' and 'Punic' is not a difference only in location. Different areas of experience are involved, documented by different kinds of evidence. Those who invoke 'Punic' are, often, historians of religious ideas. Their argument is almost exclusively linguistic: it turns on the survival of a language and of ideas associated with a language. Such ideas are plainly difficult to delimit: they are not necessarily peculiar to a region or a class; they are, rather, vehicles for the spread and assimilation of religious propaganda. S. Gsell,[1] followed by E. F. Gautier,[2] for instance, fastened on references to Punic as evidence for the survival of the ancient Carthaginian culture of Africa, and, so, as evidence of the vitality of the specifically Semitic bedrock of North African life. With the language, so they argued, went a body of distinctive religious ideas that remained radically different from those of classical Roman paganism, and akin to those of the Jews and the Arabs. Recently, Marcel Simon has ascribed the remarkable success of Judaism in North Africa, and the emergence of the more rigidly Judaistic traits in African popular Christianity, to the survival of Punic as a spoken language, closely related to Hebrew, and its adoption, as a language of culture, by the Berbers of the hinterland.[3] The success of Christianity, in the third century, has been explained by a similar kinship of ideas.[4] And, throughout, it has been assumed that Islam trumped Jews and Christians alike, in bringing a Semitic religion and a Semitic language to a Punic population.

Those who look to 'Berber' claim to be more firmly rooted: they

---

[1] S. Gsell, *Histoire ancienne de l'Afrique du Nord* IV, 1918 (1929 ³), 179 and 496–8; VI 1928 (1929 ²), 108–13, VII, 1928 (1930 ²), 107–8.

[2] E. F. Gautier, *Le Passé de l'Afrique du Nord. Les siècles obscurs*, 1942, 134–57.

[3] Marcel Simon, 'Le judaïsme berbère dans l'Afrique ancienne,' *Revue d'histoire et de philosophie religieuses* XXVI, 1946 (= *Recherches d'histoire Judée-Chrétienne*, 1962, 30–87) and 'Punique ou berbère?', *Annuaire de l'Institut de Philologie et d'Histoire Orientales et Slaves* XIII, 1955 (= *Recherches . . .* 88–100).

[4] W. H. C. Frend, *Martyrdom and Persecution in the Early Church*, 1964, esp. p. 332. It is said that this is illustrated, by the choice of 'theophoric' names: see I. Kajanto, *Onomastic Studies in the Early Christian Inscriptions of Rome and Carthage*, (Acta Instituti Romani Finlandiae II, 1), 1963, pp. 102 and 115; but not all bearers of such names need be Christians: e.g. J. Moreau, *Das Trierer Kornmarktmosaik* (Köln, 1960), plate 1; Farbtafel II, p. 21; also pp. 10–15, where the mosaic shows a Quodvultdeus at a sacrifice in a mystery-cult.

have been archaeologists and sociologists. The greatest single impetus to Dr. Frend's *Donatist Church* was the discovery of an extraordinary number of Christian churches in Southern Numidia, marked by distinctive features of native craftsmanship and, apparently, maintaining local traditions of cult-practice that stretch from prehistoric times to the sub-Islamic pieties of the modern Berbers. From the churches recorded by Berthier in his *Vestiges du christianisme antique* of 1943, Dr. Frend moved to the society of S. Numidia as a whole, in the Late Roman period, and the role of religion in this society.[1] His *Donatist Church* is suffused with the same enthusiasm for what is local, for what is continuous, for what is associated with an immemorial ethnic group such as the Berbers, that has inspired many studies of the village-life and the religious eccentricities of the present-day Maghreb. Faced by Dr. Frend's perspective, indeed, the ancient historian and the theologian cannot burk the issue by limiting themselves to sifting the evidence he presents for his interpretation of the rise of Donatism in Numidia: if they wish to challenge him, they must be prepared to take part in a debate on the factors operative in the history of North Africa, in which the pre-historian, the historian of Medieval Islam and the sociologist of modern Algeria have each got something important to contribute.[2]

Where the protagonists of both 'Punic' and 'Berber' seem to agree, however, is in their interpretation of the manner in which a resurgence of local cultures impinged on the social and political life

---

[1] A. Berthier, *Les Vestiges du Christianisme antique dans la Numidie centrale*, 1943, esp. 220–4, and Frend, *Donatist Church*, esp. 52–9.

[2] Frend, *Donatist Church*, p. xvi: 'Is Donatism part of a continuous native tradition as fundamentally unchanged as the Berbers in the outline of their daily life?' Compare E. Dermenghen, *Le culte des saints dans l'Islam maghrébin*, 1954 and G. Drague, *Esquisse d'histoire religieuse du Maroc*, 1951; but, for a shrewd criticism of this tendency to concentrate on the local, continuous peculiarities of religious life in the Maghreb, to the exclusion of its wider context, namely, the interaction of this life with the orthodox culture of the towns, see Je. Berque, 'Cent vingt-cinq ans de sociologie maghrébine', *Annales* XI, 1956, 296–324. G-C. Picard, 'Pertinax et les prophètes de Caelestis', *Revue de l'histoire des religions* 155, 1959, 46–62, at p. 57, n. 1, is highly pertinent: 'D'autre part, il ne nous paraît pas possible de considérer la Numidie comme une sorte de réserve, où la population autochtone se serait maintenue sans subir d'altération depuis l'époque préhistorique jusqu'à nos jours.' [Charles-Emmanuel Dufourcq, 'Berbérie et Ibérie médiévales: un problème de rupture: *Revue Historique* CCXL (1968), pp. 293–324.]

of Roman Africa in the fourth and fifth centuries, and in the crucial rôle of Christianity as providing the vehicle for this resurgence.

Very briefly, the expansion of Christianity in Africa in the third century, and the permanent division of the Christian Church between Catholics and Donatists, after 311, coincided with the weakening of the hold of the Romanized classes of the towns on the under-Romanized countryside. Donatism allied itself with the resurgent culture of the country-districts of Numidia, and of the lower classes of the towns: Catholicism, with the Romanized upper-classes—the great landowners and the civic notables. As the support of the Emperors identified Catholicism with the interests of the central government in Africa, so opposition to the Catholic Church became the focus of social and political grievances. The notorious Circumcellions, the wandering monks of Donatism, were implicated in peasants' revolts that shook the Roman agrarian system of Numidia in the 340's, and threatened to do so throughout the century. The Donatist hierarchy, also, supported the usurpations of Moorish chieftains, such as Firmus and Gildo. Nor was Africa alone in this. With the exception of Gaul, it is said, the resurgence of local cultures in the Late Roman Empire is associated with the rise of Christianity: in Egypt and Syria, possibly (say some) in Africa, it produced a vernacular literature.[1] In all these provinces, the rise of great local churches, often divided from the established church of the Roman Empire by trifling theological differences, provided an expression for an active or passive rejection of Greco-Roman culture, and so paved the way for an alternative to the Roman Empire in the form of Islam.

So compact a summary inevitably fails to do justice to the seminal quality of a book such as Dr. Frend's *Donatist Church*. But it is in this form that Dr. Frend's suggestions have often been repeated by many scholars—and repeated with a certitude and comprehensiveness which noticeably increases with the distance between the retailer and his contact with the evidence for the social and religious life of Late Roman Africa. Even the most learned of us have learnt to tread the straight and narrow path between right and wrong on this issue: when the author of a most valuable article says that 'Cause-and-effect connexions, beyond absolute demonstration, but fairly clear, can be drawn between Coptic and Gnosticism, Punic

[1] R. MacMullen, 'Provincial Languages . . . ,' [p. 279, n. 1] 14.

283

and Donatism',[1] I feel that this is an academically impeccable way of saying, in the words of the poet:

> 'O let us never, never doubt,
> What nobody is sure about.'

Leaving aside the total lack of epigraphic evidence for the survival of either Punic or Libyan as significant languages in the fourth century,[2] the literary evidence for the rôle of local feeling, still more of social and political motivation, in the Donatist controversy is exceedingly fragile. It has not survived the sober gaze of Professor Jones, in the *Journal of Theological Studies* of 1959;[3] I have often had occasion to dissent;[4] and Dr. Emil Tengström has now meticulously dismantled many vital links in the chain of evidence, assembled by Dr. Frend and others, for the social and political aims of Donatism.[5]

The questions posed by Dr. Frend and by other advocates of the rôle of a resurgence of local culture in the religious life of Late Roman Africa are more important than the highly debatable answers they have given to such questions. It is myopic merely to answer these answers. For the questions raised have wider implications. What is at stake is not only the relation between Christianity and local cultures in North Africa, but the relation between Christianity and classical civilization as a whole in the Latin West in the Late Roman and early medieval periods.

[1] R. MacMullen, 'A note on *Sermo humilis*', *Journal of Theological Studies*, n.s. XVII, 1966, 108–12, at p. 109.

[2] Picard, 'Pertinax . . .,' 57–8, displays equal scepticism on both Punic and Libyan; MacMullen, 'Provincial Languages . . .,' 12–13, dismisses Libyan and retains Punic with some hesitation. As a non-specialist in a highly-specialized domain, dependent on archaeological discoveries, I would only accept these negative results *salva diligentiore quaestione*.

[3] A. H. M. Jones, 'Were the ancient heresies national or social movements in disguise?', *Journal of Theological Studies*, n.s. X, 2, 1959, 280–95 (published separately, 'Were ancient heresies disguised social movements?' *Facet Books, Historical Series* I, 1966).

[4] Brown, 'Religious Dissent . . .' [p. 279, n. 1] esp. 91–5 [pp. 247–53]; see also Brown, 'Religious Coercion in the Later Roman Empire: the case of North Africa', *History* XLVIII, 1963, 283–305, at 293–7 [pp. 317–21], and *Augustine of Hippo: A Biography*, 1967, at 217 and 227–30.

[5] E. Tengström, *Donatisten und Katholiken: soziale, wirtschaftliche und politische Aspekte einer nordafrikanischen Kirchenspaltung* (Studia Graeca et Latina Gothoburgensia XVIII, 1964); see Brown, *Journal of Roman Studies* LV, 1965, 281–3 [inf. p. 335–38].

II

Let us look again at the 21 passages in which Augustine speaks of the *lingua Punica*. Two passages refer to words and constructions that are plainly Semitic;[1] but one passage makes it clear that Augustine, by himself, was not able to judge the precise meaning of a word.[2] Five passages refer to the *lingua Punica* in the dealings of the bishop with the countryside around Hippo.[3] It is a language which a bishop, Catholic and Donatist alike, would only make contact with through an interpreter. This *lingua Punica* is featureless: the passages do not reveal a specific language. What they do reveal, however, is a linguistic situation: in and around Hippo, we are dealing with a largely bi-lingual society, where a farmer, for instance, will interpret into Latin a conversation he has just had in Punic.[4] The remaining references occur largely in Augustine's sermons: they are comments on the meaning of untranslated Hebrew words in the Bible, such as mammon, Edom, Messias, through an appeal to Punic.[5] These comments are too easily dismissed as merely academic. Yet, I would suggest that they tell us something which the other passages do not: for they cast light on the motives of Augustine in referring to Punic, on what he wished to achieve, and, so, on his views on the position of the *lingua Punica* in the culture of the African church.

First, we must remember Augustine's intellectual equipment. His own schooling in Latin had done little to help him master any language, even his own, from the grammar, the syntax, the accidence, in the manner of modern linguistics. What he had always learnt was to fasten on words: 'One read Vergil, not as one might look out from a vantage point over a vast landscape, but as one might admire a necklace of pearls, passing them through one's fingers, examining one after the other.'[6] We are well on the way to the *Etymologies* of Isidore of Seville: understanding a language or a

---

[1] *Ep. ad Rom. incoh. expos.* 13; *Enarr. in Ps.* 128, 8.

[2] *de magistro* XIII, 44.

[3] *Ep. ad Rom. incoh. expos.* 13; *Ep.* 66, 2; *Ep.* 108, 14; *Ep.* 209, 3; *de haeres.* 87.

[4] *Ep. ad Rom. incoh. expos.* 13.

[5] *Loc. in Hept. I,* ad Gen. I, 24; *Qu. in Hept.* VII, 16; *Tract. in Ioh.* XV. 27; *Enarr. in Ps.* 128, 8 and 136, 18; *Serm.* 113, II, 2; *de serm. Dom. in monte* II, xiv, 47; C. Lambot, 'Nouveaux sermons inédits de S. Augustin,' *Revue bénédictine* XLIX, 1937, p. 265, lines 248–9; *C. litt. Petil.* II, civ. 229.

[6] H. I. Marrou, *S. Augustin et la fin de la culture antique*, 1938, p. 25.

culture means grasping the meaning of isolated words. Punic, therefore, usually comes to Augustine like the signposts of a foreign country: single *nomina Punica*, which he invariably handles in isolation.[1]

To this educational trait, we must add Augustine's distinctive mystique of language. He believed that the common usage of words often reflected a providential design to establish more firmly in men's minds certain profound truths. Frequently applied to Latin in his theological treatises, this habit of the *grammaticus* has led him to be acclaimed as a forerunner of linguistic philosophy.[2] Applied to Punic, it takes on a more romantic turn.

In one passage, concerning the spoken language of the country-folk of Hippo, we come across a clue to the attitude of Augustine and its possible roots. When he was still a priest in Hippo, his bishop, Valerius, had overheard countryfolk using the word 'salus' in conversation: *salus*, he was told, meant 'Three' (compare the Hebrew, *shalosh*). The information intrigued Valerius and Augustine: for every time a Punic speaker said *salus* in Latin, meaning 'Salvation', he was also saying *salus*—Three—in Punic; and so he was being reminded, by the mysterious providence of language, of the relation between Salvation and the Trinity.[3]

He was also told that these countryfolk called themselves *Chenani*. This, he thought, was a mis-pronunciation for *Cananaei*: they had come, in the distant past, from the Land of Canaan. Marcel Simon has drawn attention to the importance of this idea. The myth that the inhabitants of North Africa were either relatives of the Hebrew people, or near-neighbours, was an old Jewish tradition that appears in the *Book of Jubilees*. It had played a part in conciliating the Jewish communities of North Africa to the local inhabitants;[4] one suspects that in this passage, and in his many appeals to the Punic equivalent of Hebrew words, Augustine has stepped into the shoes of the *rabbis*[5]—he has deliberately placed the population of his diocese in the penumbra of the Chosen People.

---

[1] e.g. *Ep.* 17, 2.

[2] Marrou, op. cit [p. 285, n. 6], p. 16 and '*Retractatio*', 1949, p. 676.

[3] *Ep. ad Rom. incoh. expos.* 13.

[4] Simon, 'Le judaïsme berbère' (= *Recherches* . . . pp. 39–42) and A. Choura-qui, *Les Juifs de l'Afrique du Nord*, 1952, pp. 14–19.

[5] Jerome, *Liber hebraicarum quaestionum in Genesim*, ad Gen. XXXVI, 24 (*P.L.* 23, 993B–994A) refers to an appeal to Punic *apud Hebraeos*.

It is this perspective that determines Augustine's attitude to the *lingua Punica*. It is a learned perspective: like the Latin origin of the Rumanian nation, even when believed, it casts its pattern upon ethnic realities from a dizzy height. A similar 'imaginative nationalism' led Donatists to claim Simon of Cyrene as a fellow-*Afer*,[1] and American senators to invoke the Emperor Septimius Severus and Saint Augustine in favour of the Negro cause. As with many such 'imaginative nationalisms', it served a good purpose: as with the debate on whether Bulgarian or Serbian was most akin to the Macedonian dialect in the late nineteenth century, philology was a prelude to annexation. The *Chenani* of Hippo are Canaanites precisely because they reminded Augustine of the Canaanite woman of the Gospels: she had come to ask Christ for *Salus*—for health. Though not a member of the Chosen People, the Canaanite woman could claim to be a close relative; and, like the countryfolk of Hippo, the divine providence had prepared her to link the idea of Salvation —*salus*—with her word for Three. But there is no doubt, in this story, as to who would be the source of salvation among the Canaanites of Hippo—the Catholic bishop of the town; and no question whatsoever that, when they came to the point, they would ask for it in good Latin—for the *Salus* of Catholic baptism.[2]

This anecdote shows clearly the direction in which Augustine wished the linguistic currents of his diocese to run, at a time when, as a priest and a star-preacher, he was more directly concerned than at any other period of his life with the problems of evangelization and reform by the spoken word.[3] The *lingua Punica* has a privileged place in his mind: but only as a step towards full Latinity—in this incident, as in his sermons, 'Punic' hovers in the wings of a Latin culture.

For I would suggest that there was only one 'language of culture' in Late Roman Africa—that was Latin; that the particular form of Christianity in the Later Empire, Catholic and Donatist alike, demanded a 'language of culture'; and, so, that the rapid Christianization of Numidia involved, not a resurgence of any regional culture, but the creation of a Latin—or sub-Latin—religious culture

---

[1] *Serm.* 46, 41.
[2] 'Baptism' was spoken of by such *Punici Christiani* as *Salus: de pecc. mer. et rem.* I, XXIV, 34.
[3] Brown, *Augustine of Hippo*, 138–42; 206–7 and 235–6.

on an unprecedented scale.[1] The problems posed by the creation of a popular Latin culture are far more solidly documented in the literature of African Christianity than are the fleeting references to a *lingua Punica*.

First of all, we must envisage a missionary situation. The greatest weakness of any view that sees, in the division between Catholic and Donatist, the opening of a fissure between classes or races, is that it ignores the fluidity of the situation up to the age of Augustine. Numidia was not Christianized suddenly: most leading Donatists of the fourth century were converts direct from paganism.[2] At the end of the fourth century, Donatist and Catholic groups still faced each other on either side of a wide, neutral zone of pagans yet to be converted.[3] It is a situation which modern experience of Christian missions has shown to be more conducive to zeal than to mutual tolerance.

Now one of the distinctive features of Christianity in the ancient world as a whole, and in Africa in particular, is that it was a Religion of the Book. Like Judaism, the Christianity of the African clergy was a Law—a *lex*.[4] The bishop's authority stemmed from his preservation of his Law, and his professional activity consisted in expounding it.[5] This Law was, quite concretely, the *codex* of the Holy Scriptures. The fact that some Catholic bishops had handed on these *codices* to be burnt, during the Great Persecution of 304, branded their party, forever, as 'the *traditores*', the 'handers-over' of the Holy Books 'to alter one word of which must be accounted the greatest sacrilege'.[6] 'You come with edicts of Emperors', the Donatist primate of Carthage told the Catholics: 'we hold nothing in our hands but volumes of the Scriptures'.[7] The *panache* of this

---

[1] The important distinction between a spoken *patois* and a 'language of culture', introduced by Simon, 'Punique ou berbère?' (*Recherches* . . . 95–6) in favour of Punic, seems to me to favour only Latin: see Picard, 'Pertinax . . . ,' 58, n. 2, on the meagre quality of Punic inscriptions.

[2] Bishop Marculus: *Passio Marculi* (*P.L.* 8, 760); while Vitellius Afer— Gennadius, *de script eccles.* 4 (*P.L.* 58, 1063)—wrote '*against the pagans*'.

[3] *de catech. rud.* xxv, 48. Simultaneous attacks on rural shrines by Catholics and Donatist Circumcellions: *Serm.* 62, 13.

[4] W. H. C. Frend, 'A Note on the Great Persecution in the West', *Studies in Church History* II, 1965, ed. C. J. Cuming, 146–8, and Brown, *Augustine of Hippo*, 217.

[5] Brown, *Augustine of Hippo*, 259–63.

[6] *Acta Saturnini*, 18 (*P.L.* 8, 701B).

[7] Augustine, *Ad Don. post Coll.* I, 31.

remark is deeply revealing. It was as a Religion of the Book that the Christians of Africa thought they had been persecuted; it was as a Religion of the Book that the Donatists thought they had been betrayed; and it was as a Religion of the Book that Christianity spread into the countryside of Africa.

For, outside the educated upper-classes, the struggle between Christianity and paganism was not just a conflict of two religions: it was a conflict of two different cultures, associated with two different types of religion. Paganism, in the Roman world, like the religion of any primitive society, was inextricably embedded in the local language: the Lycaonians, in the *Acts of the Apostles*, acclaimed Paul and Barnabas as gods, Λυκαονιστί.[1] The earliest vernaculars in the Roman Empire are *pagan* vernaculars, and the revival of one language, in the third century, that of Phrygian, was a *pagan* revival.[2] Even the most imposing paganism in the Late Antique world, the Zoroastrianism of Sassanian Persia, remained largely pre-literate. It was enshrined in murmured prayers, passed on by word of mouth. Only in the sixth and seventh centuries were the Zoroastrian holy books written down, to save the traditional faith from the inroads of two literate religions, Christianity and Islam.[3]

To abandon paganism was to change one's culture: it was to forget the formulae and liturgies of one's ancient tongue, and to expose oneself to the uniformity of a written book. The situation was not very different from what can now be observed, for instance, in the paganism of New Guinea: 'To understand Tangu, to think the way they do, is to think in their language. The axioms and ideas contained within Tangu sorcery beliefs and activities are best expressed in the Tangu language, which itself expresses the way in which Tangu think about themselves and the world outside ... by teaching pidgin English, and more recently English, the (Christian) mission hopes to draw Tangu out of the confines of their language' (K. O. L. Burridge, *Mambu: a Melanesian Millennium*, 1960, 70–71).

[1] *Acts of the Apostles* 14, 11.
[2] E.g. W. M. Ramsey, 'The Tekmoreian Guest-Friends', *Journal of Hellenic Studies* XXXII, 1912, 151–70; A. Heubeck, 'Bemerkungen zu den neuphrygischen Fluchformeln', *Indogermanische Forschungen* LXIV, 1958, 13–25; MacMullen, 'Provincial Languages ...', p. 13, n. 29; and O. Haas, *Die phrygischen Sprachdenkmäler*, 1966.
[3] J. Tavadia, 'Zur Pflege des iranischen Schrifttums', *Zeitschr. deutsch. mornegländ. Gesell.* 98, 1944, 337.

Thus to participate fully in Late Roman Christianity, as a clergy-man or a monk, inevitably involved suffering the fate which Irish legend ascribed to a convert of St. Patrick: 'He baptised him and handed him the A.B.C. . . .'[1]

This Latin was more than a 'popular' Latin: it was a Latin that invited literacy—it had the simplicity and uniformity of an ideo-logical language. It had emerged, in the towns of the third century, as amazingly homogeneous: far from betraying an 'African tem-perament', the Christian Latin of Carthage was uniform with that of Rome; that of an educated Christian, uniform with that of a simple deacon.[2] This 'clerical language, with its solemn dignity, cold-blooded anger and misuse of Biblical words to interpret and criticise contemporary affairs',[3] remains common to both sides of the Donatist controversy. In the vast correspondence of Augustine, it is possible to recognize at a glance the open-letters which he wrote to his Donatist opponents: they are all in the 'professional' Latin of the African church.[4]

Behind Augustine's vast output in Hippo, we can sense the pressure of the need to extend this religious literacy as widely as possible. The recruitment of the clergy on both sides; the intro-duction of the monastic life by Augustine and his friends; the con-sequent growth of a piety based on the *Lectio Divina*—all these changes of the late fourth century placed more and more weight on the Latin language.[5] The Latin of the Scriptures might disgust the

[1] This has been clearly seen and brilliantly expressed by H. I. Marrou, *Histoire de l'Éducation dans l'Antiquité*, 1955³, 418–21 (the citation appears on p. 439). [Now see *Literacy in Traditional Societies*, ed. Jack Goody (1968), esp. pp. 2–3.]

[2] Christine Mohrmann, 'Les origines de la latinité chrétienne à Rome', *Études sur le latin des chrétiens* III, 1965, 67–126.

[3] A. Harnack, *History of Dogma* (Dover Books, 1961), V, 25.

[4] Christine Mohrmann, 'S. Augustin écrivain', *Recherches augustiniennes* I, 1958, 43–66, at p. 65.

[5] See, in general, Marrou, *Histoire de l'Éducation* . . ., 439–40 and the per-ceptive comments of P. Riché, *Éducation et Culture dans l'Occident barbare*, 1962, 133–4. For Hippo, I would agree with Courtois, 'S. Augustin . . .', o.c. [p. 280, n. 6], 282, n. 61, and *Les Vandales et l'Afrique*, 1955, 127, n. 8, that the text of *Ep.* 84, 2, should read *cum latina lingua*, not *cum punica lingua*: hence, 'sed cum latina lingua, cuius inopia in nostris regionibus evangelica dispensatio multum laborat . . .' The situation would be similar to that in which Augustine found himself on becoming a priest in Hippo in 391: his bishop Valerius, as a Greek, was handicapped by lack of a Latin education—Possidius, *Vita Augustini* V, 3.

educated pagan: but many members of the Christian clergy first learnt to read and write in this Latin,[1] such as the elderly colleague of Augustine who had 'grown up in a farm and had little book-learning'.[2] Augustine would adapt his style to such people: they were his *fratres in eloquio latino ineruditi*.[3]

The *sermo humilis*—the 'humble style'—of Augustine's sermons was far more than an exercise in inverted snobbery: it is part of an attempt to enable a bilingual society to participate in an exclusively Latin religious culture, gravitating around a Latin holy text.[4] Augustine's method of allegorical exegesis even betrays this pressure: for his approach to the Scriptures involved moving backwards and forwards throughout the whole length of the Bible in each sermon. By piling half-verse on half-verse, from Genesis to St. Paul and back again, *via* the Psalms, the bishop would create a whole skeleton of verbal echoes, well suited to introducing large areas of the text to an audience used to memorizing by ear. And, like the inspired schoolmaster that he remained, Augustine could hold the whole congregation together, with the hope that those in the back, who had heard the Passion according to St. Matthew for the first time,[5] might, one day, join the *cognoscenti* in the front, who knew why the prophets used the past tense to speak of future events, or why there were 13 Apostles and only 12 thrones.[6]

And there is no greater spur to taking an interest in a sacred text than the fact that the experts so patently disagree about it. Ever since the time of Cyprian, controversy had taken the form of bundles of citations—*testimonia*.[7] When Augustine took over the church of his Donatist opponents, he covered its walls with posters of such *testimonia* in support of his case;[8] and Donatist pamphlets are no

[1] See Rémi Crespin, *Ministère et Sainteté: pastorale du clergé et solution de la crise donatiste dans la vie et la doctrine de S. Augustine*, 1965, 116–17. This shows that the clergy was not recruited from classes that would have been literate.

[2] Possidius, *Vita* XXVII, 10.

[3] *Retract.* II, 29 on the *de agone christiano*. It is important to note that, though written in simple Latin, the ideas in this book are far from being those of 'popular' African Christianity: see Brown, *Augustine of Hippo*, 245.

[4] See esp. R. MacMullen, 'A note on *Sermo humilis*', *Journal of Theological Studies*, n.s. XVII, 1966, 108–12.

[5] *Serm.* 232, 1.

[6] *Enarr. in Ps.* 49, 9; *Serm.* 249, 3.

[7] *Testimoniorum ad Quirinum libri III (C.S.E.L.* III, 25–184).

[8] *Retract*, II, 27; cf. Possidius, *Indiculus*, 'De testimoniis Scripturarum contra Donatistas et idola'.

different.[1] By the end of the fourth century, it would have been as difficult for a Christian citizen of Hippo, Donatist or Catholic, *not* to know why the Ark of Noah was tarred inside and out,[2] what the navel of the Beloved in the *Song of Songs* stood for,[3] who was the 'strong woman' of the Book of Proverbs,[4] and why she spun wool for her husband,[5] as it would be for us *not* to recognize Mr. Wilson or President Johnson in a newspaper cartoon. Where the Bible ended, the popular song took over: Augustine wrote one such—the *Psalmus abecedarius*, '*The A.B.C. against the Donatists*', 'to reach the attention of the humblest masses and of the ignorant and obscure, and to fasten in their memories as much as we can'.[6]

The African church never lacked controversy. The arrival of the Vandals in 429 meant the arrival of yet another group of ecclesiastical opponents—the Vandals being Arian heretics—who, again, were bilingual: speaking Gothic, their language of ecclesiastical culture was almost certainly Latin.[7] Once again, the armoury of Latin controversy was trundled out: the *testimonia*,[8] and the popular song—an 'A.B.C. against the Arians'.[9]

This is true of the third missionary group in Africa. Manichaean propaganda reached all classes:[10] it was current in the villages of Numidia,[11] as well as among the intelligentsia of Carthage;[12] among humble artisans,[13] as among great landowners.[14] While in Egypt Manichean literature passed, almost immediately, into Coptic, in Africa it remained exclusively Latin.[15]

[1] See esp. J.-P. Brisson, *Autonomisme et christianisme dans l'Afrique romaine*, 1958, 145–9.

[2] *Ep. ad cath.* v, 9.

[3] Optatus of Milevis, *de schism. Don.* II, 8.

[4] *Serm.* 37, 2.

[5] *Serm.* 37, 17.

[6] *Retract.* I, 20.

[7] Victor Vitensis, *Historia Persecutionis Vandalicae* II, XVIII, 53.

[8] E.g. *Florilegia Biblica Africana saec.* v, ed. B. Schwank, Corpus Christianorum, ser. lat. 90, 1961.

[9] By Fulgentius of Ruspe; ed. Lambot, *Revue bénédictine* XLVIII, 1936, 231–4.

[10] On the composition of the Manichaean movement in Africa, see Brown, *Augustine of Hippo*, 54–5.

[11] *Ep.* 64, 3.

[12] *de util. cred.* XIV, 32.

[13] The names given in the abjuration of a Manichee: *P.L.* 42, 518.

[14] E.g. Romanianus, patron of Augustine: *C. Acad.* II, iii, 8.

[15] See, most recently, T. Save-Söderbergh, *Studies in the Coptic Manichaean Psalmbook*, 1949.

The Christian culture of Africa, therefore, was exclusively Latin. How many people did it affect? This problem cannot be solved by quantitative analysis: one cannot place those, for instance, who chose to be buried in Latin as one mass, against the untold millions who, apparently, did not.[1] We are dealing with a bilingual population. The issue, therefore, is one of direction. Which way did the cat jump? In which way did Christianity alter the balance in this bilingual situation?[2]

One feature should be stressed. The effect of religious movements is not always to group themselves around the existing contours of class and culture: it is part of their appeal that they do by-pass such divisions. This is particularly true of the fourth century: in Africa, religion became a *carrière ouverte aux talents*. The leader of the Western Manichaean movement, Faustus of Milevis, was one such autodidact: a poor man's son, 'I found at once', Augustine wrote of him, 'that the man was not learned in any of the liberal sciences save literature, and not especially learned in that. He had read some of Cicero's speeches and a very few books of Seneca, some of the poets and such writings of his own sect as had been written in Latin. . . .'[3] His religion had gained him an *entrée* into Latin culture.

Christianity, indeed, had joined hands with that other agent of social mobility in Africa—the teaching profession. In 320, a Moor, the grandson of one of the rude cavalrymen of the Emperor's *comitatus*, had settled down in Cirta as a 'professor of Roman letters'.[4] The process continued throughout the fourth century: looking through the personnel of the Donatist Church[5] and reading the sermons of African preachers,[6] one wonders whether, for the one bishop who might have entered the Church, in Gaul or Italy, as a spectacular *avatar* of the local senatorial magnate, there were not a

---

[1] As by Chr. Courtois, *Les Vandales et l'Afrique*, 1955, p. 128; his remarks on the quality of the Latin of the inscriptions are more cogent. On the problem of the development of the Latin cursive script in African inscriptions, see a mysterious recent example: P. A. Février and J. Marcillet-Jaubert, 'La pierre sculptée et écrite de Ksar Sbahi (Algérie)', *Mélanges d'archéologie et d'histoire* 78, 1966, 141–85.

[2] Cf. C. Jullian, *Histoire de la Gaule* VIII, 310, on the rôle of the Church in finally Latinizing the Gallic countryside.

[3] Augustine, *Conf.* v, vi, 11, and *Contra Faustum* v, 5.

[4] *Gesta apud Zenophilum*, C.S.E.L. XXVI, 185.

[5] See esp. P. Monceaux, *Histoire littéraire de l'Afrique chrétienne* VI, 1922.

[6] J. Leclercq, 'Prédication et rhétorique au temps de S. Augustin', *Revue bénédictine* 67, 1947, 117–31, at pp. 129–30.

score of minor clergy, in Africa, whose careers and outlook reincarnated the *grammaticus* and the small-town lawyer.

Beyond the few who actually became literate through religion, there were the listeners.[1] Christian preaching and Christian controversy—religious debates being a star-attraction in African towns of the fourth century[2]—would have had an effect similar to that of the wireless in many multi-lingual societies: its constant broadcasts would have tipped the balance in favour of the uniform language of culture. In Hippo, in the early fifth century, the works of Cicero were not available;[3] but the Latin of the Psalms had become popular songs,[4] and the Latin of the Bible so familiar that it, and not the Latin of the classics, was considered 'good' Latin.[5]

III

This, I would suggest, was the cultural function of the rise of Christianity in Late Roman Africa: far from fostering native tradition, it widened the franchise of the Latin language. Nowhere is this more true than in Numidia, where the Donatist Church was strongest. For it is highly questionable to isolate Numidia as being any more 'rural' than the other provinces of Late Roman Africa: and to persist in describing Numidian Donatism as a distinctly 'rural' religion is to misunderstand the role of the towns in the Late Roman period. The vigour of these towns should not be underestimated.[6] If there is a conflict of social groups in fourth-century Numidia, it is not between 'town' and 'country' but, perhaps, between two layers of the aristocracies of the towns. The 'traditional' local aristocracy of *curiales* and *grammatici* tended to be either pagan or Donatist, while the 'new' aristocracy of *honorati*, as dependents on Imperial patronage, followed their masters into Catholicism.[7] The Donatist

---

[1] Augustine, *Enarr. in Ps.* 121, 8: 'nos simus codex ipsorum'.

[2] E.g. Augustine's debate with a Manichee in a packed bath-house: *C. Fort.* I and Possidius, *Vita* VI, 2. The crowd gathering in a debate with a Donatist bishop: *Ep.* 44.

[3] *Ep.* 118, II, 9.

[4] *Enarr. in Ps.* 132, 1.

[5] *de doct. christ.* II, xiv, 21.

[6] P. A. Février, 'Toujours le Donatisme: à quand l'Afrique?', *Rivista di storia e letteratura religiosa* II, 2 (1966), 228–40, esp. 234 f.

[7] See the evidence ingeniously discussed by T. Kotula, *Zgromadzenia prowincjonalne w rzymskiej Afryce w epoce późnego Cesarstwa* (1965).

Church of Numidia was a church of 'great churches',[1] that is, of huge, urban basilicas, dedicated, as that of Timgad, to praising the Donatist bishop, in Latin.[2] The Latin slogans on altars, on the graves of martyrs, the Latin Biblical citations around baptisteries and above the lintels of country-churches are the shadow of this new, confident Latin culture of the Christian Church.[3] The Donatist bishops, their clergy, and their followers had gained, by their conversion to Christianity, a culture which they shared with the rest of the Latin world, and, having gained it in Latin, they not unnaturally claimed to be right, in Latin. To treat Donatism as a manifestation of 'African separatism' blunts its challenge. It does scant justice to the roots of the Donatist ideology in the common culture of Latin Christianity.[4] For the historian of the religious divisions of the Christian Church, such a view can be an easy way out: it resembles the judgement of the Yugoslav court which dismissed *The New Class* of Milovan Djilas as a manifestation of 'Montenegrin separatism'; it is a convenient way of drawing the sting of a challenge couched in terms of a universal body of doctrine, common to both sides, and so guaranteed to hurt—whether this is the 'true' Socialism of Djilas, or the 'true' Church of a Donatist. The atmosphere of Christianized Africa is not that of a region drifting out of the Roman world: it is a doctrinaire and cocksure belief that what was good for Numidia was good for the Roman Empire: 'What has been done in Africa', wrote one, 'must appear in the whole world.'[5] Tyconius was more right than he could have dreamed. For his commentary on the *Apocalypse* filtered into the Catholic tradition under the blessing of Augustine: it was vital to early medieval exegesis.[6] If the Spanish manuscript illuminations, from which the Christ in Majesty of the Romanesque tympanum

---

[1] *Enarr. in Ps.* 21, 26.

[2] Brown, 'Religious Dissent . . .', (above n. 1) 92.

[3] On the repercussions of establishing a bishop in such villages, see Brown, 'Religious Dissent . . .', 95 [p. 252], to which add the epigraphic evidence for churches built by the local population, notably *Année épigraphique* 1894, nos. 24 and 138, and 1926, no. 60, and Augustine, *Ep.* 44, VI, 14, on the loyalties surrounding such a church.

[4] An oversight handsomely remedied by W. H. C. Frend, *Martyrdom and Persecution in the Early Church*, 1964. See Brown, *Augustine of Hippo*, 212–25.

[5] T. Hahn, *Tyconius-Studien*, 1900, p. 85.

[6] Gerald Bonner, *Saint Bede in the tradition of Western Apocalyptic Commentary* (Jarrow Lecture, 1966).

derives, owe anything to the Tyconian commentary of Beatus of Liebana, then the traveller to Moissac may still see, on the great porch, a distant echo of the ecclesiological rancours of a fourth-century Donatist.[1]

There is, indeed, one facet of the rise of Christianity in Roman society, as of the rôle of religious movements in any society, which has not been stressed as strongly as it deserves. It is generally assumed, by most students of Donatism, that the function of Christianity was to provide an ideological expression for pre-existing tensions: that religion can act as the vehicle of social grievances, that it can strengthen the solidarity of submerged groups. What is overlooked is the rôle of religion as a mediator: how a religious movement, such as Christianity, can make the culture of an élite available to a wider audience, how its appeal lies partly in its ability to enable people to participate in something different from their ordinary existence. Yet a look at the sermons which African bishops preached on great occasions should convince us of this—they are glorious displays of rhetoric, the Latin language of the towns parading in its Sunday best.[2]

Perhaps the debate on the rôle of local culture in Late Roman Africa has been tied too closely to the problem of the rise of the Donatist Church. There is one point which this hypnosis with the superbly-documented age of Augustine tends to miss. The history of African Christianity remains well known to us, to the mid-seventh century at least. In all this period, from 430 to 698, there is not one mention of the *lingua Punica*.[3]

[1] H. Schlunk, 'Observaciones en torno al problema de la miniatura visigoda', *Archivo Español de Arte* 71, 1945, 241–64, at pp, 262 f.

[2] See the example in J. Leclercq, 'Prédication et rhétorique au temps de S. Augustin', *Revue bénédictine* 67, 1947, at pp. 121–5.

[3] The following recent works provide some indication of the prosperity and Latin civilization of Africa after 430: H. I. Marrou, 'Épitaphe chrétienne d'Hippone à réminiscences virgiliennes', *Libyca* I, 1953, 215–90; Chr. Courtois, 'Sur un baptistère découvert dans la région de Kelibia', *Karthago* VII, 1955, 98–126 and J. Cintras and N. Duval, 'L'Église du prêtre Félix, Région de Kelibia', *Karthago* IX, 1958, 157–265; R. Braun, ed. *Quoduultdeus: Livre des Promesses et des Prédictions* (Sources chrétiennes, 101), 1964; H.-J. Diesner, *Fulgentius von Ruspe als Theologe und Kirchenpolitiker* (Abhandlungen 2, Theologie, I Reihe, Heft 26), 1966, esp. 60–5; on secular culture, see esp. A. Cameron, 'The Date and Identity of Macrobius', *Journal of Roman Studies* LVI, 1966, 25–38 (see Brown, *Augustine of Hippo* 420, n. 13); Riché, *Culture et Education* . . ., 76–8; on Luxorius, M. Rosenblum, *Luxorius: a Latin poet among*

I should like to end by asking why this should be so.

My reason is, briefly, that it was no longer necessary. The late fourth and early fifth centuries was a period of crisis: it marks the peak of missionary activity in Numidia, and the peak of competition between Donatists and Catholics. To save a Donatist from eternal damnation it was necessary to talk to him even in the *lingua Punica*.[1] But, with the forcible elimination of the Donatist clergy, after 411, the peasantry could settle down to the normal perils of under-evangelization, perils less spectacular than evangelization by the wrong side.

Also, there was no time. In 430, Roman rule collapsed in Numidia; by the end of the century, the Vandals had as good as abandoned the province for the Carthaginian coastline. The Donatist 'holy city' of Timgad had been pillaged by mountain-tribes from the Aures and the Hodna. Throughout the sixth century, Numidia was overshadowed by these 'Moorish' kingdoms.[2] In the fourth century, these mountaineers had been beneath religion.[3] They had regarded the Donatist controversy with the same indifference as the Highland clans of the seventeenth century had regarded the literate rancours of the Lowland Scots. We can glimpse what had happened by the end of the sixth century: Gregory the Great found to his surprise that Catholic bishops of Numidia had been collaborating with their

---

the Vandals, 1961; on Dracontius, Domenico Romano, *Studi draconziani*, 1959. Finally, J. Fontaine, *Isidore de Séville et la culture classique de l'Espagne wisigothique* II, 1959, 854–61, draws attention to the importance of Africa in the late sixth century.

[1] *Epp*. 66, 2 and 209, 3. In the last case, there is no evidence that Augustine's final choice for bishop of Fussala did speak the *lingua Punica*: it was plainly an accomplishment that could be dispensed with.

[2] Chr. Courtois, *Les Vandales et l'Afrique* 315, n. 7 (on Timgad) and 325–38 (map on p. 334).

[3] Hence Augustine's accusation that the Donatist bishops had supported the Moorish usurper Firmus: *Ep*. 87, 10. This accusation is made only to a bishop of Caesarea in Mauretania. Seeing that this town had been sacked by Firmus, and that the Christian bishop had had to appeal to the Emperor to save the town from paying taxes after the disaster (Symmachus, *Ep*. 1, 64), Augustine's accusation is in deliberate bad taste. His handling of many incidents in Donatism would repay re-consideration in this light: see Brown, *Augustine of Hippo*, 228–30.

Donatist colleagues.[1] The reason is not difficult to understand: faced by the resurgence of what Dr. Courtois has called *l'Afrique oubliée*, the Forgotten Africa of the mountains and the deserts, these two groups of Latin professionals had decided that the devil they knew was better than the devil they did not know. It is a sign of the future: the Christian has already become isolated as the *Roumi*, the man of Roman faith and Roman culture, in an alien world.

The Christian Latin culture of the West was the culture of men in a hurry: the missionary had to expand, the scholar had to preserve.[2] Like the Romans of Africa in the fifth and sixth centuries, who had hastily converted the classical monuments of their towns into fortresses, these men used what was to hand—the Latin language. By contrast, vernacular cultures grew up in the East under very different conditions. Far from reflecting any conscious desire to remove the yoke of Rome, these local cultures assumed its continued existence: in the fourth, fifth and sixth centuries, they could grow up peaceably, among the placid subjects of a world well policed by the two great empires of Byzantium and Persia. At exactly the time when, in the Byzantine Empire, Greek philosophy and medicine were passing quietly into Syriac, and Syriac imagery, in turn, was colouring the hymns and liturgy of the Byzantine Church, the Latin civilization of Africa had left no alternative but barbarism. We meet a cultivated African, Donatus, throwing in the towel:

> violentias barbararum gentium imminere conspiciens . . . ferme cum septuaginta monachis copiosisque librorum codicibus navali vehiculo in Hispaniam commeavit.[3]

We are left with the old problem, that has exercised historians of the classical tradition and of the growth of the Papacy: there *is* some connection between Christianity and the survival of Roman civilization in the west. The possibility that there had existed, in Late Roman Africa, a powerful Christian Church, hostile to the Roman

---

[1] The incident has been admirably studied by R. A. Markus, 'Donatism: the Last Phase', *Studies in Church History* I, ed. C. W. Dugmore and Charles Duggan, 1964, 118–26. This article, and the same author's 'Religious Dissent in North Africa in the Byzantine Period', *Studies in Church History* III, ed. C. J. Cuming, 1966, 140–9, show how much of general importance for our understanding of the evolution and fundamental characteristics of African Christianity can be gained from careful study of the events of the late sixth century.

[2] '. . . il faut faire vite': Fontaine, *Isidore de Séville* . . . II, 884.

[3] Ildefonsus of Toledo, *de vir. ill.* 4 (*P.L.* 96 200 c).

towns, rooted in the native cultural traditions of the countryside, had seemed, for a moment, to offer an alternative to that view. I do not think that there is an alternative. Christianity won, in the West, as elsewhere in the Roman world, because it won the battle for the towns:[1] it absorbed their culture, it transmitted this culture on its own terms, to those who had not enjoyed it to such an extent, or, rather, to those who would not have enjoyed it on such easy terms in the social and cultural conditions of the Later Empire.[2] (There may be a direct connection, in the Late Roman period, between the narrowing of Latin culture in its pagan form—its 'aristocratisation'—and its widening—its 'democratisation'—in its Christian form. For the Christian Church had the best of both worlds: its urban structure and the recruitment of its bishops would constantly transmit the culture of an élite to large congregations, as Augustine, in Hippo, would spell out the sheltered mysticism of Plotinus in simple Latin.)

There is always a social and cultural history yet to be written, of the terms on which Christianity won this victory in the Roman towns: it would aim, above all, to explain the gradual realization, throughout the fourth century, of that most breath-taking of all intellectual sleights of hand—the solemn identification, by Christian apologists from Origen and Lactantius onwards, of Christianity with *true* Greco-Roman culture, and the great tradition of Greco-Roman religion with all that was barbaric, un-Roman, not *évolué*.

We have seen how this happened in one area of the Latin culture of Africa. Whether we think it was worth happening, depends on whether we take Roman civilization, in its Late Roman form, for granted as an unquestioned good thing. One may doubt it: Christianity gained respectability at the high cost of adopting a town-dweller's assumptions on the passivity of the countryside, and by committing itself, disastrously, to a town-dweller's contempt of the barbarian.[3] In Africa, it paid the heavy price of gradual extinction.

---

[1] This is not to deny the interest of the survey of W. H. C. Frend, 'The Winning of the Countryside', *Journal of Ecclesiastical History* XVIII, 1967, 1–14.

[2] On the 'aristocratisation' of culture see, for instance, R. MacMullen, 'Roman Bureaucratese', *Traditio* XVIII, 1962, 367 f. [See now P. Brown, *The World of Late Antiquity* (1971), pp. 29–33 and 93–94.]

[3] See Brown, 'The Later Roman Empire', *Economic History Review* 2 ser., XX, 1967, at pp. 331–3 [pp. 53–54], and 'Approaches to the Religious Crisis of the Third Century', *English Historical Review*, LXXXIII (1968), at pp. 542 ff. pp. 89 ff.] [See now P. B. Brown, *The World of Late Antiquity* (1971), pp. 112 and 124.]

Elsewhere in Western Europe it survived. Perhaps the price was not paid until later. The failure of so many Western missions, from the inner erosion of the great Jesuit venture in China to the rise of nationalism in the *Tiers Monde* is, perhaps, the delayed payment for the Christian victories of the fourth and fifth centuries.

RELIGIOUS COERCION IN THE
LATER ROMAN EMPIRE: THE CASE
OF NORTH AFRICA*

In our treatment of the problem of religious coercion in the Later Roman Empire we are the direct heirs of a question posed by scholars at the time of the Reformation[1]—what part did the authority of the Christian Roman Emperors play in the development of the Christian church? During the sixteenth and seventeenth centuries two possible answers emerged. First, the 'liberals', such as Erasmus and Castellion, stressed the independent powers of growth of the primitive church and minimized the intervention of the Emperors, in order to deny that the history of the Christian Roman Empire could offer any precedent for the bloody heresy-laws of their own time.[2] As Erasmus wrote to Cardinal Campeggio in 1530, 'We should not lose faith in the state of the Church. At other times it has been subject to far greater tempests, as under Arcadius and Theodosius. What a state the world was then in! Each city had its Arians, its pagans, as well as the orthodox. In Africa, the Donatists and Circumcellions were raging . . . And yet, in the midst of such great discords, the Emperor governed without the shedding of blood, and, little by little, he eliminated those monsters of heresy . . .'[3] The second answer was that of the 'reactionaries', who had come to see in the 'godly princes' of their own time the only guarantee of religious unity. They saw the Later Empire as a period of decisive secular intervention in the interests of the Christian Church: the advisers of Louis XIV cited Augustine's relations with the Donatists

* *History* XLVIII, 1963, pp. 283–305.

[1] v. J. Lecler, *Toleration and the Reformation* (transl. Westow), 1960.

[2] v. S. Castellion, *Concerning Heretics* (transl. with Introduction and references to modern editions of the passages cited, by R. H. Bainton), 1935—the best dossier of the problem of tolerance in the Later Empire.

[3] Erasmus, *Opus Epistolarum*, ed. Allen, ix. 15.

in order to justify the persecution of the Huguenots:[1] and a Protestant such as Pierre Jurieu agreed, that: 'Sans l'autorité des empereurs, il est indubitable que les temples de Jupiter et de Mars seraient encore debout.'[2]

These two views have remained the poles between which the argument on religious coercion has taken place.[3] Yet the argument remains unsatisfactory if posed in this way. The holders of either view tend to assume a rigid dichotomy between Church and State: they disagree only in their assessment of the respective rôles of what they take to be two distinct entities. Thus, in its most modern form, the problem of coercion tends to be relegated to the problem of the nature of the Later Roman state. This state is treated as an autocracy, demanding religious obedience from all its subjects: it was so when Diocletian persecuted the Christians; it continued to be so when his successors persecuted the rivals of the Christians. It is both possible for some writers to blame the Church for being corrupted by accepting the unilateral patronage of this alien autocracy, and for others to treat religious coercion as a mere 'backwash' of ecclesiastical history, made inevitable by the unregenerate, authoritarian traditions of the Roman state. In fact, such a policy of coercion involved a 'symbiosis' between the Imperial and the episcopal authority. This symbiosis is an equally important element in the history of this problem in the Later Empire: it has not received the attention it deserves. The purpose of this article is to suggest that, in North Africa in the age of S. Augustine, who was bishop of Hippo from 396 to 430, the structure and ideals of both the Church and the Empire were being transformed in the course of a long period of such a symbiosis.

The need to treat the relation between the Christian Church and lay society province by province is of long standing;[4] and in Africa the influence of local factors on the general problem of Church and State is particularly marked. The ecclesiastical life of this province

---

[1] The answer to these arguments, by P. Bayle, *Commentaire philosophique . . .*, revised edition, Amsterdam, 1713, is the classic criticism of Augustine's justification of coercion.

[2] P. Jurie, *Tableau du socinianisme*, The Hague, 1690, p. 501.

[3] E.g. the correspondence which followed the B.B.C. talk of M. Finlay on 'The Emperor Diocletian', *The Listener*, vol. 63, 1960, 10 March, pp. 447 *sq.* Correspondence, 14 April, p. 668, and 28 April, p. 758.

[4] *v.* A. Momigliano, in his Introduction to *Christianity and Paganism in the Fourth Century*, Warburg Lectures, 1963, p. 14.

is exceptionally well-documented[1] and has been the subject of excellent monographs.[2] The rise of the schismatic church of the Donatists—which had begun in Carthage in 311 and by the time of Augustine had won over the majority of African Christians[3]—created a situation which posed the problem of coercion in its classic form: that is, this church was not only prohibited but, during the episcopate of Augustine, its congregations were subjected to official pressure to join the Catholic Church.

I do not propose to deal directly with the question whether such coercion was 'effective'. Augustine claimed that, in the case of the Donatists, this policy had been justified by results;[4] but, for an historian, it is important to go outside the immediate problem of the Donatist schism and to consider the effect of the suppression of a wide variety of religious beliefs on the life of the province as a whole. We must first consider the situation created by the Imperial legislation; then, the 'meaning' of this legislation—its purpose and justification as seen by the Emperor and the bishops; and, lastly, the rôle of the bishop in applying and adapting these laws.

Around A.D. 400 the Catholic Church was distinguished from all other religions both by being privileged and by the fact that its rivals were repressed in varying degrees. 'You must know, my friends', Augustine said in a sermon, 'how the mutterings (of the pagans) join with those of the heretics and the Jews. Heretics, Jews and pagans: they have formed a unity over against our Unity.'[5] This

---

[1] Especially the works of S. Augustine: *v.* table of editions in Portalié, *Guide to the Thought of S. Augustine*, 1960, pp. 401–6, and of translations in Marrou, *S. Augustine* (Men of Wisdom), 1957, pp. 182–6. All references to Augustine's *Letters* and anti-Donatist writings are taken from the *Corpus Scriptorum Ecclesiae Latinorum* (C.S.E.L.). *The Sermons* of Augustine are in *Patrologia Latina* xxxviii and xxxix: The *Ennarationes in Psalmos* in *ibid.* xxxvi–xxxvii. Full collection of documents, including the whole surviving verbatim record of the *Collatio* at Carthage of 411, with excellent commentaries as an Appendix to Optatus of Milevis, *De schismate Donatistarum*: in *Patrologia Latina* xi. coll. 1179 *sqq.*

[2] P. Monceaux, *Histoire littéraire de l'Afrique chrétienne*, in 7 vols. 1901–23, is basic. See the vivid evocation of F. van der Meer, *Augustine the Bishop* (trans. Battershaw and Lamb), 1961.

[3] The best account is W. H. C. Frend, *The Donatist Church*, 1952. For further bibliography and alternative interpretations, see *History*, xlvi. 83–101 [p. 237–259].

[4] See especially his *Letter* 93. v. 17 (34, 2, p. 461, trans. Dods, *The Letters of S. Augustine*, i. 409–10).

[5] *Sermon* 62, 18.

state of religious discrimination has been compared to the traditional differentiation which, in the Early Empire, had existed between Roman citizens and *peregrini*.[1]

The laws on which this discrimination rested were, mostly, edited in the Theodosian Code of 438[2] and have been studied exhaustively.[3] Very briefly, these laws punished individuals for certain unlawful religious acts, withdrew civic rights from the members of certain sects, excluded others from public employment, and interfered with the property and collective worship of every non-Catholic religious body in the Empire, except the Jews. Certain rites such as those of 'black' magic had always been punished by death.[4] This penalty was gradually extended to cover pagan sacrifices[5] and, intermittently, was used against the leaders of the Manichees.[6] In this last case, the laws only continued sanctions that had been laid down by pagan Emperors like Diocletian and Maximian who had persecuted the Christians.[7] Other rites were subjected to increasing penalties: those who perpetrated heretical ordinations and ceremonies were fined,[8] and the principle was later extended to impose proscription and exile on the Donatist clergy who had 'polluted' the Catholic sacraments by re-baptism.[9] The property in which these rites took place

[1] J. Gaudemet, *L'Eglise dans l'Empire romain*, ive–ve siècles, 1958, p. 596.

[2] *Codex Theodosianus*, ed. Mommsen and Meyer, 1905: trans. C. Pharr, 1952.

[3] The most complete remains that of Jacques Godefroye (Gothofredus) *Codex Theodosianus cum perpetuis commentariis*, 6 vols., 1665, esp. *vol. vi ad lib. xvi*, of which parts are included in P. L. xi. See also: general—Gaudemet, *op. cit.*, pp. 597–652 (whose references are incomplete and inaccurate). On Donatims—F. Martroye, 'La répression du Donatisme', *Mem. Soc. Antiq. de France*, lxiii. 1913. On paganism—Martroye, 'La répression de la magie et le culte des gentils au ive siècle', *Nouv. Rev. Hist. de droit*, 1930. On magic—E. Massonneau, *La magie dans l'antiquité romaine*, 1934. On the Manichees—E. Kaden, 'Die Edikte gegen die Manichaer v. Diokletian bis Justinian', *Festschr. Lewald*, 1953, pp. 55–68. [See now P. Brown, 'The Diffusion of Manichaeism in the Roman Empire', *Journal of Roman Studies*, LIX, 1969, pp. 92–103 = pp. 94–118.] On the Jews—most recently, B. Blumenkranz, *Juifs et chrétiens dans le monde occidental, 430–1096*, 1960.

[4] *v. Cod. Theod.* ix, xvi.

[5] From at least 391: *Cod. Theod.* xvi. x. 10.

[6] *v. Cod. Theod.* xvi. v. 3 (372) and *Codex Justinianus* i. v. 11.

[7] *Lex Dei, sive Mosaicarum et Romanorum legum collatio*, xv, 3, ed. *Iurisprudentiae anteustiniana reliquiae*, ii. 2, pp. 381 sq.; cf. Valentinian, Novella xviii (445): 'superstitio paganis quoque damnata temporibus'. [Now see p. 106.]

[8] *Cod. Theod.* xvi. v. 21 (392).

[9] *v.* language of *Cod. Theod.* xvi. vi. 2 (377) and penalties in xvi. v. 52, 5 (412).

was also forfeited: pagan temples were emptied and access to them restricted,[1] idols and altars destroyed,[2] heretical churches handed over to the Catholics,[3] and illicit places of assembly confiscated.[4]

It is possible to minimize the severity of these measures in comparison with later practice. Their point of departure was limited to externals: only specific acts were punished, and the means of performing them denied. Thus, in Africa, pagans would have found their temples closed for worship, would have been savagely punished for performing sacrifices, and excluded from the Imperial service:[5] but at no time were they forced by law to join the Catholic Church. It was easy for Augustine to treat such laws as a purely external framework: they either prohibited 'impieties'[6] or they brought indirect pressure to bear on individuals, as *molestiae medicinales*—as a 'treatment by inconveniences'.[7] We are still a long way from an official policy of forcible conversion, such as the forced baptism of the Jews in Byzantium and elsewhere in the seventh century.[8]

In Africa, however, the special circumstances of the Donatist schism provoked a new departure. After 405, the laws against the Donatists are laws on 'Unity'. They are framed to force the Donatist clergy and rank and file into the Catholic Church: they override the individual will[9] and were known to provoke feigned conversions.[10] Punishments, such as the loss of civic rights, were remitted on 'penitence',[11] and in 412 and 414 a scale of very heavy fines was imposed on Donatist laymen who did not join the Catholic Church.[12]

---

[1] E.g. *Cod. Theod.* xvi. x. 18.

[2] E.g. *Cod. Theod.* xvi. x. 19 (407 or 408).

[3] E.g. *Cod. Theod.* xvi. v. 43 (407 or 408). The transfer was made direct to the Catholic church, as happened in the case of smaller sects: *v.* Augustine, *De haeresibus*, *c.* 87 (in P.L. xlii).

[4] E.g. *Cod. Theod.* xvi. vi. 2, 1 (377).

[5] For a description of the pagans in Africa, see van der Meer, *op. cit.*, pp. 37–45.

[6] Augustine, *Contra Epistulam Parmeniani*, lx, 15 (51, p. 35).

[7] A constant phrase: *v. Letter*, 185. vii. 26 (57, p. 25, l. 4).

[8] *v.* Blumencranz, *op. cit.*, pp. 97–138.

[9] The Donatists held that this distinguished the Catholic persecution from their own civil law suits for the property of their own schismatics, the Maximianists: *Gesta Collationis Carthaginensis*, iii. *die*, no. 258: P.L. xi, 1413 C.

[10] E.g. Augustine, *Letter*, 93, v. 17 (34, 2, p. 461).

[11] *Cod. Theod.* xvi. v. 41 (407).

[12] *Cod. Theod.* xvi. v. 52 (412) and 54 (414).

This new principle comes very close to the use of direct force: indeed, slaves and *coloni*, who had always been exposed to such treatment,[1] were to be 'admonished' by their lords 'with frequent strokes'.[2]

It is tempting to try to reduce to order the confusing and often inconsistent punishments contained in the Theodosian Code. Many scholars see in these the continuation of a consistent juridical attitude, which underlay the persecution of the Christians under Diocletian—the belief that only those who adhered to the official Roman religion could expect to enjoy the full benefits of Roman citizenship.[3] Certain punishments, such as *infamia*—which included disqualification from conducting a lawsuit and from holding office—may have been applied by Diocletian to the Christians, and then, by Constantine, to the heretics;[4] but the evidence for a continuous and precise legal basis of persecution in both pagan and Christian times is still lacking.[5] The language of the Theodosian Code provides only one certain conclusion: that from 379 onwards it led in the direction of religious intolerance.[6] This intolerance is often expressed in terms of excluding sects from the benefits of Roman society; but such language involves few precise legal measures and is usually applied to small, detested sects such as the Manichees.[7] To impose greater precision is, perhaps, to overlook the human element in the

---

[1] As occurred in the persecutions of the Christians in the third century. *Cf.* the sarcophagus of Elia Athanasia, which shows her being flogged: Fuhrmann, *Mem. Pont. Accademia.* iv. 1934-8, pp. 187-207 tav. 43.

[2] *Cod. Theod.* xvi. v. 52, 3 and 54, 8. Such uses of direct force were common on African estates. The Donatist bishop of Calama had rebaptized the slaves on an estate he had purchased—Augustine, *Letter* 66 (34, 2, pp. 235-6); and Augustine expected Catholic land-owners to exert what may have been similar pressure; e.g. *Letter* 58 (34, 2, pp. 216-19), *v.* Dölger, 'Christliche Grundbesitzer u. heidnische Landarbeiter', *Antike u. Christentum*, 6, 1950.

[3] The case for such a view is made by Mommsen, *Römisches Strafecht*, 1899, Book iv, sect. 2, 'Häresie und Nichtchristentum', p.p. 595-611; and has been adopted by Maissonneuve, *Étude sur les origines de l'Inquisition*, 2nd ed. 1960, esp. p. 36.

[4] *v.* Mommsen, *op. cit.* p. 593 n. 2 and p. 604.

[5] *v.* some criticisms of Mommsen's thesis, as it affects the persecution of the Christians, by Last, *s.v. Christenverfolgung*, ii (juristisch), *Reallexikon für Antike u. Christentum*, 2, 1954, col. 1216.

[6] Law of Gratian: *Cod. Theod.* xvi. v. 5: *omnes vetitae legibus et divinis et imperialibus constitutionibus haereses perpetuo conquiescant.*

[7] *v.* Kaden, *art. cit.*

situation. A policy of religious discrimination, pursued for many generations, cannot be summed up in a code of rules; it can best be understood by the historian as an 'atmosphere'. Thus, this 'atmosphere' caused long-established Roman laws—such as those against magic—to cast a considerably longer shadow under a Christian government.[1]

In Africa, this 'atmosphere' can also be seen in areas that are not directly covered by the laws. Communities have always had their own ways of dealing with minority-groups. In Hippo, for instance, Manichees and pagans could be controlled merely by a 'boycott' in a predominantly Christian town,[2] just as the Catholic minority had been subjected to a boycott imposed by the Donatist bishop.[3] Here the bishop comes into his own as the leader of public opinion: as one roundly declared, 'If the very name of a Donatist is heard in our town, he will be stoned'.[4]

The most sinister aspect of this atmosphere was the prevalence of religious rioting in Africa and elsewhere. The notorious murder of Hypatia by the Alexandrian mob was only one example among dozens.[5] It was due, partly, to the ineffectiveness of the Roman state. The policy of coercion did not in itself require a great show of force; but force was necessary to hold in check the disturbances

---

[1] Especially by the application of these laws to private sacrifices of all kinds— such as those of the Theurgists. [Now see p. 126, n. 6.] Many pagans opposed such sacrifices: v. e.g. Eunapius, *Lives of the Sophists*, ed. Loeb, p. 419: 'He (Antonius son of Eustathius) displayed no tendency towards theurgy and that which is at variance to sensible appearances, perhaps because he kept a wary eye on the imperial views and policy, which were opposed to such practices.' v. E. R. Dodds, 'Theurgy and its relationship to Neo-Platonism', *Journ. of Roman Studies*, 37, 1947, pp. 55–69.

[2] *Sermons* 182, 2 and 302, 19. [See p. 114.]

[3] *Contra Litteras Petiliani*, ii. 83, 184 (52, p. 114). He forbade the bakers to bake bread for the Catholics.

[4] *Coll. Carth.* i die. no. 178: P.L. xi. 1302A.

[5] v. Socrates, *Eccles. Hist.* vii, 15: 'And surely nothing can be further from the spirit of Christianity than massacres, fights and transactions of that sort.' Similar incidents at Bordeaux (386: a Priscillianist), Prosper of Acquitaine, *Chron.* ad. ann.: P.L. li, 586; and in Africa, at Ala Miliaria = Benian (434: a Donatist nun). v. Aug. *Letter* 91, 8 (34, 2, pp. 432–4; tr. Dods, i, pp. 387-9), a vivid description of a pagan riot at Calama, and the many outrages that followed the application of the laws against the Donatists in 405: v. Willis, *S, Augustine and the Donatist Controversy*, S.P.C.K., 1950, p. 61. [Now see P. Brown, *The World of Late Antiquity*, 1971, pp. 103–106.]

that might follow in its wake.[1] In Africa, the police and army were conspicuous by their absence.[2] The result of this weakness was a particularly venomous situation. The Emperors, in their public edicts, set a 'tone' of loftly intolerance, while leaving local groups to carry it out in their own way. The bishops played a highly dubious rôle in this situation. At a time of anti-Jewish riots that had spread with alarming rapidity from the frontier of Mesopotamia to Aquileia, the eastern sea-port of Northern Italy, Ambrose could even rebuke the Emperor for having granted military protection to a Jewish community: 'They have lost their own army, now they want to corrupt ours.'[3] Nor is Augustine exempt. In 399 he preached a rousing sermon at the time when official measures were being taken against paganism in Carthage, amid cheers of 'Down with the Roman gods';[4] and the indirect result of this clever oratory may well have been a religious riot in a provincial town, in which sixty Christians were killed.[5] In such an atmosphere, the praise lavished on an Emperor such as Theodosius I for his personal moderation in the treatment of heretics is mere special pleading.[6] The Emperors could no longer control the situation, and by their denunciations they only

[1] v. *Commonitorium* of the Catholic Council (404) in P.L. xi. 1202-3: appeal for police protection. *Cod. Theod.* xvi. ii. 31: armed force against resisting mobs. In Africa—esp. in Numidia—these incidents took place largely in the countryside, or by the impingement of rural discontent on the small towns—e.g. Aug. *Letter* 108. v. 14 (44, pp. 627-8) for the 'invasion' of Hippo by the Donatist bishop in 410. There is nothing comparable to the military measures necessary to control large, urban populations, as in Alexandria and Constantinople v. Optatus, *De schismate Donatistarum*, iii (P.L. xi. 987-1028) and Frend, *op. cit.*, p. 177-82, for a description of the most spectacular show of force against the Donatists of which we know in detail.

[2] This army was small—v. Warmington, *The North African Provinces*, c. ii, pp. 8-19, and extremely unpopular. v. Augustine, *Sermon* 302, preached after his congregation had lynched the commander of the garrison. Such troops sometimes colluded with Donatist mobs which they would not, or could not, control: Optatus, ii, 18, P.L. xi, 971 B.

[3] Ambrose, *Letter* 40, 18: for this incident and its repercussions in Italy, see L. Ruggini, 'Ebrei e orientali nell'Italia settentrionale fra il iv e il vi secolo', *Studia et documenta Historiae et Iuris*, xxv. 1959, pp. 192-207, with a complete catalogue of anti-Jewish riots throughout the Empire.

[4] *Sermon*, 24, 6 v. Lambot, *Corpus Christianorum*, xli. 1961, p. 32415.

[5] Augustine, *Letter* 50 (34, 2, p. 143).

[6] Socrates, *Ecclesiastical Hist.* v. 20 and Sozomen, *Eccl. Hist.* vii, 12, accepted, with reserves, by King, *The Emperor Theodosius and the Establishment of Christianity*, S.C.M., 1961, p. 95.

aggravated it. When the state could no longer command sufficient force to operate its own measures on its own terms, the claims of Augustine and other Christian writers that the Roman laws were fair and free from *saevitia*—from arbitrary violence[1]—contained an element of wilful naïvety.

The laws themselves would have affected different religious groups differently, according to their attitudes. Thus, the Donatists had a tradition of martyrdom which made them intensely aware of the situation,[2] and which drove some communities to expect the worst.[3] In short, they had the materials for a *prise de conscience* on the issue of coercion. They drew heavily on the Christian apologists of the time of the pagan persecutions.[4] Augustine's self-conscious justification of the Catholic policy—the only one of its kind in the literature of the Early Church—was provoked less by his own scruples than by being confronted with this articulate, Donatist attitude to the problem. On the other hand, as Augustine himself pointed out, pagans caught at illicit sacrifices, and faced with death on the charge of performing magic rites that had always been detested by their fellows, were not of the stuff of martyrs.[5]

We can study the material effects of the laws in great detail as they were applied to the Donatist Church. One feature emerges clearly: that the coercive legislation impinged directly only on the leaders of the movement and on the upper classes of provincial society. As first applied in Africa, the laws were used against the bishops and clergy of the heretical churches. This is shown by the fact that, in the brief period of repression between 405 and 409, out of some 23 Donatist sees that had been reduced to Catholic 'Unity' only three congregations had been converted of their own accord, the others having been deprived of their bishop by conversion, by driving him

---

[1] A constant theme in Augustine: *v.* esp. *Sermon* 302, 13; also in the '*Ambrosiaster*': *v.* Heggelbacher, *Vom römischem zum christl. Recht*, 1959, p. 29.

[2] *v.* An excellent reconstruction of this attitude by Frend, 'The Roman Empire in the eyes of Western Schismatics during the 4th century', *Miscellanea Historiae Ecclesiasticae* (Stockholm, 1960), 1961, pp. 9–22. [Now see P. Brown, *Augustine of Hippo*, pp. 217–221.]

[3] The Donatist congregation at Timgad thought that the Imperial commissioner intended to execute them all: Augustine, *Letter*, 204, 3 (57, pp. 318–19).

[4] Especially the arguments used by Gaudentius, the Donatist bishop of Timgad: *v.* Augustine, *Contra Gaudentium* (53, pp. 210–74: trans. in the *Anti-Donatist Writings of S. Augustine*). Gaudentius' original letter is reconstructed by Monceaux, *op. cit.* V, pp. 329–33.

[5] *Ennaratio in Psalm.* 140, c.20.

out, or by the simple means of preventing the Donatists from holding an election whenever a vacancy occurred.[1] In Mauretanian Caesarea, for instance, the Donatist bishop, Emeritus, had been excluded from his church, and his congregation had gone over to the Catholic bishop *faute de mieux*, though with such a bad grace that Augustine had wished to impress them by a debate with their former leader.[2]

We know much less about the effects of the later laws on lay society, mainly because Augustine lost interest in Donatism at that time. The edicts made everyone in authority—down to the '*seniores*', the village headmen[3]—responsible for the application of the laws.[4] The fines imposed in 412 and 414[5] ranged from fifty pounds of gold for high officials to five pounds for ordinary townsmen (with a mysterious imposition of five pounds of silver on the Circumcellions). They are exceptionally heavy by Late Roman standards.[6] We know next to nothing about their application, except that they drop dramatically from twenty to five to cover the classes that would have made up the bulk of the Donatist congregations of the towns—the *curiales*, *negotiatores* and *plebeii*. From what we know of the difficulty of collecting gold taxes from the urban populations of the Later Roman Empire, in towns considerably more developed than those of Africa,[7] we might guess that such fines would only have been used *in terrorem*. It is not surprising that the lower categories were omitted in the later laws. Of the different classes, the *negotiatores* would have been the most vulnerable. They would have had ready money for usury,[8] and would have been in constant contact with the authorities by reason of their vital rôle in the food-supply of the town and army.[9] In Hippo, the imposition of such fines might

---

[1] This evidence is derived from the roll-call of Donatist and Catholic bishops at the *Collatio* of Carthage (411): P.L. 1280–1351, *v.* Frend, *op. cit.* pp. 265–7.

[2] *Sermo ad Caesariensis Ecclesiae plebem* and *Gesta cum Emerito*, esp. c.2 (53, pp. 167–96).

[3] Frend, *op. cit.* p. 288: sententia cognitoris, *Coll. Carth.* P.L. xi. 1418.

[4] E.g. *Cod. Theod.* xvi. v. 45 (408) and 46 (409).

[5] *Cod. Theod.* xvi. v. 52 and 54.

[6] Twenty pounds of gold was a sufficiently heavy penalty to be a substitute for capital punishment: *Cod. Theod.* ix. xvii. 2 (347).

[7] *v.* A. H. M. Jones, *Ancient Economic History*, 1948, pp. 11–12. [See A. H. M. Jones, *The Later Roman Empire*, II, 1964, p. 847.]

[8] *Enn. in Ps.* 54, c.14.

[9] *v.* The excellent analysis of the repercussions of a fine of 200 pounds of gold imposed, in 385, on the *corpus mercatorum* of Milan (Ambrose, *Letter* 20) in L. Ruggini, *Economia e società nell'Italia annonaria*, 1962, pp. 106–11.

well have been yet another incident in the victimization of these tradesmen by the local garrison.[1]

The life of the rank and file would also have been affected by the confiscation of the estates of the Donatist church. The transfer of traditional property, which would have included the cemeteries, those foci of the intense family-feeling of the Africans,[2] impressed contemporaries and is mentioned in Augustine's later sermons.[3] The economic effects of these measures may be exaggerated: with the possible exception of alms-giving,[4] the transfer of this wealth would not so much have affected the poor as deprived the Donatist bishop of the means with which to 'maintain his estate' in the community. In the countryside, the *coloni*, serfs and Circumcellions were left to the discretion of the landlords, without direct intervention by the state.[5] Thus, the working of religious coercion, as it affected the Donatists, served to emphasize that cleavage between the *honestiores* and the passive poorer classes—the *humiliores*—which is the most marked feature of the 'pyramidal' structure of Late Roman society.

An even more obvious distinction existed between town and country. The population of a Later Roman town was particularly vulnerable to pressure from above: in Africa, the towns were small, manageable communities, and the population of a big city, such as Rome, Constantinople and Alexandria was organized in gilds[6] and partly dependent on privileges that could be strictly controlled.[7] While the towns were more amenable to an official line,[8] the country-side became the refuge of innumerable dissenting sects, many of

[1] *Sermon* 302, c. 16.

[2] *Sermon* 359, c. 8.

[3] E.g. *Tractatus in Johannis Evangelium*, vi. 25.

[4] Augustine, *Letter* 185, ix. 36 (57, p. 32).

[5] *v. n. supra*. Cyprian, *Letter* 55, 13 implies a similar responsibility of a lord for his tenant, at the time of the pagan persecution of Decius.

[6] E.g. *Cod. Theod.* xvi. iv. 5 (404), by which the corpora of Constantinople are made responsible for preventing their members from attending heretical assemblies. [This impression has been confirmed in greater detail by E. Tengström, *Donatisten und Katholiken*, 1964 (on which see pp. 335–6), and P. A. Février, 'Toujours le Donatisme: à quand l'Afrique?', *Rivista di storia e letteratura religiosa* II, 2, 1966, pp. 228–40—see p. 294.]

[7] E.g. Sozomen, *Ecclesiastical History*, iii, 7. The Arian Constantius II had halved the bread-ration of the people of Constantinople as a punishment for rioting in favour of their orthodox bishop.

[8] This is made plain by the anxiety expressed by the Monophysite patriarch of Alexandria during the persecution of his church, by Justinian in 539: 'he

which survived untouched into the Middle Ages.[1] The contrast continued under Islam: the inland villages of Western Syria remained Christian, while the cities of the coast became Muslim.[2]

The effects of the laws were very different at the top. The extension to them of civic disabilities usually applied only to the Manichees would have had a disastrous effect on the leading citizens of a *civitas Romana* such as Hippo. In an age in which the upper classes were especially dependent upon official privileges, titles and their ability to protect their wealth by litigation,[3] a penalty such as *infamia*, which prejudiced just these advantages, was particularly onerous.[4] The denial of the right to make donations, to receive legacies and even to make a will was aggravated by its repercussions on the family in a society where mixed marriages between Donatists and Catholics had once been common.[5] We know of attempts to make false wills,[6] and of high-ranking Donatists who may have been converted by such pressures—Celer, a local landowner in Hippo,[7] and Donatus, the Proconsul, also a landowner in Hippo and the son of a mixed marriage.[8] This sanction was too drastic to be applied

---

sighed and wept, because he knew the people of Alexandria, and that they loved pomp and honour, and he feared that they would depart from the orthodox Faith, with a view to gaining honour from the prince', History of the Patriarchs, *Patrologia Orientalis*, I, p. (203) 467.

[1] Phrygia: Montanists till the eighth century: Sozomen, *Eccl. Hist.* II, 32, 6 (fifth cent.); Theophanes, *Chronicon*, ed. C. de Boor i. 401 (eighth cent.). Egypt: Meletians from fourth to eighth centuries, *v.* Bell, *Jews and Christians in Egypt*, 1924, pp. 42-3. Syria: out of 800 villages, 1 Arian, 1 Eunomian and 8 Marcionite—Theodoret of Cyrrhus, *Letter* 81, 113 (A.D. 450). For these strange patterns of dissent, see A. H. M. Jones, 'Were the ancient heresies national or social movements in disguise ?', *Journal of Theol. Studies*, x, 1959, pp. 280-95.

[2] *v. Spuler*, 'Die west-syrische (monophysitische) Kirche uner dem Islam', *Saeculum* 9, 1958, p. 324.

[3] See the description of Augustine's patron, Romanianus, in the *Confessions* and the preface to the *Contra Academicos*: litigation, *honores* and *potestates* are all-important in his career. [See P. Brown, *Augustine of Hippo*, pp. 21, 90 and 145.]

[4] *v.* esp. M. Kaser, '*Infamia u. ignominia* i. d. röm. Rechtsquellen,' *Zeitschr. Savigny-Stift. für Rechtsgesch.* 73, 1956, Rom. Abt. pp. 272-8.

[5] *v.* Augustine, *Letter* 33, 5 (34, pp. 21-2).

[6] *Sermon* 47, c. 13.

[7] Augustine, *Letters* 56 and 57 (34, 2, pp. 213-16) and 139, (44, p. 151). [See H. Krummrey, 'Zu der Ehreninschrift für Celer aus Hippo Regius', *Helikon* v, 1965, pp. 318-319 and P. Brown, *Augustine of Hippo*, pp. 226 and 240-41.]

[8] Augustine, *Letter* 112, 3 (34, 2, p. 659).

consistently to a respectable provincial upper class. It was usually applied only to prevent donations to the Donatist church. In one such *cause célèbre*, a nobleman challenged the will of his sister, who had left her property to a Donatist bishop:[1] he had obviously intervened to keep the possessions 'in the family'. There is even evidence to suggest that such laws were handled with anxiety by both Emperors and bishops: the Catholic Council was concerned lest the law provoked too many feigned conversions among those engaged in lawsuits;[2] and an Imperial edict, which emphasized, in almost episcopal language, that the laws would not be applied to those who had shown 'penitence', may well have been a covert attempt to reassure the provincials at a time of crisis.[3]

Thus the immediate effects of the coercive legislation can best be seen at the top. The most obvious result was the effect on the Catholic hierarchy itself. The widening division between bishop and congregation is a phenomenon of Later Roman history that still needs to be explained. In a province such as Africa, as in the Greek East at the time of the Arian controversy, this split is directly connected with the problem of religious coercion. The Greek ecclesiastical historians of the time show how the heresy-laws were used as part of a game of forfeits by which bishops fought each other for the control of passive congregations. One example is plainly included by the historian as a caricature of this development. The orthodox bishop of Synnada was determined to persecute his heretical rival. Dissatisfied with the provincial governor, he went to Constantinople to appeal to the Praetorian Prefect for wider powers against the heretics. In his absence, the rival hit upon a brilliant idea: gathering his congregation, he subscribed to the orthodox creed, and took over the basilica of his persecutor. When the bishop returned from Constantinople, he found that he had been 'trumped'![4] Other bishops might have found themselves placed by the Emperor at the head of alien and hostile communities.[5] In

[1] *Contra Epistulam Parmeniani* i, 19 (51, pp. 41–2).

[2] The *Commonitorium* of the legation of the Catholic council of 404: in P.L. xi, 1203.

[3] *Cod. Theod.* xvi. v. 41 (November 407).

[4] Socrates, *Eccl. Hist.* vii, 3.

[5] v. Theodoret, *Eccl. Hist.* iv. 15 for a graphic description of the boycott of the Arian bishop of Samosata by the orthodox congregation. The same happened to Maximin of Sinitum when he became a Catholic: Augustine, *Letter* 105, ii, 4 (34 2, p. 567).

such a situation, the identification of bishop and official would have become inevitable: nor would a bishop, once imposed by force, be likely to offer a firm resistance whenever the official policy changed.[1]

Moreover the Catholic Church had always found it difficult to recruit clergy[2] and the sudden accession of new sees forced the bishops to 'scrape the barrel'. Antoninus of Fussala, Augustine's disastrous nominee to a former Donatist community, is an extreme example of the possibilities of the new dispensation. Once ordained, he victimized his flock and then absented himself to Rome in order to regain his post. Augustine implied, in his letter to the pope, that it would be the last straw for this coerced community if a bishop were again to be imposed on them: 'For threats are being made to the people . . . of legal processes and public officials and military pressure . . . In consequence, those unfortunate people, though Catholic Christians, are in dread of heavier punishment from a Catholic bishop than they feared from the laws of Catholic Emperors when they were heretics.'[3]

This demoralizing process was held in check in Africa. The Imperial legislation was usually effective only in areas where there were already strong Catholic communities capable of absorbing their 'lost sheep'.[4] The absorption would depend on the character of the bishop. Augustine, typically, covered the walls of the church of his rival with posters, showing the Scriptural testimonies on which his case rested.[5] The bishop of Hippo Diarrhytos (Bizerte)[6] and the bishop of Cuicul (Djemila)[7] built splendid new basilicas to crown their victory. The shrewdest of all was Evodius of Uzalis: knowing the intense attachment of the Donatists to the cult of martyrs and relics (Augustine once said, contemptuously, that they worshipped every bit of dust that came from the Holy Land)[8] he placed the newly discovered relics of St. Stephen, the first martyr,

---

[1] A bishop imposed by force on their own schismatic community by the Donatists became a Catholic at the time of the Imperial 'severity': Augustine, *Gesta cum Emerito* c. 9 (53, p. 192).

[2] Legation of the Catholic council to pope Anastasius (401): in P.L. xi. 1195.

[3] *Letter* 209, 9 (57, pp. 351–2). [See P. Brown, *Augustine of Hippo*, pp. 412 and 424.]

[4] *v.* Frend, *op. cit.* p. 265.

[5] *Retractationes* ii, 27.

[6] *Sermon* 359, 9.

[7] E. Albertini, *Bull. Arch. du Comité*, 1922, pp. xxvi–xxxii.

[8] *Letter* 52, 2 (34, 2, p. 150).

imported direct from Jerusalem, in the 'regained' Donatist basilica, plainly in order to cement the loyalty of its former congregation.[1] The effect of this situation on the individual can be seen in the sermons of Augustine: and especially in two long sermons in 410, in which he attempted to justify his activity—his *instantia*—to a demoralized congregation.[2] It was his duty to pasture his sheep 'with discipline'.[3] For Augustine, 'discipline' meant 'teaching by inconveniences':[4] and the context of this and other sermons makes it clear that this *disciplina* had been extended from the purely moral sphere to include a large measure of identification with the 'terror' of the Imperial laws against heresy. In this way we can sometimes glimpse our abstract categories of 'Church' and 'State' as living factors in forming the character of a sensitive man determined to be a slave to his own exercise of power: and there were many bishops who were not as scrupulous as Augustine, and who did not share his genuine concern for the inner evolution of the individual.[5]

It has been suggested that this legislation alienated whole provinces from Roman rule and so played a part in bringing about the fall of the Roman Empire. There is little evidence that this happened in Africa: the primitive Moorish kingdoms and the pirate-state of the Vandals would hardly have been greeted by settled Donatist communities as a preferable alternative to the Roman order that had formed their horizon for centuries. The last entry of a Donatist chronicle attempts to show that 666, the Number of the Beast in Revelation, applies to Genseric, the Vandal king of Carthage.[6] But it is not an irrelevant question for the future evolution of Western Europe. 'Heretical' barbarian states were emerging as viable alternatives to the Roman Empire. These *regna* had limited ideological ambitions and little interest in the intolerance of their Roman

---

[1] As is implied in the *de Miraculis Sancti Stephani*, i, c. 7: P.L. xli. 839. [See P. Brown, *Augustine of Hippo*, pp. 413–414.]

[2] *Sermons* 46 and 47 on Ezechiel 34, *de pastoribus* and *de ovibus*.

[3] *Sermon* 46, 23.

[4] *v.* Marrou, '*Doctrina* et *disciplina* dans la langue des Perès de l'Eglise', *Bulletin du Cange*, ix. 1934, pp. 5–25.

[5] An admirable passage in a letter to Paulinus of Nola: 95, 3 (34, 2, p. 508: transl. Dods, ii, p. 3), which coincides with an appeal for penalties against pagans and the maintenance of the laws against the Donatists. [See p. 278.]

[6] *Liber Genealogus* in *Monumenta Germaniae Historica* ix, Chronica Minora: *v.* Monceaux, *op. cit.* vi, 249–58. [See p. 297.]

subjects.[1] The catholic bishops realized that such states were no substitute for the Empire as champions of the Church against religious dissent. In 447, Pope Leo regretted that the dislocation of the Imperial authority in Spain had made impossible the application of the laws against the Manichees and Priscillianists.[2] An identity of interests, once stated so unambiguously, could hardly escape the notice of the possible victims of a renewed alliance of Church and Empire. The support which Jewish communities gave to the 'permissive' Arian government of Theoderic in Italy may well be connected with the fear of the re-establishment, by Justinian, of an intolerant Catholic government.[3] It was a fear well-justified by the later history of persecution in a 'Byzantinized' Catholic state, such as Visigothic Spain, in the seventh century.[4]

It is, however, not enough to describe the situation merely in terms of the effects of the laws. It is equally important to find out what the situation 'meant' to the two interested parties—the Emperors and the bishops. The attitude of the Emperors was extremely complex. Fragments of a traditional Roman attitude to religious observance appear in the laws: Donatism is described as a *piacularis doctrina*, but this is merely a conventional formula invoked to justify specific measures.[5] Again, it is possible to see the coercive legislation of the time of Augustine as an inevitable extension of the policy of Constantine, in that, once the Emperors had decided to grant privileges to the 'Catholic religion', they had to ensure that these privileges were not disputed, as they were in Africa, by the rise of a second church. Thus, a law which, in vague terms, penalizes any person who 'disagrees with the Catholic bishop', may be part of the particular application to Africa of general laws defining and strengthening the position of the *audientia episcopalis*—the bishop's

[1] Inevitably all *Cod. Theod.* xvi. v. *de haereticis* is omitted in the *Breviarium* of Alaric II. For the general tolerance of Arian rulers, see E. A. Thompson, 'The conversion of the Visigoths to Catholicism', *Nottingham Medieval Studies*, iv, 1960, pp. 9–10.

[2] Leo, *Letter* 15 (P.L. 54. 680 A).

[3] *v.* Ruggini, *art. cit.* 237–8, whose economic explanation of the loyalty of the Jewish communities to the Ostrogoths is rightly replaced by Momigliano, *Journ. Roman Studies*, 50, 1960, p. 285, by an emphasis on the tolerance they had enjoyed, for which *v.* Cassiodorus, *Variae*, ii. 27, iv. 33 and 43, v. 37 (tr. Hodgkin, *The Letters of Cassiodorus*, 1886, pp. 185–6, 251, 256–7 and 286).

[4] *v.* Thompson, *art. cit.* p. 32.

[5] *Cod. Theod.* xvi. vi. 2 (377): the confiscation of property used for heretical assemblies.

court of arbitration whose decisions had been recognized as valid by Constantine.[1] During the episcopate of Augustine, the personal piety of the young Emperor Honorius, of his sister, Galla Placidia, and of his courtiers,[2] had become an important factor in the situation. On two crucial occasions, in the issuing of the first laws of Unity against the Donatists, in 405,[3] and in the condemnation of the Pelagians, in 418,[4] Augustine was able to represent the tender feelings of the court as having played the decisive rôle: as a good Catholic, the Emperor could be expected to be shocked by heresy,[5] and to be deeply touched by outrages committed against his 'fellow-members in Christ', the Catholic bishops.[6] This emphasis on the subjective reaction of the Emperor and his servants as good 'sons of the Church' reveals a state of mind very different from that of Constantine, who had wished to impose unity on his new religion as an arbiter.[7]

Thus, the attitude of the Emperors to religious coercion is made up of many elements, which vary in importance at different times. It can only be understood in terms of the relations between such constituent parts; and to extrapolate one single idea or motive as the 'cause' of the coercive policy of the Emperors is to falsify our picture of the situation. It is necessary to insist on this complexity

---

[1] *v.* Gothofredus *ad Cod. Theod.* xvi. v. 44 (408): P.L. xi. 1220 C. The privileges of the *episcopalis audientia* should not be exaggerated. They were enjoyed by Jews and by non-Catholic bishops when they were in a majority, as in Egypt.

[2] The extraordinary mood of this court is described by a hostile pagan: Zosimus, *Historia Nova*, v and vi; *v.* Demougeot, *De l'unité à la division de l'Empire romain*, 1951 and the recent, unsatisfactory study of V. A. Sirago, *Galla Placida*, 1961; also Nordström, *Ravennastudien*, 1953, for the religious ideas expressed in the 'Mausoleum' of Galla Placida. [Now see J. F. Matthews, 'A Pious Supporter of Theodosius I: Maternus Cynegius and his Family', *Journal of Theological Studies* XVIII, 2, 1967, pp. 438–446.]

[3] Esp. Augustine, *Letter* 185, vii. 26 (57, p. 25).

[4] *v.* J. Ferguson, *Pelagius*, 1956, pp. 110–12.

[5] *Opus Imperfectum contra Julianum*, i. 10. [See P. Brown, *Augustine of Hippo*, pp. 361–362 on how this pious reaction was discreetly mobilized.]

[6] *v. Letter* 87, 8 (34, 2, p. 404).

[7] This is an extension in an ecclesiastical sense of popular views of the omnipresence and all-embracing 'sympathy' of the Emperor; *v.* Gregory of Nazianz, *Contra Julianum*, i. 80 (*Patrol. Graeca*, 35, 605) for the part this view played in the veneration of the Imperial images, and the baroque language of a later panegyricist: Agapetos, *Ekthesis* (P.G. 86. 1165 B), 'the many-eyed mind of the Emperor keeps vigil as controller throughout all things'. Senators are also treated as 'parts' of the 'body' of the Emperor: *Cod. Theod.* ix. xiv. 3.

in the face of a modern opinion that claims to have 'explained' the Imperial laws against heretics as they were applied to Africa in the fourth and fifth centuries, and later in the Eastern Empire. This 'explanation' regards the laws as measures provoked by the need to maintain public order and the values of Greco-Roman civilization in provinces whose movements of religious dissent only veiled 'particularist'—even 'nationalist'—tendencies.[1]

A *prima facie* case for such an interpretation can be made out for Africa. The Donatist extremists, the Circumcellions, appear in our sources as a menace to law and order in Numidia; and the Donatists are supposed to have supported the 'particularist' ambitions of two rebels—the Moorish counts, Firmus (in 372–5) and Gildo (in the 390s).[2] But the evidence for such a view is slender. We know very little about the true nature of the Circumcellion movement,[3] but perhaps enough to suggest that Augustine had deliberately emphasized their rôle as potential troublemakers in order to induce the authorities to suppress them as a religious group.[4] Secondly, the collaboration of individual Donatist bishops with the Moorish counts cannot be used to interpret the political aims of the Donatist church as a whole. Again, Augustine is our only direct source for such alliances; and he is aware that he is dealing with incidents that bulked large in provincial scandal, and not with a deeply-motivated political alignment.[5]

[1] Plainly expressed in judging the policy of Justinian, by E. Kaden, *L'Église et l'État sous Justinien*, 1952, p. 139: 'ces lois consolident son régne et ses conquêtes et garantissent l'unité politique et la paix intérieur, et le prémunissent contre les hérétiques qui, souvent, ne sont que des séditieux et des séparatistes sans conviction religieuse'.

[2] The most impressive statement of this interpretation is by Frend, *op. cit.* esp. ch. xiv. For my reserves, *v. History*, xliv, 1961, pp. 91–2 [pp. 250–51], and a criticism of the evidence in Jones, *art. cit. Journ. Theol. Studies*, 1959 at pp. 282–3 and 294–5. [See pp. 283–4 and 335–6.]

[3] The basic bibliography *v.* Frend, *op. cit.* pp. 346–50. Two differentiated studies by German Marxist scholars are Büttner, 'Die Circumcellionen' (in *Circumcellionen u. Adamiten*, Zwei Formen mittelalterl. Häresie , 1959, pp. 1–72) and Diesner, 'Die Circumcellionen von Hippo Regius', *Theol. Literaturz.* 7, 1960, pp. 497–508. The name *Circumcellio* it itself pejorative, the Donatists calling them *Agonistici*—'Prize-fighters of the Lord': Augustine, *Enn. in Ps.* 132, c. 6.

[4] As is implied in the Sententia Cognitoris of 411: *siquidem tam catholicae legi quam quieti publicae . . . in hac parte consulitur.* P.L. xi. 1420.

[5] *v.* esp. *Letter* 87, 10 (34, 2, p. 406) *et alia innumerabilia.* [See P. Brown, *Augustine of Hippo*, pp. 228–230 and on a revealing point of detail, p. 297, n. 3.]

It is, therefore, misleading to relegate the problem of religious coercion to a mere function of the political and social needs of the Roman Empire, and to say of the suppression of the Donatists, as P. Monceaux does, that: 'Par sa campagne contre le Donatisme, l'évêque d'Hippone a peut-être sauvé partiellement, pour trois siècles, le Catholicisme et la civilisation de la contrée.'[1] Such a judgement is merely melodramatic: it should not blind us to an element of immediate and genuine tragedy—that, in a time of unparalleled religious ferment,[2] the Emperors and the Catholic Church had combined to deny to the subjects of the Roman Empire an alternative to their own opinion in religious matters.

It would be unwise, however, to deny that the Imperial administration was forced, at times, to face the need for temporary religious tolerance. The official policy of excluding religious dissenters 'from the Roman soil'[3] was held in check by the need to avoid aggravating the provincials in times of crisis. In 409–10, during Alaric's invasion of Italy, the authorities in Africa issued a hasty edict of toleration;[4] the same happened after the battle of Adrianople (378)[5] and, indeed, continued to happen whenever a state of emergency forced the Emperors to abandon, as a peacetime luxury, the unpopular policy of penalizing their subjects on religious matters. In 574 the Caesar, Tiberius, is supposed to have said: 'Let the wars against barbarians, that surround us in every part, be sufficient for us. We cannot raise up, as well as these, another war against Christians';[6] and in 591 the Emperor Maurice refused to use armed force against a schismatic congregation in Grado for fear of alienating the population of an area disputed with the Lombards.[7] Again, a large measure of *de facto* tolerance continued to exist in the army by reason of its diverse recruitment.[8] In Africa, it is hardly a coincidence that Augustine should have addressed one of his two full

---

[1] Monceaux, *op. cit.* p. 35.
[2] 88 entries in Augustine's *De haeresibus* and 22 heresies mentioned in one law: *Cod. Theod,* xvi. v. 65 (428).
[3] *Cod. Theod.* xvi. v. 65, 2.
[4] *v. Cod. Theod.* xvi. v. 51 (August 410); *cf. Coll. Carth.*, P.L. xi. 1260
[5] *Cod. Theod.* xvi. v. 5 (Aug. 379) withdraws this rescript.
[6] John of Ephesus, *Ecclesiastical History*, iii, 37. ed. Brooks, 1936, p. 32.
[7] Gregory I, *Letters* i, 16b (*Monumenta Germaniae Historica*), 1891, pp. 22–3.
[8] *v. Codex Justinianus* i. v. 12, 17 (527): special exemption for the Gothic-Arian soldiers.

justifications of coercion to the tribune Boniface,[1] in 417. Boniface lived in a more tolerant world than Augustine: he was in command of German *foederati*—probably Arian Goths who had been approached by their 'fellow-heretics', the Donatists[2]—and was soon to marry an Arian wife.[3] These incidents reflect the constant pressure towards some form of religious coexistence exerted by the dead weight of *hommes moyens sensuels*, of predominantly lay culture. Such men continued to play a large part in the society and government of the Empire: Ausonius, in the fourth century,[4] and Procopius, in the sixth,[5] are examples of this common type. Thus, to take religious coercion for granted as an inevitable feature of Later Roman life, and to deny that such a policy of official intolerance created quite as many problems for the Imperial administration as it was ever designed to solve, would be to fall into the most subtle of all anachronisms—to treat as an irrefutable and all-embracing expression of the *Zeitgeist* what was only the most articulate current of thought of the age. To treat this current of intolerance as having played a positive rôle in maintaining the unity and stability of the Roman Empire is contrary to much evidence.

For Africa, one factor seems to have played an important part in determining the Imperial laws against heretics: the Roman state was hypnotized by its own exercise of authority and at the same time this authority could no longer be taken for granted. This is an 'imponderable' factor, in that it both goes beyond and fuses the isolated religious and political motives that we have discussed; but it is a constant theme in the wording of the laws and can help us to understand the pertinacity of the Imperial legislation. Ever since the reign of Constantine, a Christian policy had existed. In a Christianized province such as Africa such a policy had to be shown to exist. Thus, by the end of the fourth century the policy had taken on a momentum of its own. Gratian could claim to be upholding rules of impressive antiquity: 'For it is Our will that nothing shall be taught except what the uncorrupted tradition of the Evangelists

---

[1] *Letter* 185. This was written to convince non-Donatists who were unwilling to apply the laws against the Donatists: *Retractationes* ii. 73.

[2] *Letter* 185, i. 1 (57, p. 2). [See pp. 109 and 230.]

[3] *Letter* 220, 4 (47, pp. 433–4).

[4] *v.* Ausonius xx. *Gratiarum actio*, 2 (Lock, p. 222), 'securitas erroris humani'.

[5] *v.* Procopius, *Secret History*, xi. 21–33. His promised Ecclesiastical History would have been, perhaps, a history of religious coercion—even of Catholics!— under Justinian [p. 65, n. 5].

and Apostles have preserved, just as the Imperial law of Our Fathers, Constantine, Constantius and Valentinian, have decreed.'[1] The Emperors could admit no discontinuity: hence the reiteration of laws in favour of the Catholic Church in the two periods of 'direct' rule which followed the suppression of the revolts of Firmus and Gildo.[2] This reiteration, therefore, was probably not provoked by the fear of any deep-seated alliance between the Donatist church and the rebels: instead, it was part of a whole 'ideology of reconquest', which, since the third century, had marked the attempts of innumerable Emperors to assert their control of the whole Empire. In Africa this ideology had come to demand, among other things, the solemn revival by the legitimate Christian Emperors of the 'good old laws' on religion of Constantine and his successors. Honorius probably believed, quite sincerely, that his law against the Pelagian heresy was 'a law to out-do the laws of every age',[3] and that the prestige of his government in Africa—'loyal to Us in every worldly obligation'—was intimately involved in the suppression of Donatism.[4] In Africa, therefore, the problem of religious coercion was part of the general 'crisis of authority' that was so marked a feature of the last century of Roman rule in that province.

The question, then, is whether the Roman Emperors were able to assert their authority on their own terms, through their own officials, or whether they could only maintain the coercive legislation in such a way that the administration of the laws redounded to the credit, not of themselves as Roman Emperors, but of the only persons capable of securing their enforcement—the Catholic bishops. There is much evidence to suggest that the latter view is the correct one; and that, in Africa, the authoritarian action of the Roman state was ineffective without the zealous application—the *instantia*—of the Catholic Church. Thus, the law of Gratian was a mere act of self-assertion on the part of the state; it lacked effect because the Catholic Church, at that time, had not been organized to make use of the Imperial sanctions.[5] In the verbatim account of the Conference of 411 at Carthage, however, the situation has changed: the Emperor

[1] *Cod. Theod.* xvi. vi. 2 (377).

[2] E.g. *Cod. Theod.* xvi. v. 4 (376) and xvi. ii. 34 (399)—defining the privileges of the Catholic Church against heretics; *v.* Frend, *op. cit.* 199 and 249.

[3] The Sacrum Rescriptum of 30 April 418—'victura in omne aevum legem'.

[4] E.g. the Imperial rescript summoning the *Collatio* of Carthage: P.L. xi. 1260-1.

[5] *v.* Monceaux, *op. cit.*, vii. p. 4.

appears as a distant source of 'terror':[1] but the 'persecutor' proper, spontaneously denounced by the spokesmen of many small communities, is the Catholic bishop.[2]

It is not difficult to see how such a situation could have arisen. The defects of the Later Roman administration in Africa are notorious.[3] In enforcing religious legislation this administration was handicapped, at the top, by the discontinuity of its personnel—many of the provincial governors, and even the representatives of the Praetorian Prefect, were pagans[4]—and, at the bottom, by the extent to which the *officia*, ill-paid and locally recruited, were exposed to the influence of local opinion.[5] In Carthage, the most efficient *officium* in Africa seems to have consistently followed the line of least resistance, which involved supporting the Donatist primate on one occasion.[6] These defects could be partly remedied by the appointment of special agents[7] who were devout Catholics—such as the famous Imperial Commissioner at the Conference of Carthage, the *tribunus notariorum*, Marcellinus;[8] and, after 412, special *executores* were charged with putting into effect the laws against the Donatists.[9] One such was the tribune Dulcitius.[10] But in the routine business of

[1] *Coll. Carth.* iii. 25 and 26; P.L. xi. 1367 A.

[2] *Coll. Carth.* i. 139: 'Ipse est Ecclesiae persecutor in eadem civitate ubi ego episcopus sum': 1316 B; i. 143: 'Agnosco persecutorem meum': 1318 A.

[3] *Sirmondian Constitution* xiv. (407), tr. Pharr, p. 483: 'We have been impelled, therefore, by the pertinacity of the Donatists and the madness of the pagans which have been enkindled by the evil sloth of the judges, by the connivance of the office staffs and by the contempt of the municipal senates . . .' *v.* Warmington, *op. cit.* p. 102.

[4] *v.* Samuel Dill, *Roman Society in the Last Century of the Western Empire*, 2nd ed. 1899, esp. pp. 23–6.

[5] *v.* A. H. M. Jones, 'The Roman civil service: clerical and sub-clerical grades', *Journal of Roman Studies*, 39, 1949, esp. p. 53.

[6] *v.* complaints of the Maximianist council at Cabarsussa (393): P.L. xi. 1187 C. Yet they were quite aware of the official status of the Catholic Church over against the Donatists: Augustine, *Enn. ii in Ps.* 21 c. 31.

[7] *v.* W. G. Sinnigen, 'Two branches of the Later Roman secret service', *Am. Journ. of Philology*, 80, 1959, 238–58, on the *agentes in rebus* and the *schola notariorum*.

[8] *v.* Augustine, *Letter* 151 (44, pp. 382–92, tr. Dods, ii. 215–62), for a vivid description of Marcellinus' personal qualities: Monceaux, *op. cit.* vii, pp. 71–5. [See P. Brown, *Augustine of Hippo*, pp. 292.]

[9] *v. Cod. Theod.* xvi. v. 52, 1 (412).

[10] *v.* Augustine, *Letter* 204 (57, pp. 317–22) and the *Contra Gaudentium*. The 'siege' of Timgad must have been a spectacular mission: we know little about the routine duties of such *executores*.

suppression, the harsh comment of Dr. Courtois on the local power of the Roman state in Africa is quite justified: 'L'Afrique du ve siècle ne demeure romaine que par le double appui de l'aristocratie foncière et de l'Eglise catholique, qui s'accordent pour assurer à l'État le minimum de puissance indispensable à la leur.'[1]

The Donatist schism had served to heighten, on both sides, the peculiarly African preoccupation with the Church.[2] In a second-rate pamphlet, the De unitate ecclesiae,[3] we can see how this institution had come to dominate the imagination of the Christian communities: the existence, expansion and growing power of the Church in Roman society were held to be a miraculous fulfilment of the prophecies of the Old Testament. This preoccupation with the expansion of the Church lies at the root of Augustine's attitude to religious coercion.[4] For this reason, his acceptance of forced conversion, after 405, far from remaining a reluctant capitulation to necessity,[5] pushed deep roots into the main body of his thought. A less differentiated man, Optatus of Milevis, even accepted gruesome incidents in the Old Testament—such as the 'zeal of Phineas'[6] —as models of the severity that could be meted out to heretics. In the issue of religious coercion, therefore, they were in the enviable position of men who knew why history was happening. For Augustine, the coercive legislation of the Emperors against heretics, Jews and pagans was a fulfilment of the Psalm that the Kings of the

---

[1] Christian Courtois, Les Vandales et l'Afrique, 1955, p. 132.

[2] v. most recently, J. Ratzinger, Volk und Haus Gottes, 1954, which emphasizes the African background of the ecclesiology of Augustine. [P. Brown, Augustine of Hippo, pp. 212-17.]

[3] C.S.E.L. 52, pp. 231-322, as the Epistula ad Catholicos. The view that it was written by a priest for Augustine would suit its obvious popular character: v. Frend, op. cit. 237 n. 5.

[4] Rightly emphasized by R. Joly, 'S. Augustin et l'intolérance religieuse', Rev. Belge de Philologie et d'Hist. 33, 1, 1955, pp. 263-94. [See P. Brown, Augustine of Hippo, pp. 221-5, 231-2 and pp. 260-78.]

[5] Implied by Willis, St. Augustine and the Donatist Controversy, S.P.C.K., 1950, pp. 127-8.

[6] In Num. xxv. 11 (Vulgate). Optatus, De schismate Donatistarum, iii. 5: P.L. xi. 1013-14. Note that a newly-discovered catacomb in Rome contains the first representation of this scene in Christian art, and may be contemporary with Optatus: A. Ferrua, Le pitture della nuova catacomba di Via Latina, 1960, tav. xcii, and pp. 48-9.

world should serve Christ[1]—even the leniency of the laws which allowed Jewish worship had a prophetic meaning.[2] He was forced to justify the sovereign rights of the Roman state against Donatist critics:[3] but these rights remained a means to an end; ultimately the coercive legislation of the Emperors formed part of the '*prophetica veritas*'[4] of the expansion of the Church.

Thus, the attitude of the bishops and the Emperors overlapped without coinciding. This is made clear over one issue: the application of the death-penalty. Such a penalty was quite consistent with the maintenance of the authority of the state in religious matters. It continued to cover magic, and was extended to cover sacrilege[5]—attacks on clergy and churches, which were frequent enough in Africa. This drastic penalty was hardly consistent with the expansion of the Church through the 'correction' of its enemies. The execution of Priscillian, the Spanish heretic, in Trèves in 385, on formal charge of magic and obscene practices, had caused a vocal reaction largely because his death had made plain how easy it might be for unscrupulous bishops and authoritarian officials to make a permanent breach in the thin wall of principle.[6] A similar problem existed in Africa: the Circumcellions were both a religious movement, whose members courted martyrdom, and potential criminals, liable to execution for assaulting the clergy[7]—even to summary justice by the landowners as *latrones*.[8]

The correspondence of Augustine after 405 contains many references to his use of the customary right of a bishop to intercede for the condemned,[9] and of his personal influence with Imperial officials to make sure that the trials of Donatist terrorists were conducted

---

[1] Among many passages, *v. Enn. iii in Ps.* 32 cc. 13 and 14—where the idea is firmly linked to the Augustinian view of Providence: 'Sed quis fecit hoc? Forte tu, ut extollas te?'

[2] *v.* Blumencranz, *Die Judenpredigt Augustins*, 1946, p. 67—esp. *Contra Faustum* xii. 23 (C.S.E.L. 25, p. 253) and *Enn. ii in Ps.* 58 c. 2.

[3] *v.* a bloodthirsty passage in *Contra Epistulam Parmeniani* i. 8. 13 (51, p. 34).

[4] *v.* esp. *Letter* 173 to a coerced Donatist priest (44, pp. 640-8).

[5] *v.* Mommsen, *op. cit.* p. 598.

[6] *v.* Massonneau, *op. cit.* pt. ii, ch. 6, pp. 242-61.

[7] *v.* the case conducted by Augustine in 411, on the murder of a priest: *Letters* 133, 134 and 139, 1-2 (44, 80-8 and 148-52). *v.* Monceaux, *op. cit.* iv, p. 297.

[8] *Letter* 88, 9 (34, 2, p. 415).

[9] *v.* Gaudemet, *op. cit.* p. 351.

with suitable publicity,[1] above all, that the death-penalty should be avoided.[2] He was determined that the coercive legislation should be applied in Africa only in a way that expressed the principles and aided the propaganda of the Catholic Church.[3] Inevitably this determination led to disagreements with officials. In 414 Augustine was obliged to justify his general practice of intercession to Macedonius, the Vicar of Africa: Macedonius doubted whether a right to intercede was an integral part of the established religion;[4] and he thought that there were too many wicked men in the world for criminals to receive such tender treatment.[5] On one occasion we may suspect that Augustine may have brought an official snub on himself. In 408 he had written to the Proconsul, Donatus, in order to check his use of the death-penalty against Donatist rioters.[6] He reminded Donatus that only the bishops could bring such cases before the authorities, and that the Church would rather 'boycott' the Proconsul's court, by suffering in silence, than provide victims for execution.[7] The law of January 409 may well be the official answer to such blackmail: it laid down that crimes of violence against the clergy might be denounced by anyone; in this way the authorities could politely by-pass the 'bishop, the persuader of mercy' in arresting and punishing culprits.[8]

In one area, however, the constant pressure of intercession had a permanent effect: this was by the amelioration, in Africa, of the laws against the Manichees. Many Catholic bishops, Augustine among them, had once been Manichees.[9] Thus, Augustine's former acquaintance, the Manichaean Faustus of Milevis, had his capital sentence commuted on the instance of the bishops;[10] and by 404 the

---

[1] v. Letter 139, 1-2.

[2] v. Letter 133, 2 and 139, 2.

[3] Largely to avoid creating Donatist martyrs: v. Letter 139, 2. The coercion of the Donatists was not without its dark corners. Optatus of Timgad, executed as a rebel, was honoured as a martyr: Frend, p. 226. Florentius of Hippo Diarrhytus attempted to have his rival executed and kept him in prison: Coll. Carth i. 141: P.L. xi. 1318 A.

[4] Letter 152, 2, to Augustine (44, p. 394).

[5] Letter 153, 20, Augustine's answer (44, p. 419).

[6] Letter 100 (34, 2, pp. 535-8: tr. Dods, ii. pp. 26-8).

[7] Letter 100, 2, p. 537.

[8] Const. Sirm. xiv, tr. Pharr, pp. 484-5. But the date is uncertain.

[9] v. Frend, 'The Gnostic-Manichaean tradition in Roman North Africa', Journ. of Eccles. Hist. April 1953, pp. 21 sqq.

[10] Contra Faustum v. 8 (C.S.E.L. 25, p. 280).

savage laws of Diocletian had fallen into such abeyance that a Manichaean missionary could dare to use them as the basis of a histrionic public gesture—by offering to be burnt with his books if proved wrong.[1]

The conflict of principle, however, was only part of a wider ambiguity: the Imperial laws in Africa were understood in the terms in which the bishops could claim to understand them in their sermons —they were 'refracted' in the distinctive ecclesiastical atmosphere of the province. One example shows this. The suppression of paganism involved considerable action by the state: in 399 a special mission had been sent to Africa to deal with the temples there.[2] But this suppression was understood, in the popular imagination, as the fulfilment of the promises of God in the Old Testament,[3] and the credit for it was transferred from the Emperor to the bishops. In the Greek and Latin literature of the age, the destruction of the magnificent material remains of paganism is told as the story of an heroic initiative of the bishops, remotely sanctioned by Imperial mandates.[4] In the World Chronicle of Alexandria, the patriarch Theophilus is shown standing triumphant on the ruins of the Serapeum;[5] and the suppression of the great temple of the Dea Caelestis in Carthage redounded, in popular legend, entirely to the credit of the Catholic primate, Aurelius.[6]

These imponderable factors should not be ignored when we deal with the practical rôle of the bishop in applying the coercive legislation. The imagination counts for much in the life of small communities living in a time of dramatic change; and the perspective we have just described gives a sense of the direction in which change took place, which is, inevitably, lacking in purely juridical sources.

The juridical basis of the intervention of the bishop has been studied as precisely as the evidence allows.[7] It must be noted, how-

---

[1] *Gesta cum Felice* i. 12 (*ibid.* p. 815).

[2] The mission of counts Jovius and Gaudentius: *City of God*, xviii. 54.

[3] See the passages cited by A. Mandouze, 'S. Augustin et la religion romaine', in *Recherches Augustiniennes*, i. 1958, pp. 218–22.

[4] The best account is still that of Gibbon, *Decline and Fall*, c. 28.

[5] *v.* Mohrmann and van der Meer, *Atlas of the Early Christian World*, 1958, ill. 339, p. 112.

[6] *Liber de promissionibus Dei*, iii. 44, P.L. li. 835 BC.

[7] *v.* Gaudemet, *op. cit.*, pp. 613–14, and esp. Cacciari, *Exercitationes in S. Leonis Magni opera*, ii. 6 (in P.L. 55, 918 sq.). E. Volterra, 'Appunti intorno all'intervento del vescovo nei processi contro gli eretici', *Bull. dell'Ist. di diritto*

ever, that the tendency, begun by Protestant writers of the seventeenth century and continued by scholars of the secular institutions of the Later Empire, has been to limit the importance of this intervention,[1] to distinguish Later Roman practice from that of the Inquisition, and to assert the pre-eminent importance of the Roman state. Briefly, the state would punish—as a 'public crime'—what the bishops, and the bishops only, could decide to call a 'heresy'. Such a view is too formal for African conditions. It could apply in a situation where 'heresy' was a matter of expert opinion,[2] but hardly in a province where the majority of 'heretics' had, within recent memory, been declared such by the Emperor.[3] In Gaul and Italy, the treatment of heretics played a comparatively small part in the relations between a bishop and the secular authorities: these heretics were individuals without a large following, such as the Pelagians,[4] or small 'cells' consisting mainly of aliens, as were the Manichees in Rome.[5] In Africa, on the other hand, the sheer quantitative pressure of dealing with heretics caused the juridical norms to cast a different, and a longer, shadow. We can see what forms this pressure might take.

First, in a province where heresy was defined in terms of persistent refusal to communicate with the Catholic Church, only the bishop could know who had communicated, and who need no longer be liable to the Imperial laws. The bishops had issued certificates to converted Manichees, which gave formal protection from 'inconveniences by the public laws'.[6] The laws of 412 and 414, which punished the Donatist laity for not joining the Catholic Church, presumably made such a practice necessary on a large scale, and so placed at the mercy of the diligence of the Catholic bishop a body of men quite as large as his own congregation. The decrees of the

---

romano, 42, 1934, pp. 453–68, and Ennslin, 'Valentinians ii Novellen xvi. u. xviii von 445', *Zeitschr. Sav.-Stift. f. Rechtsgesch. Rom. Abt.* 57, 1937, pp. 367–378 (all connected with the treatment of the Manichees [see pp. 111–12].) General: *v.* Laprat, *s.v.* Bras seculier (Livraison au), *Dict. de droit canonique,* ii. 1937. coll. 918–96.

[1] E.g. anon. *Histoire des Inquisitions,* 1759, i. bk. 1, and Ennslin, *art. cit.*

[2] *Cod. Theod.* xvi. v. 28 (392) cited by Volterra, *art. cit.* p. 457, refers to one bishop only.

[3] *Cod. Theod.* xvi, vi. 4 (405).

[4] *v.* de Plinval, *Pélage,* 1943, ch. ix, pp. 333–84. [See pp. 188–92 and 208–214.]

[5] *v.* Gaudemet, op. cit., p. 619. [See pp. 108–13.]

[6] *Commonitorium Sancti Augustini,* in P.L. xlii. 1153–6.

Council of 418 illustrate the crucial position attained by the Catholic bishop.[1] He appears as handling the property of suppressed churches;[2] as directly responsible for summoning the Imperial *executores* to suppress heresy in his town;[3] as the only one who could know who had communicated with the Catholic Church, and who was still on what must have been a list of the names of heretics.[4]

Secondly, the dissolution of paganism: in Africa, as elsewhere, the bishop could intervene to suppress pagan festivals and shrines.[5] Because of this, much litigation arising from the dissolution would have been handled by the bishop in his *audientia*; and it has been suggested that the pressure of such business was such as to provoke a law that attempted to regulate the norms used in arbitration.[6]

Thirdly, a general power of 'vigilance and control'[7] was exercised by the bishop over the Imperial administration in this, as in many other matters. The bishops' powers against heretics are limited to this function in later laws in the East;[8] and to put this vigilance into effect would have meant, for the individual bishop, the tedious, and as we have seen, often hazardous, business of an appeal to the Emperor or the Praetorian prefect.[9] In Africa, the problem of individual appeals was largely, though not entirely,[10] avoided by the formal legations sent by the whole African council;[11] and, later, by the excellent relations between Augustine and the Imperial commissioners.[12] In local business, however, the problem of control was made more urgent by the fact that the Imperial laws could only

[1] *v.* the recent edition, Goldaraz, *Los concilios de Cartago*, 1960, pp. 154–5.

[2] Can. 24.

[3] Can. 25.

[4] Can. 25. Note that these canons are imposed in the form of sanctions for the non-performance of these duties.

[5] E.g. *Cod. Theod.* xvi. x. 19, 3 (407 or 408).

[6] *v.* Martroye, 'S. Augustin et la compétence de la juridiction ecclésiastique', *Mém. Soc. nat. des Antiquaires*, 1910, pp. 44–5.

[7] This is the term used in the fundamental study of Mocchi-Onory, *Vescovi e città*, 1934 = *Riv. di storia del diritto italiano*, iv, v, vi, 1931–3.

[8] *Codex Justinianus* i. v. 18, 12, 22 (527), as part of a general duty which included lay officials—c. 21.

[9] *Cod. Just.* i. v. 18, 12.

[10] E.g. the independent *querelae* of the bishop of Bagai, and not the legation of the Catholic Council of 404, were decisive in provoking the suppression of the Donatists: Aug. *Letter*, 185, vii. 26 (57, p. 25).

[11] *Conc. Carth.* v. (401), can. 15, ed. Goldaraz, p. 113. The effect of such formal legations should not be exaggerated.

[12] E.g. *Letter* 86 (34, 2, pp. 396–7).

directly affect the towns. When the initiative in the destruction of pagan shrines on estates,[1] and the admonition of Donatist tenants, depended on the landowners, the bishop had to act as the link between the coercive legislation and the countryside. Augustine's correspondence with landowners on the application of the laws shows how important a rôle he had come to play in the predominantly rural society of his diocese.[2]

Finally, there is the customary right of the bishop to bring to the attention of the authorities cases affecting the 'sanctity of the Christian religion'—whether to report a heretic, or a new heresy, or incidents of violence. The effect of this customary right depended on the frequency and the firmness with which it was asserted. When Augustine cited it, in his letter to the Proconsul Donatus, in 408, he did so in order to give the impression that, in Africa, the laws existed for the Catholic Church, and would be applied only when and as the Catholic Church thought fit. There is an element of special pleading in this claim; but it seems to have gained credence, even with the Donatists. In 396 Donatists could claim that the Catholic primate of Carthage had, on one occasion, intervened to suspend the heresy-laws in their interest.[3]

It is not easy to fit these fragments into a single pattern. Certain features, however, are undeniable. The rise of the bishop to predominance in the life of the Later Roman towns is a complex phenomenon, which varies from province to province and has yet to be fully understood.[4] In Africa, however, it appears that this rise to power was closely connected with the rôle of the bishop in the application of the laws against heretics. It can be seen in Augustine's lifetime. There is a great difference between his early tentative letters to local dignitaries[5] and evident reluctance to lobby indifferent governors,[6] and the dominating position which he and his

---

[1] Augustine, *Sermon* 62, c. 17, and Maximus of Turin, *Sermon* 82, P.L. 57, esp. 693 B.

[2] E.g. *Letter* 89, 8 (34, 2, pp. 424–5), and *Letter* 139, 2 (44, pp. 150–1). For a list of Augustine's country-clergy, many of whom were the clergy of estates, see Courtois, *op. cit.* p. 137. [See P. Brown, *Augustine of Hippo*, pp. 191–193.]

[3] Augustine, *Letter* 44, v. 12 (34, 2, p. 119): the language suggests personal intervention to 'quash' an imperial law.

[4] *v.* Gaudemet, *op. cit.* pp. 350–6, Mocchi-Onory, *op. cit.* and the excellent study of Steinwenter, 'Die Stellung der Bischöfe i. d. byzantinischen Verwaltung Aegyptens', *Studi P. de Francisci*, i. 1956, pp. 77–99.

[5] E.g. *Letters* 33, 34, 35 (34, 2, 18–31).

[6] *Sermon* 302, c. 17.

colleagues came to exercise at the time of the Conference of 411. The edict of the Vicar of Africa, in 414, can place the 'most holy priests' before the Emperor as those who labour for the salvation of heretics;[1] and, in 420, Augustine can intervene in the last days of Donatism in Timgad.[2] A generation earlier, he had been forced to accept this see, ruled over with regal pomp by Optatus—'the king of all reptiles[3]'—as one of the 'great churches' of his rivals.[4] It is an index of the speed with which certain aspects of the Christianization of the Empire took place.

This sudden rise can also be seen in terms of the power it replaced. The Emperor had become a distant figure; and the traditional authorities of the African towns had, perforce, to remain neutral in the suppression of religious dissent. Many such *ordines* were heavily compromised: some, as in Calama and Madaura, were pagan,[5] others, as in Hippo, intermarried with Donatists;[6] one, that of Cirta, lost its favourite bishop, Petilian, and had to submit with a good grace to Augustine—they were, they said, like the drunken student, Polemo, brought to their senses in the lecture-room of Xenocrates![7] It would be impossible to expect public inscriptions such as had coincided with the persecution of Christians in the previous century to be erected now by the *ordines*.[8] The mould of religious uniformity which had been broken in the towns could only be refashioned around the bishop. Already, in his debates with the Manichees, Augustine stands for the *civitas* against a stranger;[9] and in Hippo Diarrhytos, the congregation of Bishop Florentius is quite content to name the new basilica that they themselves had built, the '*Basilica Florentia*'.[10]

It is now understood that the decline of the municipal classes in the Later Roman Empire is not a purely economic phenomenon, the result only of the weight of their fiscal obligations.[11] This class

[1] Aug. *Letter* 153, 17 (44, p. 446).
[2] In the *Contra Gaudentium*.
[3] *Contra Ep. Parmeniani*, ii. 3, 7 (51, p. 51, 26).
[4] *Enn. ii in Ps.* 21, c. 26.
[5] Calama: *Letter* 91 (34, 2, pp. 427-35); Madaura: 232 (57, pp. 511-17).
[6] *Letter* 33, 5 (34, 2, pp. 21-2).
[7] *Letter* 144 (44, p. 263).
[8] *v.* Warmington, *op. cit.* p. 30.
[9] *Gesta cum Felice*, i. 18 (C.S.E.L., 25, p. 826, 11). [See pp. 112-13.]
[10] *Sermon* 359, c. 9.
[11] *v.* Dill, *op. cit.* Bk. iii, ch. 2, pp. 245-81.

was threatened quite as much by the process by which the real lines of division in the towns had ceased to coincide with the traditional, privileged position of the *curia*.[1] A generation of religious intolerance crystallized yet another line of division that ignored the *curia*. Augustine had to defend a pagan who had recently conformed 'of necessity' against the Christian congregation: they had challenged his right to hold high office in the town.[2]

In Africa, therefore, the abstract problem of the relation of Church and State can be seen as a practical problem in the relation between the central policy of a Christian Emperor and the meaning which this policy took on in the local life of a bishop's community. Often in history one group has risen to power by using and interpreting in its own sense the authority of a state too weak to impose its will in its own way. This is the last time in Roman history that energetic local men in that 'Commonwealth of Cities' will stamp their own meaning on the *Pax Romana*. The process did not pass unnoticed. In 404, Felix the Manichee stood before Augustine: he used the word '*virtus*' to describe the bishop's position, in a way strangely reminiscent of the *virtù* of Macchiavelli—that mysterious quality of power that determines the rise and fall of states: '*Non tantum ego possum contra tuam virtutem, quia mira virtus est gradus episcopalis; deinde contra leges Imperatorum . . .*'[3]

[1] *v.* A. H. M. Jones, *The Greek City*, 1940, p. 207. [A. H. M. Jones, *The Later Roman Empire*, II, 1964, pp. 757–763.]
[2] Ed. Morin, in *Miscellanea Agostiniana*, i. 1930, pp. 589–93.
[3] *Gesta cum Felice*, i. 12 (C.S.E.L. 25, p. 813).

Review of:
KIRCHE UND STAAT IM SPÄTRÖMISCHEN REICH: AUFSÄTZE ZUR SPÄTANTIKE UND ZUR GESCHICHTE DER ALTEN KIRCHE
By Hans-Joachim Diesner. Pp. 167. Berlin: Evangelische Verlagsanstalt, 1963.*

The appearance of collected articles by a leading East German scholar provides a welcome opportunity to assess the contribution of a distinctive viewpoint to the study of the Early Church. The author enters on ground shared by all Patristic scholars: his subjects are almost all of them churchmen, ranging from Ambrose to Severinus of Noricum. The heart of the book, however, is devoted to North Africa on the eve of the Vandal invasion: there is an analysis of the situation of the population (pp. 127–39), of the Circumcellions (pp. 53–90); and welcome studies of the relations of Augustine with the fateful politicians of the last days of Roman rule (pp. 91–126). Compared with Soviet historians of an earlier generation, whose work is doctrinaire and mainly limited to juridical sources (e.g. Mashkin, in *Vestnik drevnei istorii*, 1937 and 1949), this collection shows a deliberate sophistication and a new catholicity in the choice of problems.

None the less, the overall impression is disheartening. There is a constant, disquieting hiatus between professions of the need for a correct historical method and the actual quality of the work in which this method is applied. For instance, the social structure of the groups involved with Ambrose in Milan is mentioned as a problem, previous treatments are dismissed, but no positive results are forthcoming: *les savants ne sont pas curieux*. The attitude struck in this passage (p. 31) contrasts unfavourably with the daring hypotheses on just this topic, advanced after long study, by Lelia Ruggini (*Economia e società nell'Italia annonaria*, 1962, pp. 106–11).

* *Journal of Theological Studies* n.s. xv, 1964, pp. 409–11.

By contrast, the analysis of the Circumcellions—especially, *Die Circumcellionen von Hippo Regius* (pp. 78–90)—brings valuable contributions to the debate. The distinction which emerges between Circumcellions and 'Circumcellion-like' groups does justice to the complexity of the phenomenon, and carries conviction. It is a pity that such a differentiated treatment should be rendered inconclusive by unanalysed concepts. *Pro nobis fabula narratur*: even the word 'movement' applied by historians to the Circumcellions contains the insidious *praeiudicium* that their activity must have been directed 'against' something. A man hit by a random snowball assumes, only too readily, that it is deliberately aimed at himself; and, with the Circumcellions, one is constantly tempted to argue backwards, from the impingement of their activity on organized provincial life, and, so, to assume without question that the origin of such activity must lie in a reaction to Roman society. In fact, we know so little about the origin of the Circumcellions: but enough, perhaps, to suggest that we are dealing with a 'crisis', such as frequently affects the religion of primitive communities; and that the social repercussions and intentions of this religious 'crisis' were largely wished upon it by the more easily shocked, or the less scrupulous, members of the African episcopate. (Cf. K. Burridge, *Mambu, a Melanesian Millenium*, 1960, esp. pp. xviii–xix, and 242 seq., for a brilliant and sensitive analysis of the way in which a religious crisis, of profound psychological significance, achieved importance, in the eyes of Europeans, mainly as an 'Anti-European movement'. See also W. Lindig, in *Chiliasmus und Nativismus*, ed. W. Mühlmann, 1961, pp. 27–28.) Thus, the fact that the inhabitants of a village near Hippo could become members of a sect dedicated to the continence of Abel (Aug. *de haeres.* c. 87) may throw quite as much light on the possible origins of the Circumcellions as any study of the relation of classes in Roman Africa.

Where the reviewer would differ *toto caelo* from the author is over his use of Patristic texts as evidence of the social *Haltung* of their authors. In so doing, he seems to ignore the complexity of mind of a Late Roman bishop, often an over-educated man, in whom a heavy ballast of *idées reçues* could coexist with self-conscious thought. Thus, to say that Ambrose's deeper relation to the social aspirations of his age is reflected in the fact that his *Besitzlehre* is more 'radical' than that of Augustine, is really tantamount to saying only that Ambrose's *Besitzlehre* is the more platitudinous: such 'radicalism'

333

appears, too often, in Ambrose's works, as a textbook dictum unrefined by experience. Such *idées reçues* are not revealing; and summary judgements based upon them are no substitute for the long task of finding out exactly what Ambrose or Augustine took for granted, and what they felt challenged to think out for themselves. Indeed, for a scholar who asserts so frequently, against his critics (as on p. 59), the need to seize the 'whole' Augustine, the author's use of the corpus of Augustine's writing is surprisingly limited: a chance remark in a work such as the *De Genesi ad litteram* will often throw a more true light on Augustine's instinctive social attitudes than do the flamboyant caricatures sketched in his anti-Donatist polemics.

In his Preface, the author shows that he is concerned with the moral aspect of a social crisis: 'Vielleicht liegt die Hauptschwäche der Kirche dieser Zeit nicht in einer *gleichwie* gearteten Säkularisierung . . . sondern *nur* in der Vernachlässigung einfachster, urchristlicher Formen der Nächstenliebe' (p. 14). His explanation is interesting: the social dichotomy of rich and poor was not only maintained by the Catholic Church, it was reinforced by a moral dichotomy, by which ascetic bishops, withdrawn from the world, left no time for the humble business of loving their neighbours. Aspects of this symptom are relentlessly pursued in Augustine (pp. 46–52), in Salvian (pp. 149–54), and in Severinus and his biographer, Eugippius (pp. 155–67); it amounted, in many, to a 'Spaltung des Bewusstseins'—a state of mind which the author handles with a trace of fellow-feeling (p. 14). The reviewer would disagree only by seeking to understand this dichotomy partly in terms of inner tensions within the system of Christian ethics. Norman Baynes has brilliantly exposed the 'Double Life' of the Byzantines—one for the perfect, the other for the common man. A society that wanted nothing less than saints seems to have paid insufficient attention to the gradual improvement of sinners.

The time may well have come for a modern version of Lecky's *History of European Morals;* though we must wait a little longer before any contribution of positive value to this crucial theme comes from the tradition of scholarship represented in these essays.

Review of:
EMIN TENGSTRÖM, DONATISTEN UND
KATHOLIKEN: SOZIALE, WIRTSCHAFTLICHE
UND POLITISCHE ASPEKTEN EINER
NORDAFRIKANISCHEN KIRCHENSPALTUNG
(Studia Graeca et Latina Gothoburgensia, xviii). Göteborg:
Acta Universitatis Gothoburgensis, 1964.*

This book is the fruit of a 'silent discussion' with a seminal work on
the relation of social and religious movements in the Later Empire,
The Donatist Church (1952) of W. H. C. Frend. T. dismantles many
vital links in F.'s thesis: the evidence presented for revolutionary
aims among the Circumcellions and for an alliance of the Donatists
with local rebels is dissolved; the statistical argument for the predominance of Donatism in a distinctive geographical area is diluted;
the preponderance of Donatism in the countryside and of Catholicism in the towns receives a different explanation; a novel hypothesis
is advanced to explain the collapse of Donatism after 411. A critical
reassessment of this calibre has been long overdue.

According to T., the preponderance of Donatism in the countryside was due, not to any innate alliance with the Berber peasantry,
but to the success of Catholic persecution in the towns. Having
arrived, independently, at similar conclusions—*History* XLVIII
(1963), 283–305 [pp. 301–331]—I cannot but feel reassured by T.'s
meticulous scholarship. T.'s picture is essentially fluid: the distribution of the two churches was determined, not by static barriers
of class or race, but by the effectiveness of the use of force by either
side—a sad, but convincing, picture of the relations of two bodies
of Christians. Much attention has been devoted to the social con-
comitants and consequences of religious dissent in the Later Empire. This book is a welcome contribution to the obverse of that
problem, the social consequences of religious intolerance. If there

* *Journal of Roman Studies*, LV, 1965, pp. 281–83.

is a 'movement' in North Africa in the age of Augustine, it is not, as we had thought, the 'movement of protest' of Donatists and Circumcellions, but the active pressure exerted by Catholic bishops and Emperors, called by Augustine, euphemistically, *instantia*.

It is a pity that T. did not consider the role of the Catholic bishops in this situation. A détente between Christians in Africa was always possible; it happened, later, with the connivance of Catholic bishops, as soon as the wedge of persecution was withdrawn (v. R. A. Markus, 'Donatism: the last phase', *Studies in Church History*, vol. 1, ed. C. W. Dugmore and C. Duggan, London and Edinburgh, 1964, pp. 118–26). Perhaps the active policy of internal reform, pursued from the outset, by Augustine and Aurelius, might have proved too unpopular if it had not been linked with an external campaign: 'Cupio lucra exteriora, sed timeo plus damna interiora' (Augustine, *Sermo*, 46, 15)—a not uncommon motive for aggression.

T.'s hypothesis on the social reasons for the resistance and decline of Donatism is ingenious. Briefly, the tax-system of the fourth century was too rigid to permit any further disturbance of the peasantry on religious grounds. The great landowners were not, as F. assumed, active Catholics: they were the principal protectors of their Donatist *coloni*, and especially of the labour-force needed to harvest the olive-crop, identified by T. with the Circumcellions. For persecuted *coloni* would have left them with deserted holdings, for which they were responsible by the *adiectio sterilium*. Thus, according to T., the great penal law of Jan. 30, 412—*Cod. Theod.* XVI, 5, 52—was deliberately supplemented the next day by *Cod. Theod.* XI, 1, 31, reversing the policy of *adiectio*. From then onwards, the landowners were free to coerce their *coloni* without fear of fiscal losses; and so the fate of the Circumcellion gangs, and with them, of Donatism, was sealed. I remain unconvinced. (i) T. makes important use of a hitherto undiscussed passage—Praedestinatus, *De haeres.* 61 (*PL* 53, 608 D)—to localize the Circumcellions in Numidia Superior. But he must establish their social origin by arguing that the clubs with which they were armed were their professional tools, used to beat down the olives. This is rather like concluding that a riot-squad armed with pickaxe handles was a gang of roadmenders. As a predominantly religious group, the C. may have used clubs to avoid shedding blood with the sword, a Christian decency continued by warrior-bishops in the Middle Ages, and ascribed to the Catholics in a Donatist text: *Sermo de passione Advocati et Donati*, VI, *PL* 8, 755 C. The social origins of the C. remain opaque; and any attempt to understand them in terms of such origins may be misplaced (see my remarks in *J.Th.S.* n.s. XV (1964), 410 [see sup. p. 333]) [see, now, Salvatore Calderone, 'Circumcelliones', *La Parola del Passato*, CXIII, 1967, pp. 94–109] (ii) *Cod. Theod.* XI, 1, 31, need not bear such a general interpretation, as it merely precedes a new assessment. T.'s interpretation ascribes to Honorius an improbable degree of ingenuity and freedom in framing his policy towards Africa. The laws of this time reflect, rather, the success of the African *possessores* in extorting redress of their grievances while their province was indispensable. If any factor was decisive, after 411, it may have been the atmosphere of public emergency created by the Sack of Rome. This calamity only brought short-term benefits to pagan opinion: in the long run, it greatly strengthened the hands of the bishops in bringing a chastened *res publica terrena* into line with the Heavenly Jerusalem.

T. limits himself strictly to a criticism of specific cruxes in the literary evidence. (His method is similar to that of Jones, *J.Th.S.* n.s. X (1959), 280 98.) This is not enough. The relation of religious to social change can only be seized cumulatively; the problems posed by such a relationship cannot be so easily 'verbalized' and solved by the analysis of a few texts. Thus, T.'s criticism misses the centre of gravity of F.'s thesis—the genesis of Donatism in the religious and social changes of Numidia in the third century; for this is based on a sense of archaeological evidence. When, in fact, did the Donatists evangelize the countryside, and how? This, the decisive question, will only be answered with a spade.

T. has effectively closed some approaches to Donatism and opened new ones. But any debate that treats social and political factors in isolation is liable to remain a chopping at twigs. For the formation of religious groups with distinctive attitudes affect a society as much as the more obvious relations of race or class. F.'s book is seminal because he saw the dividing line between Catholic and Donatist clearly in general terms. The last chapter of *The Donatist Church* remains a classic description of two opposed views on the relation of 'the church' to 'the world'; and F.'s interpretation of the Donatist schism in terms of the ethnic and social divisions of North Africa is a secondary, and more arguable, elaboration of that fundamental juxtaposition. The central insight can be extended beyond Africa (*Miscellanea Historiae Ecclesiasticae*, 1961, 9–22), and has led to a fruitful alliance of Christian and Jewish studies (*Journ. Eccl. Hist.* IX (1958), 141–58, cf. M. Simon, 'Le Judaïsme berbère dans l'Afrique ancienne', *Rev. d'hist. et de philos. relig.* XXVI (1946), 1–31, 105–45). The historian of Donatism must start, not with the social history of North Africa, but with the implications of two distinct views of the rôle of a religious group in society: the one, that the group exists above all to defend its identity—to preserve a divinely-given law, *Machabaeico more*; the other, that it may dominate, 'baptize' and absorb, by constraint if need be, the society in which it is placed. The controversy of the age of Augustine decided in which of these two forms Christianity would come to predominate in Western Europe: 'if it arose in Syria, it was in and through Africa that it became the religion for the world' (Mommsen, *The Provinces of the Roman Empire*, II, 343).

INDEX